PRAYING
FOR THE
IMPOSSIBLE

Books by Dutch Sheets

Authority in Prayer
Becoming Who You Are
The Beginner's Guide to Intercessory Prayer
Dream
The Essential Guide to Prayer
God's Timing for Your Life
How to Pray for Lost Loved Ones
Intercessory Prayer
Intercessory Prayer Study Guide
Intercessory Prayer, Youth Edition
The Pleasure of His Company
River of God
The Ultimate Guide to Prayer
Watchman Prayer

PRAYING
FOR THE
IMPOSSIBLE

TWO CLASSICS IN ONE VOLUME

DUTCH SHEETS

BETHANYHOUSE
a division of Baker Publishing Group
Minneapolis, Minnesota

© 1996, 2006 by Dutch Sheets

Previously published in two separate volumes:
Intercessory Prayer © 1996 by Dutch Sheets (Previously published by Regal Books; Bethany House edition published 2016)
Authority in Prayer © 2006 by Dutch Sheets

2-in-1 edition published 2019

Published by Bethany House Publishers
11400 Hampshire Avenue South
Bloomington, Minnesota 55438
www.bethanyhouse.com

Bethany House Publishers is a division of
Baker Publishing Group, Grand Rapids, Michigan

Printed in the United States of America

All rights reserved. No part of this publication may be reproduced, stored in a retrieval system, or transmitted in any form or by any means—for example, electronic, photocopy, recording—without the prior written permission of the publisher. The only exception is brief quotations in printed reviews.

Library of Congress Cataloging-in-Publication Data
Names: Sheets, Dutch, author.
Title: Praying for the impossible : two classics in one volume / Dutch Sheets.
Description: Minneapolis : Bethany House Publishers, 2019. | Includes bibliographical references and index.
Identifiers: LCCN 2019007173 | ISBN 9780764233296 (trade paper: alk. paper)
Subjects: LCSH: Prayer—Christianity.
Classification: LCC BV210.3 .S54725 2019 | DDC 248.3/2—dc23
LC record available at https://lccn.loc.gov/2019007173

Unless otherwise indicated, Scripture quotations are from the New American Standard Bible, © 1960, 1962, 1963, 1968, 1971, 1972, 1973, 1975, 1977, 1995 by The Lockman Foundation. Used by permission.

Scripture quotations identified AMP are from the Amplified Bible. Old Testament copyright © 1965, 1987 by the Zondervan Corporation. The Amplified New Testament copyright © 1958, 1987 by the Lockman Foundation. Used by permission.

Scripture quotations labeled AMPC are from the Amplified® Bible, Classic Edition copyright © 1954, 1958, 1962, 1964, 1965, 1987 by The Lockman Foundation. Used by permission.

Scripture quotations labeled KJV are from the King James Version of the Bible.

Scripture quotations identified The Message are from *The Message.* Copyright © 1993, 1994, 1995 by Eugene H. Peterson. Used by permission of NavPress Publishing Group.

Scripture quotations labeled NIV are from the Holy Bible, New International Version®.

NIV®. Copyright © 1973, 1978, 1984 by Biblica, Inc.™ Used by permission of Zondervan. All rights reserved worldwide.

Scripture quotations identified NKJV are from the New King James Version of the Bible. Copyright © 1979, 1980, 1982 by Thomas Nelson, Inc. Used by permission. All rights reserved.

Scripture quotations labeled TLB are from The Living Bible, copyright © 1971. Used by permission of Tyndale House Publishers, Inc., Wheaton, Illinois 60189. All rights reserved.

The New Testament: An Expanded Translation by Kenneth S. Wuest. © Copyright Wm. B. Eerdmans Publishing Co. 1961. All rights reserved.

The Bible: James Moffatt Translation by James A. R. Moffatt. Copyright © 1922, 1924, 1925, 1926, 1935 by Harper Collins San Francisco. Copyright © 1950, 1952, 1953, 1954, by James A. R. Moffatt.

Cover design by Eric Walljasper

In keeping with biblical principles of creation stewardship, Baker Publishing Group advocates the responsible use of our natural resources. As a member of the Green Press Initiative, our company uses recycled paper when possible. The text paper of this book is composed in part of post-consumer waste.

19 20 21 22 23 24 25   7 6 5 4 3 2 1

INTERCESSORY
PRAYER

HOW GOD CAN USE YOUR PRAYERS TO

MOVE HEAVEN AND EARTH

"*Intercessory Prayer* is one of the best books I have ever read on the subject in more than 34 years of walking with Jesus. I specifically want to encourage all young people to read this foundational and revolutionary book on prayer."

Ché Ahn
President, Harvest International Ministry
Senior Pastor, Harvest Rock Church

"*Intercessory Prayer* is illuminating and motivating. Dutch Sheets sheds fascinating light on this sometimes mysterious subject. Readers will want to pray more, and they will see more results."

Dr. Bill Bright
Founder and President
Campus Crusade for Christ International

"My heart flooded with excitement as I read *Intercessory Prayer*. What a blessing it is to have this instructive, God-inspired manual revealing the ways God works through His people. The Body of Christ will be richer in knowledge and depth of intercession, equipped to hit the bull's-eye."

Bobbye Byerly
Former U.S. National President, Aglow International

"*Intercessory Prayer* is bold, visionary and pushes us out of our comfort zones. Read it, read it again, and then get on your knees and expect God to move heaven and Earth through you. Thank you, Dutch, for your inspiration to believe God for miracles and then watch them happen. I'm praying for revival in Hollywood, and I know that we'll see God bring it."

Karen Covell
Founding Director, Hollywood Prayer Network
TV Producer and Author, *How to Talk About Jesus Without Freaking Out* and *The Day I Met God*

"If you are looking for a textbook on prayer, this is the best! Dutch Sheets's fresh insights will inspire your faith, deepen your understanding, and equip you to fulfill your destiny as one of God's praying people."

Dick Eastman
International President, Every Home for Christ

"*Intercessory Prayer* has deservedly become a popular classic. This engaging and practical book has contributed enormously to the prayer movement of the last decade. Although thousands of books have been written about prayer, I tend to recommend just four titles wherever I go: *Letters to Malcolm* by C. S. Lewis, *Prayer: Finding the Heart's True Home* by Richard Foster, *The Soul of Prayer* by P. T. Forsythe, and the book you are now holding in your hands. May it impact your life the way it has impacted mine."

Pete Greig
Cofounder, 24-7 Prayer
Author, *God on Mute: Engaging the Silence of Unanswered Prayer*

"Dutch Sheets is one of the most exciting teachers I have ever heard. He explains God's heart for prayer in a clear, concise, powerful way. Dutch makes praying with impact something that is within everyone's reach. I heartily recommend it."

Jane Hansen
International President, Aglow International

"Every praying Christian and intercessor should read this book! *Intercessory Prayer* will revolutionize your prayer life. It contains a depth of revelation found in no other book about intercession."

Cindy Jacobs
Cofounder, Generals International

"This book is for those who need answers from God, which as yet haven't come. Why? Sheets clearly explains the struggle of prayer that enforces the victory of Calvary. Authority is the issue. Warring and winning are born of worship and waiting. This book shows that the choice is ours."

Freda Lindsay
Cofounder/Chairman of the Board Emeritus
Christ for the Nations, Incorporated

"Few times in history does an author capture the heart of God and create a classic that will affect generation after generation. Dutch Sheets has accomplished that with *Intercessory Prayer*. I was privileged to go with Dutch to all 50 states of our nation. What he writes in this book was demonstrated in every state. I do not know anyone who has an intercessory burden like Dutch Sheets. After you read this book, you will understand how to stand, make decrees and become the lightning of God in the earth."

Chuck D. Pierce
Author, *God's Unfolding Battle Plan*

"Biblical, practical, workable, humorous and God-honoring—Dutch explains the why and how of effective intercessory prayer. You will want to refer to this as a resource book many times as you draw closer and closer to God. I read it through without stopping!"

Quin Sherrer
Author, *Lord I Need to Pray With Power*

"I am always amazed at how practical and understandable God's Word is when it is explained by Holy Spirit-anointed teachers. I believe God has inspired the truths shared in this book to release an army of intercessors to strategically and powerfully work together with God at this time. I strongly recommend it to all who want to make a difference for the kingdom of God."

Willard Thiessen
President of Trinity Television and Host of *It's a New Day*

To the Sheets team—Ceci, my wife and best friend;
Sarah and Hannah, our two precious daughters;
and yours truly—lovingly dedicate this labor of love to Jesus.
"Thank You, Sir, for the price You paid and the
passion that still motivates You. You're our Hero.
It is fun and a great honor to serve and represent
You on the earth. We look forward to many more
wonderful times and days with You!"

P.S. "We hope You like the book—we did it for You!"

Contents

Acknowledgments   13

Foreword by C. Peter Wagner   15

1. The Question Is . . .   19

   The right answer begins with the right question.

2. The Necessity of Prayer   27

   God chose, from the time of the Creation, to work on the earth through humans, not independently from them.

3. Re-Presenting Jesus   43

   Intercession can be summarized as mediating, going between, pleading for another, representing one party to another.

4. Meetings: The Good, the Bad and the Ugly   57

   Intercessors meet with God; they also meet the powers of darkness.

5. Cheek to Cheek   71

   He put His tear-stained cheek next to ours and "bore" our punishment for sin.

Contents

6. No Trespassing   89

"No dumping allowed, Satan. Trespassers will be violated."

7. Butterflies, Mice, Elephants and Bull's-Eyes   107

The Holy Spirit empowers the Butterfly Anointing so that we don't confuse the mice with the elephant.

8. Supernatural Childbirth   123

There is a prayer that births, bringing forth spiritual sons and daughters.

9. Pro Wrestlers   151

Step into the ring and face the powers of darkness.

10. Most High Man   177

The sin of pride, passed on from Lucifer to humans in the Garden, is what Satan uses to blind humanity.

11. The Lightning of God   201

We let the "Son" shine forth through us, directing His light to desired situations, allowing it to "strike the mark."

12. The Substance of Prayer   217

You must release the power of God inside of you on a consistent basis.

13. Actions That Speak and Words That Perform   239

Our words or actions impact the heavenly realm, which then impacts the natural realm.

14. The Watchman Anointing   259

To the degree we are ignorant of our adversary, he will gain on us, prey on us and defraud us of what is ours.

Discussion Leader's Guide   287

Notes   293

Bibliography   301

Scripture Index   305

Subject Index   309

Acknowledgments

Thanks . . .

To Jesus for being and giving us so much to write about.

To my wife, Ceci, and my daughters, Sarah and Hannah, for believing in me and loaning me to this endeavor. I love you more than you'll ever know.

To my secretary, Joy Anderson. Thanks for the many extra hours and excellent editorializing.

To the rest of my great staff: Bob, David, Warren, Gerri, LeRoy and Linda, for picking up the slack while I "vanished" into a book.

To the many who have helped birth this book through prayer.

To the church I pastor, Freedom Church, for aiding me in this endeavor through prayer and moral support; for allowing me to disappear for a few weeks; and just for being all-around great sheep.

To Karen Kaufman, my editor at Regal, for the many hours of diligent labor trying to satisfy this rookie writer and bring alignment between my conversational communicative style and Regal's formal grammatical style. Thanks for your expertise, for understanding my reasoning and for helping make this a better book.

Foreword

The modern prayer movement began around 1970. True, it had been burning brightly in Korea for some decades previously, but it was around 1970 that it started to spread worldwide. In recent years the expansion of the prayer movement has been exponential. Quality of prayer is increasing along with quantity of prayer. Flames of prayer are being lit in virtually every church movement on every continent. Pastors are giving prayer a higher priority, children are praying fervently and effectively, prayer movements and prayer ministries are proliferating, theological seminaries are introducing courses on prayer, and even secular magazines have been featuring cover stories about prayer.

I am one of those who has been deeply touched by the contemporary prayer movement. For a good bit of my ministry career, prayer was boring to me. Oh, I knew the Bible taught that we must pray and that God answers prayer. I also knew prayer was included as a normal part of the day-by-day routine of Christian individuals, families and churches. But I would look forward to a prayer meeting with about as much enthusiasm as I look forward to visiting the dentist. No longer!

It was the sovereign hand of God that drew me into what would become an intense involvement with the worldwide prayer movement back in 1987. Since then, I have researched prayer diligently. I have improved my personal prayer life greatly. I have taught prayer seminars and seminary courses on prayer. I helped to coordinate prayer activities for the A.D. 2000 Movement and I have written several books on prayer. The reason I mention these things is not to blow myself up as some sort of spiritual giant, which I am not. It is rather to display some credentials as a backdrop to a statement I am about to make.

As a professional scholar, I accept the responsibility of keeping abreast of the literature relating to prayer to the best of my ability. My personal library currently includes many shelves of books about prayer, and the number continues to increase rapidly. Looking over that section of my library, which I can see from where I am now sitting, I see no book that compares to this one written by my good friend Dutch Sheets.

I know every book has its own unique features. But *Intercessory Prayer* is in a category by itself. In my opinion, Dutch Sheets has provided, more than any other contemporary author, what could be considered the standard biblical theology for the world-wide prayer movement. I was thrilled as I first read page after page of solid biblical teaching about the many facets of prayer. As I did, I was pleasantly surprised to come across concept after concept that I had not considered before. Few things I have read have turned on more lights than *Intercessory Prayer*. Others have agreed with me, since the book has sold hundreds of thousands of copies.

It is a danger, I realize, to classify anything as "theology." To many, reading theology is about as interesting as watching lawn bowling. But Dutch Sheets is one of those theologians who are also dynamic communicators. Instead of making simple things complicated, like some theologians, he knows how to make complicated things simple.

Sunday after Sunday, Pastor Dutch preaches to hundreds in Freedom Church, one of Colorado Springs's most dynamic churches. As he does in his sermons, Dutch brings to life every point he makes through real life stories, some about his own experiences and some about the experiences of others. Every one of them shows how God can be glorified through the prayers of any believer.

If you want new power in your prayer life and in the prayer life of your group, you have the guidebook you need in your hands. Your prayers will have more power to the degree they have more substance. You will not read far before you realize you are absorbing some of the most substantial teaching about prayer available today. As I have done, you will thank God and thank Dutch Sheets for this outstanding book.

C. Peter Wagner
Presiding Apostle
International Coalition of Apostles

1

The Question Is . . .

No Hope

I knew the person I was going to pray for was very ill. What I didn't know was that she was comatose with a tracheostomy in her throat, a feeding tube in her stomach and had been in that condition for a year and a half. Seeing her for the first time was like expecting a prescription and receiving brain surgery. Her sister, who had asked me to visit this young lady, had not given me the whole story for fear I wouldn't go at all. She knew if she could just get me there once, I'd probably go back. She was right!

The doctors gave Diane (not her real name) no hope for living, let alone coming out of the coma. Even if she did regain consciousness, she would basically be a vegetable because of her extensive brain damage, or so the doctors believed.

Have you ever stood beside someone in this kind of condition and asked God for a miracle? To stand beside death and ask for life can be intimidating. It can also teach us a lot—about life, about death, about ourselves and about our God. Especially when we stand beside the same person 60 to 70 times, for an hour or more each time, throughout the course of a year.

Confronted With the Unexpected

It didn't work out as I expected. Life rarely does, does it?

I expected the Lord to heal this young lady through our prayers in a dramatic, easy, quick way. After all, that's how it happened with Jesus.

- I didn't expect to invest three to four hours of my life each week for a year (including the travel time).
- I didn't expect humiliation and insults from the staff of the nursing home where she stayed.
- I didn't expect to cry so much.
- I didn't expect to be so bold at times.
- I didn't expect to be so intimidated at times.
- I didn't expect it to take so long.
- I didn't expect to learn so much!

The Miracle

Yes, God restored Diane! He healed her brain, the outer layer of which the doctors said had been totally destroyed by a virus. Every part of it was covered with infection. "No hope," they said.

The front page of the *Dayton Daily News* (not the real place or newspaper) read, "Woman Awake, Alive, Healthy After Two Years in Coma." The doctors called it a "medical miracle." "We have no explanation," they said, though they stopped short of giving God the glory.

It actually happened on a Saturday morning when she was all alone. Earlier that week Diane had been moved from the nursing home to a hospital for treatment of an infection. After administering more tests, the doctors determined her condition had grown worse and informed her family that she would probably die soon.

When Diane's sister relayed this information to me, I dashed off to the hospital.

Knowing comatose people can often hear and understand everything happening around them, I spoke much to her. As we later learned, because of the damage to her brain Diane was not hearing me. But on this Wednesday afternoon, I spoke to her as usual.

"This nightmare is almost over," I said with tears streaming down my face. "Nothing can keep us from receiving our miracle. Nothing!"

The memory is forever imprinted on my mind. As I exited the hospital weeping, I remember saying to myself again and again, "Nothing can keep us from our miracle. Nothing!"

It was not just a strong hope I had at this point but a great faith. I had turned to God many times throughout the course of that year asking Him if He had really sent me to this little girl. Each time I received His assurance: "I sent you. Don't quit."

The Power of Persistence

Now, I've been accused of being quite a stubborn fellow, and I suppose that's true. In fact, I've "stubborned" myself into a lot of trouble, including two major concussions playing football when a couple of fellows had more size and muscle behind their "stubborn" than I did.

Stubbornness, however, can be channeled into a righteous force called persistence or endurance. I've found it to be one

21

of the most important spiritual attributes of the Christian life. Charles Spurgeon said, "By perseverance the snail reached the ark."[1]

A lack of endurance is one of the greatest causes of defeat, especially in prayer. We don't wait well. We're into microwaving; God, on the other hand, is usually into marinating. So I persisted for a year, and as I did my faith grew until I knew deep inside we were going to win. My motto had become Galatians 6:9: "Let us not lose heart in doing good, for in due time we shall reap if we do not grow weary."

My persistence was rewarded when, three days after that Wednesday in the hospital, Diane woke up with full restoration to her brain. News about the miracle spread to other nations. In fact, the nursing home where she had stayed received inquiries from Europe wanting to know about her incredible recovery.

Every hour and every tear I had invested became worth the wait when I saw Diane awake and heard her speak the words, "Praise the Lord."

What did I learn from that year-long endeavor? Much, plus a whole lot! And I'm still learning.

> In "The Last Days Newsletter," Leonard Ravenhill tells about a group of tourists visiting a picturesque village who walked by an old man sitting beside a fence. In a rather patronizing way, one tourist asked, "Were any great men born in this village?" The old man replied, "Nope, only babies."[2]

I've learned that no one is born a prayer hero. They are shaped and refined on the practice field of life.

A Hollywood talent judge said of Fred Astaire, one of the top singers, dancers and actors of all time: "Can't act. Can't sing.

Can dance a little."[3] I'm sure Satan has passed his judgment on me at times in my life: "Can't preach. Can't lead. Can pray a little." Thank God for His grace, patience and commitment to me. I've stumbled forward more than backward in life.

So Many Questions

From this and other prayer journeys—from failures as well as victories—from hundreds of hours of study, I've formed some thoughts to share with you. I believe they will answer many questions, such as:

- Is prayer really necessary? If so, why? Isn't God sovereign? Doesn't that mean He accomplishes what He wants, when He wants? If so, why pray?
- Is God's will for a Christian automatically guaranteed or is it linked to prayer and other factors?
- Why does it often take so long to get a prayer answered? Why is persistence required? Jacob wrestled with God. Is that what we are to do in prayer? I don't like the thought of wrestling with God, do you?
- What about prayer for the lost? How can I be more effective? I get a little frustrated trying to think of new ways to ask God to save people, don't you? I thought He *wanted* to save them. Then why do I feel as though I'm trying to talk Him into it? Is there a better way? Do I ask for their salvation again and again or simply petition Him once and then just thank Him in faith?
- What about spiritual warfare? If Satan is defeated and Christ has all authority, shouldn't we just forget about the devil? Does God bind the devil or do we?
- What exactly is intercessory prayer? And don't just tell me it's "standing in the gap." Enough religious quotes

and spiritual jargon. I know the thought is taken from the Bible, but what does it mean?

- What about protection? Is everything that happens to me or my family simply allowed by God? Or is there something I need to do to procure our safety?
- How do we "bear one another's burdens" (Gal. 6:2)?
- Is there a right time for answers to prayer or does the timing depend on me?

Are you getting tired of all these questions? I know I am—so I'll stop. You may even be tired of asking yourself some of them. I know I was. Many people stopped asking them long ago, and probably stopped praying, too.

Please don't do that!

Keep asking! I've discovered that the right answer begins with the right question. I've also discovered that God is not offended by a sincere question. He won't satisfy the skeptic and He is not pleased with unbelief, but He loves an honest seeker. Those who lack and ask for wisdom He does not rebuke (see Jas. 1:5). He is a good Dad. Will you pray this prayer with me?

Father, we need more understanding—not more knowledge. We have so much of it now that we are becoming confused. Yes, and even cynical at times because our knowledge has not always worked. In fact, Father, our Bibles often seem to contradict our experiences. We need some answers. We need a marriage of theology and experience.

We've been encouraged by the stories of other great prayer warriors—the praying Hydes, the David Brainerds, the Andrew Murrays and the apostle Pauls. But frankly, Lord, it gets a bit frustrating when our prayers don't seem to work. And intimidating as well because we don't know if we will ever be able to pray two to three hours a day, as these great intercessors did. We need more than inspiration now. We need answers.

So, as Your disciples did, Lord, we say, "Teach us to pray." We know it often requires hard work, but can't it also be fun? We know there will be failures, but how about a few more successes? We know "we walk by faith, not by sight" (2 Cor. 5:7), but couldn't we see a few more victories? . . . Souls saved? . . . Healings?

We are tired of cloaking our ignorance in robes of blind obedience and calling it spirituality. We are tired of religious exercises that make us feel better for a while but bear little lasting fruit. We are tired of a form of godliness without the power.

Help us, please. In Jesus' name we pray. Amen.

2

The Necessity of Prayer

Because I Said So!

"Because I said so!"

Don't you just hate it when that's the reason given for doing something? Not only is it frustrating, but it's also a motivation killer. It's one thing when the question "Why?" stems from a rebellion-rooted resistance, but when one sincerely doesn't understand why, this answer can be a real bummer. I remember having my knuckles rapped with a ruler for asking the simple question, "Why?"

Whack! "Because I said so! Now be quiet and do it."

I still wish I could rap that teacher's knuckles with a yardstick and not tell her why! (Don't worry, we'll deal with forgiveness and inner healing another time.)

None of us wants to do something just because someone else said so. Oh, I know God requires things of us at times without the full knowledge of why, but they are usually occasional obedience and trust issues—not the way He expects us to live life on a regular basis. We are not programmed robots who never ask why. He does not require an ostrich mentality of us: head in the sand, blind to the truth, the issues, the facts.

I Wonder Why

God has given us a Bible full of answers to the *whys* of life. The one I'm interested in is: Why pray? I'm not speaking of why in the sense of needing this or that. Obviously we ask because we want or need something. I'm speaking of why in the context of God's sovereignty.

Do my prayers really matter all that much? Isn't God going to do what He wants anyway? Most people, even if only sub-consciously, believe just that. The proof is in their prayer life, or lack thereof.

Can my prayers actually change things? Does God *need* me to pray or does He just *want* me to pray? Some would argue an omnipotent God doesn't "need" anything, including our prayers.

Can God's will on Earth be frustrated or not accomplished if I don't pray? Many would brand me a heretic for even rais-ing the question.

But these and other questions deserve answers. I've discovered that understanding the why of doing something can be a great motivating force. The opposite is also true.

As a kid I wondered why the sign said "No diving" in the shallow end of the pool. Then one day I hit my head on the bottom. I don't do that anymore.

I used to wonder why I shouldn't touch the pretty red glow on the stove. I found out.

I wondered why a fellow in front of me in the woods said, "Duck."

I thought, *I don't want to duck. I don't have to duck.* Then the branch whopped me upside the head. Now I duck.

I Need to Know

Someone said, "To err is human, to repeat it is stupid." I'm sure I've even qualified for that once or twice, but not with these three *because now I know why!* However, we're not talking about bumps, burns and bruises here; we're talking about eternal destinies. We're talking about homes, marriages, the welfare of people we love, revival in our cities—the list continues.

When God says, "Pray," I want to know it will matter. I'm not into religious exercises and my time is valuable—so is yours. Was S. D. Gordon right or wrong when he said, "You can do more than pray *after* you have prayed, but you cannot do more than pray until you have prayed. . . . Prayer is striking the winning blow . . . service is gathering up the results"?[1]

If God is going to do something regardless of whether or not we pray, then He doesn't need us to ask and we don't need another waste of time. If it's all *que sera, sera,* then let's take a siesta and let it all just happen.

If, on the other hand, John Wesley was correct when he said, "God does nothing on the earth save in answer to believing prayer," I'll lose a little sleep for that. I'll change my lifestyle for that. I'll turn the TV off, and even miss a meal or two.

- I need to know if that cyst on my wife's ovary dissolved because I prayed.
- I need to know if I was spared in the earthquake because someone prayed.
- I need to know if Diane came out of her coma with a restored brain because we prayed.

- I need to know if my prayers can make a difference between heaven and hell for someone.

Is Prayer Really Necessary?

The real question is: Does a sovereign, all-powerful God need our involvement or not? Is prayer really necessary? If so, why? I believe it is necessary. Our prayers can bring revival. They can bring healing. We can change a nation. Strongholds can come down when and because we pray. I agree with E. M. Bounds when he said:

> God shapes the world by prayer. The more praying there is in the world the better the world will be, the mightier the forces against evil. . . . The prayers of God's saints are the capital stock of heaven by which God carries on His great work upon earth. God conditions the very life and prosperity of His cause on prayer.[2]

I couldn't agree more—and want to share with you why I believe this is so. If you concur with me, you'll pray more. You will most likely pray with greater faith, too.

God's Original Plan

The answer to why prayer is necessary lies in God's original plan when He created Adam.

I used to think Adam had to be pretty awesome. I now know he was, as my kids would say, "way awesome." (For those who don't have teenagers or young kids, "way" means "very" or "totally.")

The name Adam means "man; human being."[3] In other words, God made man and called him "Man." He made a human and called him "Human." He made an adam and named him "Adam." In fact, oftentimes when the Bible uses the term "man" the actual Hebrew word is *adam*, spelled just like our English word. I share this simply to say that Adam represents all of us. What God intended for Adam, He intended for the entire human race.

What was God's intention? Initially, He gave Adam and Eve and their descendants dominion over the entire earth and all creation as we see in Genesis 1:26–28:

> Then God said, "Let Us make man in Our image, according to Our likeness; and let them rule over the fish of the sea and over the birds of the sky and over the cattle and over all the earth, and over every creeping thing that creeps on the earth." And God created man in His own image, in the image of God He created him; male and female He created them. And God blessed them; and God said to them, "Be fruitful and multiply, and fill the earth, and subdue it; and rule over the fish of the sea and over the birds of the sky, and over every living thing that moves on the earth."

We see this also in Psalm 8:3–8:

> When I consider Thy heavens, the work of Thy fingers, the moon and the stars, which Thou hast ordained; What is man, that Thou dost take thought of him? And the son of man, that Thou dost care for him? And Thou hast made him a little lower than God, and dost crown him with glory and majesty! Thou dost make him to rule over the works of Thy hands; Thou hast put all things under his feet, all sheep and oxen, Yea, and the beasts of the field, the birds of the heavens, and the fish of the sea, Whatever passes through the paths of the seas.

Adam, God's Re-Presenter on Earth

The Hebrew word *mashal*, translated "rule" in verse 6 of this passage, indicates that Adam (and eventually his descendants) was God's *manager* here, God's *steward* or *governor*. Adam was God's *mediator, go-between* or *representative*.

Psalm 115:16 also confirms this: "The heaven . . . the Eternal holds himself, the earth he has *assigned* to men" (*Moffatt Translation*, emphasis added). This translation communicates with greater accuracy the meaning of the Hebrew word *nathan*, otherwise frequently translated "given." God didn't give away ownership of the earth, but He did assign the responsibility of governing it to humanity.

Genesis 2:15 says, "Then the LORD God took the man and put him into the garden of Eden to cultivate it and keep it." The word "keep" is a translation of the Hebrew word *shamar*, which means "to guard or protect."[4] It is the primary word used for a watchman in the Scriptures. Adam literally was God's watchman or guardian on the earth.

No serious student of the Bible would argue that Adam was God's representative here. But what does it actually mean to represent someone? The dictionary defines "representation" as "to present again."[5] Another way to say it might be to "re-present" someone. A representative is one who re-presents the will of another. I, for example, am honored to represent Christ often throughout the world. I hope I *present* Him *again* as I speak in His name.

The dictionary also provided these meanings: "to exhibit the image and counterpart of; to speak and act with authority on the part of; to be a substitute or agent for."[6] Sounds very similar to what God told Adam, doesn't it?

Now, it's no small task to re-present God. Therefore to help us humans more adequately carry out this assignment, God made us so much the same as Himself that it was illusionary. "And God created man in His own image, in the image of God He created him; male and female He created them" (Gen. 1:27).

32

The Hebrew word for "image" is *tselem*, which involves the concept of a *shadow*, a *phantom* or an *illusion*.[7]

An illusion is something you think you see, but on closer observation you discover that your eyes have tricked you. When the rest of creation saw Adam, they must have done a double take, probably thinking something along these lines: *For a moment I thought it was God, but it's only Adam.* How's that for re-presentation? It's pretty heavy theology, too!

We are also told that Adam was *similar* to or *comparable* to God. The Hebrew word *demuuwth*, translated "likeness" in Genesis 1:26, comes from the root word *damah*, meaning "to compare."[8] Adam was very much like God!

Psalm 8:5 actually says human beings were made just "a little lower than God." God even gave us the ability to create eternal spirits, something He had entrusted to no other creature! Later, the same verse says humanity was crowned with God's very own glory.

Speaking of heavy theology, the definition of the Hebrew word *kabowd*, which is translated "glory," literally means "heavy or weighty"![9] This, of course, is linked to the concept of authority. We still use the picture today when we refer to one who "carries a lot of weight." Adam carried the weight on Earth. I don't know what he weighed but he was heavy. He represented God with full authority! He was in charge!

The Greek word for "glory," *doxa*, is just as revelatory. It involves the concept of recognition. More precisely, it is that which causes something or someone to be recognized for what it really is.[10] When we read in Scripture that humankind is the glory of God (see 1 Cor. 11:7), it is telling us God was *recognized* in humans. Why? So that humans could accurately *represent* Him. When creation looked at Adam, they were supposed to see God. And they did! That is, until Adam sinned and fell short of the glory of God. God is no longer recognized in fallen humankind. We must be changed back into God's image "from glory to glory" (2 Cor. 3:18) for this recognition to be realized again.

My purpose is not to overwhelm or impress you with a lot of definitions, but rather to broaden your understanding of God's plan for humankind at the Creation. Therefore, let's summarize what we've said using a compilation of the preceding verses and definitions:

> Adam was comparable to or similar to God—so much like God that it was illusionary. God was recognized in Adam, which meant that Adam "carried the weight" here on Earth. Adam represented God, presenting again His will on the earth. Adam was God's governor or manager here. The earth was Adam's assignment—it was under Adam's charge or care. Adam was the watchman or guardian. How things went on planet Earth, for better or worse, depended on Adam and his offspring.

Please think about that. If the earth remained a paradise, it would be because of humankind. If things became messed up, it would be because of humankind. If the serpent ever gained control, it would be because of humankind. Humanity really was in charge!

Why would God do it this way? Why would He take such a risk? From what I know about God in the Scriptures and from my personal walk with Him, I find only one conclusion: God wanted a family—sons and daughters who could personally relate to Him, and vice versa. So He made our original parents similar to Himself. He put His very life and Spirit into them, gave them a beautiful home with lots of pets, sat down and said, "This is good." Daily He communed with them, walked with them, taught them about Himself and their home. He said, "Give me some grandsons and granddaughters." God was now a dad, and He was thrilled!

Granted, this is the Sheets's paraphrase, but it doesn't really change the Scriptures—it is leading us to a conclusion about the necessity of prayer.

God Works Through the Prayers of His People

Let's move on to this conclusion. Because we are talking about "weighty" stuff, such as glory crowns, illusions and people creating eternal things, how is this for heavy? So complete and final was Adam's authority over the earth that he, not just God, had the ability to give it away to another! Listen to the words of Satan in Luke 4:6–7 as he tempted Jesus: "I will give You all this domain and its glory; for *it has been handed over to me, and I give it to whomever I wish.* Therefore, if You worship before me, it shall all be Yours" (emphasis added).

The part about the domain being handed over to him was true and Jesus knew it. He even called Satan "the ruler of this world" three times in the Gospels (see John 12:31; 14:30; 16:11).

And here comes heavy number two: So complete and final was God's decision to do things on Earth through human beings that it cost God the Incarnation to regain what Adam gave away. He had to become a part of the human race. I can't think of a more staggering truth. Certainly nothing could give weightier proof of the finality of this "through humans" decision God made. Without question, *humans were forever to be God's link to authority and activity on the earth.*

Here we have, I believe, the reason for the necessity of prayer. God chose, from the time of the Creation, to work on the earth through humans, not independent of them. He always has and always will, even at the cost of becoming one. Though God is sovereign and all-powerful, Scripture clearly tells us that He limited Himself, concerning the affairs of Earth, to working *through* human beings.

Is this not the reason the earth is in such a mess? Not because God wills it so, but because of His need to work and carry out His will through people.

Is this not the story woven throughout the Scriptures:

- God and humans, for better or worse, doing it together?
- God needing faithful men and women?
- God needing a race through whom to work?
- God needing prophets?
- God needing judges?
- God needing a human Messiah?
- God needing human hands to heal, human voices to speak and human feet to go?

Doesn't He need us to ask for His kingdom to come, His will to be done (see Matt. 6:10)? Surely He wouldn't want us to waste our time asking for something that was going to happen anyway, would He?

Didn't He tell us to ask for our daily bread (see Matt. 6:11)? And yet, He knows our needs before we even ask.

Didn't He tell us to ask that laborers be sent into the harvest (see Matt. 9:38)? But, doesn't the Lord of the harvest want that more than we do?

Didn't Paul say, "Pray for us that the word of the Lord may spread rapidly and be glorified" (2 Thess. 3:1)? Wasn't God already planning to do this?

Are not these things God's will? Why, then, am I supposed to ask Him for something He already wants to do if it's not that my asking somehow releases Him to do it? Let's look briefly at three more biblical passages that support this.

Elijah's Fervent Prayers

In 1 Kings 18, we find the story of God needing and using a person to accomplish His will through prayer. It is the account of Elijah praying for rain after three years of drought. James 5:17–18 also mentions this occasion, and we know from his account that not only did Elijah's prayers bring rain, but they also stopped the rain three years earlier. We know we're in trouble when the prophets are praying for drought!

In verse one of 1 Kings 18, after three years of this judgment, God spoke to Elijah and said, "Go, show yourself to Ahab, and I will send rain on the face of the earth." Then at the end of this chapter, after several other events have occurred, Elijah prays seven times and finally the rain comes.

According to the statement in verse one, whose idea was it to send rain? . . . Whose will? . . . Whose initiation? Answer: God's, not Elijah's.

Then why, if it was God's will, idea and timing, did it take a human's prayers to "birth" the rain? (Elijah was in the posture of a woman in that culture giving birth, symbolizing the concept of travailing prayer.)

Why did Elijah have to ask seven times? Seven is the biblical number of completion, and I'm sure God was teaching us that we must pray until the task is accomplished. But why would this or any other prayer endeavor require perseverance, when it was God's will, idea and timing?

And finally, did Elijah's prayers really produce the rain or was it simply coincidental that he happened to be praying when God sent it?

James clarifies the answer to this last question. Yes, "the effectual fervent prayer" of this man stopped and brought the rain:

> Elijah was a man with a nature like ours, and he prayed earnestly
> that it might not rain; and it did not rain on the earth for three

years and six months. And he prayed again, and the sky poured rain, and the earth produced its fruit.

Jas. 5:17–18

The only logical answer to the question of why Elijah needed to pray is simply that *God has chosen to work through people.* Even when it is the Lord Himself initiating something, earnestly desiring to do it, He still needs us to ask. Andrew Murray succinctly speaks of our need to ask: "God's giving is inseparably connected with our asking. . . . Only by intercession can that power be brought down from heaven which will enable the Church to conquer the world."[11]

As to Elijah's need for perseverance, I don't want to comment extensively at this time, but for now suffice it to say that I believe our prayers do more than just petition the Father. I've become convinced that in some situations they actually release cumulative amounts of God's power until enough has been released to accomplish His will.

Daniel, a Man of Prayer

Another example that supports our premise of the absolute need for prayer is found in the life of Daniel. In 606 BC Israel had been taken captive by another nation because of its sin. Years later in Daniel 9 we're told that while reading the prophet Jeremiah, Daniel discovered it was time for Israel's captivity to end. Jeremiah had not only prophesied the captivity of which Daniel was a part, but he also prophesied the duration: 70 years.

At this point Daniel did something very different from what most of us would do. When we receive a promise of revival, deliverance, healing, restoration, etc., we tend to passively wait for its fulfillment—but not Daniel. He knew better. Somehow he must have known that God needed his involvement because he said, "So I gave my attention to the Lord God to seek Him by prayer and supplications, with fasting, sackcloth, and ashes" (Dan. 9:3).

No verse in Daniel, as there is with Elijah, specifically says Israel was restored because of Daniel's prayers, but with the emphasis given to them, the insinuation is certainly there. We do know that the angel Gabriel was dispatched immediately after Daniel started praying. However, it took him 21 days to penetrate the warfare in the heavens with the message to inform Daniel that "your words were heard, and I have come in response to your words" (Dan. 10:12). I can't help wondering how many promises from God have gone unfulfilled because He can't find the human involvement He needs. Paul E. Billheimer says:

> Daniel evidently realized that intercession had a part to play in bringing the prophecy to pass. God had made the prophecy. *When it was time for its fulfillment He did not fulfill it arbitrarily outside of His program of prayer. He sought for a man upon whose heart He could lay a burden of intercession. . . . As always, God made the decision in heaven. A man was called upon to enforce that decision on earth through intercession and faith.*[12]

God Needs Our Prayers

Another Scripture strongly supports our contention that even though God's existence and character are completely independent of any created thing (see Acts 17:24–25) and God already has all resources in His hands (see Job 41:11; Ps. 50:10–12), God needs our prayers:

> "And I searched for a man among them who would build up the wall and stand in the gap before Me for the land, that I would not destroy it; but I found no one. Thus I have poured

out My indignation on them; I have consumed them with the
fire of My wrath; their way I have brought upon their heads,"
declares the Lord GOD.

Ezek. 22:30–31

The implications of these verses are staggering. God's holiness, integrity and uncompromising truth prevent Him from simply excusing sin. It must be judged. On the other hand, not only is He holy, but He is also love and His love always desires to redeem, to restore and to show mercy. Scripture tells us that God takes no pleasure in the death of the wicked (see Ezek. 33:11).

The passage is clearly saying, "While My justice demanded judgment, My love wanted forgiveness. Had I been able to find a human to ask Me to spare this people, I could have. It would have allowed Me to show mercy. Because I found no one, however, I had to destroy them."

I don't like the implications of this passage any more than you do. I don't want the responsibility. I don't like to consider the ramifications of a God who has somehow limited Himself to us earthlings. But in light of these and other passages, as well as the condition of the world, I can come to no other conclusion.

Either God wants the earth in this condition or He doesn't. If He doesn't, which is certainly the case, then we must assume one of two things. Either He is powerless to do anything about it, or He needs and is waiting on something from us to bring about change. Peter Wagner agrees with this when he says:

We must understand that our sovereign God has for His own reasons so designed this world that much of what is truly His will He makes contingent on the attitudes and actions of human beings. He allows humans to make decisions that can influence history. . . . Human inaction does not *nullify* the atonement, but human inaction can make the atonement *ineffective* for lost people.[13]

This truth could intimidate us with the responsibility it implies, or even condemn us because of our lack of prayer. But another possibility exists as well. A responsibility can also be a privilege; a responsibility can be enjoyable. If allowed, this revelation can elevate us in our hearts to new positions of dignity alongside our heavenly Father and Lord Jesus. Jack Hayford said, "Prayer is essentially a partnership of the redeemed child of God working hand in hand with God toward the realization of His redemptive purposes on earth."[14]

Let's rise to the occasion and embrace the incredible invitation to be co-laborers with God . . . to be carriers of His awesome Holy Spirit and ambassadors for His great kingdom. Let's represent Him!

Awaken us to our destiny, Lord!

Questions for Reflection

1. How complete was Adam's (humankind's) dominion upon the earth? Can you explain how this relates to the necessity of prayer in order for God to work?

2. What did God mean when He said we were made in His image and likeness?

3. How does the story of Elijah's praying for rain (see 1 Kings 18) reinforce our assertion that God works through prayer? How about Daniel's prayer for the restoration of Israel?

4. What is the root meaning of "glory"? How does this relate to prayer and representation?

5. How does it feel to be a partner with God?

3

Re-Presenting Jesus

Looking for Answers

When you don't know what you're looking for, you'll probably never find it. When you don't know what you're doing, you probably won't do it well.

I remember sitting in English class one day during high school. I never was very good in English—too busy doing important things such as playing football and running track. It was Friday afternoon and we had a big game that night. You can probably guess where my mind was.

After I spiked the ball into the end zone, listening to the deafening roar of the crowd, my mind gradually drifted back to my English class. The teacher was saying something about a "present participle."

Now, I had no idea what a participle was, but it didn't sound good to me. And I knew the fact that it was "present" either meant it was a current situation or something present in the room.

"Dutch," my teacher said, probably realizing I had been elsewhere, "can you find the present participle for us?"

I didn't know whether to look on the floor, the ceiling or out the window. Trying to appear as innocent, intelligent and concerned as possible, I looked around the room for a few seconds before responding, "No, ma'am, I don't see that participle anywhere. But don't worry, I'm sure it will turn up somewhere."

I never did figure out what that present participle was, but it must not have been as bad or serious as I thought because when I said that everyone sort of laughed. I was relieved, having added a little peace of mind to an obviously troubled teacher and bluffed my way out of a potentially embarrassing situation.

What is intercession anyway?

No, it's not.

I know you said prayer or something similar. But technically speaking, intercession isn't prayer at all. Intercessory prayer is prayer. Intercession is something a person does that he or she can do in prayer. That's about as confusing as a present participle, isn't it?

Think of it this way: Agreement isn't prayer, but there is the prayer of agreement. Faith isn't prayer, but there is the prayer of faith. In the same way that a person can't intentionally pray a prayer of agreement until he or she understands the meaning of agreement, a person won't be very effective in intercessory prayer until he or she understands the concept of intercession.

Are you still with me?

Before we define intercession—so that we can define intercessory *prayer*—we're not only going to do so literally, but also in the context of (1) God's plan for humankind at the time of the Creation, (2) the disruption of that plan by the Fall and (3) God's solution. In other words, we're going to see the concept of intercession in these settings and allow them to help us define it. This will accomplish three things:

1. It will help you understand the concept of intercession so that you can understand intercessory prayer.
2. It will enable you to see Christ's role as THE intercessor. (Our intercessory *prayer* will always and only be an extension of His intercessory *work*. This is crucial and will become clearer as we progress.)
3. With that kind of knowledge, it will make you the most spiritual person in your prayer group!

Defining Intercession

Let's look first at the literal concept of intercession; then we'll think about it in the context of the Fall.

According to Webster, "intercede" means "to go or pass between; to act between parties with a view to reconcile those who differ or contend; to interpose; to mediate or make intercession; mediation."[1]

Using the same source, "mediate" means "between two extremes; to interpose between parties as the equal friend of each; to negotiate between persons at variance with a view to reconciliation; to mediate a peace; intercession."[2]

Please notice that these terms are largely synonymous with some of the same words used to define each—"between," "interpose" and "reconcile." Notice also that one is used to define the other: "mediation" defines "intercession" and "intercession" defines "mediation."

As can be clearly seen from these definitions, the concept of intercession can be summarized as mediating, going between, pleading for another, representing one party to another for, but not limited to, legal situations.

Intercession happens in our courts daily with lawyers interceding for clients.

Intercession happens in contractual meetings daily with attorneys representing one party to another.

Intercession happens in offices and business meetings daily as secretaries or other associates "go between," representing one to another. Nothing spiritual about it.

It involves delegation.

It involves authority.

It boils down to representation. As we discussed in the previous chapter, to represent means to re-present, or present again.

Many years ago my dad hired an intercessor (we called him a lawyer) to represent him in court. Dad had been stopped by some policemen, beaten up quite badly and thrown in jail—all of this with my mother and then three-year-old sister watching. The policemen thought he was someone else! Dad was actually on his way home from a church service where he had preached that night, which added to the irony and injustice of the entire ordeal.

Our attorney went *between* Dad, the judge, the other lawyer and the policemen. He listened to the case, gathered proof, found out what Dad wanted and then *re-presented* it in court. He *mediated* well.

We won.

All intercession is not in the sense of an attorney. That's only one example. Any work of representation or mediation between is intercession.

Now, let's think about this concept in light of the Creation and the Fall. Adam was supposed to represent God on planet Earth—managing, governing or ruling for Him. God told Adam what He wanted and Adam re-presented Him to the rest of the earth. Adam was a go-between for God. Literally, Adam was God's intercessor or mediator on the earth.

Christ, the Ultimate Intercessor

Adam, of course, failed and God had to send another human, called the "last Adam," to do what the first Adam was supposed to do and fix what the first Adam messed up. So Christ came to re-present God on the earth. He became the intercessor or mediator, going between and re-presenting God to humanity.

According to John 1:18, Jesus exegeted God for us: "No one has seen God at any time; the only begotten God who is in the bosom of the Father, He has explained Him." The Greek word translated "explained" is actually *exegeomai*, from which we get our English word "exegete."[3]

You have probably heard of the small child who "was drawing a picture and his teacher said, 'That's an interesting picture. Tell me about it.'

'It's a picture of God.'

'But nobody knows what God looks like.'

'They will when I get done,'" said the young artist.[4]

Jesus came and drew us a picture of God! Now we know what He looks like.

But that's not the only direction of His interceding. Great irony exists in the fact that Man who was meant to be God's intercessor, mediator or representative on Earth now needed someone to mediate *for him*. He who was made to represent God on the earth now needed someone to represent him *to* God. Christ, of course, became that representative, intercessor or mediator. Not only did He represent God to man, but He also represented man to God. This God-man was the attorney for both sides!

He is the ultimate, final and only go-between. He is "the Apostle [God to the human race] and High Priest [the human race to God] of our confession" (Heb. 3:1). He is Job's great go-between, hanging between heaven and Earth, placing one hand on God and the other on humans (see Job 9:32–33).

Are you getting the picture? Christ's intercession, in keeping with its literal meaning, was not a *prayer* He prayed, but a *work* of mediation He did.

And I hope you're ready for this: I don't believe the intercession attributed to Him now in heaven on our behalf is prayer either. I'm certain it refers to His work of mediation (see 1 Tim. 2:5), to His being our Advocate with the Father (see 1 John 2:1). He is now functioning as our representative, guaranteeing our access to the Father and to our benefits of redemption.

In fact, He tells us in John 16:26 that He is not doing our asking or petitioning of the Father for us: "In that day you will ask in My name, and I do not say to you that I will request the Father on your behalf." So what is He doing as He makes intercession for us? He is mediating, or going between, not to clear us of charges against us as He did to redeem us from sin, but to present each of us to the Father as righteous and one of His own.

When I approach the throne, He is always there saying something such as: "Father, Dutch is here to speak with You. He isn't coming on his own merits or righteousness; he is here based on Mine. He is here *in My name*. I am sure You remember that I've *gone between* You and Dutch and provided him with access to You. He has a few things to ask You."

Can't you just hear the Father say in response, *Of course I remember, Son. You've made him one of Ours. Because he came through You, Dutch is always welcome here.* He then looks at me and says, *Come boldly to My throne of grace, Son, and make your request known.*

Jesus isn't *praying* for us; He is *interceding* for us so that we can pray. This is what is meant by asking "in His name."

Let's look at one more aspect of Christ's intercession in the context of the Fall. Basically, humanity needed two things after the Fall. They needed someone to "go between" themselves and

God to *reconcile* themselves to God; they also needed someone to "go between" themselves and Satan to *separate* themselves from him. One was a uniting, the other a disuniting. One reestablished headship, the other broke headship. It was a twofold work of intercession.

We needed both. Jesus did both. As the intercessor-mediator, He went between God and humanity, reconciling us to the Father; and between Satan and humanity, breaking Satan's hold. This was the redemptive *work* of intercession and it is complete. Therefore, in the legal sense of humanity's redemption, Christ is the *one and only* intercessor. This is why the Scriptures say, "For there is one God, and one mediator also between God and men, the man Christ Jesus" (1 Tim. 2:5). The verse could just as easily read, "one intercessor."

This revelation is critical. It means our *prayers* of intercession are always and only an extension of His *work* of intercession.

Why is this so important? Because God won't honor any intercession except Christ's, and also because this understanding will make our *prayers* of intercession infinitely more powerful.

Let's return to our conversation in the throne room. I am there asking the Father to extend mercy and bring salvation to the people of Tibet. The Father could reply, "How can I do this? They are sinners. They worship false gods, which is really worshiping Satan. And besides, they don't even want Me to do this. They themselves have never asked."

I answer, "Because Jesus *interceded* or *mediated* for them, Father. I am asking based on what He did. And He needs a human on Earth to ask for Him because He is in heaven now. So, as He taught me, I'm asking for Your Kingdom to come and Your will to be done in Tibet. I'm asking for some laborers to be sent there. I'm asking these things for Christ and through Christ. And I am asking You to do it based entirely on the redemptive work He has already done."

The Father replies, "RIGHT ANSWER! You heard the man, Gabriel. What are you waiting for?"

Distributors for God

When I say our *prayers* of intercession are an extension of His *work* of intercession, the difference is in distributing versus producing. We don't have to produce anything—reconciliation, deliverance, victory, etc.—but rather we distribute, as the disciples did with the loaves and fishes (see Matt. 14:17–19). *Our calling and function is not to replace God, but to release Him.*[5] It liberates us from intimidation and emboldens us to know that:

- The Producer simply wants to distribute through us.
- The Intercessor wants to intercede through us.
- The Mediator wants to mediate through us.
- The Representative wants to represent through us.
- The Go-between wants to go between through us.
- The Victor wants His victory enforced[6] through us.
- The Minister of reconciliation has given to us the ministry of reconciliation (see 2 Cor. 5:18–19). We now represent Him in His representation ministry. *God continues to incarnate His redemptive purposes in human lives.*[7]

We don't deliver anyone, we don't reconcile anyone to God, we don't defeat the enemy. The work is already done. Reconciliation is complete. Deliverance and victory are complete. Salvation is complete. Intercession is complete! Finished! Done! WOW! What a relief. And yet . . .

We must ask for the release and application of these things. So, let me offer the following as a biblical definition of intercessory prayer: *Intercessory prayer is an extension of the ministry*

50

of Jesus through His Body, the Church, whereby we mediate between God and humanity for the purpose of reconciling the world to Him, or between Satan and humanity for the purpose of enforcing the victory of Calvary.

Christ needs a human on the earth to represent Himself through just as the Father did. The Father's human was Jesus; Jesus' humans are us, the Church. He said, "As the Father has sent Me, I also send you" (John 20:21).

The concept of being sent is important and embodies the truths of which we have been speaking. A representative is a "sent" one. Sent ones have authority, as long as they represent the sender. And the importance or emphasis is not on the sent one but on the sender. The setting of conditions and the ability to carry out or enforce them is all the responsibility of the sender, not the sent one. For example, an ambassador representing one nation to another is a sent one. He has no authority of his own, but he is authorized to represent the authority of the nation sending him.

Jesus was a sent one. That is why He had authority. He received it from the Father who sent Him. Forty times in John's Gospel alone He mentions the important fact of being sent by the Father. The result of this arrangement was that, in essence, He wasn't doing the works, but the Father who sent Him (see John 14:10).

The same is true with us. Our authority comes from being sent ones, representing Jesus. As long as we function in that capacity, we function in Christ's authority. And, in essence, we're not really doing the works; He is.

Let me illustrate. In 1977, while praying about an upcoming journey to Guatemala, I heard the words: *On this trip, represent Jesus to the people.*

At first I rebuked the voice, thinking it was an evil spirit trying to deceive me. But the voice came again, this time adding the words: *Be His voice, be His hands, be His feet. Do what you know He would do if He were there in the flesh. Represent Him.* Suddenly I understood. I was not going to represent myself or the ministry with which I was working. In the same way that Jesus represented the Father—speaking His words and doing His works—I was to represent Jesus. And if I really believed I was functioning as an ambassador or a sent one, then I could believe it wasn't my authority or ability that was an issue but Christ's—I was simply representing Him *and what He had already done.*

A Galilee Jesus Became a Guatemala Jesus

Once in Guatemala I traveled with a team to a remote village far from any modern city. There was no electrical power, no plumbing, no phones. Our purpose in being there was to build shelters for the villagers whose adobe homes had been destroyed in the devastating earthquake of 1976. It had killed 30,000 people and left 1,000,000 homeless. We had trucked in materials and were building small, one-room homes for them during the daylight hours. In the evenings we would hold services in the center of the village, preaching the gospel of Jesus Christ to them, explaining that His love was motivating us to spend our time, money and energies helping them.

We had been ministering for one week with very few people coming to Christ. The people were listening, but not responding.

I was to preach on the final night of our trip. Just as the service was about to begin, a team member told me about something he and others had found on the far side of the village—a little girl, six or seven years old, tied to a tree.

Not believing what they were seeing, they asked the family that lived there, "Why is this small girl tied to that tree?" It was obvious she lived there, much like a dog, in the back yard—nasty, filthy, helpless and alone.

"She is crazy," the parents replied. "We can't control her. She hurts herself and others and runs away if we turn her loose. There is nothing else we can do for her, so we just have to tie her up."

My heart broke as the member shared what he had seen. It was on my mind as we began the service. A few minutes into my message, standing on a folding table under the stars, the same voice that had spoken to me before the trip began speaking to me again.

Tell them you are going to pray for the little insane girl across the village tied to the tree. Tell them you are going to do it in the name of this Jesus you've been preaching about. Tell them that through Him you are going to break the evil powers controlling her—that when she is free and normal, they can then know that what you are preaching is true. They can believe that the Jesus you are preaching about is who you say He is.

I responded to the voice in my heart with fear and trembling. I believe the words were something like, *WHAT DID YOU SAY???*

Same instructions.

Being the man of faith that I am, I replied, *What is plan B?*

Rebellion and failure, came the response. *Remember what I said to you before the trip began? Represent Jesus.*

Faith began to rise. *The emphasis is not on me in this situation,* I thought, *but on the One who sent me. I am simply His spokesman. I merely release what He has already done. He has finished the work of delivering this little girl; my prayers release the work. I'm only a distributor of what He has already produced. Be bold, sent one. Enforce the victory!*

With new assurance I began informing the people about what I was planning to do. They nodded in recognition as I mentioned the girl. Expressions of intrigue turned to astonishment as they listened to my plans.

Then I prayed.

On a moonlit night in a tiny, remote village of Guatemala with a handful of people as my audience, my life changed forever. Jesus came out of hiding. He became alive: relevant . . . sufficient . . . available! A "hidden" Jesus emerged from the cobwebs of theology. A yesterday Jesus became a today and forever Jesus. A Galilee Jesus became a Guatemala Jesus.

And a new plan unfolded to me. A new concept emerged—Jesus and me.

The Heavenly Pattern

For the first time I understood the heavenly pattern: Jesus is the Victor—we're the enforcers; Jesus is the Redeemer—we're the releasers; Jesus is the Head—we're the Body.

Yes, He set the little girl free.

Yes, the village turned to Christ.

Yes, Jesus prevailed through a sent one.

So the partnership goes on—God and humans. But the correct pattern is critical: My *prayers* of intercession release Christ's finished *work* of intercession.

His work empowers my prayers—my prayers release His work.

Mine extends His—His effectuates mine.

Mine activates His—His validates mine.

In Kingdom Enterprises we're not in the production department. We're in distribution . . . BIG difference. He's the generator. We're the distributors.

Awesomites Re-Presenting His Awesomeness

I think this makes us His co-laborers. What do you think? I think Christ is awesome and wants us to be "awesomites."

Humble awesomites representing His awesomeness, but awesome nonetheless. More than conquerors! Christ and His Christians, changing things on the earth.

There are many wounded and hurting individuals "tied to trees" around the world. You work with some, others live across the street. One of them probably just served you in a check-out line, seated you in a restaurant or served you food. Their chains are alcohol, drugs, abuse, broken dreams, rejection, money, lust . . . well, you get the point.

Plan A is for supernatural but ordinary people like you and me to: (1) wholeheartedly believe in the victory of Calvary—to be convinced that it was complete and final, and (2) to rise up in our role as sent ones, ambassadors, authorized representatives of the Victor. Our challenge is not so much to liberate as to believe in the Liberator; to heal as to believe in the Healer.

Plan B is to waste the Cross; to leave the tormented in their torment; to scream with our silence, "There is no hope!"; to hear the Father say again, "I looked, but found no one"; to hear the Son cry once more, "The laborers! Where are the laborers?"

Come on, Church! Let's untie some folks. Let's tell them there is a God who cares. Let's represent—let's mediate—let's intercede!

"Can anyone find the present participator?"

Questions for Reflection

1. Define intercession and intercessory prayer. What is the difference? Why is this important?

2. How are intercession and mediation related?

3. Can you explain what I meant when I said Christ was THE intercessor and that our *prayers* are an extension of His *work*?

4. Explain the two aspects of Christ's intercession—reconciling and separating—relating it to humankind's twofold need created by the Fall.

5. What is the significance of being a "sent one"?

6. Do you know anyone chained to a "tree"? Please help them.

4

Meetings: The Good, the Bad and the Ugly

Boy Meets Girl

"Dutch Sheets, I want you to *meet* Celia Merchant." The world suddenly stood still and my life changed forever.

The second most important *meeting* of my life was taking place—only my introduction to Jesus ranked higher. It was 1977 and I was a student in Bible college.

Having just enjoyed a time of private prayer, I emerged from the prayer room to see two individuals carrying a large folding table. One of them was a male friend of mine, the other was the most beautiful young lady I had ever laid eyes on.

Oh, it wasn't the first time I had seen her, but it was my first face-to-face encounter. Weak-kneed and tongue-tied, I nearly tripped over myself grabbing her end of the table. With a gallant demonstration of chivalry and muscle, I relieved her of her burden and nearly knocked the other guy off his feet showing how fast I could carry that table.

He then introduced me to what had to be my missing rib, and I knew life would never be right if I didn't marry this woman! I told God as much. Fortunately, He agreed and so did she. Life is good!

I sure am glad I spent that time in prayer. I would not have wanted to miss that *meeting*!

Boy Meets Baseball

I had another memorable *meeting* when I was in the sixth grade. This one wasn't so pleasant. It would also remain with me the rest of my life, however. A baseball *met* my front teeth. The baseball won—they usually do. I have two nice caps on my front teeth today as a result of that *meeting*.

I thought about revealing that I was trying to teach another kid to catch a baseball when it happened, but that would be too embarrassing. I won't mention that I was demonstrating what not to do when the accident happened. But I will say that when teaching your kids the fine points of baseball, show them what to do—not what not to do. Doing it backward leads to unpleasant *meetings* and cosmetic smiles.

God Meets a Mate, Satan Meets His Match

A figure hangs on a cross between heaven and Earth. Two *meetings* are about to take place—one good and pleasant, one ugly and violent. A Man is about to *meet* His bride and a serpent is about to *meet* a curveball to the teeth:

> For this reason a man shall leave his father and mother and shall be joined to his wife, and the two shall become one flesh. This

mystery is great; but I am speaking with reference to Christ and the church.

Eph. 5:31–32

Arise, O LORD; save me, O my God! For You have smitten all my enemies on the cheek; You have shattered the teeth of the wicked.

Ps. 3:7

Such beauty, such ugliness . . . union, disunion . . . joining, breaking . . .

Actually, many other *meetings* could be mentioned as taking place through the Cross:

- Mercy *met* judgment.
- Righteousness *met* sin.
- Light *met* darkness.
- Humility *met* pride.
- Love *met* hate.
- Life *met* death.
- A cursed One on a tree *met* the curse that originated from a tree.
- The sting of death *met* the antidote of resurrection.

All the good guys won!

Only God could plan such an event—let alone have it turn out perfectly. Only He could marry such extremes in one oc-currence. Who but He could shed blood to create life, use pain to bring healing, allow injustice to satisfy justice and accept rejection to restore acceptance?

Who could use such an evil act to accomplish so much good?

Who could transform an act of amazing love into such vio-lence, and vice versa? Only God.

So many paradoxes. So much irony.

59

Don't you find it fascinating that the serpent who accomplished his greatest victory from a tree (of the knowledge of good and evil) suffered his greatest defeat from a tree (the Cross of Calvary)?

Don't you find it ironic that the first Adam succumbed to temptation in a garden (Eden) and the last Adam overcame His greatest temptation in a garden (Gethsemane)?

Can God ever write a script!

Perhaps you have guessed by now that hidden somewhere in these three stories—my wife, the baseball and the Cross—are pictures of intercession. In fact, I've actually used one of the definitions of the Hebrew word for "intercession," *paga*, 23 times thus far. I'll continue to use it more than 30 additional times by the end of this chapter. How's that for redundancy?!

Intercession Creates a Meeting

The Hebrew word for "intercession," *paga*, means "to meet."[1] As we have already seen by studying the English word, intercession is not primarily a prayer a person prays, but something a person does that can be done through prayer. This is also true in the Hebrew language. Although the word "intercession" has come to mean "prayer" in our minds, its Hebrew word does not necessarily mean "prayer" at all. It has many shades of meaning, all of which can be done through prayer.

Throughout the remainder of the book, we will look at several of these meanings, and then put them into the context of prayer. As we do, our understanding will increase of what Christ did for us through His intercession and what our re-presenting of it on the earth through prayer really entails. As the opening stories imply, the first usage of *paga* we will explore is "to meet."

Intercession creates a *meeting*. Intercessors *meet* with God; they also *meet* the powers of darkness. "Prayer meetings" are aptly named!

A Meeting for Reconciliation

Similar to Christ's, often our *meeting* with God is to effect another *meeting*—a reconciliation. We *meet* with Him asking Him to *meet* with someone else. We become the *go-between*: "Heavenly Father, I come to you today (a *meeting*) asking You to touch Tom (another *meeting*)." On the opposite end of the spectrum, as Christ did through spiritual warfare, our *meeting* with the enemy is to undo a *meeting*—a breaking, a severing, a disuniting. All of our praying intercession will involve one or both of these facets: reconciliation or breaking; uniting or disuniting.

First, we will look at a couple of Scriptures that describe what Christ did when He *met* the Father to create a *meeting* between God and humanity. Then we will look at the warfare aspect. Psalm 85:10 states, "Lovingkindness and truth have met together; righteousness and peace have kissed each other." Let's examine more fully this beautiful description of the Cross.

God had a dilemma seen through four words in this verse. He not only is a God of *lovingkindness* (which represents His mercy, kindness, love and forgiveness), but He is also a God of *truth* (which represents His integrity and justice). He does not merely represent *peace* (safety, wholeness and rest), but also *righteousness* (holiness and purity), without which there can be no peace.

The dilemma is this: A truly holy, righteous, just and true God cannot simply forgive, grant mercy to or bestow peace on a fallen humanity without compromising His character. Sin cannot be excused. It must be judged and with it the sinner. So, how can this holy, yet loving, God marry the two? THE CROSS!

On the Cross lovingkindness and truth *met*. Righteousness and peace kissed each other. And when they did, so did God and humanity! We kissed the Father through the Son! We *met* Him through the blood of Christ! Jesus grabbed our end of the table and was introduced to His bride.

61

In one sovereign, unsearchable act of wisdom, God satisfied both His love and His justice. He established righteousness as well as peace. *Who is like unto You, O Lord? Who can describe Your great mercy, Your awesome power, Your infinite wisdom?* When this took place, Christ's ministry of reconciliation was being accomplished: "Who reconciled us to Himself through Christ . . . namely, that God was in Christ reconciling the world to Himself" (2 Cor. 5:18–19).

Because we now represent Christ in His intercession, let's apply these verses to ourselves. Verse 18 says He "gave us the ministry of reconciliation." In other words, through our praying intercession, we release the fruit of what He did through His act of intercession. We bring individuals to God in prayer, asking the Father to *meet* with them. We, too, have been given the ministry of reconciliation. Whether for a person or a nation, regardless of the reason, when we're used to create a *meeting* between God and humans, releasing the fruit of Christ's work, *paga* has happened.

It might be as you are prayer-walking through your neighborhood, asking God to *meet* with families and save them.

It could be a prayer journey into another nation. Our church has sent teams of intercessors into some of the darkest countries upon the earth for the sole purpose of prayer—creating *meetings* between God and humanity—divine connections through human conduits.

Meetings That Heal

I have witnessed miracles of healing as God *met* with people. In 1980 I was on another of my many journeys into Guatemala. On one occasion my wife, another couple and I were ministering to an elderly lady who had recently been saved. We had gone to her home to share some teaching with her.

Approximately six months earlier this lady had fallen from a stool and severely broken her ankle. As is often the case with the elderly, the fracture was not healing well. Her ankle was still badly swollen and she was in much pain. While we visited with her, the other gentleman and I both sensed that God wanted to heal her ankle—right then.

After sharing this with her and obtaining her agreement, we asked her to prop her leg on a stool. I began to pray, sort of.

Has God ever interrupted you? He did me on this occasion. (Oh, that He would always be so "unmannerly"!) When I stepped *between* her and God to effect a *meeting*, the presence of God came so powerfully into the room that I stopped in mid-stride and mid-sentence. I had taken one step toward her and uttered one word, "Father."

That's all He needed!

It's as though He was so eager to touch this dear lady that He couldn't wait any longer. I realize that what I'm about to say may sound overly dramatic, but it's exactly what took place.

The presence of the Holy Spirit filled the room so strongly that I froze in my tracks, stopped speaking and began to weep. My wife and the other couple also began to weep. The lady we were ministering to began to weep. Her foot began to bounce up and down on the stool, shaking uncontrollably for several minutes as she had a powerful encounter with the Holy Spirit— a *meeting*! The Lord healed her and filled her with His Spirit.

On the same visit to Guatemala, my wife and I, along with the couple previously mentioned, were asked to pray for a woman hospitalized with tuberculosis. We found her in a ward with approximately 40 other women, the beds being only about three feet apart. It was simply an area in the hospital where the doctors and nurses could attend the very poor. Not even partitions separated the women. And yes, this woman was coughing her tuberculosis all over those around her.

As we talked and prayed with her, we noticed the lady in the next bed observing us closely. When we finished she asked if we would be willing to pray for her. Of course we were glad to and inquired about her need. She pulled her arms out from under the covers and showed us her two hands, curled back toward her body, somewhat frozen in that position. They were totally unusable. Her feet were also the same way.

While in the hospital for back surgery, the doctor had accidentally cut a nerve in her spinal cord, leaving her in this condition. There was nothing they could do to correct the problem.

Compassion filled our hearts as we asked the Lord to *meet* her need. Nothing noticeable happened, but we encouraged her to trust the Lord and drifted across the room to see if we could share Jesus with anyone else. No hospital employees were present, so we had relative freedom to do as we pleased.

Just as we began to visit with another lady across the room, we heard a sudden commotion and someone screaming, "Milagro! Milagro! Milagro!" We turned to look and saw the lady moving her hands wildly, opening and closing them, wiggling her fingers, kicking her feet under the covers and shouting the Spanish word for miracle. A *meeting* had taken place!

I don't know who was more surprised—the lady who was healed, the other ladies in the room or me. I hoped for a miracle but I don't think I believed for one. I remember thinking, *This sort of thing only happened during Bible days.*

The next thing we knew, every woman in the room was begging us to minister to them. We went from bed to bed—just like we knew what we were doing—leading women to Christ and praying for their recoveries. I remember thinking, *This is wild. Is it real or am I dreaming? We're having revival in a hospital ward!* Several were saved, the lady with tuberculosis was also healed and another lady who had been scheduled for exploratory surgery the following morning was instead sent home healed. In general, we just had a good time! We even sang a song or two. Probably shouldn't have because a hospital employee heard us, came to the room and asked us to leave. She left but we didn't. Too many women were begging for prayer. A few minutes later she returned and "graciously" escorted us out of the hospital.

What on earth can turn a sad, hopeless, disease-filled ward into a church service? God! God *meeting* with people. And prayer *meetings* create God *meetings*!

I don't want to mislead you into thinking that miracles will always happen as easily as they did on these two occasions. However, we can bring individuals into contact with God and that is the very meaning of the word "intercession." It often requires much intercession; but whether it takes days or minutes, it's always worth the effort. The important thing is that we do it.

She-Bear Meetings

Let's progress in our thinking to the breaking aspect of inter-cession *meetings*—enforcing the victory of Calvary. I call this "the bear anointing" because of Proverbs 17:12: "Let a man *meet* a bear robbed of her cubs, rather than a fool in his folly" (emphasis added).

I've never met a she-bear in the wild with or without her cubs, and I hope I never do. But a wise old woodsman, instructing me in the art of surviving bear encounters, gave me the following piece of wisdom: "Son, try to avoid them, if possible! But if you can't and it's a female you run into, don't ever get between mama and her cubs. Because if you do there's fixin' to be a *meeting*, and you're gonna be on the receiving end!"

Now, before I'm lynched for contextual murder of the Scriptures, let me say I am not insinuating that this verse is talking about prayer. I am saying, however, that the word for "meet" is our Hebrew word translated "intercession," *paga*. Other

Hebrew words could have been used, but this one was chosen partly because it often has a very violent connotation. In fact, *paga* is frequently a battlefield term (for examples, see Judg. 8:21; 15:12; 1 Sam. 22:17–18; 2 Sam. 1:15; 1 Kings 2:25–46).

Intercession can be violent!

Meetings can be unpleasant! Some can be downright ugly!

Such as the one Satan had with Jesus at Calvary when Christ interceded for us. Satan had come between God and His "cubs." He ought not to have done that! Satan's worst nightmare came true when, with 4,000 years of pent-up fury, Jesus *met* him at Calvary. The earth rocked, and I do mean literally, with the force of the battle (see Matt. 27:51). The very sun grew dark as the war raged (see v. 45). At the moment of what Satan thought was his greatest triumph, he and all his forces heard the most terrifying sound they had ever heard: God's laugh of derision (see Ps. 2:4)!

The laughter was followed by the voice of the Son of man crying with a loud voice, "*Tetelestai*." This Greek word is translated "It is finished" in John 19:30. Please don't think Jesus was talking about death when He spoke that word. No way! *Tetelestai* means to fully accomplish something or bring it to its completed state,[2] as the word "finished" would imply, but it was also the word stamped on invoices in that day meaning "Paid in full."[3] Jesus was shouting, "The debt is paid in full!" Hallelujah!

Christ was quoting from Psalm 22:31 when He chose this statement. Three of His seven sayings on the cross come from this psalm. The Hebrew word He quoted from this verse is *asah*. He may have actually been speaking Hebrew, using this very word, even though John recorded it in Greek. The word means, among other things, "to create."[4] It is used in Genesis, for example, when God created the earth. I believe that not only was Christ saying, "The debt is paid in full," but also, "Come forth, new creation!" No wonder the earth shook, the sun reappeared, the centurion was terrified (see Matt. 27:54) and Old Testament saints were resurrected (see Matt. 27:52–53). Don't tell me God doesn't have a flare for the dramatic. The Cross defines drama.

And yes, behind the scenes it was violent. Captives were rescued (see 1 Pet. 3:19; 4:6; Isa. 61:1), bruises were inflicted (see Gen. 3:15; Isa. 53:5; 1 Pet. 2:24), keys were exchanged, authority was transferred (see Matt. 28:18).

An interesting word is used in 1 John 3:8 that adds insight to what happened at the Cross. The verse reads, "For this purpose the Son of God was manifested, that he might destroy the works of the devil" (KJV). "Destroy" is the Greek word *luo*, which has both a legal and a physical meaning. Understanding its full definition will greatly enhance our knowledge of what Jesus did to Satan and his works.

The legal meaning of *luo* is (1) to pronounce or determine that something or someone is no longer bound; (2) to dissolve or void a contract or anything that legally binds.[5] Jesus came to dissolve the legal hold Satan had over us and to pronounce that we were no longer bound by his works. He "voided the contract," breaking Satan's dominion over us.

The physical meaning of *luo* is to dissolve or melt, break, beat something to pieces or untie something that is bound.[6] In Acts 27:41, the boat Paul traveled on was broken to pieces (*luo*) by the force of a storm. In 2 Peter 3:10, 12, we're told that one day the elements of the earth will melt or dissolve (*luo*) from a great heat. Jesus not only delivered us legally, but He also made certain that the literal consequences of that deliverance were manifested: He brought healing, set captives free, lifted oppression and liberated those under demonic control.

Enforcing the Victory

Our responsibility is to enforce the victory as we also *meet* the powers of darkness. It is interesting to know that Jesus used the same word, *luo*, to describe what we, the Church, are to do through spiritual warfare. Matthew 16:19 tells us, "I will give you the keys of the kingdom of heaven; and whatever you shall bind on earth shall be bound in heaven, and whatever you shall loose on earth shall be loosed in heaven." The word "loose" in this verse is *luo*.

Now, the question is, "Did Christ *luo* the works of the devil or do we *luo* the works of the devil?" The answer is yes. Although Jesus fully accomplished the task of breaking the authority of Satan and voiding his legal hold upon the human race, someone on Earth must represent Him in that victory and enforce it.

With this in mind and remembering that the Hebrew word for "intercession," *paga*, means to *meet*, let's state it this way:

> We, through *prayers* of intercession, *meet* the powers of darkness, enforcing the victory Christ accomplished when He *met* them in His *work* of intercession.

This is exactly what took place in Guatemala when we prayed for the little girl tied to a tree, mentioned in the previous chapter. We *met* the powers of darkness and enforced the victory of the Cross.

Several years ago in Guatemala, a friend of mine pointed out a vibrant, healthy young woman and told me the following story. When he first saw her just a few months prior to this time, she was paralyzed from the neck down. She could move her head slightly, but could not speak. "The young lady has been this way for two years," my friend was informed by her pastor. "And the puzzling thing is that the doctors can find nothing physically wrong with her to create such a problem."

My friend, who was visiting the church as a guest speaker, discerned that the cause was demonic. Not knowing the church's position about such matters, he discreetly approached this wheelchair-bound young lady, knelt next to her and whispered in her ear. As he did, he was *going between* (intercession) her and the powers of darkness, *meeting* them with the power of Christ. He prayed, "Satan, I break (*luo*) your hold over this young lady in the name of Jesus. I command you to loose (*luo*) your hold over her and let her go." (Parenthetical words are mine.)

No manifestation or immediate change occurred. A week later, however, she was able to move her arms a little. The following week she was moving her arms normally and her legs slightly. The recovery continued for a month until she was totally free and well.

She then told my friend the following details about the cause of her condition and why the doctors could find no reasonable explanation. "A teacher in my school who was also a witch doctor made a sexual advance toward me, which I refused. He grew angry and told me that if I didn't have sex with him, he would place a curse on me."

She knew nothing about such things and didn't think much about it. A short time later, however, this condition of paralysis came upon her. Her inability to speak prevented her from communicating with anyone about what had taken place.

What happened to bring about this girl's freedom? An individual stepped *between* this young lady and the powers of darkness, *meeting* them in the name of Jesus, enforcing His victory. That . . . is intercession!

A *meeting* can be a good and pleasant experience or it can be a violent confrontation between opposing forces. The intercessor is either going to *meet* with God for the purpose of reconciling the world to the Father and His wonderful blessings, or he is going to *meet* Satanic forces of opposition to enforce the victory of Calvary. The purpose will vary, but one thing is certain: The prayers of an understanding intercessor WILL create a *meeting*. And when the *meeting* comes to a close, something will have changed.

Don't be intimidated by the size of the giant. Jesus has qualified you to represent Him. And don't be intimidated by past failures. Be like the small boy playing in the backyard with his bat and ball:

"I'm the greatest baseball player in the world," he said proudly. Then he tossed the ball in the air, swung and missed. Undaunted, he picked up the ball, threw it into the air and said to himself, "I'm the greatest player ever!" He swung at the ball again, and again he missed. He paused a moment to examine bat and ball carefully. Then once again he threw the ball into the air and said, "I'm the greatest baseball player who ever lived." He swung the bat hard and again missed the ball.

"Wow!" he exclaimed. "What a pitcher!"[7]

Deny unbelief access. You can do it!
Let's have a prayer *meeting*!

Questions for Reflection

1. In what way does a meeting picture intercession? How does *paga* establish the correlation between the two?

2. Explain the two opposite kinds of meetings discussed in this chapter. How does each one represent Calvary?

3. Define *luo* and comment on Christ doing it and the Church doing it.

4. Think of someone you know who needs a meeting with God. How and when can you help facilitate this?

5. Don't you think God will be thrilled when you do number 4?

5

Cheek to Cheek

Lean on Me

Charlie Brown was pitching and doing a lousy job. Lucy was giving him grief, as usual. Finally, he could bear the misery and humiliation no longer. In an expression of exasperation that only Charlie Brown could think of, he stood on his head right there on the pitcher's mound.

As Lucy's degrading mockery continued, the ever-loyal Snoopy did the unexpected. He walked onto the pitcher's mound and stood on his head beside Charlie Brown, sharing his humiliation.

Sound biblical? The Bible says, "Weep with those who weep" (Rom. 12:15) and "Bear one another's burdens" (Gal. 6:2). Although this involves "standing on our heads" together—sharing each other's pain, it does NOT convey the full scope of these verses. We're not merely to *carry* burdens for our brothers and sisters in Christ; we're to *carry them away*. . . . Big difference! One involves sharing a load; the other involves removing a load.

Actually, two words are used for "bearing" in the New Testament. One word could be construed to mean standing beside a brother or sister in times of need to strengthen and comfort. The other, however, means something entirely different.

The first one, *anechomai*, means "to sustain, bear or hold up against a thing,"[1] much as a person would tie a stake to a tomato plant to sustain it from the weight it carries. The strength of the stake is transferred to the plant and thus "bears it up." When the Lord commands us to bear with one another in Colossians 3:13 and Ephesians 4:2, He isn't simply saying, "Put up with one another."

Although He is telling us to do that, He is also saying, "Stake yourselves to one another." In other words, we're to come alongside a weak brother or sister who is "weighted down" and say, "You're not going to fall and be broken or destroyed, because I'm staking myself to you. My strength is now yours. Go ahead, lean on me. As long as I can stand, you will."

What a wonderful picture for the Body of Christ. Fruit will result.

> Jackie Robinson was the first black to play major league baseball. While breaking baseball's color barrier, he faced jeering crowds in every stadium. While playing one day in his home stadium in Brooklyn, he committed an error. His own fans began to ridicule him. He stood at second base, humiliated, while the fans jeered. Then shortstop "Pee Wee" Reese came over and stood next to him. He put his arm around Jackie Robinson and faced the crowd. The fans grew quiet. Robinson later said that arm around his shoulder saved his career.[2]

Sometimes the world is more biblical than we are!

Carry the Burden Away

The second word is *bastazo*, meaning "to bear, lift or carry" something, with the idea being to carry it *away* or *remove* it.[3]

It is used in Romans 15:1–3 and Galatians 6:2, which we will look at shortly.

An amazing and little-understood aspect of intercession is exemplified by Christ in which He performed both of these bearing concepts. We have already established that His intercession for us was not a *prayer* He prayed, but a *work* He did. It was a work of "going between" to *reconcile* us to the Father and *break* Satan's dominion. And, of course, understanding His work in this area paves the way for an understanding of ours.

The intercessory work of Christ reached its fullest and most profound expression when our sins were "laid on" Him and He "bore" them away:

> All we like sheep have gone astray; we have turned every one to his own way; and the LORD hath *laid on* him the iniquity of us all . . . he hath poured out his soul unto death: and he was numbered with the transgressors; and he *bare* the sin of many, and made *intercession* for the transgressors.
>
> Isa. 53:6, 12 KJV, emphasis added

The Hebrew word *paga* is used twice in these two verses. Isaiah 53 is one of the most graphic Old Testament prophecies of Christ's cross. *Paga* is translated "laid on" once and "intercession" once. Both instances refer to when our sins, iniquities, diseases, etc., were placed upon Him. The New Testament describes this identification accordingly: "He made Him who knew no sin to be sin on our behalf, that we might become the righteousness of God in Him" (2 Cor. 5:21).

Christ then "bore" our sins and weaknesses away, "as far as the east is from the west" (Ps. 103:12). He is not still carrying them—somewhere, somehow, He disposed of them. The Hebrew word for "bore" or "bare" in this chapter is *nasa*, meaning "to bear away"[4] or "remove to a distance."[5] (We would spell the KJV "bare" today "bear.")

As already mentioned, the Greek counterpart, *bastazo*, means essentially the same. This connotation of bearing something to get rid of it becomes increasingly significant as we discuss our role in this facet of Christ's ministry of intercession. It is imperative to know that we don't simply carry someone's burden. We *stake (anechomai)* ourselves to the person and *carry the burden away (bastazo)*, helping them *get rid of it*!

The Scapegoat

The concept of a scapegoat comes from this redemptive intercessional work of Christ and illustrates well our concept of carrying something away.

A scapegoat takes someone else's blame and resulting consequences. My older brother, Tim, who is now a pastor in Ohio, was an expert at diverting blame to me when we were kids. I was always perfectly innocent as a child, never doing anything wrong. He was always the troublemaker.

Mom and Dad were forever taking his side—they could never see through his falsities and manipulation nor believe that I was so perfect. My entire childhood was one of enduring false accusation—being Tim's scapegoat! I've spent the last 20 years as an adult seeking inner healing for this injustice.

Of course you know that none of that is true—I was only almost perfect. But at least it allows me to get even with Tim for the few times he did successfully divert blame my way and it also illustrates my point. (By the way, I never did this to him.)

In the Old Testament, two animals were used on the Day of Atonement. One was sacrificed; the other was used for the scapegoat. After the high priest placed his hands on the scapegoat's head, confessing the sins of the nation, it was released into the wilderness never to be seen again. It symbolized

Christ the scapegoat crucified outside the city *bearing away* our curse.

Christ the scapegoat bearing our curse is well illustrated by a story I read in the book *What It Will Take to Change the World* by S. D. Gordon. The following is my paraphrase of this story about a couple who discovered that their 14-year-old son had lied to them. The young boy, whom we'll refer to as Steven, had skipped school three consecutive days. He was found out when his teacher called his parents to inquire about his well-being.

The parents were more upset by Steven's lies than his missing school. After praying with him about what he had done, they decided on a very unusual and severe form of punishment. Their conversation with him went something like this:

"Steven, do you know how important it is that we be able to trust one another?"

"Yes."

"How can we ever trust each other if we don't always tell the truth? That's why lying is such a terrible thing. Not only is it sin, but it also destroys our ability to trust one another. Do you understand that?"

"Yes, sir."

"Your mother and I must make you understand the seriousness, not so much of skipping school, but of the lies you told. Your discipline will be that for the next three days, one for each day of your sin, you must go to the attic and stay there by yourself. You will even eat and sleep there."

So young Steven headed off to the attic and the bed prepared for him there. It was a long evening for Steven and perhaps longer for Mom and Dad. Neither could eat, and for some reason when Dad tried to read the paper the words seemed foggy. Mom tried to sew but couldn't see to thread the needle. Finally it was bedtime. About midnight as the father lay in bed thinking about how lonely and afraid Steven must be, he finally spoke to his wife, "Are you awake?"

"Yes. I can't sleep for thinking about Steven."

"Neither can I," answered Dad.

An hour later he queried again, "Are you asleep yet?"

"No," answered Mom, "I just can't sleep for thinking about Steven all alone up in the attic."

"Me neither."

Another hour passed. It was now 2:00 A.M. "I can't stand this any longer!" murmured Dad as he climbed out of bed grabbing his pillow and a blanket. "I'm going to the attic."

He found Steven much as he expected: wide awake with tears in his eyes.

"Steven," said his father, "I can't take away the punishment for your lies because you must know the seriousness of what you have done. You must realize that sin, especially lying, has severe consequences. But your mother and I can't bear the thought of you being all alone here in the attic, so I'm going to share your punishment with you."

Father lay down next to his son and the two put their arms around each other's necks. The tears on their cheeks mingled as they shared the same pillow and the same punishment . . . for three nights.[6]

What a picture! Two thousand years ago God crawled "out of bed" with His blanket and pillow—actually three spikes and a cross of crucifixion—"staked" His tear-stained cheek next to ours and "bore" our punishment for sin. His attic was a tomb, His bed a slab of rock and the cheek next to His was yours—yours and mine.

That's right. Christ was not alone on the cross. We were with Him. He was actually there to join us in our sentence of death. No, we may not have been there physically, but we were there spiritually (see Rom. 6:4, 6). And of course, as He hung there

He was "bearing" some things. Our sins were being "laid on" Him and He was carrying them away.

Christ didn't quite finish the job, however.

Wait! Before you "stone" me with letters and phone calls, please look at Colossians 1:24: "Now I rejoice in my sufferings for your sake, and in my flesh I do my share on behalf of His Body (which is the church) in filling up that which is lacking in Christ's afflictions."

Our Part

What could possibly be lacking in Christ's afflictions? Our part. In fact, the *Amplified Bible* actually adds those words: "And in my own person I am making up whatever is still lacking and remains to be completed [on our part] of Christ's afflictions, for the sake of His body, which is the church." Ours isn't exactly the same as His was, of course: carrying another's sin, curse or blame. "But He, having offered one sacrifice for sins for all time" (Heb. 10:12) took the sins of the world upon Himself. Nonetheless, there is a "sharing" and "a filling up that which is lacking in Christ's afflictions."

That which is lacking is really the point of this entire book, not just this chapter. It's the "re-presenting" of which we have spoken. It's the mediating, the going between, the distributing, the enforcing. It's our part.

Let's look, then, at our part in this *bearing* aspect of Christ's work of intercession. We have already mentioned the "staking" facet in Colossians 3:13 and Ephesians 4:2. Let's examine the other aspect in Romans 15:1–3 and Galatians 6:2, then we will see how the two work together in our intercession:

> Now we who are strong ought to *bear* the weaknesses of those without strength and not just please ourselves. Let each of us

please his neighbor for his good, to his edification. For even Christ did not please Himself; but as it is written, "The reproaches of those who reproached Thee fell upon Me."

Rom. 15:1–3, emphasis added

Bear one another's burdens, and thus fulfill the law of Christ.

Gal. 6:2, emphasis added

As mentioned earlier, the Greek word for "bear" in both verses is *bastazo*, which, synonymous with the Hebrew *nasa*, means "to lift or carry," conveying the idea of removing or carrying away. In implementing Christ's priestly ministry of intercession, we're not simply to carry burdens *for* others; we're to carry them *away from* others—just as Jesus did.

Please remember, however, we're not literally *re-doing* what Christ did; we're *re-presenting* what He did. There's a big difference between the two. We're representing Him, extending His work—He who bore our infirmities, diseases, sins, reproaches and rejection when they were "laid on" *(paga)* Him.

He is the balm of Gilead (see Jer. 8:22), but we apply this healing salve.

He is the fountain of life (see Jer. 2:13; 17:13), but we are dispensers of His living water.

His is the comforting shepherd's staff (see Ps. 23:4), but He allows us the privilege of extending it.

Yes, not only did He bear our weaknesses, but He's also still "touched with the feeling of our infirmities" (Heb. 4:15 KJV). And He wants to touch us with the same compassion that we, too, might be bearers.

Think about it: the great Healer "healing" through us; the great High Priest "priesting" through us; the great Lover "loving" through us.

He inaugurated the new covenant with His blood (see Heb. 12:24), but in reference to *our part*, He has "made us able ministers of the new testament" (2 Cor. 3:6 KJV—"testament" is just a KJV word for "covenant").

Yes, Christ has made us "able ministers." And if I understand the word correctly, ministers administer something. What do we administer? The blessings and provisions of the new covenant.

And who secured and guarantees those benefits? Jesus, of course. Then this verse is just another way of saying that we have been made able distributors of what Christ already accomplished.

Released Through Others Coming to Your Aid

This verse came alive for me when my friend Mike Anderson made the following statement: "Sometimes the covenant of the Lord is released to you through others coming to your aid." At the time, Mike and his wife were missionaries in Jamaica. The statement was made on the heels of a life-and-death struggle they had just experienced with their son who had contracted a critical illness. The young child, two or three years old, had regressed for several days to a point of near death. That's when Mike called me and a few other individuals in the United States.

I knew something fairly serious had to be occurring when the prayer meeting I was leading was interrupted to inform me about an emergency phone call from Jamaica.

"I'm sorry to interrupt your meeting, Dutch," my friend Mike began, "but I desperately need your help."

"What is it?" I asked.

"It's my son, Toby," Mike replied. "He is deathly ill with a raging fever. The doctors haven't been able to find the cause. They've done all they know to do, but nothing seems to help. It is questionable whether or not he can survive another night in his condition. I have been praying and praying for him but can't seem to break this attack. The Lord has now revealed to me that his condition is being caused by a strong spirit of infirmity, which He actually allowed me to see as I was praying. I have not been able to break its power over my son, however, even though I've warred against it for hours. But I feel the Lord has shown me that if some strong intercessors join me, we can break this attack."

Mike and his wife, Pam, are strong in the Lord. They pray. They have faith. They understand authority. They were not in sin. Why then, you might ask, could they not get the breakthrough they needed on their own?

I don't know. But I suspect the Lord wanted to teach them (and those of us praying with them) the principle I'm now sharing with you.

The people I was meeting with and a few others Mike had called went into prayer. We asked God to meet (*paga*) with this child. We said essentially, "Father, allow us to move into our priestly role as intercessors (*paga*), enforcing the victory of Jesus in this situation, re-presenting or administering the blessings of the new covenant. Stake us to Toby and allow us, along with Christ, to be touched with the feeling of this infirmity. Lay on (*paga*) us this burden that we might bear (*nasa, bastazo*) it away. We ask this in Jesus' name—based on who He is and what He has done, Father."

We then bound the power of Satan over this child's life—in Christ's name, of course, because it was His victory we were "administering." Then we growled with "the bear anointing" (see chapter 4). No, we didn't really, but lighten up and enjoy the symbolism. Besides, I think maybe there was a growl in the Spirit! Perhaps a roar would be more accurate because the Lion of the tribe of Judah roared through us. He does "roar out of Zion," you know (see Joel 3:16; Amos 1:2). And we are certain He did because Mike called back a few hours later and said, "Almost immediately after I contacted several of you to pray with me, the fever broke and my son began to improve. Within a few hours he was well and released from the hospital."

Praise God! The Body of Christ had functioned as the Lord intended, and Jesus was glorified.

Mike continued, "I asked the Lord why I needed others to help me break this attack against my son. He reminded me of the story of Joshua and the army of Israel coming to the aid of the Gibeonites, who were helplessly outnumbered by five armies." Mike then recounted the story from Joshua 9 and 10 for me, which I'll briefly summarize for you.

The Gibeonites were one of the Canaanite tribes that Joshua and Israel were supposed to destroy. They had deceived the Israelites, however, into believing they had come from a far country in order to enter a covenant with them. Joshua and the Israelites neglected to pray about this and were therefore deceived into a binding, covenantal agreement. (Have you ever "forgotten" to pray about something and gotten into trouble?)

Even though it was born of deceit, the covenant was still valid and made Israel an ally of Gibeon. Therefore, a few days later when five armies marched against Gibeon, they called upon Joshua for help—based on the strength of covenant. Even though the agreement was conceived in deception, Joshua and his army traveled all night to arrive in time and rescue the Gibeonites. The entire story is an incredible demonstration of the power of covenant.

After calling my attention to this story, Mike then spoke these words to me: "Dutch, after reminding me of this story, the Lord planted the following thought in my heart as to why I needed help overcoming this spirit: 'Sometimes the covenant of the Lord is released to you through others coming to your aid!'"

Isn't that profound? The Almighty administering the blessings of the covenant through us. That's what intercession is all about. *Paga*: He "lays on" us someone else's need. *Anechomai*: We "stake" ourselves to that person. *Bastazo*: We "carry away" the weakness or burden.

Enforcing and Treading Upon the Enemy

A further profound picture of this partnership between Christ and the Church is exemplified in this same story of Israel and the Gibeonites. It's found in Joshua 10:22–27. Joshua is an Old Testament picture or type of Christ, and Israel pictures the Church. Joshua's name, which is actually the Hebrew equivalent to the name Jesus, had been changed earlier in his life to paint this picture. It had formerly been Hoshea.

After Joshua and the army of Israel defeated the five Canaanite armies in defense of the Gibeonites, the kings of these armies fled to hide in a cave.

Upon discovering them, Joshua ordered the kings to be brought to him and made them lie down on the ground. He was about to enact a very familiar custom, which was to place his foot on their necks or heads to display his conquest. Oftentimes the defeated army, or armies in this case, would then be paraded before the conquering king or general, observing him as he "displayed" his conquest. This is what Colossians 2:15 is referring to when it says of Christ, "When He had disarmed the rulers and authorities, He made a public display of them, having triumphed over them through Him."

Joshua, however, is about to do something very different and very prophetic. Rather than place his foot on the necks of these kings, as was the typical custom, Joshua summoned some of his soldiers and had them do it. No more literal picture of Christ and the Church, His army, could have been given to us. In fulfillment of this prophetic picture, when Jesus defeated Satan and his principalities and powers, the rulers of the darkness of this world, He, too, called His army to Him and said, "You put your feet on the necks of these enemies."

When Ephesians 2:6 says that He "raised us up with Him," Christ is saying, "It's not only My victory, but it's also yours."

He is also saying, "What I have done, you must enforce. I have put them under My feet legally—under My authority—but you must exercise that authority in individual situations, causing the literal fulfillment of it."

That is why Romans 16 says, "And the God of peace will soon crush Satan under *your* feet" (v. 20, emphasis added). And Luke 10:19 tells us, "Behold, I have given *you* authority to tread upon serpents and scorpions, and over all the power of the enemy, and nothing shall injure you" (emphasis added). This is what happened when we helped Mike: an enforcing and a treading.

Sometimes a "laying on" requires a "treading upon"!

Psalm 110, a futuristic Messianic psalm relating to Christ, also pictures our partnership with Him. It foretells that Christ would, after His resurrection, ascend to the right hand of the Father. According to the New Testament, at the time of His ascension and enthronement, He had *already* placed all other authorities under His feet:

And He put all things in subjection under His feet, and gave Him as head over all things to the church.

Eph. 1:22

For He has put all things in subjection under His feet. But when He says, "All things are put in subjection," it is evident that He is excepted who put all things in subjection to Him.

1 Cor. 15:27

But Psalm 110 informs us that He would still be *waiting* for them to become His footstool: "Sit at My right hand, *until* I make Thine enemies a footstool for Thy feet" (Ps. 110:1, emphasis added).

Wait a minute. Do we have a contradiction between this Messianic prophecy and the New Testament verses that say after He ascended to the Father's right hand they were *already* under His feet? No. Then why the seeming inconsistency? *Are* they under His feet or *will* they be placed there? The answer is YES! They are *legally* through the Cross. They will be *literally* as we do "our part." Verses 2 and 3 of Psalm 110 describe our part:

> The LORD will stretch forth Your strong scepter from Zion, saying, "Rule in the midst of Your enemies." Your people will volunteer freely in the day of Your power; in holy array, from the womb of the dawn, Your youth are to you as the dew.

The word "power" in this passage, *chayil*, is also translated "army."[7] Christ is looking for a volunteer army that will stretch forth His strong scepter of authority, ruling in the midst of their enemies, enforcing His great victory. So, once again, did He place all other authorities under foot or do we? YES! He did; we enforce. He conquered Satan and his kingdom; we enforce the victory.

As we stated, sometimes a "laying on" results in a "treading upon."

In other words, at times when Christ lays a prayer mission or burden on us (*paga*) that we might bear it away (*nasa, bastazo*), the task involves warfare. No serious Bible student could study the word "intercession" (*paga*) and separate it from the concept of warfare. This will be obvious as we focus more directly on spiritual warfare in upcoming chapters.

Both the Hebrew and Greek words used for "tread," *darak* (Hebrew)[8] and *pateo* (Greek),[9] involve the concept of violence or war. The Hebrew word *darak* actually came to be used for "bending the bow"[10] when about to shoot an arrow and is still used today in Israel for the command, "Load your weapons." Both words are used for treading or trampling in a wine press, a fittingly used symbolism of Christ overcoming His enemies in Isaiah 63:3 and Revelation 19:15.

The verse in Revelation says, "And from His mouth comes a sharp sword, so that with it He may smite the nations; and He will rule them with a rod of iron; and He treads the wine press of the fierce wrath of God, the Almighty." We in America even have a verse from the famous hymn "The Battle Hymn of the Republic" taken from these two verses of Scripture: "He is trampling out the vintage where the grapes of wrath are stored, He has loosed the fateful lightning of His terrible swift sword."[11]

It's amazing to me that these same two words are used to describe not only Christ at war, but also our warfare. Let me give you one such reference. In Joshua 1:3, the Lord said to Joshua, "Every place on which the sole of your foot treads, I have given it to you, just as I spoke to Moses." The word "tread," of course, is *darak*. God wasn't telling Israel that everywhere they walked or stepped was theirs. He had already marked off the perimeters of the inheritance. He was saying symbolically, "Every place that you are willing to load your weapons and take, I'm going to give to you."

So, one more time, was God giving or were they taking? YES! And just to prove my point, remember that the previous generation under Moses was afraid and wouldn't *darak* (load their weapons and fight) and God wouldn't give.

Please don't think for a moment that it's any different for us today. These things happened to Israel as types or shadows for us (see 1 Cor. 10:6, 11). That which our Joshua-Jesus has and is giving to us won't automatically come to us either, just because we belong to Him. We, too, must take "the weapons of our warfare" (2 Cor. 10:4) and *darak*!

This is intercession, as it was through Christ and is through us. Oftentimes it is to be done for our brothers and sisters as we, like Christ, climb into their attics of despair, place our cheeks next to theirs and carry away the burdens or weaknesses.

- May Christ live *through you*!
- May that which is lacking in Christ's afflictions—our part—be lacking no more!
- May the scepter be extended from us as we rule in the midst of our enemies, making them His footstool!
- May the terrifying roar of the Lion of Judah resound from the Church!
- May the covenant of the Lord be administered in the earth!

I read the following father-and-son story that serves as a fitting end to this chapter:

> In spite of repeated warnings, a small boy continued coming home late after school. One morning his parents informed him that there was no more grace—he must arrive on time that evening. He was late again.
>
> At dinner that night the young man discovered his punishment. On his plate was only a piece of bread. The boy was shocked and dismayed. After waiting a few moments for the full impact to do its work, the father took the boy's plate and gave him his fill of meat and potatoes.
>
> When the boy was grown to manhood he said, "All my life I've known what God is like by what my father did that night."[12]

To be like Christ will cost us. Our cause is costly. The work of intercession has a price. Let's pay it. Let's push back from our bountiful table once in a while and show someone what God is like.

Questions for Reflection

1. Explain the two types of bearing in the Scriptures. How do they pertain to intercession? What does *paga* have to do with bearing?

2. Can you explain how the scapegoat is a picture of intercession?

3. How does the account of Joshua and the Israelites in Joshua 10:22–27 picture the partnership between Christ and the Church?

4. In what way does Psalm 110 picture the relationship between Jesus and the Church?

5. Have you told Jesus yet today that you love Him?

6

No Trespassing

Protective Boundaries

"No dumping allowed. Trespassers will be violated."

I used to laugh every time I drove by the sign. This wasn't a homemade sign. It was a professionally made metal sign posted by a city in Oklahoma (I won't tell you which one). It was even the fancy kind with fluorescent letters that could be easily seen at night. But those who made it were confused and instead of saying "Trespassers (or Violators) will be prosecuted," they worded it "Trespassers will be violated."

I hope they were merely confused. Perhaps they weren't. Maybe in that town the law violated lawbreakers instead of prosecuting them. I decided I didn't want to find out.

There is an aspect of intercession that relates to protection: protective boundaries—posting signs in the spirit, if you please: "No dumping allowed, Satan. Trespassers will be violated."

In the nineteenth chapter of Joshua, the word *paga* (intercession) is used several times. The passage is describing the dimensions or boundaries of each of the tribes of Israel. It is translated several ways in different translations, including "reached to," "touched," "bordered," "boundary." *The Spirit-Filled Bible* says *paga*, when used in this context, is the extent to which a boundary reaches.[1]

Does it surprise you that the word used for "intercession," *paga*, is also translated "boundary"? It really shouldn't. It only seems logical to me that perimeters of protection be linked to prayer. I want to state emphatically: We CAN build boundaries of protection[2] around ourselves and others through intercession. What a comfort to know that this truth is inherent in the very meaning of the word.

Many Christians believe that protection from accidents, destruction, satanic traps and assaults, etc., is automatic for the Christian—that we do nothing to cause it—that it is based on the sovereignty of God alone. In other words, when God wants to protect us from these things, He does; when He chooses not to, He allows them to happen.

This belief simply means that whether or not we are delivered from destructive things is based entirely on God, not us. Those who adhere to this teaching usually believe nothing can happen to a Christian that is not allowed by God. Others go so far as to say this is true for everyone, not just Christians. They believe God is in control of everything that happens on Earth.

That God is not directly in control of *everything* that takes place on Earth can be seen in the simple facts:

- He would never decide a person should be raped or abused.
- He would never desire that the innocent suffer.
- He would never will murder, pillage, racial genocide and a thousand other things.

Governing Principles

Whether or not God directly controls every event in the life of a Christian can be answered by stating that the basic laws of sowing and reaping, cause and effect, individual responsibility and the free will aren't negated when we come to Christ. *All* promises from God are attached to conditions—governing principles. Most, if not all, of these conditions involve responsibility on our part. Protection is no exception.

Most of us don't like that. It threatens us and somehow weakens God in our minds to imply He's not in total control of everything. And the majority are greatly offended if anything is taught implying that a failure to receive protection, provision, healing, an answer to prayer, or anything else from God could be our fault.

I can understand how it might threaten us—I'm threatened by me—but I don't understand why it offends. Are any of us claiming perfection? Aren't all of us going to fail once in a while? Then why are we offended when a teaching suggests that these imperfections and failures might hinder us?

Why are we offended and opposed to a teaching that says our unbelief kept us from receiving something when so often the Bible says if we believe and do not doubt or waver we'll receive (see Matt. 17:20; 21:21; Mark 11:22–24; Jas. 1:6–7)?

Why are we offended when it is implied that our inability to persevere created lack when the Bible says that we "through faith *and patience* inherit the promises" (Heb. 6:12, emphasis added)?

Why are we confused or angry when it is suggested that our not doing something caused failure when the Bible says if we're "willing *and obedient*" we'll eat the good of the land (Isa. 1:19 KJV, emphasis added)?

As many as 80 percent of those who consider themselves born again don't tithe, thereby opening themselves to a curse. Yet they are offended when someone implies that their lack of provision might be their own fault (see Mal. 3:8–12).

We don't forgive and still have the gall to think God will hear and answer our prayers (see Mark 11:25–26).

Often, we eat poorly, don't exercise and abuse our bodies in other ways. Then we blame our sicknesses on God's will.

We don't properly train our children, yet we're offended with the suggestion that their rebellion might be our fault (see Deut. 6:7; Prov. 22:6).

We don't abide in Christ and His Word. Still we blame it on "God's will" when we "ask what we will" and it isn't done (John 15:7 KJV).

We know faith comes through hearing and meditating on God's Word (see Rom. 10:17), and most of us do very little of that. But let someone imply that we didn't receive a promise because of unbelief and we're irate.

The Scriptures teach that "He that dwelleth in the secret place of the most High" (KJV) receives the protective promises of the remainder of Psalm 91 . . . that I have an armor I must wear and carry, including the shield of faith, to ward off Satan's fiery darts (see Eph. 6:13–18 KJV) . . . that Satan goes about like a roaring lion seeking whom he may devour and that I am to resist him (see 1 Pet. 5:8; Jas. 4:7) . . . and yet, let someone suggest that my lack of protection from some destructive happening could be my own fault and I'm offended. How about you?

I'm certainly not implying that God *never* allows us to walk through difficulties, that *all* our problems are because of disobedience or that *all* unanswered prayer is because of unbelief. I'm simply saying that many of our failures and difficulties are our fault, not "God's will"; we have a part to play in the securing of protection and other heavenly provisions.

Let's try to lay down our fears, insecurities and tendencies toward offense. Let's accept the fact that the Scriptures are filled with principles that put responsibility on us, which must be met to receive God's promises. Let's realize this doesn't cancel grace and promote salvation by works. Grace does not imply "no responsibility" on our part. Let's realize the love of God is unconditional, but His favor and blessing are not.

Let's cast off all laziness, complacency and apathy. Let's realize we will fall short at times and not feel condemned when we do. *Let's!*

Building Boundaries Through Prayer

If you're still willing to finish this book after such a dissertation—back to protection. You've probably guessed by now that I don't believe it is automatically ours just because we are Christians. We must do things to secure it, one of which is building boundaries (*paga*) of protection through prayer.

I heard a minister in Fort Worth, Texas, tell the story of another pastor who years ago received divine protection as a result of prayer-building walls or boundaries of protection (*paga*). This pastor had developed the discipline of beginning every day with an hour of prayer.

One particular day, however, he felt a strong leading of the Holy Spirit to pray longer, so he continued for a second hour. After two hours he still felt the need to keep on praying, so he persevered for a third hour, asking for God's protection and blessing on his day, as well as for other things. He then felt released from the need to pray longer, so he stopped.

That evening as he was mowing his lawn, he felt something repeatedly brush up against his leg. He looked down and saw a coiled rattlesnake trying to strike him, but it just couldn't hit him. Instead, it kept brushing either side of his leg.

Why had the man felt the need to pray longer that morning? What was he doing? Among other things he was building "boundaries" of protection through prayer—*paga*.

Some would say, of course, that God doesn't need three hours of prayer to protect one from a rattlesnake. I would agree. He didn't "need" seven days of marching around Jericho to tear it down either, but He chose to do it that way. He doesn't "need" to spit in a person's eye to heal them, but He did once. Why He requires things to be done certain ways, we don't always know, but we do know that for us *obedience is the key*. If He says "three hours" then three hours is exactly what it will take.

Dwelling in the Secret Place

Consistency is also a key when it comes to prayer for protection. We must "dwell" in the secret place to "abide" under the Almighty's protective shadow: "He that dwelleth in the secret place of the most High shall abide under the shadow of the Almighty" (Ps. 91:1 KJV). Jesus equated the "secret" place to the prayer closet in Matthew 6:6. The word "dwell" in Psalm 91:1 is *yashab*, which means "to remain or abide; to dwell in or inhabit."[3] The point is that it must be a lifestyle, not a once in a while activity. We must make the secret place our habitation or "dwelling" place. Many believers' prayer lives are too sporadic to build solid walls of protection.

The word "abide" in this same verse is *luwn*, which means, among other things, "to spend the night."[4] Let's read it with that meaning: "He that dwelleth in the secret place of the most High, shall *spend the night* under the shadow of the Almighty." In other words, prayer is like the Word of God—we don't read enough today for the entire week. We must have "daily bread" or manna. Likewise, we must go to the secret place daily and when we do we can "spend the night" there. Tomorrow, however, we must go again. Consistency is a key.

I heard a visiting minister in Eaton, Ohio, share this testimony of God's protection in World War II. He served on a ship and every day he and a few other sailors would have a prayer time, seeking God for protection for themselves and the ship. What were they doing? Building boundaries (*paga*) of protection.

"In one battle," he related, "an enemy plane dropped a bomb onto the deck of our ship. Instead of exploding, however, to everyone's astonishment the bomb bounced off the deck and into the water, just like a rubber ball would!" This minister went on to say that in battle after battle they and the ship were miraculously spared.

Well-Timed Times to Pray

Boundaries of protection! No trespassing! Life in the secret place!

This facet of intercession is not only to be something we do on a *general* regular basis for our family and loved ones. There are also *specific* times when the Holy Spirit will alert us to particular situations that need protective prayer. These are what the Scriptures call *kairos* times.

There are two Greek words for "time." One is *chronos*, which is time in general, the general "time in which anything *is* done."[5] The other word, *kairos*, is the strategic or "right time; the opportune point of time at which something *should be* done."[6]

A window of opportunity would be *kairos* time.

A well-timed attack in war would be *kairos* time.

When someone is in danger or about to be attacked by Satan, that is a *kairos* time.

What time it is would be *chronos* time.

The Bible speaks of well-timed (*kairos*) temptations (see Luke 4:13; 8:13). No doubt coincidental temptations occur—a person just happening to be in the wrong place at the wrong time—but there are also well-planned, well-timed temptations.

It pays to be alert, both for ourselves and for others. I've had the Holy Spirit prompt me to pray for individuals, especially young believers, with the thought, *It's a* kairos *time of temptation for them.* This is what took place in Luke 22:31–32 when Jesus interceded for Peter, praying that his faith not fail him after he denied Christ. It worked.

Is it possible that some who have fallen away from Christ would not have if someone had interceded for them?

The Scriptures also inform us of strategically timed persecution (see Acts 12:1; 19:23). This is usually to discourage, to distract or, in extreme cases, to destroy us. In these references, during times of renewal and success in the Early Church, Satan launched orchestrated attacks of persecution. They failed.

Is it possible that much successful persecution against the Church could be stopped or rendered unfruitful if we were alert and interceded against it?

Often we forget the instruction to not lean on our own understanding, and fail to acknowledge Him in our intercession (see Prov. 3:5–6). We do not wait for or listen to the promptings of the Holy Spirit, usually to our own hurt. We forget that "we wrestle not against flesh and blood" (Eph. 6:12 KJV) and that the "weapons of our warfare are not carnal" (2 Cor. 10:4 KJV). We are so afraid of becoming demon conscious (putting an overemphasis on them) that we become demon unconscious. Sometimes our quest for balance gets us out of balance.

Ephesians 6:18, the context of which is spiritual warfare, says that we are to "be on the alert . . . for all the saints" and "pray at all times [*kairos*] in the Spirit." He is not telling us here to pray all the time, which would be *chronos*, but to pray at all strategic times (*kairos*). In other words, we are in a war and if we are alert He will warn us of the well-timed attacks (*kairos*) of the enemy so that we can create a boundary (*paga*) of protection by praying.

Kairos, a Time to *Paga*

One morning several years ago as I was praying, the Lord gave me a mental picture. Some might call it a vision. Whatever it is called, I saw something: a rattlesnake coiled at my dad's feet. Seemed like a *kairos* time to me! I spent about 15 minutes praying earnestly for his protection until I felt released from the urgency.

The next day he called me—he was in Florida, I was in Texas—and said, "You'll never guess what happened yesterday. Jodie [my stepmother] went out back to the shed. Before walking in as she normally would, she pushed the door open, stopped and looked down. There where she was about to step was a coiled rattlesnake. She backed away carefully, came and got me and I killed it."

I said to Dad, "Yeah, I know."

Surprised, he asked, "How did you know?"

"I saw it in the spirit," I responded, "and prayed for your protection. You owe me." (No, I didn't really say the part about owing me. I acted real humble and said something like, "Praise God" or "Praise Jesus." You know how we do it!)

What was I doing as I prayed for him? Setting boundaries (*paga*) of protection around him and Jodie.

How did I pray? I asked the Father to protect them. I bound any attempt of Satan to harm them. I quoted a verse or two of Scripture promising protection. Then I prayed in the Spirit.

Gail Mummert, a member of our fellowship in Colorado Springs, shared this remarkable testimony of protection during a *kairos* moment in Lancaster, Texas:

> As we were driving home in threatening weather, my husband, Gene, turned on the radio for a local report.

Funnel clouds had indeed been spotted nearby. After arriving home, things grew strangely calm.

In a short while, the wind started to blow fiercely. Trees were bent over and the very walls of the house began to flutter. Windows rattled and hail beat on the carport.

"Get into the hall and close the doors," my husband shouted. "Get pillows, blankets and a flashlight."

"Nana, I'm scared," cried our five-year-old grandson, William.

"Jesus will take care of us. Don't be afraid," I told him.

Suddenly sirens began to go off in our small town. The walls moved as though they weren't anchored to anything. "If we're not in a tornado, we're close," shouted Gene as he ran into the hall.

"Link arms and sit on the floor," I said.

"I love you," Gene said to us as he surrounded us with blankets and pillows, covered us with his body and enveloped us with his arms.

A mighty rushing wind was all around us and sucked us together into a ball. "Pray! Keep praying," he said.

"God Almighty, help us!" we screamed.

Explosion!

Windows shattered, glass flew everywhere. Another explosion. The walls caved in. Debris shot everywhere like arrows toward their target.

"Jesus, help us! You are our Savior! You are our King!" my voice cried. I looked up—the roof was falling on us. A ladder crashed down on my husband's back.

"Now start praising Him," Gene shouted through the wind. The next blast was the worst. There was nothing we could do. Only He could help us. Everything was out of control, but we knew the sovereignty of God. We knew we were at the point of death, but we shouted, "Thank You, Jesus! Thank You, Lord!"

Suddenly, peace filled me like a flood. A sweet voice filled my heart, "I've heard your cry for help. I've bent the heavens for you. No matter what happens around you, I'm here protecting you." Tears flooded my face and I knew Jesus was protecting us. It seemed His arms had surrounded us. I knew we would be safe.

The tornado was over. The rain beat down on us with a force I had never felt before. We were safe. "Mama, I see the sky," little William said.

"William, that's because the roof is gone. We probably won't have any walls, either," Gene informed him.

"I'm so thankful we're okay," our daughter Wendy cried. "Jesus protected us, didn't He?" Though buried under tons of debris, our hair covered with insulation and glass, we were okay. Just a few minor injuries.

Talk about walls of protection! Several people were killed and many injured in that devastating tornado, but the everlasting arms of the Lord protected the Mummert family. Gail was privileged to share her entire story with *The Dallas Morning News*. The newspaper even printed her testimony about the protection of the Lord.

I had a friend in Dallas several years ago who experienced an interesting answer to prayer in a *kairos* situation. She had gone early one morning to visit her son and daughter-in-law. The son worked an all-night shift, so, awaiting his return from work, his wife and mother visited for a while. As time wore on and the son didn't arrive, Mom began to feel uneasy. Something didn't seem right.

Thinking that perhaps he was still at work, they called his place of employment, "No," they were told, "he has already left." Becoming more alarmed the mother said, "I'm concerned. Let's drive toward his place of work."

She had assumed her son had left work at his normal time and should have been home by then when, in fact, he had left just moments before their call. But the Lord was directing even in that because, though he was not in any danger yet, the Holy Spirit knew a *kairos* moment was coming for this young man, and He wanted this praying mother there when it happened.

As Mom and daughter-in-law drove toward his workplace on a busy Dallas parkway, they saw him coming from the other direction on his motorcycle, traveling around 40 to 50 miles per hour. As they watched, he fell asleep and veered off the road, hit the curb and flew 40 or 50 feet through the air. He was not even wearing a helmet.

As the boy was moving through the air, Mom was praying, "*Jesus, protect my son!*" She continued to pray as they turned around and drove back to him. A crowd had already gathered around him, and they ran to the scene, wondering what they would find.

They found a miracle! No injuries—no bones broken, no lacerations, no internal injuries. Just a dazed young man wondering what had happened.

Paga happened . . . *Kairos paga* happened! Boundaries happened. A mother picked up on the warning from the Holy Spirit and was therefore in the right place at the right time.

Does this mean that if you weren't there praying when someone you loved had an accident, you're to blame for their injury or death? Of course not. If we all played that guessing game, it would drive us insane. It simply means we must be alert, and when warnings do come from the Holy Spirit, we must respond by praying—building some boundaries.

I heard a guest lecturer at Christ for the Nations in Dallas, Texas, tell another interesting story involving not a *kairos moment*, but a *kairos season* of building boundaries (*paga*) of protection.

He had a vivid reoccurring dream, which he felt strongly was a warning from the Lord, of his married daughter dying. In the dream he was not shown how her death happened, but he felt strongly that Satan had a well-laid plan to take his daughter's life. So as not to alarm her, he told only his son-in-law and the two of them began to intercede (*paga*) daily for her safety. They were building boundaries (*paga*) of protection around her.

This minister related how several times a day—while he worked, drove his car, walked, whenever it came to mind—he would bind Satan's plan to take his daughter's life. "How would he do this?" some might ask. "What did he say?" He probably said things like:

- "Father, I bring my daughter to You." That is creating a "meeting" (*paga*) with God.
- "I ask You to protect her from any trap Satan has set for her. You said You would deliver us from the snare of the trapper" (see Ps. 91:3). That is building "boundaries" (*paga*) of protection.
- "Thank You for laying this prayer burden on me that I might lift off and carry away from her (*nasa*) this assignment of death." That's having someone else's burden or weakness "laid on" (*paga*) us.
- "Satan, I bind this plan of yours and break any hold you may have gained in this situation. Your weapons against her won't prosper and you're not going to take her life." That is "meeting" (*paga*) the enemy to break.
- "I do this in the name of Jesus!" That's basing all our *prayers* on the *work* Christ has already done. It's *representing* Him

101

. . . administering what He has already accomplished . . . *enforcing* His victory.

About a month later—remember, I said this was a *kairos season* and I said he prayed *daily*—his daughter received a promotion at work. With the promotion came a life insurance policy that mandated a physical exam.

At one point in the process, after a blood sample had been taken, a doctor addressed her in a near panic with the question and comments, "Lady, what have you been doing in your diet? We can find no potassium in you at all! You should be dead. There is no reasonable explanation as to why you're alive. When this deficiency occurs, a person normally feels fine but suddenly drops dead. We must get you to the hospital immediately and begin to replenish the potassium."

She lived, of course. She had been on a strange diet for several weeks, during which she had eaten only one or two kinds of food. Though there was no reasonable explanation as to why she lived, we know the spiritual explanation: a boundary (*paga*) of protection built in the spirit through prayer.

Under the Shadow of the Most High. Keep Out!

Perhaps the most amazing example of *kairos*-timed intercession in my life happened on one of my journeys to Guatemala. I was one of 40 to 45 individuals traveling to a remote place on the Passion River in the Peten Jungle. Our mission was to build a combination clinic and outreach station on the river. We were to be constructing two buildings as well as doing a little preaching in the nearby villages.

It was an amazing trip. We ate monkey meat and boa constrictor. We killed huge tarantulas, a nine-inch scorpion and a coral snake in our camp. I was attacked by ants that, unbeknownst to us, had taken refuge in the lumber we were hauling and sleeping on as we traveled all night up the river. We flew in old, rickety army planes and landed on fields from which goats had to be cleared prior to our arrival. (None of this has anything to do with prayer, but it lets you know how incredibly brave I am and how much I've suffered for the cause of Christ.)

Our leader, Hap Brooks, had me leading songs from the front of our long dugout canoe as we journeyed up and down the river. His favorite was "It's a Good Life Livin' for the Lord." He also made me utter my famous Tarzan call, which was incredibly good and would reverberate across the river and into the jungle. Natives from the villages would stand on the banks and listen. Having never seen or heard of Tarzan, of course, they were not terribly impressed—in fact they sort of had that "who is that idiot?" look on their faces. That is, until the animals in the jungle began to come to me! They had the same expression. (This has nothing to do with prayer, either, but it lets you know how incredibly talented I am.)

Back to the purpose of the story. Prior to leaving for the jungle, we spent our first night (Friday) in Guatemala City, the capital of Guatemala. We had arranged months earlier for the Guatemalan airlines to fly us the following day into the jungle. On our arrival at the airport Saturday afternoon, we were informed that they had changed their plans and would fly us to our destination not that day but the next.

Feeling an urgency to go as scheduled due to the limited amount of time to accomplish our mission, our leaders pressed the airlines for three hours to honor their original agreement.

"No," the manager said in his broken English, "we take you tomorrow."

"But you agreed months ago to take us today," we argued.

"We have no pilot available," they countered.

"Find one," we pleaded.

"What is your hurry? Enjoy the city," they encouraged us.

And so it went for three hours, in and out of offices, meeting with one official, then another. Finally, in exasperation, one of them threw up his hands and said, "Okay, we take you now! Get on that plane—quickly!"

We all ran to the plane, throwing our bags and tools into the baggage area ourselves. We wanted to leave before they changed their minds.

That night, while we were 250 miles away, an earthquake hit Guatemala City and killed 30,000 people in 34 seconds! Had we stayed in the city one more night—as the airlines wanted us to—some of our team would have been killed and others injured. We know this for certain because on our return to the city we saw the building we had stayed in the night before the earthquake—and would have been staying in again had we not left on Saturday—with huge beams lying across the beds.

The connection between all this and our subject is that an intercessor from our home church back in Ohio had received a strong burden to pray for us on the second day of our journey. For *three hours* she was in intense intercession for us. Can you guess which three hours? Yes. The three hours that our leaders were negotiating with the airline officials.

We didn't know that our lives would have been in jeopardy had we stayed another night in Guatemala City, but God did. This intercessor didn't know it either. She only knew that for some reason she had a strong burden to pray for us. She was alert, as Ephesians 6:18 instructs us, and perceived the *kairos* time. There isn't a doubt in my mind that she helped create the protection and intervention we experienced.

There is a life in the secret place, but it's not automatic for believers. Although we are promised protection from our enemy, we have a definite part to play in the securing of it for ourselves and for others. The intercessor knows this and leaves nothing to chance, posting signs for all the forces of hell to see: "Under the shadow of the Most High. Keep out!"

Questions for Reflection

1. How is the connection between *paga* and protection made?

2. Is all protection automatic for Christians? Is everything that happens to us allowed by God, or do our actions and prayers have a part in it? Explain.

3. Comment on consistency in prayer as it relates to protection.

4. Explain the difference between *chronos* and *kairos* and how this relates to intercession.

5. Have you posted any "No Trespassing" signs lately?

7

Butterflies, Mice, Elephants and Bull's-Eyes

A Happening by Chance

I was riding high, literally. About 200 feet high, as a matter of fact. I was parasailing in Acapulco.

My wife, Ceci, and I were on the last day of our three-day vacation in this tourist hot spot. I had been watching this activity, seeing the boats pull individuals from off the beach, up into the air and across the beautiful waters. These airborne sailors would soar effortlessly for 5 to 10 minutes, enjoying their freedom from the bonds of the earth, and then be swung back onto the beach. To the amazement and cheers of us less-adventurous earthlings, they would land softly and accept our applause. They didn't even get wet.

For two days I watched this. Now I've always wanted to parachute—actually, wondered what it would be like is closer to the truth—but was smart enough to not do it before I married.

My wife has since asked me not to, which is now my face-saving excuse. *But maybe this would satisfy my curiosity*, I thought as I watched this activity. Finally, I decided I wasn't quite that curious.

We men have a constant need to impress the ladies in our lives, demonstrating our fearlessness and ability to rise to any challenge.

"Wow, that looks pretty awesome," my wife said.

"Aw, it doesn't look that difficult," I replied in my best matter-of-fact "any guy could do it" voice. "All you do is run off the beach and let the boat do the rest. I'd do it, but you probably wouldn't want me to. Besides, it's not worth the money."

To my absolute horror, she responded excitedly, "Oh, I wouldn't mind. In fact, I'd love to see you do it and it's not really that expensive. Give it a try!"

Oh, my dear heavenly Father, I cried inwardly, *get me out of this!*

Get yourself out of it, I heard in my heart. *You got yourself into it.*

"Oh, you're just saying that for me, dear," I responded to her. "I know you would really be terrified if I did this, but thanks for thinking of me. I won't put you through it, though."

"No, really, I *want* you to. It would make a great picture and, besides, what could go wrong?" she asked. "Go for it."

"Okay," I said foolishly. "Yeah, what could go wrong?"

There are times in your life when the thing to do is fake an injury, come up with an unexplainable headache or simply humble yourself, admit you're an egotistical male liar and repent of your sin. But I decided to save face. Now tell me, with God's sense of justice and humor, do you really think He was going to allow that?

It was the final morning of our stay. We were to leave in an hour or so. I was in my street clothes, shoes and all. Even kept my watch on. After all, you didn't even touch the water. I should have known this didn't always go as planned when they made me sign that release form but . . .

I was the first of the day. Takeoff was fairly routine and within seconds I was 200 feet high, enjoying a bird's eye view of the beach. Being the first of the day, they were pulling me along the beach, only about 50 or so yards out from the shoreline so that they could advertise for their day's business.

I actually began to enjoy it. It was a real high (pun intended). People along the shore began to wave at me and cheer me on. I was the center of attention for everyone. I, of course, waved back in a "not too demonstrative, this is no big deal" sort of way. Just being cool.

Suddenly, I had the strange sensation the water was getting closer. A second later I knew it was getting closer. Another second and I *lighted upon* the water with a great splash. "How the mighty have fallen!"

This is impossible, I thought. *This is a dream. A BAD dream.* Remembering that I had never tasted salt water in a dream, it didn't take me long to realize that it wasn't a dream at all and that it was very possible. I swam to the boat, which had experienced engine failure, and climbed aboard. Now I was totally cool—wet and cool!

The driver of the boat finally got it started again and we drove back to the starting point. With my best "it's no big deal, in fact, it was kinda fun" swagger, I waded back onto the beach. To this day I don't think my wife knows how I really felt. Like most women she never picks up on it when my male ego is asserting itself. Why, just the other day when she thought we needed to stop and ask for directions . . .

I can hear the wheels of your mind turning. You are wondering what part of this story could possibly have anything to do with intercession, except for a couple of fleeting seconds when I was in SERIOUS prayer. Actually, another of our definitions of *paga* is used, which is "to light upon."[1] The concept, of course, is landing on or coming to a certain place, and the inference is that it is happening by chance. We might, therefore, use the phrase "chance upon" or "happen upon." I'll give you the reference for this shortly and explain its connection to prayer, but first let's look at a couple of other introductory points.

Our Helper

This chapter is about our Helper, the Holy Spirit. Without any doubt the greatest single key to successful intercession is learning to cooperate with the Holy Spirit, allowing Him to be all He was sent to be in us. Jesus called Him our "Helper" in John 14:26: "But the Helper, the Holy Spirit, whom the Father will send in My name, He will teach you all things, and bring to your remembrance all that I said to you."

Some translations use the word "Comforter" instead of "Helper," but the word is *Parakletos* and means "one called alongside to aid, help or support."[2] It is such a powerful word that the *Amplified* version uses seven words to communicate its rich meaning: "Comforter (Counselor, Helper, Intercessor, Advocate, Strengthener, Standby), the Holy Spirit." I want to focus on Him as our "Helper" and "Intercessor."

We read in Romans 8:26–28 that He wants to help us in our prayer lives:

> And in the same way the Spirit also helps our weakness; for we do not know how to pray as we should, but the Spirit Himself intercedes for us with groanings too deep for words; and He who searches the hearts knows what the mind of the Spirit is, because He intercedes for the saints according to the will of God. And we know that God causes all things to work together for good to those who love God, to those who are called according to His purpose.

Notice that verse 28 begins with the word "and," which is a conjunction connecting verse 28 to verses 26 and 27, making it dependent on what is said there. In other words, all things DON'T work together for good in the lives of Christians unless certain conditions are met. All things CAN work together for our good, and God's will is for all things to work together for our good, but this isn't automatic. We have a part to play. It happens as verses 26 and 27 are being implemented.

I don't believe the intercession of the Holy Spirit spoken of in these verses refers only to "tongues." However, most of us in Pentecostal and charismatic circles believe it has to include this gift, which we believe allows the Holy Spirit to literally pray through us. It is not my intention in this book to prove this, nor am I implying that those who do not practice it are second rate in their praying.

If you do not pray in this way, it is my strong desire not to offend you. I have great love and respect for my non-charismatic brothers and sisters in Christ. Yet, it is impossible for me to share what I believe the Lord has taught me concerning this passage without referring to praying in tongues, or as the Scriptures also word it, "praying in the Spirit."

I will, therefore, be saying a good bit about this. From this point on, however, in an effort to be as inclusive and inoffensive as possible, I will only use the phrase "praying in the Spirit." To charismatic readers, when you see this phrase, please know that I am including "tongues." To the rest of you, please interpret with your belief of what it means to "pray in the Spirit."

This passage says that the Holy Spirit wants to help us in our "weakness." The word in Greek is *astheneia* and means literally "without strength" or ability.[3] An "inability to produce results" is the concept communicated by the word.

Have you ever felt an inability in your prayer life to produce results? Have you ever come up against a "mountain" you couldn't move? I recall that happening to me a few years ago, or was that a few hours ago? It's a fact of life.

The Lord then says in this verse that one of the reasons we have this "inability to produce results" is because we don't always "know how to pray as we should." The word "should" here is a very important word. *Dei* is primarily a legal term meaning "that which is necessary, right or proper in the nature of a case; what one must do; that which is legally binding for someone."[4]

For example, Luke 18:1 tells us, "Men *ought* always to pray, and not to faint" (KJV, emphasis added). The verse does not mean, "It would be a good idea to pray." It is declaring, "It is absolutely necessary—binding upon you—that you pray."

Jesus used the word when He said of the woman bent over from a spirit of infirmity, "And ought not this woman, being a daughter of Abraham, whom Satan hath bound, lo, these eighteen years, be loosed from this bond on the sabbath day?" (Luke 13:16 KJV). His reason that she should be loosed from this spirit was her being "a daughter of Abraham." In other words, she had a covenantal right to it. Because He had the ability to give her what she had a covenantal right to, He said in essence, "Is it not necessary and binding upon me that I deliver this daughter of Abraham from this infirmity?"

Now that we understand the strength of the word, let's put it back into Romans 8:26. The Lord is saying that we don't always know what needs to happen in a given situation. We don't always know what is necessary or right.

I find myself wondering at times, *How do I pray for this person or situation, Lord? What needs to happen?*

At other times I have felt led by the Holy Spirit to pray for someone, yet had no way at that moment of knowing why the person needed prayer.

Sometimes mature intercessors are prompted by the Lord to pray, and not only do they not know what they are praying for, but they also don't know for whom they are praying. They just feel a burden to pray. Talk about a weakness—an inability to produce results. Talk about not knowing what is "necessary, right or proper" in a situation.

What do we do in these circumstances? This is when the Holy Spirit wants to help us. He will lead us as we pray, perhaps revealing things about the situation to us, or bringing Scriptures to our minds so that we can pray them in the situation. He will certainly help us by empowering our prayers. But another way He wants to help us is by literally praying through us as we pray in the Spirit.

The Right Place at the Right Time

This now brings us to *paga* and the definition mentioned earlier: "light upon" or "light on *by chance*." The setting where the word is used this way is in Genesis 28:10–17.[5] The passage is describing Jacob's flight from Esau after conniving from him his birthright. After traveling all day Jacob needed a place to spend the night "because the sun was set." Verse 11 says he "lighted upon" (KJV) a particular place and there he spent the night. Notice that Jacob had not predetermined to spend the night there; he didn't choose the place in advance, but was guided *by chance*—"because the sun was set."

The place as it turns out was a very special place, Bethel, which means "house of God." Jacob actually referred to it as a "gate of heaven." Even though most translations say Jacob lighted on "a" place, the literal Hebrew wording is "the" place. What was simply *a* place to Jacob, chosen by chance, was *the* place to the Lord and sovereignly chosen by Him. It was there that Jacob had a mighty, life-changing encounter with God.

It was there that he saw the angels ascending and descending from heaven. It was at that time that God extended to him the same covenant He had made with Abraham, and informed Jacob that through his lineage He would save the world. He also promised great blessing to Jacob, to protect him and bring him back to his homeland safely. In short, it was a place where Jacob's entire destiny was foretold and his history shaped.

Nice story but how does that relate to intercession and to Romans 8:26–28? I'm glad you asked!

Like Jacob, who was not guided to this special place by his own reasoning or understanding, we are not always able to be directed in prayer by ours either. Consequently we often feel weak and anemic in our ability to produce results. At times it seems the process is hit and miss, as though we have to land or "light upon" the situation correctly "by chance."

That's okay. It's one of the primary meanings of *paga*.

And it isn't really hit and miss because what is by chance for us is not to our Helper, the Holy Spirit. In fact, *paga* also means "bull's-eye."[6] They still use the word this way in Israel today. Close your eyes and fire! When we allow Him to intercede through us, just as He sovereignly guided Jacob to the right place at the right time, He will cause our prayers to light upon (*paga*) the right person or place, in the right way, at the right time, bringing forth the will of God in situations. And that's right good!

- Bethels will occur!
- Meetings with God will occur!
- Heaven's gates will open!
- Destinies will be written!
- History will be shaped!

"Too dramatic," you say? If you said that, you don't know God well enough. Or perhaps you don't believe strongly enough that we can involve the miracle worker in our praying. I submit to you that one of the reasons we don't see more miracles is because we don't expect more miracles. Our Bible—on both sides of the Cross—presents a lot of them. They come from God, however, and the way to see more of them is to involve Him in more situations. Praying in the Spirit does this.

The Butterfly Anointing

At times when I'm praying in the Spirit I feel like a butterfly looks. Have you ever observed a butterfly flying from one location to another? They flutter this way and that, up and down, "herky-jerky." It appears they do not have the slightest idea where they are going. They almost look drunk. When I begin to pray in the Spirit, not knowing what I'm saying, sometimes with my mind wandering this way and that, I feel as though I'm trying to move in the "butterfly anointing."

Where am I going?

What am I doing?

Will I land in the right place, on the right person?

Is this really accomplishing anything?

But just as surely as that butterfly knows exactly where it's going, so too the Holy Spirit directs my prayers precisely! They WILL "light upon" correctly.

This truth is profoundly illustrated by a story I heard a minister from Cleveland, Tennessee, relate that happened in one of his meetings. He was ministering in a small church in Canada. He did not know anyone in the church well, as it was his first time there. About 15 minutes into his message, he heard the Holy Spirit speak inwardly to him, *Stop your message and begin to pray in the Spirit.*

I'm sure you can imagine the awkwardness of such a thing, especially since he really didn't know these people. The leading of the Holy Spirit was so strong, however, that he obeyed.

"You'll have to excuse me," he said, "but the Lord has just instructed me to stop my message and pray in the Spirit." He began to pace the platform, praying in the Spirit audibly.

Five minutes went by. Nothing.

Ten minutes went by. Nothing.

Fifteen minutes went by. Still nothing.

I don't know about you, but I would be feeling pretty nervous by that time. I would have been looking for that button on the podium I've longed for a time or two that I could push to disappear through a trap door! Talk about a weakness—an inability to produce results (*anaideia*). He hadn't even the slightest idea what this was all about.

Talk about not knowing how to pray as he should—what was necessary, right or proper (*dei*)!

Talk about needing to light upon by chance. Talk about the butterfly anointing!

Twenty minutes.

The people had simply sat and watched and listened. Suddenly a woman in the back began to scream, leaped to her feet and ran to the front of the church.

"What is happening?" the minister asked.

"My daughter is a missionary deep in Africa," the lady began. "So deep, in fact, that it takes 3 weeks to get where she is. You have to travel by automobile, then a boat, ride an animal and walk for a total of 21 days. My husband and I just yesterday received a telegram from the people she works with informing us that she had contracted a fatal disease that runs its course in 3 days. If she was in civilization it could be treated, but it would take too long to get her there. 'She'll probably die within 3 days,' they told me, 'and all we can do is send you her body as soon as possible.'"

"The last time my daughter was home," the lady continued, "she taught me some of the dialect of the people with whom she works. And you just said, in that dialect, 'You can rejoice, your daughter is healed. You can rejoice, your daughter is healed.'"

And she was!

WOW! Now that is *PAGA*! That is lighting upon the right person at the right time in the right way. That is Holy Spirit help. That is the butterfly anointing.

Why did it take 20 minutes? Because it's a long way from Canada to Africa and it took the Holy Spirit awhile to flutter like a butterfly all that way?! Well, maybe not. I'm not sure why it took 20 minutes. There are several reasons why I believe perseverance is often necessary in prayer, but that is for another chapter. (Persevere and you will come to it.)

Taking Hold of Together With Against

Another tremendous way the Holy Spirit aids us in our intercession is hidden in the meaning of the word "helps." "And in the same way the Spirit also *helps* our weakness" (Rom. 8:26, emphasis added). The Greek word is *sunantilambanomai*. I think you have to speak in tongues just to say this word. There must be a revelation in it somewhere. It is a compound word made up of three words. *Sun* means "together with," *anti* means "against," and *lambano* means "to take hold of."[7] Putting them together, a very literal meaning of the word would be "take hold of together with against."

How's that for help?

In situations where we're experiencing an inability to get results, the Holy Spirit not only wants to direct our prayers precisely, causing them to light upon correctly, but He also wants to take hold of the situation together with us, adding His strength to ours. "'Not by [your] might, not by [your] power, but by My Spirit,' says the Lord of hosts" (Zech. 4:6) will the mountain be moved.

Although the context of 2 Corinthians 12:9 is not prayer, praying in the Spirit is perhaps the greatest example of when His strength is made complete in our weaknesses. When we realize our weaknesses, our inability to produce results, it causes us to look to Him for help. If we allow Him to pray through us, He will take hold together with us. We just have to believe that when the Holy Spirit takes hold, something is going to move!

Please notice that both the word "helps" and its literal definition "takes hold *together* with against" implies not that He is doing it *for* us, but *with* us. In other words, this isn't something the Holy Spirit is simply doing in us, with or without our participation. No, we involve Him by praying in the Spirit, which is actually allowing Him to pray through us.

Several years ago my wife, Ceci, developed a troubling pain in her abdomen. It began as a minor discomfort and grew in intensity over the course of a year, at which time she went to have it checked. The doctor found an ovarian cyst about the size of a large egg. He informed us that surgery was necessary to remove it and possibly the ovary as well.

The doctor was a believer and understood spiritual principles, so I talked with him about giving us a little time to pray for healing. "Doc," I said, "if you can give us some time I think we can get rid of it by prayer."

Being fairly confident that the cyst was not malignant or life threatening, he replied, "I'll give you two months. If you don't get it your way, we'll get it mine."

"Fair enough," I agreed.

We prayed for Ceci with every biblical method we knew of: laying on of hands, elders anointing her with oil, the prayer of agreement, speaking the Scriptures, binding, loosing, casting out and, like good charismatics, we even knocked her on the floor and let her lie there awhile—sometimes you just have to try everything! The next time you speak with someone who insinuates they always know exactly what needs to happen in prayer and spiritual warfare, tell them Dutch Sheets doesn't believe it. (They will then ask you who Dutch Sheets is, but don't be intimidated by that.)

No change in her condition occurred, and I realized we were going to have to obtain this healing through perseverance and laying hold by faith (see 1 Tim. 6:12). That, by the way, is the way most answers to prayer come—not as instant miracles, but through fighting the fight of faith and patience.

I felt I needed to spend an hour a day praying for Ceci. I began my prayer times by stating my reason for approaching the Father. Then I referred to the Scriptures on which I was basing my petition. I would quote them, thanking the Father for His Word and Jesus for providing healing. This usually took no more than five or six minutes. I prayed in the Spirit for the remainder of the hour. This went on for a month.

Some would believe that to be an unreasonable amount of time to pray for something—an hour a day for a month. Others would say God doesn't need that long to heal someone. I'm only telling you what worked for me. And I've discovered that He does not have only one way of doing things, even the same things. His creative varieties never seem to end. The key for us is always obedience.

After a couple of weeks of this, one afternoon the Lord showed me a picture as I was praying in the Spirit. I saw myself holding this cyst in my hand squeezing the life out of it. I did not yet know that the literal meaning of "helps" in Romans 8 was "taking hold of together with against," but the Holy Spirit was teaching me a wonderful truth.

I knew, of course, that I couldn't really get my hands on the cyst, but He was showing me that as I allowed Him to pray through me, HE was "lighting on" and "taking hold with me against" the thing. Obviously, it was His power making the difference.

It sort of reminds me of the mouse and elephant who were best friends. They hung out together all the time, the mouse riding on the elephant's back. One day they crossed a wooden bridge, causing it to bow, creak and sway under their combined weight. After they were across, the mouse, impressed over their ability to make such an impact, said to the elephant, "We sure shook up that bridge, didn't we?"

Kind of reminds me of some of our advertisements and testimonials. You'd think He was the mouse and we were the elephant. (Maybe that's why we don't shake many bridges.)

After seeing the picture of myself squeezing the life out of the cyst, I asked Ceci if there was any change in her condition. "Yes, the pain is decreasing," she informed me.

The doctor's response was, "If the pain is decreasing, the cyst must be shrinking. Keep doing whatever it is you're doing."

I tried hard to make sure I wasn't conjuring up any mental images, but twice more the Holy Spirit showed me this same picture. Each time the cyst was smaller. The last of them, which was the third time overall, was about a month into the process. In the picture the cyst was about the size of a quarter and as I prayed it vanished in my hand. I knew the Lord was letting me know the work was finished. Even though Ceci said there was still a very small amount of discomfort, I could not bring myself to pray about it any further. I knew it was done.

Three days later she informed me that all the pain and discomfort was gone. The subsequent ultrasound confirmed what we already knew in our hearts—no more cyst!

You know what happened, don't you? *PAGA!*

- A "taking hold of together with against" happened.
- A "Bethel" happened.
- A "lighting on" happened.
- A "laying on" and "bearing away" happened.

- A "meeting" happened.
- An "enforcing" happened.
- A "representation" happened.

Intercession happened! And it can happen through you!

The butterfly anointing combined with the bear anointing and a serpent was defeated again. (Please don't give this book to any super-religious people or any of the ministries called to fix all of us "crazimatics." They'd put my bear into hibernation and transform my butterfly into a worm again.)

The most important point I want to communicate to you through this book is that God wants to use YOU. You don't have to be a pastor or prophet. You don't have to be Brother or Sister Well Known. You don't have to know Greek from Swahili. You simply have to be a believer in Jesus—one of His chosen representatives—one called and authorized to administer the blessings of the new covenant—a Christian.

God the Father wants to release the *work* of Jesus through your *prayers*. The Holy Spirit wants to help you. Bethels are waiting to be discovered. Histories are waiting to be written, destinies shaped.

Don't be intimidated by your ignorance, "not knowing what is necessary, right or proper." Don't allow your weaknesses to paralyze you into inactivity. Rise up! Better still, allow your Helper to rise up in you! Together, you can shake any bridge!

Just make sure you know who the mouse is.

Questions for Reflection

1. Can you explain the connection between Genesis 28:10–17 and Romans 8:26–27? Be sure to include comments on *paga*, the butterfly anointing and praying in the Spirit.

121

2. What does the Holy Spirit do to "help" us in our weaknesses?

3. Think of situations where you don't know how to pray as you should. Make a decision to allow the Holy Spirit to help you. Decide when you're going to give Him the opportunity to do so.

4. If you had it to do over again, would you still choose Jesus? (What a dumb question!)

8

Supernatural Childbirth

(Warning: This chapter could drastically alter the
population of the kingdom of darkness and increase
the need for new-convert classes.)

The Coach

I coached my wife, Ceci, through 65 hours of labor during
the births of our two daughters, Sarah and Hannah. Told her
exactly what to do and when—for about the first 10 minutes.
She then assumed the roles of coach, player, umpire, referee
and any other position that presented itself. Being the intelligent man I am and loving life as I do, it didn't take me long to
discern that the only way to survive this "bonding" effort was
compliance—quick and without questions.

It was an education. I had no idea she was such a capable
instructor. We have it all on video, which can be ordered through
Dutch Sheets Ministries, P.O. Box . . . just kidding!

I learned all about how to do what I did in those first 10 minutes from several weeks of classes on "natural childbirth." After the first 10 minutes, I didn't need the training. Everything came quite naturally.

This chapter is about "*super*natural childbirth." My success rate was poor in praying for the lost, as was everyone else's I knew. So I thought I'd see what the Bible had to say about it: not much! At least not directly. Nowhere does it say to ask God to save someone. This puzzled me. How could something so important have so little said about it? It seemed that general principles of prayer would have to be applied to intercession for the lost.

I did find one verse that said, "Ask of me, and I shall give thee the heathen for thine inheritance" (Ps. 2:8 KJV). But I knew this was a prophetic Old Testament verse referring to the Father telling Jesus to ask. I figured Christ had already done this and the Father had probably said yes.

I found that we were to ask for laborers to be sent into the harvest (see Matt. 9:38). But that wasn't asking God to save anyone; it was asking for workers. I also discovered some things concerning spiritual warfare, which we will look at in a later chapter, and I found a few Scriptures concerning travail.

Travail, What Is It?

Travail, what was it, anyway? What did it do? I knew what I thought it was, but I wasn't satisfied. *Is it a valid form of prayer?* I wondered. *Is there really a prayer that births?*

Yes, I now believe, although it is not easy to define and explain. And it is controversial. How can a mere human have a part in birthing spiritual life? What do groaning, weeping and hard work have to do with it?

One segment of the Body of Christ probably believes they already have an adequate understanding of what it is. Another

Supernatural Childbirth

has likely heard enough to think they don't want to know any more about it. And there's probably a group who have heard nothing about it. I appeal to all three: Read on with an open mind.

This chapter becomes quite theological and perhaps requires deeper thinking than others. But please realize that the word "theology," contrary to popular belief, is not a swearword, nor does it mean "boring." It actually means "the science or study of God."[1] And I'm sure I've read somewhere in the Bible, "*Study to show yourself approved unto God.*" So don't be hesitant to do some. "He who studieth this chapter, yea verily, shall be truly awesome" (Additions 1:1).

This prayer called travail always puzzled me. I was raised in a stream of the Body of Christ that believed in it, although it didn't occur often. The few times I did see what I was informed was travailing intercession, it involved a little old lady who was also one of the few prayer warriors in the church. It seemed to me that it was treated as a sort of mystical thing no one really understood (such as where babies came from), very few ever did (and those only rarely), but everyone revered.

It Happened to Me

It actually happened to me once, although I didn't make the kind of noise I'd heard others make. (Those I had heard sounded a lot like my wife when she was in labor.) I was probably 9 or 10 years old and it occurred while praying for an unsaved aunt.

One night as I lay in bed, I felt a strong burden to pray for her salvation. I remember getting out of my bed, onto my knees and weeping uncontrollably, asking God to save her. I was so young and it was so long ago that I can't remember how long it lasted—probably 30 minutes to an hour. Finally, the burden lifted and I went to sleep.

My aunt lived about an hour and a half away from us. For some "unknown" reason, however, she called us later that week and said she wanted to come to our church that Sunday morning. We did not know at the time that she was actually coming to the service planning to give her life to Christ, and did. I was amazed. I had travailed for her, and that very same week she drove the long distance to give her heart to the Lord.

Travail was wonderful but I didn't understand it. And I only did it once. I couldn't help wondering why something that helped people get saved happened so infrequently. But the truth was, this sort of intense and anguishing prayer just didn't seem to "come upon" anyone very often. Because that defined travail to us, we just had to wait and be patient—like the troubling of the pool of Bethesda in John 5.

I didn't question the concept—I knew that would be irreverent. *God forbid that anyone would have questions about something so spiritual!* The things we couldn't explain, we treated as too holy to question. We were supposed to act as if the questions weren't there—admitting them might be too disrespectful. So we didn't let God or anyone else know we had them. (I still think I can fool God once in a while!)

The Thomas Anointing

Then one day I discovered that the disciples asked Jesus a lot of questions when they didn't understand things. Sometimes the questions even seemed a little irreverent, implying that His teaching skills weren't all that great. They would ask about His parables and question some of His difficult sayings. Oh, they couched their words in nice language, calling Him "Master" and such, but you know as well as I that they were really saying, "What in the world are you talking about?"

Once when He told them to eat His flesh and drink His blood, a group of them told Him it was "a hard saying." We know what they really meant: "This is weird stuff." That bunch finally left Him.

On another occasion Christ was waxing eloquent about the disciples not being troubled because there were lots of houses where His Father lived. He was going to go there, build a few more for them, then come back and take them there. And of course, they knew the way to this place . . . (see John 14:1–4). About this time Thomas—thank God for Thomas—said what all of them were thinking: "Time out, Jesus. We don't have the foggiest idea what You're talking about. We don't even know *where* You're going, let alone *how to get there.*" I'm sure Christ's answer really helped, "I'm the way, You go through Me." I don't think the disciples understood a lot of what Jesus said until later.

As the Twelve usually did, I still most often do the safe, reverent and spiritual thing: I act like I understand, even when I don't. It keeps me ignorant but I look good, which is what really matters! Once in a while, however, the Thomas anointing comes and I just go ahead and tell God He has done a poor job of explaining something . . . such as travail.

As I thought about this subject of travail, I decided to allow some of the nagging questions I had buried to go ahead and surface: *If travailing intercession really helps get people saved, then why is it so hard to do and why does it happen so seldom and why do only a few do it and why does it have to be so loud and strange and why didn't You say more about what it is and how to do it?*

That's lousy English, but it's a great question!

Spiritual Experiences Versus Physical Façades

I would like to suggest two things at this point. First, I believe biblical travail is an important, if not essential, part of intercession for the lost. Second, I don't believe it is defined by groaning, wailing, weeping and hard work. Natural travail certainly is, and spiritual travail *can* include these things. I do not believe, however, that it *must* include them, and I'm convinced it is not defined by them. In fact, I believe a person can travail while doing the dishes, mowing the lawn, driving a car—anything a person can do and still pray.

We in the Church have done with this subject what we do with many. By our very natures we have a need to see or feel something in order to believe in it. Thus, *we tend even to judge what is happening in the spirit by what we see naturally.*

For example, if we pray with someone for salvation or repentance, we tend to believe the person who weeps is probably receiving more than the one who doesn't. We even say things such as, "The Holy Spirit really touched him or her." This is because we see his or her reaction.

In actuality, however, I have observed some who did not cry or show any emotion while praying who were totally transformed. On the other hand, I have witnessed some who sobbed and wept in seeming repentance, much like Judas (see Matt. 27:3–5), but experienced no change whatsoever. Again, the point is, *you cannot judge what is happening in the realm of the spirit by what takes place in the natural realm.*

We in charismatic and Pentecostal circles have a phenomenon we call being "slain in the Spirit." Although this is not a biblical term and the practice is certainly abused, I believe people can and do fall under the power of God. We have, however, done a similar thing with this experience. During a meeting where this particular phenomenon is happening, we tend to believe those who fall down are receiving more from the Lord than those who do not. At times we even judge whether anything at all is happening by whether or not people fall down.

I have been in meetings where I have observed this happening to the degree that I am certain the emphasis and goal became getting people to fall down, rather than a faith that allowed the Holy Spirit to do whatever He wanted, however He wanted. In other words, *we began to judge what was happening in the spirit realm by what we saw naturally.* This is dangerous. It leads to extremes, imbalanced teaching, wrong expectations and striving after the flesh.

In any spiritual release of power and anointing, the possibility of a physical manifestation always exists—that is biblical. People may weep. People may at times fall down under the power of God. People may laugh, perhaps hilariously. They may even appear drunk. Sometimes when God moves there is a physical manifestation; oftentimes there is not. But *we can never ever judge what is happening in the spirit by what we see in the natural.*

Travail, a Spiritual Happening

This is also true with travail. When choosing the term, the Holy Spirit uses a *physical* phenomenon—childbirth—to describe a *spiritual* happening or truth. In doing so, His emphasis is not on the physical realm but the spiritual. And the comparison is not meant to be literal or exact. In other words, the Holy Spirit is not trying to describe what is happening *physically* but rather *spiritually* when He uses the word "travail." It isn't a natural birth, but a spiritual one.

The emphasis is meant to be on the *spiritual* power released to give birth *spiritually*, not the *physical* phenomenon that might accompany it (groanings, weepings, crying out, etc.). Most of us who have been associated with travailing prayer have made what happens physically the focal point, thereby missing the spiritual point that something is being born of the Spirit.

It's easy to find out if you have made this mistake. Ask yourself the question and answer it honestly: When you hear the word "travail" in the context of prayer, do you think first of *what* is taking place in the spirit (a birthing), or *how* it is happening outwardly (in the body)? Most of you probably answered with the latter—how. The rest of you—well, I'm suspicious. You most likely relied on the theology of the little boy in Sunday school who was asked what a lie was. "It is an abomination unto God," he replied, "and a very present help in time of trouble."

Most of us have unconsciously defined a work of the Spirit by a work of the body. It would probably be wise to use different verbiage, perhaps "birthing through prayer," rather than the word "travail" to aid in changing this. This phrase would be acceptable biblically because, as we will see later, the Hebrew words for "travail" actually mean "give birth" or "bring forth." The translators, not necessarily the Holy Spirit, decided when to use the term "travail."

In defining travail outwardly we have not only missed the real issue, but we have also unconsciously accepted what I believe is a lie of Satan: Only a few people can really travail, and then only rarely. I do not believe this is true. In fact, I believe all of us can involve ourselves in travailing (birthing) intercession, and do so regularly. The key is to realize that the emphasis is on birthing something spiritually, not on what happens to us as we do it. (Please remember, I have said travailing intercession can include strong physical manifestations, but it doesn't have to and isn't defined by them.)

The Birthing Prayer

For the sake of changing our mindset, from this point on in the chapter, I will use the words "birthing prayer" interchangeably with "travail" in referring to this type of intercession.

Having said all that, let me say plainly and emphatically: There is an aspect of prayer that births things in the Spirit. We are "birthers" for God. The Holy Spirit wants to "bring forth" through us. Jesus said in John 7:38, "From his *innermost being* shall flow rivers of living water" (emphasis added). "Innermost being" is the word *koilia*, which means "womb."[2] We are the womb of God upon the earth. We are not the source of life, but we are carriers of the source of life. We do not generate life, but we release, through prayer, Him who does.

David and Polly Simchen, members of our church in Colorado Springs, recently received the answer to more than four years of prayer for the salvation of their son, Jonathan. Polly, and a few of her friends, demonstrated throughout this course of time one of the most tenacious and thorough examples of intercession I have ever witnessed, including this concept of birthing. The following are some excerpts from Polly's testimony. They are somewhat lengthy but filled with pertinent illustrations of things I intend to discuss in this and other chapters (emphasis added):

> We gave Jonathan to God before he was ever born and raised him in church, but at 17 years of age, through a combination of several well-laid plans of the enemy, he began to wander away from God. It wasn't long before he was living a life of total rebellion, characterized by drugs and all the things that accompany such a lifestyle. Through these things, his diabetes became a greater problem, and at times he would end up in the hospital, only to get out and go back to running and doing drugs.
>
> About that time Pastor Dutch began teaching the church about intercession. Though initially devastated and at times frozen with fear, we began to learn more

and more. As my friends and I would intercede together, God gave instructions of how to pray, along with many uplifting promises and words of encouragement.

We would *paga*, asking the Holy Spirit to *hover*—around his bed as he slept, in his car, wherever he was—and *birth life* into him. I did this daily.

Many times, for seasons almost daily, we anointed his room, his doors and windows, his bed, his car, his clothing and anything else he came in contact with. Many times I would go into his room and sing in the Spirit for an hour or more. I sang things like, "The name of Jesus is exalted in this place—over this bed, over these things, these clothes, everything!" I sang, "Jonathan has a destiny I know he will fulfill." My friends Shirley and Patty and I would sometimes pray four to six hours late at night.

On one occasion Pastor Dutch taught about prayer cloths. Immediately I thought, *We can do that for Jonathan!* Pastor Dutch, David and I together laid hands on a prayer cloth, releasing God's power and anointing into it, agreeing that the anointing would break the yoke of drugs, sin, ungodly friends, perversion and anything else that needed breaking. We cut the cloth into about 12 pieces and put them under his sheets, inside his pillow, hidden in the flaps of his wallet, sewed into the cuff of his pants, under his pocket, inside holes in his walls and inside the tag on the tongue of his shoes. With each one we would *declare*, "The anointing breaks the yoke."

At times it seemed things would get worse; it was like Jonathan was on a mission to destroy his life. But we stood fast in loving him, speaking God's plan over his life, anointing and singing over his room and car, interceding daily and declaring Scripture after Scripture. We also declared and called forth every word and promise God had ever given to us about Jonathan. The more we declared the Scriptures, the more our faith grew. Every few months we would take a new prayer cloth to Pastor Dutch and repeat the process.

We also involved ourselves in *spiritual warfare* for Jonathan. We cursed the power of drugs and asked God to remove every ungodly influence in his life—although we always prayed for the salvation of his friends, three of whom have also come to Christ. God took our fears and converted them into fighting!

In January of this year, 1996, we received a word from a friend, saying God was about to *"tip the bowl"* of our prayers. Pastor Dutch had taught us about that, and we could hardly wait.

In February 1996, after more than four years, we could see God was dealing with Jonathan. He wanted his life to be straight. He started to read his Bible and became concerned about the salvation of his girlfriend. He began to hate the power drugs had over his friends. Then one night at one of our prayer meetings, he prayed a prayer of recommitment to Christ. We watched in amazement as the things of the world began to fall away from Jonathan and the things of the kingdom of God became clear and appealing. Just last week (May 1996), his girlfriend also gave her life to Christ. Does God answer prayer? You bet He does!

Throughout four years of intercession, the Lord taught us much about prayer and gave us great encouragement along the way—a pastor who cared and taught us, friends who cared and prayed, prophetic words concerning Jonathan's call and God's hand on him. He even allowed my husband, David, to see the angel that would ride in Jonathan's car everywhere he went, even twice when he spent the night in jail. All fear left and we were able to fully trust God.

Thank you, Pastor Dutch, and Ceci too, for everything you have done. We are so thankful to God for the miracle that has taken place in our precious son. No one could ever convince us prayer doesn't work! God is faithful and we are forever grateful!

As stated earlier, I will examine more fully many of the ways in which Polly prayed, which I italicized, throughout the remainder of this book. At this point, however, let's examine this amazing facet of prayer—travail. May the Holy Spirit give us ears to hear.

Can we demystify this subject of travail? I believe we can. The following passages either directly mention travailing (birthing) prayer or the context and wording implies it:

1 Kings 18:41–45: "Now Elijah said to Ahab, 'Go up, eat and drink; for there is the sound of the roar of a heavy shower.' So Ahab went up to eat and drink. But Elijah went up to the top of Carmel; and he crouched down on the earth, and put his face between his knees. And he said to his servant, 'Go up now, look toward the sea.' So he went up and looked and said, 'There is nothing.' And he said, 'Go back' seven times. And it came about at the seventh time, that he said, 'Behold, a cloud as small as a man's hand is coming up from the sea.' And he said, 'Go up, say to Ahab, "Prepare your chariot and go down, so that the heavy shower does not stop you." So it came about in a little while, that the sky grew black with clouds and wind, and there was a heavy shower. And Ahab rode and went to Jezreel." (The posture of Elijah in this passage is that of a woman in his day while giving birth. We are meant to see that Elijah was actually

in travailing [birthing] prayer. James 5:16 KJV also refers to this event and calls it "fervent" prayer.)

Psalm 126:5–6: "Those who sow in tears shall reap with joyful shouting. He who goes to and fro weeping, carrying his bag of seed, shall indeed come again with a shout of joy, bringing his sheaves with him."

Isaiah 66:7–8: "Before she travailed, she brought forth; before her pain came, she gave birth to a boy. Who has heard such a thing? Who has seen such things? Can a land be born in one day? Can a nation be brought forth all at once? As soon as Zion travailed, she also brought forth her sons."

John 11:33, 35, 38, 41–43: "When Jesus therefore saw her weeping, and the Jews who came with her, also weeping, He was deeply moved in spirit, and was troubled. . . . Jesus wept. . . . Jesus therefore again being deeply moved within, came to the tomb. Now it was a cave, and a stone was lying against it. . . . And so they removed the stone. And Jesus raised His eyes, and said, 'Father, I thank Thee that Thou heardest Me. And I knew that Thou hearest Me always; but because of the people standing around I said it, that they may believe that Thou didst send Me.' And when He had said these things, He cried out with a loud voice, 'Lazarus, come forth.'"

Matthew 26:36–39: "Then Jesus came with them to a place called Gethsemane, and said to His disciples, 'Sit here while I go over there and pray.' And He took with Him Peter and the two sons of Zebedee, and began to be grieved and distressed. Then He said to them, 'My soul is deeply grieved, to the point of death; remain here and keep watch with Me.' And He went a little beyond them, and fell on His face and prayed, saying, 'My Father, if it is possible, let this cup pass from Me; yet not as I will, but as Thou wilt.'"

Romans 8:26–27: "And in the same way the Spirit also helps our weakness; for we do not know how to pray as we should, but the Spirit Himself intercedes for us with groanings too deep for words; and He who searches the hearts knows what the mind of the Spirit is, because He intercedes for the saints according to the will of God." (The context of this passage is travail—see Romans 8:22–25. The Lord speaks of all creation and us groaning and travailing, then speaks of the Holy Spirit doing it in us.)

Galatians 4:19 KJV: "My little children, of whom I travail in birth again until Christ be formed in you."

Although these passages do not fully explain *what* it is or *how* it is done, some things are clear:

- The Holy Spirit is involved.
- It is associated with spiritual reproduction.
- It aids in the maturing process of believers.
- It can be very intense, involving fervency, tears and even groaning.
- Assuming Christ was in travail at Lazarus's tomb and Elijah was in birthing prayer on the mountain, it is involved in producing physical miracles, not just the new birth.

The Holy Spirit, God's Birthing Agent

It will help to keep us from error and alleviate some of your concerns if I state clearly up front, we don't birth anything spiritually; the Holy Spirit does. He is the birthing agent of the Godhead (see Luke 1:34–35; John 3:3–8). He is the power source of the Godhead (see Acts 1:8; 10:38; Luke 4:14, 18). He is the power behind Creation, which, as we will see, is likened to a birthing (see Gen. 1). He is the one who supplies power to God's will, giving it life and substance. He gives birth to the will of God. He is the one who breathes God's life into people, bringing physical and spiritual life (see Gen. 2:7; Ezek. 37:9–10,

14; Acts 2:1–4). Concerning salvation, we call this the new birth or the new creation.

Therefore, anything we might accomplish in intercession that results in a birthing would have to be something that causes or releases the Holy Spirit to do it.

For example, Elijah as a human being couldn't birth or produce rain. Yet, James tells us his prayers did. Paul couldn't create the new birth or maturity in the Galatians, yet Galatians 4:19 implies that his intercession did. We cannot produce spiritual sons and daughters through our human abilities, yet Isaiah 66:7–8 tells us that our travail can. If we cannot create or birth these and other things through our own power or ability, then it seems fairly obvious that our prayers must in some way cause or release the Holy Spirit to do so.

Understanding, then, that it is the Holy Spirit's power actually doing the work, I want to say unequivocally that *there is a prayer that births*.

If this is indeed so, we should be able to find some references that use the same words to describe what the Holy Spirit does in birthing or bringing forth life as are used to describe what our prayers accomplish. Can we? Yes! And the contexts make very clear what the Holy Spirit actually does to release this life-giving power.

Genesis 1:1–2 says, "In the beginning . . . the earth was without form, and void" (KJV). The words "without form" are the Hebrew word *tohuw*, which means "a desolation; to lie waste; a desert; a worthless thing";[3] "confusion";[4] "empty (barren); a formless, lifeless mass."[5] The basic concept is lifelessness or sterility; no order, no life. Verse two goes on to tell us "the Spirit of God moved upon the face of the waters." What does it mean when it says the Holy Spirit moved?

We use the term today in Christian circles when we speak of the Holy Spirit moving in a service. We say things such as,

"The Lord really moved today," or "The Holy Spirit was moving mightily." But what do these and similar statements mean? We have an ethereal concept of what it means to us: We are implying that He was doing something; He was active. But what was He doing? Was He moving from one place to another? Was He moving upon the hearts of people? What does the word "move" mean in these contexts?

Actually, this usage of the word finds its roots here in Genesis. The Hebrew word used for "moving," *rachaph*, literally means "to brood over."[6] The *Amplified* translation actually uses the words "was moving, hovering, brooding over." The margin of the *New American Standard* also uses the word "hovering." So, *rachaph* is a hovering or brooding over something.

Webster's Dictionary defines "brood" as "offspring; progeny; that which is bred or produced."[7] A hen's brood, for example, is her chicks that she has produced. It comes from the root word "breed," which we know means giving birth to something.

In using this term to describe Creation, the Holy Spirit is using the analogy of "birthing" something. He was "bringing forth" life. A Hebrew scholar informed me that *rachaph* is, indeed, a reproductive term in the Hebrew language that can be used to describe a husband hovering over his bride. Pretty graphic, but it confirms that *rachaph* is literally a reproductive term. One lexicon defined it as "brooding and fertilizing."[8]

We know from the New Testament that Jesus was calling forth life in this Genesis setting. We are told that all things were created by His Word (see John 1:1–3; Col. 1:16). But it was the Holy Spirit that brooded or hovered over the earth, releasing His creative energies or power at the words of Jesus, giving birth to what Christ spoke.

Psalm 90:2 confirms this, actually calling what the Holy Spirit did at Creation a birthing. The verse uses two important Hebrew words, *yalad*[9] and *chuwl*.[10] It reads, "Before the mountains were born [*yalad*], or Thou didst give birth to [*chuwl*] the earth and the world, even from everlasting to everlasting, Thou art God."

Although the words are not translated as such in this verse, they are the primary Hebrew words for travail. Each one is translated variously in the Old Testament: "bring forth," "born," "give birth to," "travail," and others (see Deut. 32:18; Job 15:7; 39:1 for examples). Regardless of how they are translated, the concept is that of giving birth to something. It is not always referring to a literal, physical birth, but is often used in creating. We do the same thing in our vocabulary. We might say an idea, vision or nation was "born" or "conceived." We're obviously not speaking of a physical birth, but of something new coming into being. In much the same way, Psalm 90:2 likens the Genesis Creation to a birthing.

Hovering Over and Bringing Forth

Now, let's make the prayer connection. These are the very same words used in Isaiah 66:8: "As soon as Zion *travailed* [*chuwl*] she also *brought forth* [*yalad*] her sons." This is extremely important! *What the Holy Spirit was doing in Genesis when He "brought forth" or "gave birth to" the earth and the world is exactly what He wants to do through our prayers in bringing forth sons and daughters.* He wants to go forth and hover around individuals, releasing His awesome power to convict, break bondages, bring revelation and draw them to Himself in order to cause the new birth or new creation in them. Yes, *the Holy Spirit wants to birth through us.*

Marlena O'Hern, of Maple Valley, Washington, tells of doing this for her brother. We'll share more details about this in chapter 10, but Marlena had been praying for her brother, Kevin, for about 12 years. Not realizing how to pray scripturally and specifically, she often grew frustrated and made the mistake of trying to pressure him into doing what was right, which would only make things worse.

Early in 1995 she heard me teach about intercession for the lost. She, her husband, Patrick, and their children all began to pray for Kevin. One of the things they prayed was that the Holy Spirit would hover over him. In about two weeks, Kevin was born again and is serving the Lord today.

The second example of the Holy Spirit hovering and bringing forth life out of lifelessness is in Deuteronomy 32:10–18. All four of the previously mentioned Hebrew words are used in this passage: *tohuw, rachaph, yalad* and *chuwl*. In this passage Moses is recounting to the Israelites their history and speaks of Israel as an individual, obviously referring back to Abraham, the father of the nation. In verse 10, Moses says God found him in a *tohuw* situation—in other words, lifeless or barren.

Abraham was in the same barren condition the earth was in prior to the Creation. Neither he nor Sarah had the ability at this point to produce life. They were sterile, lifeless. We are then told in verse 11 that like an eagle hovers (*rachaphs*) over its young, the Lord hovered over them. The Holy Spirit brooded over Abraham and Sarah, releasing His life and power, giving them the ability to conceive!

We read in Hebrews 11:11 that by faith Sarah received *dunamis* (the miraculous power of the Holy Spirit)[11] to conceive. As He hovered, God was actually birthing a nation in them. The renewing the Holy Spirit did to their bodies as He hovered was so real that it was after this point that a king wanted Sarah as his own wife because she was so beautiful. Also, Abraham received a lasting change and had other children after this.

Later in the passage (Deuteronomy 32:18) *yalad* and *chuwl*, the primary Hebrew words for "travail" or "giving birth," are used: "You neglected the Rock who *begot* you and forgot the God who *gave you birth*" (emphasis added). The identical words are chosen in this passage to describe the Holy Spirit's hovering over Abraham and Sarah to bring forth life as were used in the Genesis Creation and in Isaiah 66:8. *The hovering that brought forth natural Israel will also bring forth spiritual Israel.*

Our third example of the Holy Spirit's bringing forth life as He hovered or brooded over is found in Luke 1:35, the conception of Christ in Mary. The angel of the Lord came to Mary telling her that she would bear a child. She responded by asking, "How can this be, since I am a virgin?" (v. 34).

The answer was, "The Holy Spirit will come upon you, and the power of the Most High will overshadow you." "Overshadow" is the Greek word *episkiazo*, which means "to cast a shade upon; to envelope in a haze of brilliancy; to invest with supernatural influence."[12] It is in some ways a counterpart for the Hebrew word *rachaph*. Thayer says it is used "of the Holy Spirit exerting creative energy upon the womb of the Virgin Mary and impregnating it."[13]

The word is only used three times in the New Testament. At the transfiguration of Jesus in Matthew 17:5, the passage says the cloud of the Lord "overshadowed" them. It is also used in Acts 5:15 when people were trying to get close to Peter—in his shadow—that they might be healed. Have you ever wondered how Peter's shadow could heal anyone? It didn't. What was actually happening was that the Holy Spirit was "moving" out from Peter—hovering—and when individuals stepped into the cloud or overshadowing, they were healed.

Perhaps you have seen this phenomenon. I have. I've been in services where God was moving in such a strong way that before people were ever prayed for or touched by anyone, they were saved, healed or delivered. They came under the *episkiazo* or hovering of the Holy Spirit.

Maybe you've been in a meeting where the Spirit of the Lord began to hover over the whole room and move in a particular way. At times God has even done this over entire communities. In many of the classic revivals of the past, stories are told of an individual driving close to a church where God has been moving in mighty ways and the person begins to weep, goes to the church, walks inside and says, "Something drew me here and I want to get saved."

What happened? The moving or hovering of the Holy Spirit became so great that He brooded over an entire geographical area to bring forth life. I believe this will even happen over nations as more and more prayer is generated for the unreached people of the earth. There has never been a time in history with the amount of prayer that is currently being offered for the lost. The Spirit of the Lord is being released through this intercession to hover over not only cities, but entire nations. We will see dramatic revivals as this hovering continues and intensifies through the prayers of the saints.

Can a Land Be Born in One Day?

I was preaching in Ohio in 1990, shortly after the fall of the Berlin Wall and some of the Communist nations in Europe. This was the season, you will recall, when governments were falling like dominoes and events were happening weekly that would normally have taken decades to occur. It was indeed extraordinary.

As I preached under a very strong anointing, the Holy Spirit came upon me and I began to prophesy. In the course of my message, I said, "Just as you have seen nations fall politically in a day, so you will see nations fall before Me spiritually and be born again in a day." Even as I said this, I found myself wondering if it could really happen. After the service I went to the Lord in prayer, saying, "Father, I do not want to speak in Your name when it is not You. Nor do I want to hype Your people with sensational statements. I need to know if that was You speaking through me."

The Lord's answer to me was surprising. He gave me the reference Isaiah 66:7–8 in which I knew verse 8 said, "As soon as Zion travailed she also brought forth her sons." What I did not realize until looking up the reference was that the preceding verse is a question: "Can a land be born in one day? Can a nation be brought forth all at once?" "As soon as Zion travailed she also brought forth her sons" is actually an answer to this question.

I knew the Lord was assuring me that He was, indeed, declaring through me that nations would be born again in a day. There would come such a move of the Spirit, such a hovering and brooding, such a power released by the Spirit of God over areas that entire nations would come to Christ overnight. I don't know if overnight is literal or figurative, but I'll accept either, won't you?

The passage in verse 8 informs us that this will be through the travail of Zion. If Zion includes the Church, which it certainly does (see Ps. 87; Heb. 12:12; 1 Pet. 2:4–10), and those being born are sons and daughters of Zion, this is a promise that not only pertains to Israel, but also to us, the Body of Christ. *We can birth sons and daughters through travail.*

A Sense of Birthing

Carol Millspaugh, also of our fellowship in Colorado Springs, tells of an experience she had in Germany several years ago. At the time, she worked in counseling, first as a psychotherapist, then in full-time ministry as a Christian counselor. Carol would spend time interceding for her clients' situations and for their salvation.

One particular couple she counseled had many problems: addictions, eating disorders, family problems, and others.

Neither were believers; in fact the wife was an atheist. Carol said she felt as though she were pregnant with them, that she was carrying them in her spirit. She would intercede for them daily, often moaning and crying for hours. This went on for several months.

During her times of intercession, the Lord would reveal things about them to Carol and she would share this information with them on an individual basis. Carol wasn't aware of it initially, but the Lord was preparing them for salvation.

Then one day the Spirit powerfully hovered over them during their session, enabling them to be able to hear and understand as Carol shared Scriptures with them. The next time she met with them, both of them received the Lord together. Carol said a strong sense of a birthing was happening. Then began the time of growing and maturing as Carol nurtured them and helped them find solid biblical teaching and Christian relationships.

Based on these examples from the Scriptures—Creation, the birth of Israel and Christ's conception—I would like to offer the following as a definition of spiritual travail: "Releasing the creative power or energy of the Holy Spirit into a situation to produce, create or give birth to something." Travailing intercession would simply be prayer that causes this. At the risk of redundancy, I want to restate this phrase, using it to offer a formal definition of travailing intercession: *"A form of intercession that releases the creative power or energy of the Holy Spirit into a situation to produce, create or give birth to something."*

I use the words "produce" and "create" because travail is spoken of in the Scriptures not only in the context of someone being born again, but also of bringing forth other things. For example, when the Holy Spirit was hovering through Peter, He was bringing forth healing (see Acts 5:15). Through Elijah it was rain (see 1 Kings 18:45); through Paul it included maturity (see Gal. 4:19).

144

Christ's Travail

Let's look at the two previously mentioned examples from Christ's ministry where He was involved in travail or birthing prayer. The first is John 11:33–44, the resurrection of Lazarus. Just before going to the tomb, verse 33 says Jesus "was deeply moved in spirit, and was troubled." A more literal translation of this phrase is that Jesus "was moved with indignation in His spirit and deeply troubled Himself."[14]

The word "troubled" is *tarasso*. It means "to stir up or agitate," like an agitator in a washing machine. Jesus was stirring up the anointing within Himself. Verse 38 literally says He again was moved with indignation.

According to these verses, the tears Christ shed were not merely tears of sympathy, but of indignation and the stirrings of His spirit. We also know they were taking place in the context of prayer because verse 41 informs us that before raising Lazarus from the dead, Jesus said to the Father, "I thank Thee that Thou heardest Me." He then gave the command, "Lazarus, come forth."

Although it cannot be conclusively proven, I believe Christ was in strong travail, releasing the life-giving power of the Holy Spirit before He ever gave the command, "Lazarus, come forth." As I stated earlier, I do not believe it is *necessary* to weep and groan, etc., in order to release the birthing power of the Holy Spirit (travail). It *can* and *will* happen at times, however, when we move into deep intercession, as it did in this circumstance with Jesus.

This is what took place when I interceded for my aunt. I was involved in a form of travail. Although not groaning, I was weeping heavily. It was obviously not the emotion that caused her salvation, but my response to the prompting of the Holy Spirit, allowing Him to move through me. This released Him to go hover around my aunt, enveloping her with His power and life, convicting her of sin and possibly breaking some strongholds.

145

It doesn't always happen quickly. Occasions do occur when we move into a time of intercession and almost immediately see the results, as was the case with my aunt. However, as with Polly and her son, a season of prayer is usually necessary when, on a regular basis, we allow the Spirit of God to intercede through us. This releases Him to go hover around an individual with His life-giving power, doing what is necessary to cause the person to be born again.

Another occasion when Jesus was involved in travail was in the Garden of Gethsemane. Without any question, Christ's redemption of humanity—the work of intercession—began with His travail in the Garden. Isaiah prophesied of Him, "He shall see of the *travail* of His soul, and shall be satisfied" (Isa. 53:11 KJV, emphasis added).

In fulfillment of this, Jesus cried out in Gethsemane, saying, "My soul is exceeding sorrowful, even unto death" (Matt. 26:38 KJV). It was in the Garden of Gethsemane that redemption began and the victory of the entire ordeal was won.

We know that redemption was beginning in this travail for a couple of reasons. Luke tells us Jesus began to shed great drops of blood. Jesus was not simply sweating so profusely that it was like a person bleeding. He was literally bleeding through the pores of His skin, a medical condition known as hematidrosis. We must understand that when the blood of Christ began to flow, redemption was beginning, for it is through the shedding of His blood that we have the cleansing from sin (see Heb. 9:22).

We also know that redemption was beginning in the Garden because when Jesus said, "My soul is exceeding sorrowful, even unto death," the word used for "death" is *thanatos*. This word is often used for death as the result and penalty of sin.[15] This is the death Adam experienced when he fell.

Two other words could have been used that mean simply physical death. When *thanatos* is used, however, it frequently implies death as a result of sin. For Christ to use this word quite possibly meant that the sin of the world was already being laid upon Him.

Through these two occurrences, we see that the redemption that ended at the cross most likely began in the Garden travail. I believe the term "travail" was used, not so much because He was working hard, but because He was bringing forth the new birth. It also seems logical that because our intercession releases the fruit of this birthing, it too is called travail.

Bringing Forth the Fruit of Calvary

In summary, the Holy Spirit desperately wants to release His creative, birthing powers through us, bringing forth the fruit of Calvary. He wants to use us in *tohuw* (lifeless, fruitless, desolate, barren) situations, releasing His life into them:

- As He did at Creation. But through our intercession, He wants to bring forth "new creations" in Christ Jesus.
- As with Israel when He hovered over the barren bodies of Abraham and Sarah, bringing forth a nation, He wants to bring forth "spiritual Israel" from us.
- As with Mary when He hovered, bringing forth or conceiving the Christ in her, He desires to bring forth Christ in people through our intercession.
- As happened with Lazarus's resurrection, through our intercession He wants to bring forth spiritual life from death.
- As in Gethsemane when the fruit of our redemption was pressed from the vine, Christ Jesus, He wants the fruit of that work to be pressed forth again through our intercession.
- As through Peter people were healed, He wants to heal people through our intercession. He wants to hover around them, releasing His life.

Not only does He want to do this for salvation and healing, but travail is also to be done for maturing and developing believers. Paul said in Galatians 4:19, "My little children, of whom I travail in birth again until Christ be formed in you" (KJV). He called them his children because he had travailed once until they were born again. Then he said he was in travail "again" until Christ was formed in them. These people were already born again. Paul was obviously referring to their maturing process. This is an aspect of intercession we can involve ourselves in to help believers mature.

Hospitals have intensive care units where the staff is able to keep a close eye on patients who have undergone organ transplants. Even when the operations are successful, it is routine procedure to classify these patients as being in "critical, but stable condition" and keep them in ICU until they gain strength.

Spiritual organ transplants occur as people become Christians and receive new hearts. To grow strong in the Lord, they must receive intensive nurturing. It is exciting to be part of the birthing process—praying them into the kingdom of God. However, it is also necessary to intercede for them through their critical but stable condition stage.[16]

When the Lord first taught me this truth, I was counseling with four or five people who were in very difficult situations. Three of them were extremely suicidal. I was spending hours each day with these people, trying to help them through their situations. There were times when they would call me saying they were going to take their lives right then. I remember one of these people calling at 2:00 A.M., saying, "I have a gun to my head right now and I'm going to blow my brains out." It was a stressful season, to say the least.

It was at that time the Lord revealed to me this concept of our prayers releasing the Holy Spirit to hover around individuals, birthing life in them. He clearly spoke these words to my heart:

If you spent a fraction of the time releasing My Holy Spirit to go and hover around them bringing life as you do talking to them, you would see many times the results.

I know a good deal when I hear it! I began to spend a couple of hours every day praying for them. Most of my prayer was in the Spirit. I would simply say, "Father, I bring so and so before You now, asking that as I pray the Holy Spirit would be released to go hover around so and so, bringing forth Christ." Then I would usually just begin to pray in the Spirit. I saw immediate results. Maturity came quickly. Almost overnight bondages began to fall off. Victories occurred in their lives. It was remarkable.

What was taking place? The Holy Spirit was being released through my prayers to go hover—*rachaph, episkiazo*—around these individuals, releasing His power and life.

Releasing the Rain of the Spirit

The Bible speaks of travailing for other things as well. In 1 Kings 18, Elijah prayed fervently seven times for rain. We are told in this passage that the posture he maintained while praying was the position of a woman in that day giving birth.

The symbolism is clear. Elijah was in travail. He was birthing something. Without any question, the posture of Elijah is to symbolize this for us. Why else would God give us the position he was in while praying? And please don't miss the implication of this passage. *Even though it was God's will to bring the rain and it was also God's time for the rain, someone on Earth still had to birth it through prayer.*

In this example, travail released literal rain. We could take the story to its fullest symbolic picture and say that our travail releases the rain of the Spirit. I'm sure that would be valid because the physical drought pictured Israel's spiritual dryness,

149

and the rain pictured God's ability to bless again after the purging of the idolatry earlier in the chapter.

Our prayers can and do cause the Holy Spirit to move into situations where He then releases His power to bring life. We do have a part in producing the hovering of the Holy Spirit. The power that created the universe through His "*rachaph*-ing" has been deposited in the Church—while untold millions await their births into the kingdom of God.

Like Elijah, we must take up our position, believing that the prayers of mere men can accomplish much. We must release the power of the Holy Spirit through our intercession to hover, bringing forth the fruit of what Christ has already done. We are an integral part of the Father's birthing process into the kingdom of God.

As I said while coaching my wife, "Come on, Church, *push!*"

Questions for Reflection

1. How have we defined travail improperly and how has this hindered intercession?

2. Explain the connection between Genesis 1:1–2; Deuteronomy 32:10–18; Luke 1:35 and travail.

3. What do we mean when we speak of the "moving" of the Holy Spirit?

4. When and where can one travail? For what can one travail? Can you think of a situation in which God might want to do some birthing through your prayers?

5. Does God answer prayer?

9

Pro Wrestlers

Brother Wonderful and His Interpreter

"Resist the devil and he will flee from you! How many of you talk to the kingdom of darkness once in a while?" I asked in my most anointed preaching voice.

I was on a roll. Preaching up a storm, as we said back in Ohio, where I was raised. I was fresh out of Bible school and feeling like God's latest addition to the Brother Wonderful Fraternity of World Changers International. Had those people right where I wanted them—hanging on every word. If Mom could have seen me then! She and God would probably have found a place for me at the Lord's right hand—next to James and John.

The only problem was that I was in Guatemala preaching through an interpreter.

"So," you might ask, "why should that be a problem?"

Because my interpreter didn't seem to share my theology, and her convictions ran deep. She looked at me indignantly and said in no uncertain terms, "I won't say that!"

Her words kind of interrupted my eloquent flow. "Huh?" I replied.

"I won't say that."

"What do you mean you won't say it? You're supposed to say what I say."

"Well, I won't say it."

"Why not?"

"I don't believe in it."

"Well, the Bible says to do it."

"Where?"

"James 4:7."

Now, keep in mind that we were standing in front of a church full of people who were watching this obviously unpleasant verbal exchange between Brother Wonderful and his interpreter.

They hadn't prepared me for this in Bible school. As I stood wondering what to do next, she began to look for James 4:7 . . . Took her forever to find it. She then read it to the audience, I think. She may have been telling them how stupid I was for all I know.

We tried to continue. She wouldn't allow me to quote any other verses, though. As I would mention one, she would take her time finding it and read it, I think . . . Didn't take me long to figure out she didn't know her Bible very well, however, so I started paraphrasing verses so that she wouldn't recognize them as Scripture. After she had unknowingly said the verse, I would look at her with a smug smile and say, "That was found in . . ." At which time she would bore into me with very unspiritual eyes.

We just never did seem to get that flow back.

Laying Hold of the Victory

Intercession, according to our definition, involves two very different activities. One is a *reconciling*, the other is a *separating*.

152

One is a *tearing away*—a disuniting, the other a *joining to*—a uniting. This is what Christ did through His work of intercession, and it's what we do in our continuation of it. In light of this, it is important to realize that much of our intercession must be a combination of the two.

It is often not enough to simply ask the Father to do something, although this is most Christians' total concept of prayer. Many times it is necessary to accompany asking with a spiritual "warfare" or "wrestling," enforcing the victory of Calvary. As Arthur Mathews said, "Victory is an accomplished fact, but it does need a man to lay hold of that victory and precipitate a confrontation with the enemy, and resist him."[1]

Jack Hayford, in his book *Prayer Is Invading the Impossible*, says:

> To see both sides of Jesus is to see both sides of prayer. It is to see the need for compassion, for care, for concern, for weeping with those that weep, for sympathy, for groaning, for aching deeply because of what you sense transpiring in human lives. And it is to learn the place and time for anger, when we see Satan's wiles successfully destroying; for indignation, when the adversary's program violates territory that is rightfully Christ's; for boldness, when demonic hordes announce their presence; for attack, when the Holy Spirit prompts an advance.[2]

As with my interpreter in Guatemala, many don't believe in spiritual warfare. They believe Jesus took care of the devil and we don't need to concern ourselves with him. Others believe our actions, holy lifestyles, obedience and, I suppose, other things bind the devil, but we don't address him or his demons. Still others believe we can deal with or address evil spirits, but only in people. We cannot, they would say, command or rebuke demons in places or situations.

This book is not meant to offend those who disagree, nor is it to defend my position on this subject. It would take an entire book—perhaps several—to adequately prove the validity and demonstrate the how-tos of spiritual warfare. Several wonderful books are available that thoroughly defend and explain the subject. I have listed several in the bibliography at the end of this book. My intent in this book is to establish the absolute connection between spiritual warfare and intercession, especially for—but not limited to—warfare for the unsaved.

Paga Involves Warfare

To be sure, extremes do exist. I heard someone recently describe a cartoon. It portrayed the devil with 40 to 50 strands of rope around him and several individuals next to him discussing the situation.

"What do we do now?" one asked.

"I say we bind him again!" was the response of another.

Although imbalances occur, nonetheless, it is impossible to separate the word "intercession," *paga*, from warfare. Fifteen times it is used in this context.[3] I tell you emphatically, *violence and war are rooted in the very meaning of the word.* It is translated in various ways when speaking of warfare: "attack," "fall upon," "strike down," "impinge," as well as others (see Judg. 8:21; 1 Sam. 22:11–19; 2 Sam. 1:11–16; the essence is the same in all of them—people in battle attacking one another). Hear me clearly: *Paga* involves warfare!

Again, Jack Hayford says, "But there is a way to face impossibility. *Invade it!* Not with a glib speech of high hopes. Not in anger. Not with resignation. Not through stoical self-control. But with violence. And prayer provides the vehicle for this kind of violence."[4]

When we try to separate warfare from intercession, we do so to our own detriment. Much time and energy is wasted dealing with symptoms, when in many situations the real cause of the problem is spiritual or demonic: "For we wrestle not against flesh and blood, but against principalities, against powers, against the rulers of the darkness of this world, against spiritual wickedness in high places" (Eph. 6:12 KJV). We must guard against an overemphasis upon Satan and demons, but we in America err in the other direction. Most people stop in Ephesians 6:12 after the words "we wrestle not."

Ignorance Is Costly

Our ignorance of Satan and his tactics, as well as how to deal with them, is costly for us. Second Corinthians 2:11 tells us, "In order that no advantage be taken of us by Satan; for we are not ignorant of his schemes." The context is forgiveness, but a general principle is also revealed in this verse.

The word "ignorant" is the Greek word *agnoeo*. It means "without knowledge or understanding of."[5] Our English word "agnostic" is derived from it. Technically, an agnostic is not a person who is unsure if he or she believes in God. We now use the word this way; but in actuality, an agnostic is a person who does not know or understand, regardless of the subject. We also get the word "ignore" from the same root. In this verse we're urged not to ignore or be an agnostic—without understanding—where the devil is concerned.

"Schemes" is the word *noema*. It literally means "thought."[6] The verse is essentially saying, "Don't be without understanding of the way Satan thinks." *Noema* came to also mean "plans, schemes, plots, devices" because these things are born in the thoughts of the mind. For greater insight, let's insert all of them into the verse: "Don't be without understanding of the way your enemy thinks and operates—of his plans, plots, schemes and devices." Is there not also a subtle promise here? If God suggests we are not to be ignorant of Satan's schemes, He must be willing to reveal them to us.

What if we are unaware of his schemes? He'll take "advantage" of us. The word is *pleonekteo*, which is a compound word meaning literally "to have or hold the greater portion" (*pleon*—"the greater part"; *echo*—"have or hold").[7] It is easy to see why this is a word for "covet." It also means "overreach."[8] In boxing, the person who has the longer reach has the "advantage" and usually gets in more blows. The word is also translated "make a gain"; Satan makes a lot of gains on those who are unaware of his ways. Bullinger says it means "to make a prey of, to defraud."[9]

Let's put all these definitions together: "To the degree we are ignorant of the way our adversary thinks and operates—of his plans, plots, schemes and devices—to that degree he will gain on us, prey on us, defraud us of what is ours and have or hold the greater portion."

The greater portion of what? Whatever! Our homes, marriages, families, communities, money, government, nation, and more.

Twenty-five years ago the Church in America was without understanding of what Satan was planning, and he got the greater portion of our schools. The same could be said of our government.

Have you ever been taken advantage of? Have you ever received the smaller portion? In my Bible college days, we had a way of enlightening the superspiritual who thought it necessary to intercede for the world while giving thanks for a meal. They were ignorant of our scheme when we asked them to pray over the food. While they traversed the globe, we enjoyed the greater portion of their meals! It was a real test of their true spirituality. (I am deeply embarrassed by this abominable practice in my past and would never do it today. But for those of you who feel you must intercede over your food, save it for your prayer closet!)

Paul was taken advantage of in 1 Thessalonians 2:18. Satan gained on him (*pleonekteo*) in the ongoing war over spreading the gospel: "For we wanted to come to you—I, Paul, more than once—and yet Satan thwarted us." We know Paul won more battles than he lost. But he was human and at times Satan succeeded in thwarting his plans. Please notice it doesn't say God changed His mind about where Paul was to go. It clearly says that Satan hindered him. Those people who would have us think Satan can do nothing except what God allows, and that we are to ignore him, should reread these two verses. God doesn't ignore the devil and neither should we. And he certainly does a lot of things God doesn't "allow" him to do.

The only sense in which it can be said that God allows everything that happens on Earth is that He created the laws and principles—sowing and reaping, cause and effect, and the free will of humans—that govern the earth. We, however, implement these principles and determine much of what we reap and experience. Satan, too, understands these laws and uses them to his advantage whenever possible.

Satan's Hidden Schemes Prevail

I heard a minister in Tulsa, Oklahoma, tell of the deliverance of a person for whom he had prayed at length. It seems this person could never achieve any stability in life or in his walk with the Lord. He would find a job, then quickly lose it; then walk with the Lord for a while, then turn away. This cycle repeated itself again and again with no amount of prayer seeming to make a difference.

One day as the minister prayed for this young man, the Lord showed him a picture of three demons that were following the fellow everywhere he went. They were not in him, but always there to influence him. The minister saw names over each demon, describing what they did. One at a time he bound them in Jesus' name and commanded them to leave the young man alone.

From that moment on, everything changed. Stability came. Success followed. Eventually the young man became a wealthy businessman as well as a minister. And he is still walking with God today. It is always good and right to ask the Father to strengthen and mature individuals, but this man needed something more: someone to exercise authority and enact a deliverance. His instability was the symptom of demonic influence that he was not strong enough in himself to overcome. Satan had the advantage and as long as his schemes remained hidden, he prevailed.

Although some issues concerning spiritual warfare are open for debate—certainly it is a subjective area—others are a certainty:

- We are in a very real war (see 2 Cor. 10:4; 1 Tim. 1:18).
- We are soldiers in this war (see Ps. 110:2–3; 2 Tim. 2:3–4).
- We are to wrestle against all levels of the kingdom of darkness (see Eph. 6:12).
- We are to resist the devil (which would in most situations be his demons) and he will flee from us (see Jas. 4:7; 1 Pet. 5:9).
- We are to tread on Satan and his demons (i.e., exercise authority over them—see Luke 10:19; Rom. 16:20).
- We are to cast out demons (see Mark 16:17).
- We have authority to bind (forbid) and loose (permit) when dealing with the agents and gates of hell (see Matt. 16:19).
- We have powerful weapons designed to overcome the kingdom of darkness (see 2 Cor. 10:4; Eph. 6:10–20).

This is by no means an exhaustive list of warfare Scriptures. To be sure, God doesn't give us detailed formulas for doing all the previously mentioned warfare acts. God is not into formulas in any area of biblical truth. He is concerned with relationship and He gives us principles that must be applied as the Holy Spirit leads us.

For example, the Lord does not give us a particular formula for a worship service. It is not important that we worship in exactly the same way, but that we worship. He does not give exact formulas for church government or placing pastors. Every stream of the Body of Christ seems to do it differently. What matters is not that we all govern the same, but that we have godly government.

I'm not implying absolutes don't exist in Scripture; I am simply saying that rarely do they appear in the area of method. There is nothing sacred or unsacred about the method. What is important is that we walk according to the revelation of the Scriptures we have been given, and that we do this by the direction of the Holy Spirit. He alone knows exactly what is needed in each situation.

Be a Pro Wrestler

Likewise, in spiritual warfare the point is not so much how we wrestle, but that we wrestle. None of these assertions from Scripture about warfare are defensive in nature. They are all offensive. We are to aggressively deal with the forces of darkness whenever the challenge or opportunity arises. Five times the word "against" is used in Ephesians 6. The word in Greek is *pros*, which is a strengthened form of *pro*.

Pro means "in front of,"[10] either literally or figuratively (in the sense of superior to). We use the concept today in the word "professional," or in its shortened form "pro." A pro athlete is one who is "in front of" or "superior to" others. *Pros* also has the connotation of stepping forward and facing toward something or someone.[11] The symbolism in this Ephesians passage is of a wrestler stepping forward and facing his opponent. God

159

is saying to us, "Step forward and face the powers of darkness. Be a pro wrestler!"

Don't be like the bodybuilder visiting Africa, who was asked by a village chief what he did with all his muscles. The bodybuilder thought an exhibition might better serve to explain it, so he proceeded to flex his bulging calves, thighs, biceps and triceps, demonstrating how he performed in competition. After admiring this amazing specimen for a few moments, the chief inquired, "What else do you use them for?"

"That's about it," answered the muscular man.

"That's all you use those huge muscles for?" reiterated the chief.

"Yes."

"What a waste," muttered the chief in disgust. "What a waste."

So many of us are like this bodybuilder. We're strong in the Lord, well equipped to deal with our adversary, but we never use our strength or our weapons. Step into the ring!

As we wait upon the Lord, He will show us which strategy or method of warfare to use. God is a God of relationship. He is a Father who is passionately in love with His family and He prioritizes love over labor. It is our relational aspect of our walk with Christ that prepares us for the warring aspect.

Devotion to Christ, the Springboard for Everything

It is interesting, even paradoxical, but true, that warfare is often born from worship. *Out of our waiting often comes warring.* It is the simplicity and purity of devotion to Christ that must be the springboard for everything we do. "But I am afraid, lest as the serpent deceived Eve by his craftiness, your minds should be led astray from the simplicity and purity of devotion to Christ" (2 Cor. 11:3).

Our depth of revelation in any other area of truth does not diminish the need for simple, pure devotion to Christ. In fact, it increases it. The larger the tree, the deeper must go the roots. Likewise, the more we spread ourselves upward and outward into the multidimensional aspects of the Kingdom, the more we must allow the decomplicating effect of our relationship with Christ to go downward.

The context of 2 Corinthians 11:3 is deception. To whatever degree Satan can distract us from our relationship with Christ, to that degree we are walking in deception, regardless of how much other revelation we may be walking in.

I want to mention three of the Old Testament words for "waiting" upon the Lord, each of which has a different shade of meaning. The first one is *dumiyah*, which means "silently waiting with a quiet trust."[12] The thought conveyed is a strong, calm, quiet trust in the Lord. David said in Psalm 62:1–2, "My soul waits in silence for God only; from Him is my salvation. He only is my rock and my salvation, my stronghold; I shall not be greatly shaken."

The second word, *chakah*, means "adhere to" or "long for."[13] "Our soul waits for the LORD; He is our help and our shield" (Ps. 33:20). This is what David felt when he said, "My soul thirsts for God" (see 42:2; 63:1). He was *chakah*—longing for God's company.

The third word, *qavah*, means "to wait for . . . with eager expectation."[14] It also means "to bind something together by twisting" or braiding.[15] The main thought, then, for *qavah* is "eager expectation and oneness; a joining, a braiding together." The following verses are examples of this:

> Wait for the LORD; be strong, and let your heart take courage;
> Yes, wait for the LORD.
>
> Ps. 27:14

Yet those who wait for the LORD will gain new strength; they will mount up with wings like eagles, they will run and not get tired, they will walk and not become weary.

Isa. 40:31

Let's summarize the three meanings, putting them all together: "Silently waiting with a strong, calm trust, longing for His presence and eagerly expecting Him—for you know He'll show up—anticipating and then experiencing the oneness that results as your hearts become entwined." Hallelujah!

Psalm 37:7, 9, 34 demonstrates how waiting upon the Lord can relate to warfare:

Rest in the LORD and wait patiently for Him; do not fret because of him who prospers in his way, because of the man who carries out wicked schemes. . . . For evildoers will be cut off, but those who wait for the Lord, they will inherit the land. . . . Wait for the Lord, and keep His way, and He will exalt you to inherit the land; when the wicked are cut off, you will see it.

Waiting upon the Lord brings with it the ability to possess our inheritance. "Inherit" is the word *yaresh*, also translated "possess," and means "legally an heir; military invasion in order to seize."[16] Those who wait upon the Lord inherit and possess—worship and warfare! It's like David waiting upon the Lord, longing for Him, worshiping Him, writing songs to Him, and the next minute rising up, grabbing a lion by the mane and ripping his head off! Warring and winning were born from worshiping and waiting.

Looking Good, Lacking Anointing

When Mary was seated at the feet of the Lord and Martha was busy in the kitchen (see Luke 10:40), the passage says Martha was distracted with all her preparations. The word "distraction" is the word *perispao*. It means literally "drag around in circles."[17] The word for "preparations" is the New Testament word for "ministry"—the same word we would use for a person in the ministry. Even pure ministry for Jesus can become a weight we drag around.

Spiritual warfare and prayer in general can also become a weight we drag around. It often loses its life, becomes legalistic and a chore—something required and endured. We become so busy *for* Him that we don't have time to be *with* Him. We're dragging our ministry around in circles, going nowhere and accomplishing nothing for the kingdom of God.

Several years ago I was going through a difficult place in my life. Al Straarup, a dear friend of mine, called me and said, "I was praying for you with a friend this morning and God gave him a picture."

I thought, *Thank You, Jesus. Here comes my answer.*

Al continued, "There was a circle on the ground." (I was ready for a great revelation—the wheel in the middle of a wheel or something!) "You were walking on that circle."

I replied, "Yeah? Yeah?"

He said, "That's it. You were just walking in circles."

"That's my word from God?" I asked.

He responded, "Yeah, that's it. Sorry."

I hung up the phone and said, "I guess it's true. That's what I'm doing, Lord—walking in circles . . . busy, but going nowhere." I stepped off that treadmill and into the presence of the Lord. I stopped walking and started waiting.

Jesus looked at Martha and said, "Mary has chosen the good part, which shall not be taken away from her" (Luke 10:42). "Good part" is the word *agathos*. It's contrasted to another word for "good" in Greek—*kalos*, which means something is "constitutionally good"[18] or, in other words, is made well.

But *kalos* doesn't necessarily imply any practical usefulness or benefit. It may simply look good. Nothing is wrong with it, but it may not have any practical purpose.

On the other hand, *agathos*—the word for "good part" that Mary chose—is a word that means "good and profitable; useful; beneficial."[19] It is often translated "good works." The Lord is saying, "If you spend time waiting upon Me, seated at My feet, it puts something in you. You will not only look good, but you'll also be good for something." We often look good, but lack anointing. We must wait in His presence and allow all ministry, including our warfare, to be born of relationship.

God's Timing, God's Terms, God's Method

Waiting upon the Lord will keep us from becoming reactionary to the devil. Our response is not to the devil. We do nothing on his terms, nor are we to do anything in his timing. God chooses the times and the terms of battle. He told Joshua at Jericho (see Josh. 6), as he was on his face in worship, "Seven days, Joshua. Not a moment before. Don't do anything until I tell you." He was saying, "I choose the timing of battle."

God chose the terms, also. "Take no prisoners—only Rahab escapes. The spoils are to be given to Me. I choose the terms— you don't, Satan doesn't, no one else does. If you do it My way, you'll always win. Do it the devil's way and you will find yourself walking in circles." God chose the timing, the terms and the method. Warfare is not a responsive reaction but responsible action. It must be born from obedience, not necessity. We follow our Captain, not our foe.

The Lord told David to go to battle when the wind blew in the treetops, not until then (see 2 Sam. 5:24). He told Saul to wait seven days for Samuel to come and offer the sacrifice (see 1 Sam. 13:8–14). The enemy was encamped about them and the people were getting nervous, so Saul finally said, "I'm going to have to offer this sacrifice myself—do it my way—because we've got to get on with the battle here." Samuel showed up immediately after the sacrifice and gave him God's perspective: "You blew it, Saul, and the kingdom is going to be taken from you and given to someone after my heart. I can't have a warrior or leader who is reactionary—who leads the people according to his own wisdom and ideas. It has to be My way. You wait on Me!"

At times, God may say that worship is the key, as it was for Jehoshaphat on the battlefield (see 2 Chron. 20:1–30) and for Paul and Silas in the jail (see Acts 16:16–36). As we ministered on the streets of the Mardi Gras several years ago, the Lord led us on one occasion, 200 strong, to march silently down the street. An awesome fear of the Lord and presence of God began to hover over the entire area. The Lord had established His awesome presence and silenced His foes. A literal hush came to the streets.

On another occasion, however, He led us to march down the middle of Bourbon Street singing the poignant worshipful song "Emmanuel" by Bob McGee. This time a spirit of conviction began to hover over the street as we sang this powerful song that speaks of humanity's true destiny. As before, a silence came. It seemed as though the Lord had totally taken charge. At one intersection, which was blocked off for foot traffic, we gathered in a circle on our knees and continued to sing. As we knelt worshiping, a man literally ran into our circle, crying out that he wanted to know God.

That's praise warfare! It's also intercession (*paga*)—attacking the enemy. As Christ is enthroned in worship, Satan is dethroned in the heavenlies (see Ps. 22:3; 149:5–9). As we lift up the Son, we pull down the serpent.

The strategy of the Holy Spirit at other times might be love—acts of kindness, giving, forgiving. I was part of a reconciliation ceremony at Confluence Park in Denver, Colorado, on November 12, 1992, between Native Americans and several European Americans. I emceed the gathering, in fact, which was sponsored by Reconciliation Coalition, a ministry led by Jean Stephenson.

The strategy was really quite simple: repent and ask their forgiveness for stealing their land, breaking covenants and killing their ancestors. When one of them, on behalf of his people, extended forgiveness to us and welcomed us to this land, *something broke in the spirit realm*. It was a cold, dreary day, but the moment he spoke those words the sun broke through the clouds and shone upon us. That day marked the beginning of a major work of reconciliation between these two people groups. Why? Our act of humility and love, along with theirs, was also an act of warfare that tore down strongholds in the spirit realm. . . . Warfare through humility. . . . Violent love. Paradoxical, isn't it?

On other occasions the Holy Spirit may lead a person to join with others in agreement to break the back of the enemy. John G. Lake, a missionary to South Africa in the first half of this century, tells the story of a fever epidemic that in a single night struck a portion of South Africa. The devastation was such that in one month a fourth of the entire population of that region died. There were not caskets enough to meet the need and people were being buried in blankets, so great was the devastation.

Lake tells of a powerful intercessor who began to pray. For days—all day long and into the night—he stationed himself under a tree and prayed against the plague. Several times Lake asked the man, "Are you getting through?"

He would reply, "Not yet." But one day he said to Lake, "I feel today that if I had just a little help in faith my spirit would go through." Lake got on his knees and joined the man in prayer. What happened next is amazing. It is recorded in Lake's own words:

> As we prayed, the Spirit of the Lord overwhelmed our souls and presently I found myself, not kneeling under the tree, but moving gradually away from the tree. . . . My eyes gradually opened, and I witnessed such a scene as I never witnessed before—a multitude of demons like a flock of sheep! The Spirit had come upon him also, and he rushed ahead of me, cursing that army of demons, and they were driven back to hell, or the place from whence they came. Beloved, the next morning when we awoke, that epidemic of fever was gone.[20]

A Time to Shout

Truly, there is a time for aggressive, violent spiritual warfare in intercession. I realize many would shrink from such extreme action in prayer—running and shouting at the enemy. There is, however, a time for such spiritual intensity. More than once I have found myself shouting at spiritual powers or mountains of adversity while in intercession. I'm not spiritually ignorant enough to believe a certain volume level is required to rebuke evil forces, but the Scriptures do allow for it and even suggest that, at times, it unleashes something in the Spirit:

- Zerubbabel shouted grace to a mountain (see Zech. 4:7).
- Israel shouted at Jericho (see Josh. 6:16).
- Gideon's army shouted before the battle (see Judg. 7:20).
- Jesus shouted on the cross (see Matt. 27:50).
- Israel shouted when the Ark of the Covenant would lead them to a new place: Let God arise, let His enemies be scattered (see Num. 10:35; Ps. 68:1).

I'm not trying to start the First Church of the Screaming Warriors, but I am trying to demonstrate that warfare, even intense and sometimes loud warfare, is valid. Joash, the king of Israel, was rebuked and suffered defeat because of his lack of spiritual intensity in striking with the arrows (see 2 Kings 13:14–19). At other times, the strategy of the Lord may be to simply speak the Word as a sword or make biblically based declarations into the situation. When led by the Holy Spirit, this strategy is devastating to the enemy.

On one occasion I was trying to mediate a peace between three parties. The circumstance had reached a potentially violent point, and I had been assured by one party that on the following morning he was going to get physical. I knew he meant it and that someone would be hurt and others would be in jail. I was up quite late praying, pleading with God to stop this when, at around 2:00 A.M., the Lord shocked me with these words: *Why are you begging Me to do this? You know My will in this situation. And the problem is being caused by a spirit of anger and violence. Bind it! Declare My Word and will into the situation.*

I did and went to bed. The next morning, for some "unexplainable" reason, without any discussion, everyone had a change of heart. Peace and harmony ruled where the night before violence and anger had reigned. What had happened?

Paga happened.

Calvary happened.

Psalm 110:2 happened: "The Lord will stretch forth Thy strong scepter from Zion, saying, 'Rule in the midst of Thine enemies.'"

Seizing and Securing Our Inheritance

A word of caution is necessary at this point. As we involve ourselves in spiritual warfare, it is imperative that we remember we are not trying to defeat the devil. He is already defeated. We do not re-defeat, we re-present, the victory of the Cross. All that we do in our praying intercession must be an extension of what Christ did through His work of intercession.

Christ *paga*'ed the devil. He attacked him and crushed his headship over the earth (see Gen. 3:15). The Hebrew word for "head" in this verse, *rosh*, is actually speaking of headship or authority.[21]

Psalm 2:9, speaking prophetically of Christ, says, "Thou shalt break them with a rod of iron, Thou shalt shatter them like earthenware." The crushing of Genesis 3:15 and the breaking and shattering of Psalm 2:9 all have essentially the same meaning: to break something into pieces and scatter it. Christ shattered and scattered the headship of the serpent like a broken piece of glass. It was a total defeat.

But what Christ did, we must release and enforce. What He provided for us, we must seize by faith with spiritual weapons. Timothy was told in 1 Timothy 6:12, "Fight the good fight of faith; take hold of the eternal life to which you were called, and you made the good confession in the presence of many witnesses." Timothy already had eternal life, yet he was told to "take hold of" it.

Is that interesting to you? You can have it and not have it. You can own it and not possess it. The word is *epilambanomai* and means "to seize"[22] something. Like Israel in the Old Testament, who had been given their inheritance by God yet still had to take it, so it is with us. Their inheritance was not necessarily their possession. Ours won't automatically fall into our laps either, just as theirs didn't.

Moffatt translates the verse as "Fight in the good fight of the faith, *secure* that life eternal to which you were called" (emphasis added). Wuest's translation reads, "Take possession of the eternal life into a participation of which you were called."

As one would seize and secure territory in war, so we must seize and secure our inheritance in Christ. Who are we to seize it from? Certainly not God! We must take it from the world, the flesh and the devil.

Jack Hayford gives an enlightening amplification of Matthew 16:18–19, based on what the Greek literally says:

> Whatever you may at any time encounter (of hell's counsels which I'm declaring my church shall prevail against), you will then face a decision as to whether you will or won't bind it. What transpires will be conditional upon your response. If you do personally and consciously involve yourself in the act of binding the issue on earth, you will discover that at that future moment when you do, that it has already been bound in heaven![23]

Amazing! So much depends on our obedience and responsible action. Our inheritance in Christ is not guaranteed or automatic.

She Stepped Forward

Sue Doty shared the following testimony regarding doing spiritual warfare in her city. She stepped forward!

> I sensed the Lord wanted me, along with a team of intercessors, to go on a prayer walk over a specific route, but that some preparation was necessary. First, I talked with my pastor about this and then went to drive along the route I knew we were to prayer-walk. As I approached a theater (X-rated movie house, video shop and bookstore), the Holy Spirit started to give me specific instructions. He told me to cast out the spirits of pornography and lust, and I did so. He also told me to pray in the Spirit. After a short time I was released

from praying, and I continued on the rest of the route before going home.

On that Friday the Lord revealed to me what had actually happened. I turned on the local news to hear that this particular theater had been ordered by the city to close its doors. The day after I had been there to pray, the city conducted a surprise inspection. The theater was cited for several violations and its doors were immediately closed and locked.

What was so remarkable was that the city had already inspected the building a short time before and it had passed inspection. But without warning, and for no apparent reason, it was being inspected again. God had really moved! The theater did meet code violations and was re-opened for a short period of time before a judge ordered it to close for one year. Now the property is up for sale.

I had taken the course "Intercessory Prayer—The Lightning of God" by Dutch Sheets and I knew many charges had been placed in the wall, but this was the *kairos* time and the wall fell under the power of God. [By "charges" she is referring to the *dunamis*—dynamite—of the Holy Spirit that I teach about in the previously mentioned course.]

A Legal Breaking of Headship

"But why would warfare ever be necessary if Christ defeated Satan and his demons?" many ask. "Didn't Christ take away his power, disarm him and destroy his works? Didn't He deliver us from Satan's power?"

The answer to these questions lies in an accurate understanding of what Christ actually did when He defeated Satan.
Satan's destruction wasn't a literal one, but rather a legal breaking of his headship or authority. Nowhere does the Bible say
Christ delivered us from Satan's power. It says He delivered us
from his *exousia*—authority—or in other words, the right to
use his power on us:

> "For He delivered us from the domain [*exousia*] of darkness,
> and transferred us to the kingdom of His beloved Son."
>
> Colossians 1:13

> "Behold, I have given you authority [*exousia*] to tread upon
> serpents and scorpions, and over all the power [*dunamis*] of
> the enemy, and nothing shall injure you."
>
> Luke 10:19

> "When He had disarmed the rulers and authorities, He made
> a public display of them, having triumphed over them through
> Him." The word "disarmed" is the Greek word *apekduomai* and
> means Christ divested Himself of the rulers and authorities.[24]
> That's theological jargon for "He whipped them!"
>
> Colossians 2:15

*Power never was and never will be the issue between God
and Satan.* Authority was the issue—the authority Satan had
obtained through Adam. Jesus did not come to get back any
power, nor to remove Satan's power. He came to regain the
authority Adam lost to the serpent and break his headship
over the earth.

Satan still has all the inherent powers and abilities he has
always had. He "prowls about like a roaring lion" (1 Pet. 5:8).
And, contrary to what some teach, he still has his teeth. He
still has "fiery darts" (Eph. 6:16 KJV). If you don't believe this,
try going without your armor. What he lost was the right

(authority) to use his power on those who make Jesus Lord. However, Satan is a thief and a lawbreaker and will use his power or abilities on us anyway if we don't understand that through Christ we now have authority over him and his power. *Authority is the issue.* Power does the work, but authority controls the power.

This truth is well illustrated in the battle between Israel and Amalek in Exodus 17:8–13. In this famous passage Moses went to the top of a hill with the staff of God in his hand while Joshua led the army on the battlefield below. As long as Moses held up the rod of God, Israel prevailed; when he lowered it, Amalek prevailed.

The victory was not decided by the strength or power of Israel's army. If this had been the case, they would not have faltered when the staff was lowered. Nor was it a morale thing—they weren't watching Moses for inspiration while in hand-to-hand conflict! An unseen battle in the heavenlies actually decided the outcome on the battlefield. And when the rod, representing the rule or authority of God, was lifted by the authorized leader of Israel, Joshua and the army prevailed. In other words, it was not power on the battlefield—though it was necessary—that was the deciding factor, but authority on the mountain. *Authority is the key issue; power never has been.*

Approaching the Father

One final thought in introducing this subject of warfare: It is important to know that in our wrestling we are not to wrestle with God. I don't know about you, but the very thought terrifies me! The verses most often used to teach that we should are from Genesis 32:22–32, where Jacob wrestled all night with the angel of the Lord. Many a dynamic message has been preached using the words of Jacob as an example for what we should do in prayer: "I will not let you go unless you bless me" (see v. 26). I've done it myself.

However, Scripture does not present this wrestling match as an example of how we are to pray. The reason it lasted so long is (1) God allowed it—the angel could have flipped Jacob into orbit had he wanted to. He once sent one angel to destroy an army (see 2 Chron. 32:21); (2) God and Jacob were after different things. Jacob wanted protection from Esau; God desired a nature change in Jacob.

Notice what, on the surface, seemed like a ridiculous question the angel asked Jacob: "What is your name?" Doesn't it seem strange to you that in the midst of this wrestling match they began to have a nice little conversation trying to get acquainted? That is not really what was happening. God was trying to get Jacob to acknowledge the truth about his nature, which was described by his name. The *Amplified* translation demonstrates this clearly: "[The Man] asked him, What is your name? And [in shock of realization, whispering] he said, Jacob [supplanter, schemer, trickster, swindler]!" (Gen. 32:27).

That's all the Lord needed: revelation and confession. Immediately grace was released and a nature change occurred. His name was also changed to Israel. A study of Jacob from this point on shows the great difference in his nature.

"But Jacob prevailed," some might say.

Only by losing. The only way to win a wrestling match with God is to lose. If you win, you lose; if you lose, you win. The only way to find our lives is to lose them (see Matt. 16:24–26; Luke 9:23–25). Jacob lost Jacob and found Israel. Such sweet defeat!

The point of our study, however, is to reveal that this story is not an example of how we are to petition our heavenly Father. We are to approach Him with bold confidence (see Heb. 4:16), knowing He is our Friend and Father. We are to ask "according to His will" (1 John 5:14), not try to wrestle from Him something He might not want to give. We are laborers together with Him (see 2 Cor. 6:1), not warring against Him. We storm the gates of hell (see Isa. 28:6; Matt. 16:18), not the gates of heaven.

Persistence in prayer is necessary, but it is not to overcome God's reluctance. This is vital to know and remember. It is impossible to ask in faith, which is a requirement, if a person does not believe it is God's will to do what he or she is asking. Why then, is persistence necessary? That is for another chapter. He who persists will find it!

The purpose of this chapter, however, is to say: *There is a warfare or wrestling necessary at times in our intercession. Paga* includes the concept and the Scriptures teach it. We must do it with balance and understanding, but *we must do it*! To ignore Satan is to abdicate to Satan.

In the next chapter, we will apply this concept of warfare to doing it for the lost. We have a vital role to play in setting the captives free. Let's make a gain on the kingdom of darkness!

Questions for Reflection

1. What are the two opposite activities usually needed in intercession? Why are both necessary? Does the meaning and use of *paga* reinforce this?

2. Explain 2 Corinthians 2:11. How does it reinforce the fact that we're not to ignore Satan?

3. Can you explain the connection between worship, waiting and warfare? How does Joshua picture this? Similarly, what insights can be gleaned from Mary and Martha concerning this?

4. Why would spiritual warfare ever be necessary if Christ defeated and destroyed the powers of darkness? Include comments on the difference between authority and power.

5. Are we supposed to wrestle with God in prayer? Explain.

6. Define the word *pro* from Ephesians 6, commenting on its connection to spiritual warfare.

7. Why is it important to choose preaching interpreters carefully? (Hint: "I won't say that.")

10

Most High Man

Peeling Off the Veils

I watched the cesarean section delivery of a baby on television once. It was on one of those educational channels that enlighten us to some of the things we need to know to survive in life. Thank God for cable!

I also saw a face-lift on the same channel. They peeled the skin right off the face! Then they sucked up a bunch of cellulite. I don't know what kind of cells those are, but they also sucked up some fat—I knew what that was. Seemed to me they should have left the "lite" cells and sucked up the fat cells, but I reckon they had some reason for doing what they did. The things we do to look better. Believe me, now I know why they say beauty is only skin deep.

The delivery of the baby fascinated me the most. I always figured they just cut the skin and out plopped the baby. No way! They pert-near (that's Texan for nearly) turned that poor woman inside out. Pulled out and pointed out things I didn't even know I had (!)—ovaries and stuff like that. When they finally got to the baby, it was all they could do to pull it out. I don't know why it held on like it did. If it had been seeing what I was seeing, it would have wanted out of there fast.

Anyway, all of us need to be educated on the finer points of C-sections and face-lifts. And if you're gonna read a book by someone, you probably want to know that person is well versed in many areas of life. We don't need no more dumb authors!

Hopefully by now you know there is a method to my madness and somehow—perhaps minutely—but somehow, this relates to intercession.

The Bible says there is a veil that keeps unbelievers from clearly seeing the gospel:

> And even if our gospel is veiled, it is veiled to those who are perishing, in whose case the god of this world has blinded the minds of the unbelieving, that they might not see the light of the gospel of the glory of Christ, who is the image of God.
>
> 2 Cor. 4:3–4

My lexicons told me the word "veil" means "to hide, cover up, wrap around."[1] The Greek word is *kalupsis*. They said the inside of a tree is veiled by bark; the inside of a human body is veiled by skin. I understood immediately!

The New Testament word for a "revelation" is simply *kalupsis* with the prefix *apo* added—*apokalusis*. *Apo* means "off or away,"[2] so literally a revelation is an unveiling, an uncovering. As I watched those surgeries, I received a revelation of the inside of a human body—at least some of it.

The Veil in the Unbeliever

This chapter is all about spiritual warfare for the lost. It is perhaps the most important in the book. The primary purpose of the previous chapter was to prepare us for this one. We have a part to play in lifting the veil off the mind of the unbeliever. Second Corinthians 10:4, which we will elaborate on later, speaks of strongholds that are a part of this veil. We participate in the destruction of these fortresses. Strongholds are not demons; they are places from which demons rule.

We will look closely at several words from these two passages to gain a more thorough understanding of what is being said. The passage in 2 Corinthians 4:3–4 tells us there is a veil or covering over the minds of unbelievers that keeps them from clearly seeing the light of the gospel. It is important to know *they don't see the gospel because they can't see it. They don't understand it because they can't understand it.* They must have an unveiling—a revelation.

Recently, I was visiting with a brother in Alaska who was telling me about a friend to whom he has been witnessing. He said, "It's just like you teach, Dutch. The man actually said to me, 'I know there is something to what you're saying because it's obvious what it has done for you. *But I can't yet fully see it*'" (emphasis added).

In times past it always seemed difficult for me to understand how some people could hear and reject powerful gospel presentations. Now I know. When "hearing" it, they didn't hear what I heard, see what I saw or understand what I understood. What the unbelievers heard was filtered through a belief system—a veil—that caused them to hear something totally different. The fourth verse of 2 Corinthians 4:4 clearly states this: "that they might not *see* the light of the gospel of the glory of Christ, who is the *image* of God" (emphasis added). They simply do not see the same "image" of Christ that we do. To clearly see Him is to love and want Him. We'll describe some of the components of this "stronghold" in more detail later in the chapter. At this point it is imperative to establish that it exists.

A Distorted Perspective

This distorted perception of the unbeliever is well illustrated by the story of a woman driving home alone one evening when she noticed a man in a large truck following her. Growing increasingly fearful, she sped up, trying to lose her pursuer, but it was futile. She then exited the freeway and drove up a main street, but the truck stayed with her, even running red lights to do so.

In a panic, the woman wheeled into a service station, jumped from her car and ran inside screaming. The truck driver ran to her car, jerked the back door open and pulled from the floor behind her seat a man that was hiding there.[3]

The lady was fleeing from the wrong person. *She was running from her savior!* The truck driver, perched high enough to see into her back seat, had spied the would-be rapist and was pursuing her to save her, even at his own peril.

As was this lady's, the perspective of unbelievers is distorted. People run from the pursuit of a God who is desiring to save them from destruction. Those of us who know Him realize we love God because He first loved us. When sinners, however, hear of a loving God who wants only their best and died to provide it, they often see instead only the promise of loss and a lack of fulfillment.

Letting in the Light

The word "light" in 2 Corinthians 4:4 is *photismos*, which means "illumination."[4] It is similar to another word in Ephesians 1:18, "enlightened," which is the word *photizo*—"to let in light."[5] We can almost see the English words "photo" or "photograph" in these Greek words; they are, indeed, derived from them. What happens when one takes a photo? The shutter on the camera opens, letting in light, which brings an image.

If the shutter on the camera does not open, there will be no image or picture, regardless of how beautiful the scenery or elaborate the setting.

The same is true in the souls of human beings. And this is exactly what is being said in these two verses in 2 Corinthians 4. It sounds like photography language. It makes no difference how glorious our Jesus or how wonderful our message—if the veil (shutter) is not removed, there will be no true image (picture) of Christ.

Oh, sometimes we talk people into a salvation prayer without a true revelation (unveiling), but there is usually no real change. That is why fewer than 10 percent—I've heard figures as low as 3 percent—of people who "get saved" in America become true followers of Christ. The reason is that there is not true biblical repentance, which only comes from biblical revelation.

Repentance does not mean to "turn and go another way"—a change of direction. That's the Greek word *epistrepho*, often translated "converted" or "turn," and is the *result* of repentance. Repentance—*metanoia*—means to have "a new knowledge or understanding"—a change of mind.

In biblical contexts, repentance is a new understanding that comes from God through an unveiling (revelation). It is the reversing of the effects of the Fall through Adam. Humanity chose their own wisdom, their own knowledge of good and evil, right and wrong. Humanity now needs a new knowledge—from God. Paul said in Acts 26:18 that he was called "to open their eyes"—enlightenment, unveiling, revelation, repentance—"*so that* they may turn [*epistrepho*][6] from darkness to light."

Information Versus Revelation

We need to understand—and I'm afraid most do not—the difference between *information* and *revelation*. Information is of the mind; biblical revelation, however, involves and affects the mind, but originates from the heart. Spiritual power is only released through revelation knowledge. The written word (*graphe*)[7] must become the living word (*logos*).[8] This is why even we believers must not just read but also abide or meditate in the Word, praying as the psalmist: "Open my eyes, that I may behold wonderful things from Thy law" (Ps. 119:18). The word "open," *galah*, also means "unveil or uncover"[9]—revelation.

Information can come immediately, but revelation is normally a process. As the parable of the sower demonstrates, all biblical truth comes in seed form. Early in my walk with the Lord, I was frustrated because the wonderful truths I had heard from some outstanding teachers were not working for me. When I heard the teachings, they had seemed powerful to me. I left the meetings saying, "I will never be the same!" But a few weeks and months later, I was the same.

As I complained to God and questioned the truth of what I had heard, the Lord spoke words to me that have radically changed my life: *Son, all truth comes to you in seed form. It may be fruit in the person sharing it, but it is seed to you. Whether or not it bears fruit depends on what you do with it.* Spiritual information seeds must grow into fruit-producing revelation.

Knowledge or information alone, which is what humans have glorified and where they have begun their quest for meaning ever since the Fall, does not produce salvation. It does not necessarily lead to a true knowledge of God. Jesus said to the Pharisees, "You search the Scriptures, because you think that in them you have eternal life; and it is these that bear witness of Me" (John 5:39).

The Pharisees knew the Scriptures (*graphe*) probably better than you or I, but they did not know God. Many theologians today know the Scriptures thoroughly but don't know God well. Some, perhaps, do not know Him at all. They couldn't sit quietly in His presence for two hours without being bored silly. They have much information, but little or no revelation. Revelation makes the Scriptures "spirit and life" (John 6:63 AMPC). It makes them live.

Why is this so important? Because we are forever short-circuiting God's process and, in so doing, short-circuiting the results. It is revelation that leads to biblical faith and true change. Without it we are simply appealing to a fallen, selfish, humanistic mind that is always asking, "What's in it for me?" When we appeal to this mentality through human wisdom and intellect alone, we often preach a humanistic, "What's in it for them" gospel, and we produce—at best—humanistic, self-centered converts.

If, on the other hand, we preach a pure gospel, including repentance and the laying down of a person's own life (lordship of Christ), unbelievers are sure to reject it unless they receive a biblical revelation. In fact, our gospel is often ridiculous or moronic to them: "But a natural man does not accept the things of the Spirit of God; for they are foolishness to him, and he cannot understand them, because they are spiritually appraised" (1 Cor. 2:14). The word "foolishness" is *moria*, from which we get the word "moron."

Birthing True Repentance

What is the solution? We must allow the Holy Spirit time to birth true repentance in them through God-given revelation. This produces God-centered Christians, not self-centered ones. God knows we could use some of those, especially in America.

Two or three years ago, a lady we'll call Sarah related to me a testimony of praying for her sister and brother-in-law. Although generally nice people, "they were very anti-Christian, and were my husband's and my greatest persecutors spiritually, mocking and making fun of us."

Sarah had been praying for them *for 20 years*, but they had shown no interest in the gospel. "Because of their attitude toward God and the gospel," Sarah admits, "I had developed a hard heart toward them. I was religiously proud against them and praying out of a wrong motive."

After listening to me teach on intercession, Sarah's hope was renewed and the Holy Spirit prompted her with the question, *When are you going to do this for your family?* She repented of her attitude, got her heart right and forgave them for their attitude toward God. Then she began to pray as I had instructed.

Sarah's need to repent personally and change her own attitude is a valuable lesson for us. Attitudes in our own hearts often keep God from being able to answer our prayers. Isn't it ironic and tragic that our own sin might hinder our prayers for another sinner? Jesus said, "First take the log out of your own eye, and then you will see clearly to take the speck out of your brother's eye" (Matt. 7:5). You may need to forgive your spouse, child or loved one before God can use you to deliver him or her.

Sarah prayed several things and remembers praying specifically "for the veil to be lifted off of their eyes so that they can see and understand the truth of the gospel." Also, she prayed "that they would come to Christ together so that one would not persecute the other."

A couple of months later—remember, before applying these principles and dealing with her own heart she had prayed for *20 years*—Sarah called to speak with her sister. She heard this amazing report: Earlier that day her brother-in-law had awakened and felt they should go to church. (They *never* went to church.) So they found a small church and, during the altar call, *both of them gave their lives to Christ.* She then apologized to Sarah for the way they had treated her—their attitudes totally changed. They are still walking with the Lord. About nine months later, Sarah's father also came to the Lord.

This will work for you, too!

Blinded by Pride

How does Satan blind the mind of the unbeliever? What gives place to this veil? I believe the Lord has shown me a valuable clue. The word "blinded" in 2 Corinthians 4:4 (KJV) is *tuphloo*, which means "to dull the intellect; to make blind."[10] The root word, *tupho*, has the meaning of making smoke,[11] and the blindness in this passage is like a smoke screen that clouds or darkens the air in such a way as to prohibit a person from seeing. This made sense to me, but it didn't seem to fully answer how he did it. Then I made a fascinating discovery.

From this same root comes a word (*tuphoo*) that is used for being high-minded, proud or inflated with self-conceit.[12] The picture is of one who is "puffed up," much like smoke puffs up or billows. When I saw the connection between the words "blindness" and "pride," a major missing link was supplied for me. I realized immediately it was the sin of pride, passed on from Lucifer to humankind in the Garden, that Satan uses to blind them. I realized that most rejection of Christ, whether from the works motivation of most false religions or the simple fact most people just don't want to give lordship of their lives to another, is due to pride. It is the ultimate enemy of Christ and will ultimately be dealt with in finality when every knee bows and every tongue confesses that Christ is Lord. Pride will be dealt its final blow!

The captain of a ship on a dark night saw faint lights in the distance. He told his signalman to send the message: "Change your course 10 degrees south."

Immediately he received the response: "Change your direction 10 degrees north."

The proud captain was angry that he was being challenged, so he sent a further message: "Change your course 10 degrees south. This is the captain speaking!"

He received the response: "Change your direction 10 degrees north. I'm Seaman Third Class Jones."

The captain, thinking he would terrify this insubordinate sailor, wired a third message: "Change your direction 10 degrees south. I am a battleship."

The final reply came: "Change your course 10 degrees north. I am a lighthouse."[13]

The Male Pride Factor

God, the light of the world, is forever trying to get fallen humanity to alter their course. Arrogant humans, who have chosen to captain their own lives, usually charge on to their own destruction.

This pride factor also answered my question of why, regardless of where I went in the world, I found more women saved than men. I knew it couldn't be because they were smarter! The reason is that this root of pride is stronger in men than in women—most men at least. Some of us in the ultra-humble class no longer have a problem with it.

The reason pride is stronger in men is *that which was strongest in us in a pure form before the Fall became strongest in a perverted form after the Fall.* The motivation in men that found its greatest fulfillment in covering, nurturing, protecting and caring for—leading from a servant motivation—turned inward at the time of the Fall.

The desire to lead became a desire to dominate or lord over, a giving nature turned into a getting nature and a secure humility was transformed into an insecure pride. To see how we men were supposed to cover and lead, we need only to look at Jesus, who led and walked in amazing authority and power, yet from a pure serving motivation.

Counselors will counsel many more women than men because it is so difficult for a man to say, "I need help." Women are usually the first to say, "I'm sorry" or "I was wrong." Men are usually more competitive. Women are usually more giving and selfless. Why are these things true? The pride factor in men.

Praying for the Lost

This understanding of the blinding ability of pride is a tremendous clue in how to pray for the lost. It is mentioned again, along with several other important insights, in 2 Corinthians 10:3–5:

> For though we walk in the flesh, we do not war according to the flesh, for the weapons of our warfare are not of the flesh, but divinely powerful for the destruction of fortresses. We are destroying speculations and every lofty thing raised up against the knowledge of God, and we are taking every thought captive to the obedience of Christ.

Most Christians have interpreted these verses, especially verse five, as something we are to do for ourselves. Although I have no problem with doing it for ourselves, the context is certainly that of spiritual warfare for others. *The Living Bible* makes this very clear. As you read it in this paraphrase, notice also the references and inferences to the root of pride we saw in 2 Corinthians 4:4.

> It is true that I am an ordinary, weak human being, but I don't use human plans and methods to win my battles. I use God's mighty weapons, not those made by men, to knock down the devil's strongholds. These weapons can break down every proud argument against God and every wall that can be built to keep men from finding Him. With these weapons I can capture rebels

and bring them back to God, and change them into men whose hearts' desire is obedience to Christ.

As we observe these verses more closely, we'll see that the Lord gives us not only a solution for the pride problem, but also identifies and offers God's remedy for other aspects of the stronghold. This passage is both fascinating and enlightening.

Notice first that God tells us what should be obvious: The weapons of our warfare are not carnal or fleshly. This simply means they aren't human. God knows we often overlook the obvious, so He states it clearly. We will never win people on an intellectual basis, nor will we do it through innovative techniques or methods alone. We certainly won't do it by nagging them, putting notes in their sandwiches or berating them with statements such as "When are you going to get right with God?"

When we approach people on a human basis, especially if they feel we are pressuring them, we generally make things worse. This is because the root of pride in them that says, *I don't want anyone else controlling me or telling me what to do*, rises up and defends itself. If we attack this pride on a human level, we will only strengthen it.

God's Holy Detonators

On the other hand, we have weapons that are "divinely powerful" to pull down strongholds, if we would only realize it. God says, "Instead of using yours, I'll let you use Mine. Yours won't work, Mine will." The word "powerful" is *dunatos*[14] and is actually one of the New Testament words for a miracle. These weapons empowered by God will work miracles. The word is also translated "possible." I like that. Do you have anyone that seems impossible? Will it take a miracle? With this power, they become possible. And, of course, this is the Greek word from which we get the word "dynamite." This stuff is explosive!

This dynamite is explosive for the "destruction of fortresses" or, as the *King James* translation says, is capable of "pulling down strongholds." "Destruction" and "pull down" are the word *kathairesis*. This important and powerful word has a couple of pertinent meanings. One of them is "to bring down with violence or demolish" something.[15] With this powerful, miracle-working dynamite behind our weapons, we can become demolition agents violently tearing down Satan's strongholds.

I remember as a small child watching the destruction of an old brick school. I was fascinated as the huge cement ball, attached to a gigantic crane, was swung time after time into the building, crashing through walls and ceilings, bringing incredible destruction. I suppose this would be, in one sense, a viable picture of our warfare as we systematically—one divine blow at a time—work destruction on the strongholds of darkness. It truly does usually happen this way—a systematic, ongoing, one-blow-at-a-time war against Satan's stronghold.

Yet, I saw another huge building in Dallas, Texas, demolished several years ago. This edifice was much larger than the school I had seen destroyed as a child. This one covered nearly an entire city block, or at least it seemed that way to me. The demolition crew didn't use a wrecking ball for this one. And it didn't take days—it took seconds. They used dynamite, strategically placed by experts to demolish this major structure in less than 10 seconds.

I like to think that this in some ways can also be a picture of our intercession. Unlike this physical building, we don't usually see the answer in seconds—we may be strategically placing the dynamite of the Spirit for days, weeks or months. But every time we take up our spiritual weapons and use them against the strongholds of the enemy, we are placing our explosive charges in strategic places. And sooner or later the Holy Detonator of heaven is going to say, "Enough!" There will be a mighty explosion in the Spirit, a stronghold will crumble to the ground, and a person will fall to his knees.

Mary's *Paga*

Eva Popham from Ohio shared the following testimony with me of this very thing happening to a lady to whom she ministered:

> When Sandra Sims and I first saw Mary in the nursing home, she was demon possessed. Whenever we would come down the hall toward her, she would begin to shake, make violent noises and say things such as, "I know who you are. I know who you represent. I don't want you here." She would use a lot of profanity and disgusting, vile language.
>
> Everyone at the nursing home was afraid of Mary. No one, from the cleaning staff to nurses, would enter her room alone and no one wanted to take care of her because of her violent nature. Thus, she did not receive very good care. When it was absolutely necessary to enter her room, several of the staff would go together. Mary would not allow anyone to touch her or get near to her.
>
> We prayed and fasted for Mary on a consistent, regular basis. It was a couple of months before Mary would even allow us to enter her room. We prayed that God would remove all calluses and pain from her heart [*logismos*] so that the demons would no longer have anything to hang on to.

God showed us that Mary had been severely abused as a child. We would bind Satan from exercising power over Mary and declare that he could not speak to her [*noema*]. We asked for a hedge of protection to be around her and for God to give her dreams and visions as well as for angels to minister to her. We bound up the evil forces that were already in her so that they could no longer operate.

For approximately eight months after we were first able to enter her room, we consistently prayed and fasted for her as well as ministered to her. At this time I gave a testimony at our church, Love and Faith Christian Fellowship in Cincinnati, Ohio, about reaching out to Mary. I asked everyone to please pray for her. We joined together in prayer for Mary during that service, and many continued to pray for her. Pastor Mike Murray was given a picture of her to pray over. We continued to pray for God's perfect will to be done in Mary's life. We bound Satan and prayed for all of his doors to be closed in her life.

Sandra and I ministered to Mary's hurts and she eventually let her anger go by an act of faith [another *logismos*]. She willed for her life to be changed. There was nothing left for the enemy to have as a stronghold in her.

About two weeks later Mary gave her life to the Lord! Today she is dramatically different: She lets people love her and touch her; her voice is becoming more and more soft and gentle; there is even a marked difference in her before-and-after pictures. It's like the real Mary is just now finally appearing. The presence of God is on her now.

> The head nurse of the nursing home called Sandra and me into her office to give us a thank-you gift for what we have done with Mary. She told us the staff had all been asking, "What have they been doing with Mary? She is so different!" Because she is no longer violent, the staff is no longer frightened of her, so they are beginning to properly care for her.

Hallelujah! That's *paga*! That's a demolition!

I will be explaining the italicized words *logismos* and *noema* as we progress—they are specific components of the stronghold. But first . . . along with demolish, there's another interesting meaning to *kathairesis*. It was used figuratively of "removal from office."[16] Wow! Is that ever what we're after! . . . A new Lordship . . . A different ruler. Our weapons, charged with God's authority, can enforce the breaking of the headship of the serpent. Jesus legally broke it; we can see it become literal through our prayers. Hallelujah!

The Stronghold, Satan's Prison Within

But just what does this word "stronghold" that we throw around so pervasively in the Body of Christ actually mean? The word is *ochuroma*, coming from the root word *echo*, which means "to have or hold."[17] This word for "stronghold" (KJV) or "fortress" (NASB) is literally a place from which to *hold* something *strongly*. It is also the word for a fort, a castle or a prison.

I've seen pictures of foxholes and trenches hastily dug in times of war to maintain a position. That's a hold. On the other hand, I toured a huge castle on top of a mountain in Salzburg, Austria, several years ago. From this seeming impregnable fortress on a hill, someone had ruled the territory. That's a stronghold!

In essence, Satan has a place of strength *within* unbelievers from which he can hold on to them strongly. They are prisoners, captives, slaves. Christ was sent "to proclaim release to the captives" (Luke 4:18). I can guarantee you, however, that as His proclamation goes forth now, it will be through the mouth of the Church!

Now we come to verse five of 2 Corinthians 10, an extremely important verse. Let's read it again: "We are destroying speculations and every lofty thing raised up against the knowledge of God, and we are taking every thought captive to the obedience of Christ." It is important to know that "destruction" in verse four and "destroying" in this verse are the same words.

The KJV does a most unfortunate thing in using two totally different words, "pulling down" and "casting down." It is necessary to know these are the same words in order to realize the Holy Spirit is carrying on the same thought. Verse four says our divinely empowered weapons can demolish strongholds, and verse five is going to elaborate more fully just what the strongholds are that we're going to demolish. In other words, *He describes for us exactly what comprises the stronghold or prison!* This is critical information as we begin to war for the lost.

Specifically, He shares with us three major components of the fortress. These are the things we will begin to call out and demolish as we war over individuals with our divinely empowered weapons. I believe this can be done over people groups as well, but the context here seems to indicate that it is speaking primarily of individuals.

Mindsets

The first aspect of the stronghold He mentions is "speculations"—*logismos*. This word speaks not of the scattered individual thoughts of humans, but of their calculative reasoning, their wisdom or logic.[18] Our word "logic" is actually derived from this Greek root. *Logismos* is the sum total of the accumulated wisdom and information learned over time. It becomes *what one really believes*—the person's mindset. Moffatt calls them "theories." Humanity, before the Fall, got their wisdom and logic—their beliefs—from God. Now, James 3:15 tells us they come from the earth, the soul or intellect, and demons.

These *logismos* would include philosophies (whether formally identified or unnamed personal ones), religions, humanism, atheism, Hinduism, Buddhism, Islam, racism, intellectualism, Judaism, materialism, roots of rejection, perversions—anything that causes a person to think a certain way.

How do these *logismos* blind individuals? How do they veil truth? The way the human mind functions dictates that when people hear the gospel, *before they even have time to think or reason about it*, it is filtered through the subconscious where all other information—including these *logismos*—is stored. This means that unbelievers don't hear what we are saying; they hear what we are saying *plus* what they already believe.

For example, I was sharing the gospel with a girl who had been horribly abused. "God is love," I said. "He loves you so much He sent His Son to die for you."

She did not hear only what I said. She also heard in her mind— I know because she said to me—"Oh? If He is love, why would He have allowed me to have been so abused? Doesn't sound like a loving God to me." That is a *logismos*—a belief, a philosophy, her wisdom, her logic. Someone will need to intercede for her and help tear it down.

On another occasion I was sharing the gospel with a fellow who had a *logismos* I call "good-ole-boy-ism." He was just too nice a guy to think he needed saving. "I'm a pretty good guy," he said. "I don't cheat on my wife, beat my kids, lie, curse or steal. I don't think God would send me to hell."

How does the gospel break through these arguments? Certainly the gospel of truth itself has power to break down some of this when anointed by the Holy Spirit. But it usually takes a long period of time—*if* you can get them to listen. It is much wiser to plow the ground ahead of time, preparing for the reception of the seed by pulling down these strongholds.

Perhaps you already know what these *logismos* are in the person for whom you are praying. If not, ask the Holy Spirit to reveal them to you. He will. And when He does, call them by name, quoting 2 Corinthians 10:3–5. Say, "In the name of the Lord Jesus Christ I am destroying you, stronghold of . . ." Do it daily until the person comes to Christ.

All Pride That Rises Up

The second part of the stronghold we must demolish is "every *lofty thing* raised up against the knowledge of God" (v. 5, emphasis added). I like using the KJV for this verse because it uses "high thing" to translate the Greek word *hupsoma*, which is actually the same root word for "Most High" God. It actually means "any elevated place or thing."[19] This is referring to the same root of pride we discovered hidden in the word "blinded" in 2 Corinthians 4:3–4. It is the "most highness" that came to humanity at the Fall when Adam and Eve bought the lie "You too shall be as God" (see Gen. 3:5).

Humankind, like Satan, attempted to exalt themselves to a place of equality with the Most High. We became not the Most High, but our own most high, filled with pride. One leading lexicon even defined *hupsoma* as "all pride that rises up."[20] The word would then encompass all mindsets that exalt themselves against the knowledge of God.

The good news is that we can also tear down this stronghold in people through spiritual warfare so that they can humble themselves and bow their knees to Christ. Listen to this entire verse (2 Cor. 10:5) again in *The Living Bible*:

> These weapons *can* break down *every* proud argument against God and *every* wall that can be built to keep men from finding Him. With these weapons I *can* capture rebels and bring them back to God, and change them into men whose hearts' desire is obedience to Christ (emphasis added).

I like the "cans" and "everys" in the verse. The Lord doesn't wish us luck or tell us that we will win a few once in a while. He lets us know we *can* break down *every* proud argument and *every* wall; we *can* capture rebels! And we must!

Thoughts and Temptations

Considering the third aspect of strongholds, the Lord tells us we can "take every thought captive to the obedience of Christ." The word "thought" is *noema*, which also means plans, schemes, devices or plots. It refers to the spontaneous thoughts and temptations Satan uses to assault the unbelievers, as well as the schemes and plans he uses to keep them in darkness. In intercession we must declare boldly that no weapon of Satan's will prosper. We must bind his plans and stand against them through prayer. We can and should pray that the unbeliever be shielded from Satan's thoughts and temptations.

Marlena O'Hern, of Maple Valley, Washington, had been praying for her brother, Kevin, to be saved for approximately 12 years, with no seeming results. She basically prayed things such as "Lord, come into his life," or "Lord, reveal Yourself to him." As with many of us, she didn't realize there were more specific biblical ways to pray.

Also, similar to the rest of us, she sometimes grew frustrated and tried to take things into her own hands, saying things such as, "You just need to give your life to the Lord" or "You have to quit doing the stuff you're doing." Predictably, this would only result in her seeing the pride and rebellion in Kevin rise up, actually making things worse. "Then I would really feel like I had blown it," she said.

"Kevin was heading down a rocky road. He had major problems, including drugs, depression and extreme anger," Marlena relates.

Early in 1995 she took a class of mine in which I taught these principles about praying for the lost. Marlena shared them with her husband, Patrick, and their children. They began to pray the principles over Kevin. They specifically prayed the following (all parenthetical remarks are mine):

- That God would lift the veil over him (revelation and enlightenment)
- For the Holy Spirit to hover over him and protect him
- For godly people to be in his pathway each day
- To cast down anything that would exalt itself against the knowledge of God, specifically pride and rebellion (This would include the *hupsoma* aspect of the stronghold.)
- To take down all known strongholds—thought patterns, opinions on religion, materialism, fear (This is the *logismos* dimension of the stronghold.)
- To bind Satan from taking Kevin captive; to bind all wicked thoughts and lies Satan would try to place in Kevin's mind (These would be the *noema* aspect of the stronghold.)
- That the armor of God would be placed on him

After two weeks of praying in this way, Kevin overdosed on drugs and, in his time of need, cried out to God. "The Lord met him in a powerful way. The veil was definitely lifted and he had a revelation of God. He now has an understanding of the Word and responds to it. The confusion is gone! Kevin separated himself from the world and his former friends. He is now pursuing God and Christian relationships. His focus is on pleasing God, knowing Him more and more. He is even considering missions."

"We know that we are of God, and the whole world lies in the power of the evil one" (1 John 5:19). Yet we have been given authority! We can turn unbelievers "from darkness to light and from the dominion of Satan to God" (Acts 26:18). We are called to enforce and make effectual the freedom Christ procured.

The unbeliever cannot war for himself. He cannot and will not overcome the strongholds of darkness, and he will not understand the gospel until the veil lifts. We must take our divinely dynamic weapons and fight. The powers of darkness will resist, but "do not be afraid of them; remember the Lord who is great and awesome, and fight for your brothers, your sons, your daughters, your wives, and your houses" (Neh. 4:14).

Questions for Reflection

1. What is meant by the word "veil" in 2 Corinthians 4:3? How does this apply to unsaved people? Can you explain how this is related to a biblical revelation?

2. What is meant by Satan's "blinding" the minds of unbelievers? How is this connected to the Fall of humanity? How is this significant where men (versus women) are concerned?

3. Explain the meaning of enlightenment. Can you describe the analogy to this and photography?

4. What is the true meaning of repentance? How is this connected to biblical revelation?

5. Define a stronghold. Now describe the three aspects of the stronghold in unbelievers and how intercession can be applied to each.

6. Who are you going to do this for? Will it work for them? Hallelujah!

11

The Lightning of God

Strike the Mark

This was about the coolest thing I had discovered since baseball. I was in the fifth grade, and in that ornery, but not mean, "can't stand baths," "all girls have cooties" stage of life. I had recently procured my first magnifying glass.

I'm not sure how I discovered I could hold a magnifying glass at just the right angle to the sun and catch a piece of paper on fire. I didn't do anything majorly bad, like the time I nearly burned the science classroom down with my volcanic exhibition. Never did figure out why that teacher gave me a C just because he had to run to the window with a burning volcano and throw it outside. Looked pretty real to me. Nor was it like the time I burned the kitchen cabinets because I forgot about the french-fry grease. I didn't get a grade on that endeavor, although my mom's response was very educational.

This was nothing like those incidents. I just burned a piece of paper on the playground. Then this brilliant idea leaped up

amic psyche. I called my friends over, assuring
ly cool demonstration to show them. Looking
of the mean guys in the class, I said to him in
re the lucky guy" tone of voice, "Duncan, hold
y~   t. I want to show you something."

Duncan didn't leave his hand there very long. He chased me all around that playground! Some guys just can't take a joke.

Is there a picture of intercession hidden anywhere in this? Yes. One of the ways *paga* is translated is "strike the mark." The reference is Job 36:32: "He covers His hands with the lightning, and commands it to *strike the mark*" (emphasis added). When God releases His light, causing it to flash forth from His presence like lightning, its striking the desired target is likened to intercession.

Although the word *paga* is not used, Habakkuk 3:4 also speaks of light flashing forth from the hand of God: "His radiance is like the sunlight; He has rays flashing from His hand, and there is the hiding of His power." The *Amplified* translation is also very descriptive: "And His brightness was like the sunlight; rays streamed from His hand, and there [in the sunlike splendor] was the hiding place of His power."

We are like a magnifying glass in one sense—no, we don't add to or magnify God's power—but we do let the "Son" shine forth through us, directing His light to desired situations, allowing it to "strike the mark."

Have you ever seen a tree struck by lightning? If so, you've seen a picture of intercession. I do lots of praying in a woods nearby. At times I come across trees struck by lightning. The lightning is so hot it literally changes the molecular structure of the trees and twists the trunks until they look like the stripes on a candy cane. The temperature in a lightning bolt can reach 30,000 degrees Celsius (45,000 degrees Fahrenheit), hotter than the surface of the sun. That's hot stuff! And God uses this to picture His judgments!

If I have my theology st[...]
than the creation. That mea[...]
greater than a lightning bolt. N[...]
"As wax melts before the fire, so le[...]
God. . . . The mountains melted like [...]
the Lord. . . . He raised His voice, the ear[...]
97:5; 46:6).

"For our God *is* a consuming fire!" (Heb. 12[...]
added).

To explain this chapter adequately, I need to lay a goo[...]
dation. Therefore, I want us to look at quite a few Script[...]
that associate God with light or lightning. One of the purpos[...]
of looking at so many is to demonstrate the consistency and
prevalency of this theme. I hope you don't get bored with the
Bible. If you do, you probably should skip this chapter. Better
yet, repent and read on!

God Is Light

The following verses associate God with light or lightning, and
there are numerous others that could be given. I have italicized
various words or phrases to call your attention to the theme
of light:

> 1 John 1:5: "And this is the message we have heard from Him
> and announce to you, that *God is light*, and in Him there is no
> darkness at all."

> Hebrews 1:3 AMPC: "He is the sole expression of the glory of
> God [*the Light-being, the outraying or radiance of the divine*],
> and He is the perfect imprint and very image of [God's] nature,
> upholding and maintaining and guiding and propelling the uni-
> verse by His mighty word of power. When He had by offering
> Himself accomplished our cleansing of sins and riddance of

esty on

dwells
see. To

with His

)efore
l they

ice of
? *and*

raight, the Creator must be greater ... s the power or energy in God is ... o wonder the Scriptures say, ... the wicked perish before ... wax at the presence of ... h melted" (Ps. 68:2; ... 29, emphasis ... d foun- ... ures

... Peter and his companions had been overcome with sleep; but when they were fully awake, they saw His glory and the two men standing with Him." (We read in the margin of the NASB that the word "gleaming" means literally "*flashing like lightning.*" Wuest also translates it this way. No wonder Peter wanted to build tabernacles there!)

Revelation 21:23: "And the city has no need of the sun or of the moon to shine upon it, *for the glory of God has illumined it, and its lamp is the Lamb.*"

(See also 2 Cor. 3:7.)

Sometimes this light, lightning or glory of God is released from His mouth and often called a sword. The first four verses identify God's words or mouth as His sword. The remaining verses make the connection to light or lightning:

Ephesians 6:17: "And take the helmet of salvation, and the *sword* of the Spirit, which is the *word* of God."

Revelation 2:16: "Repent therefore; or else I am coming to you quickly, and I will make war against them with the *sword of My mouth.*"

Revelation 19:15: "And *from His mouth comes a sharp sword,* so that with it He may smite the nations; and He will rule them with a rod of iron; and He treads the wine press of the fierce wrath of God, the Almighty."

(See also Heb. 4:12.)

Psalm 29:7 AMPC: "*The voice of the Lord splits and flashes forth forked lightning.*"

Ezekiel 21:9–10, 15, 28: "Son of man, prophesy and say, 'Thus says the Lord,' Say, 'A *sword, a sword* sharpened and also polished! Sharpened to make a slaughter, polished to *flash like lightning!* . . . I have given *the glittering sword.* Ah! It is made for *striking like lightning*, it is wrapped up in readiness for slaughter. . . . And you, son of man, prophesy and say, 'Thus says the Lord God concerning the sons of Ammon and concerning their reproach,' and say: 'A *sword, a sword* is drawn, polished for the slaughter, to cause it to consume, that it may be *like lightning.*"

Deuteronomy 32:41 AMPC: "If I whet My *lightning sword* and My hand takes hold on judgment, I will wreak vengeance on My foes and recompense those who hate Me." (Sometimes movies can have interesting parallels to Scripture. Luke Skywalker from *Star Wars* isn't the only one who overcomes evil with a sword of light. God has the real one!)

(See also Ps. 18:13–14; Hos. 6:5 NIV.)

Thus far, we have God associated with light or lightning, which sometimes shines forth as His glory. It is released from His mouth at times, becoming a powerful weapon. The following

Scriptures speak of God's light in the context of Him dealing with His enemies:

Psalm 97:3–4: "Fire goes before Him, and burns up His adversaries round about. *His lightnings lit up the world*; the earth saw and trembled."

Revelation 8:5: "And the angel took the censer; and he filled it with the fire of the altar and threw it to the earth; and there followed peals of thunder and sounds and *flashes of lightning* and an earthquake."

Revelation 16:18: "And there were *flashes of lightning* and sounds and peals of thunder; and there was a great earthquake, such as there had not been since man came to be upon the earth, so great an earthquake was it, and so mighty."

(See also Ps. 78:48; Rev. 11:19.)

These last few Scriptures associate the release of God's light in the context of deliverance of His people:

Psalm 18:14: "And He sent out His arrows, and scattered them, and *lightning flashes* in abundance, and routed them."

Psalm 77:17–18: "The clouds poured out water; the skies gave forth a sound; Thy arrows flashed here and there. The sound of Your thunder was in the whirlwind; The *lightnings* lit up the world; the earth trembled and shook."

Psalm 144:6: "*Flash forth lightning* and scatter them; send out Your arrows and confuse them."

(See also Ps. 27:1.)

According to all these and other fascinating Scriptures, God is light and at times this light or glory flashes forth from Him as bolts of lightning. Many times the Bible says that in order to deal with His enemies—whether for Himself or His people—God simply releases this glory or light into the situation. It flashes forth like lightning and *PAGA* HAPPENS! God's power "strikes the mark."

This happened once several thousand years ago when there was a coup attempt in heaven. Lucifer, inflated with pride, decided he would exalt himself to God's position. "Not!" as my kids would say.

Bad idea, Satan.

This war didn't last long—about as long as it takes for a lightning bolt to flash its brilliant light across the sky. Jesus said it this way in Luke 10:18–20 (Sheets's paraphrase): "Don't get excited, guys, just because demons are subject to you in My name. That's no big deal. I watched Satan cast from heaven. It didn't take long—lightning flashed and he was gone. Get excited because you have a relationship with God."

Light Overcomes Darkness

We don't know that lightning literally flashed when Satan was ousted, but for some reason Jesus used this picture. He said it was "like lightning" (v. 18). I believe it actually flashed. It doesn't really matter, however, because whether or not it literally flashed, the analogy is certainly given of light overcoming darkness.

In fact, I don't necessarily think that in all of the previously mentioned references, literal lightning bolts were observable in the natural realm of sight. At times there certainly were, as when Christ's clothes were glowing and flashing at His transfiguration or when His glory lights the throne room of heaven.

The point, however, is not what can be seen with the human eye, but what happens in the spiritual realm: Light overcomes darkness. And the light is more than a symbolic representation of God's goodness or purity; it represents His power or energy. So whether the lightning itself is literal or symbolic, the results are the same: God's power overcoming the kingdom of darkness.

This analogy of darkness and light is prevalent throughout Scripture. Another powerful example of God's light prevailing over the darkness of Satan is at the Cross. John 1:4–5 says, "In Him was life and the life was the light of men. And the light shines in the darkness, and the darkness did not comprehend it."

The word "comprehend" is the Greek word *katalambano*, which can mean either "comprehend" or "apprehend."[1] Many scholars believe it should be translated with the latter word in this passage because the powers of darkness were not trying to comprehend or understand Christ. They were trying to apprehend or overpower Him, much like a policeman would apprehend a criminal. This makes much more sense to me.

Wuest translates verse 5 accordingly: "And the light in the darkness is constantly shining. And the darkness did not overwhelm it." Moffatt says it this way: "Amid the darkness the light shone, but the darkness did not master it." The Cross was a war—light overcoming darkness. God arose and His enemies were scattered.

Bob Woods, in *Pulpit Digest*, tells the story of a couple who took their son, 11, and daughter, 7, to Carlsbad Caverns. As always, when the tour reached the deepest point in the cavern, the guide turned off all the lights to dramatize how completely dark and silent it is below the earth's surface. The little girl, suddenly enveloped in utter darkness, was frightened and began to cry. Immediately was heard the voice of her brother: "Don't cry. Somebody here knows how to turn on the lights."[2]

All creation was terrified, groping in the darkness of sin. Two thousand years ago, God announced to His groping and frightened humans, "Don't cry. Somebody here knows how to turn on the lights."

I believe Satan has some reoccurring nightmares. One of them is when the light—lightning—flashed in heaven and kicked him out. He probably hates thunderstorms. Why, they even sound like the majestic voice of God!

"The Lord also *thundered* in the heavens, and the Most High uttered His *voice*, hailstones and coals of fire. And He sent out His arrows, and scattered them, and *lightning flashes* in abundance, and routed them" (Ps. 18:13–14, emphasis added).

"The *voice* of the Lord is upon the waters; the God of glory *thunders*, the LORD is over many waters" (Ps. 29:3, emphasis added).

Imagine Satan's horror when the light of God flashed forth at the Cross, the same light that had expelled him from heaven. I can just hear him screaming, "Oh, no. Hear it comes again! He wouldn't let me have heaven and He won't let me have Earth either."

The Lightning Anointing

Yes, at the Cross the counterfeit "angel of light" met Mr. Light Himself and nothing has been the same since! The great "light" being even reproduced Himself into a bunch of little lights— "For you were formerly darkness, but now you are light in the Lord; walk as children of light" (Eph. 5:8)—filling them with His very glory!

For the first time Satan understood Isaiah 60:1–3:

Arise, shine; for your light has come, and the glory of the LORD has risen upon you. For behold, darkness will cover the earth, and deep darkness the peoples; but the LORD will rise upon you, and His glory will appear upon you. And nations will come to your light, and kings to the brightness of your rising.

Bummer! he must have thought.

For the first time he understood that the Old Testament temple was a picture of us, this new race of people called Christians ("little Christs"), and that the glory of God was in every one of them. *"Major bummer!"*

Which brings things back to us. Please read the following statements carefully, making each connection. If intercession is pictured by God's lightning striking the mark . . . and if Christ's work of intercession when He met Satan, breaking his headship, was light overcoming darkness . . . and if our praying intercession simply releases or re-presents Christ's . . . then I think it safe to say that our intercession releases the lightning of God to flash forth into situations, bringing devastation to the powers of darkness:

- Calvary flashing forth again
- The light of the world shining again
- The royal priesthood proclaiming the excellencies of Him who called them out of darkness into His marvelous light (see 1 Pet. 2:9)
- The laser of prayer burning intensely
- The lightning sword of the Spirit flashing brightly
- Jesus and the Father are glorified in the Church (see Eph. 3:21)!

We have looked at the "bear anointing" and the "butterfly anointing"—maybe this is the "lightning anointing"!

In John 1:5, which we quoted earlier, the phrase "the light shines in the darkness" could just as accurately read "the light is constantly shining," due to the tense and mood of the verb. Some translations actually do translate it this way. The light that overcame darkness is still shining—the victory lives on. Yet it must be released through the Church!

In his first All-Star game, Roger Clemens, the great pitcher for the Boston Red Sox, came to bat for the first time in years due to the American League's designated hitter rule. After watching a blazing fastball by Dwight Gooden whiz past him, Clemens turned and asked the catcher, Gary Carter, "Is that what my pitches look like?"

"You bet it is!" responded Carter.

From then on Clemens pitched with far greater boldness, having been reminded of how a good fastball can be so overpowering to a hitter.[3]

We often forget how powerful the Holy Spirit in us is . . . how destructive to darkness is His lightning sword. It has supernatural power to overcome the works of darkness—when we release it with confidence.

Dutch Meets Goliath on Bourbon Street

I led an outreach of 200 students from Christ for the Nations Institute to Mardi Gras in 1979. We focused most of our ministry on Bourbon Street, where the biggest portion of the partying occurs. I have seen few places where darkness rules so dominantly as it does at this continuous celebration of evil.

We had many hours of prayer and preparation before going on this outreach, and were assured in our hearts that we had established victory in the Spirit. The light had preceded us. We felt we were going physically only to reap the spoils. We saw dozens of people come to Christ and experienced many dramatic events as time and time again light triumphed over darkness. It was not without its tests, however. One of the events that impacted me greatly was an encounter we had with a demonized man who intended to do some of us bodily harm— kill us.

I spent most of my time walking the length of Bourbon Street interceding for the "troops" as they witnessed and prayed with folks. One evening my partner and I crossed the street to speak with two of our students, who happened to be carrying a sign that read, "God Loves You!"

As we stood talking, a giant of a man, whom we'll call Goliath, came at us seemingly out of nowhere. He was about 10 feet tall (at least 6' 6") and weighed 500 pounds (at least 260 pounds). He was dressed from head to toe as a Roman soldier—or maybe as a Philistine soldier—and carried a long whip he was cracking as he came up to us. His lips were covered with bloody froth and blood was trickling out of the corners of his mouth.

He approached us, cracking the whip and growling like a mad dog. The area around us cleared as people backed off and watched. Goliath then began to shout in a deep, raspy voice, "God is love, huh? I'm gonna kill you!"

This is not good, I perceived quickly, being the astute man I am. I wanted to speak some powerful Scripture as a sword, but the only verse that came to mind was, *To live is Christ; to die is gain.* It just didn't seem like the one I wanted!

As I stood wondering why one of the other three team members didn't do something, the reason suddenly occurred to me—I was the leader! Being the wise leader that I am, I shouted, "Every man for himself." Then to myself I added, *Legs, don't fail me now!* I felt more like the butterfly anointing than the lightning anointing.

Of course, I didn't really say and do those things, but there was a strong fear that tried to rise up in me. What did I actually do? I PAGA'ed—big time *paga*! And when I glanced at the other three, their lips were silently moving. They were *paga*'n too!

It was *paga* times four. Magnifying glass, don't fail me now!

As we stood and bound the powers of darkness in this man in the name of Jesus, within seconds he began to change. His countenance changed, his voice changed and his attitude changed. The demons controlling him had been overcome. Light prevailed. The man actually appeared confused. He looked at us with a strange expression, muttered something about going ahead with what we were doing and walked away slowly as the crowd watched in amazement.

Light overcame darkness. God's power "struck the mark" (*paga*), quieting the evil spirits and saving us from embarrassment and probable injury.

Later that night as we all gathered and shared our war stories of the day, all were amazed as we related how fearless, confident and in control we were as "Goliath" confronted us. "Never a doubt," we all assured the group. "Never a doubt." May God forgive us!

Living Temples That Carry Glory

My father, Dean Sheets, who pastors in Ohio, saw light overcome darkness while he was on a missions trip to Haiti. He was preaching the gospel and praying for the sick according to Mark 16:15–18. As you are probably aware, the national religion of Haiti is voodoo; consequently, demon activity is prominent and strong. The powers of darkness have been given free reign.

Dad felt specifically led by the Holy Spirit to pray for blind individuals, so he invited them forward. Twenty people responded. As he stood before them one at a time, waiting for direction from the Holy Spirit, he was given the same instruction for 19 of the 20: "Cast out the spirit causing the blindness." Each time he did they were healed instantly, seeing perfectly.

Paga! Light striking the mark, penetrating darkened eyes, bringing sight.

What many believers are not aware of is that we are filled with the very glory and light of God. When the apostle Paul, inspired by the Holy Spirit, said, "Do you not know that you are a temple of God, and that the Spirit of God dwells in you?" (1 Cor. 3:16), he used the Greek word *naos* for "temple,"[4] which always referred to the holy of holies. He was literally saying, "Don't you know you are the holy of holies?"

The word "dwells" is taken from the Old Testament word *shakan*, which means "dwelling or abiding."[5] The "*shekinah* glory" was the abiding or dwelling glory found in the holy of holies. Paul was saying that in Christ the *shekinah* glory of God now *shakans* in us (see 1 Sam. 4:4; 2 Sam. 6:12–19). We are the new holy of holies, a temple of living stones not made with hands, but by God Himself. Second Corinthians 4:6–7, in the KJV, says it this way:

> For God, who commanded the light to shine out of darkness, hath shined in our hearts, to give the light of the knowledge of the glory of God in the face of Jesus Christ. But we have this treasure in earthen vessels, that the excellency of the power may be of God, and not of us.

Israel carried the Ark of the Covenant, representing the presence and glory of God, into battle (see Josh. 6:6). When the Ark set out, the shout would go up, "Rise up, O LORD! And let Thine enemies be scattered, and let those who hate Thee flee before Thee" (Num. 10:35). Psalm 68:1, a warfare verse, is a quote of this verse in Numbers. That same presence and glory now abides in us. The message we are to understand is that the key to victory is carrying this presence of God into battle with us. He rises and scatters His enemies *through us*! We are now His carriers!

Release the Light

Arise, shine, Church, for your light has come and the glory of the Lord has risen upon you. Darkness, indeed, does cover the earth and deep darkness the peoples, but it is a defeated darkness. Nations are looking for the light, kings for the brightness of our rising (see Isa. 60:1–3). We are soldiers of the light. We must boldly release the power of the Most High into situations, allowing the victory of Christ access. He has given us

His light, He has given us His sword, He has given us His name. Use them!

Position yourself toward the Son and allow Him to shine through you, striking the mark! Wield the laser sword of the Spirit. We often forget how powerful the Holy Spirit in us is—how destructive to darkness is His lightning sword. It has supernatural power to overcome the works of darkness—when we release it with confidence.

Station yourself spiritually in front of your rebellious children and ask God to send a bolt of meekness to them. Aim the light of liberty at their addictions, whether they be drugs, sex, alcohol, or whatever. Be aggressive in the spirit.

Spouses, ask God to shine forth into the lives of your mates, breaking through the darkness of deception and liberating them.

Pastors, call upon the Holy Spirit to flash, breaking strife, division and complacency over your congregations. While you are waiting for God to do something, He may be waiting on you. Release the light! Call it forth in Jesus' name.

As the Israelites carried the presence and glory of God into battle, so must we. All that was in the Ark of the Covenant is in us: the Bread of Life, the rod of priestly authority and the law of God. And the glory that was upon it now shines through us. Act like it! Strike with the sword—speak the Word! "Let God arise" through your intercession "and His enemies be scattered."

Questions for Reflection

1. How is *paga* related to lightning?

2. Explain the connection between God's light/lightning and His judgments. Can you explain how this happened at the Cross?

3. What is the relationship between God, light, His sword and our intercession?

4. Where is the holy of holies? How does this relate to intercession?

5. Think of a situation where light overcame darkness. How did God do it? Now, think of a current situation in which intercession can be used to see the same results.

6. Do you like representing Jesus?!

12

The Substance of Prayer

Two frogs fell into a can of cream,
or so it has been told.
The sides of the can were shiny and steep,
the cream was deep and cold.
"Oh, what's the use," said number one,
"It's plain no help's around.
"Good-bye, my friend, good-bye, sad world"
and weeping still he drowned.

But number two, of sterner stuff,
dog paddled in surprise.
The while he licked his creamy lips
and blinked his creamy eyes.
"I'll swim at least a while," he thought,
or so it has been said.
It really wouldn't help the world
if one more frog were dead.

An hour or more he kicked and swam,
not once he stopped to mutter.
Then hopped out from the island he had
made of fresh churned butter.

(Author unknown)

Lessons From Three Men and a Frog

I first heard this witty poem 20 years ago in a message by John Garlock, one of my professors at Christ for the Nations Institute, on the subject of tenacity. There aren't many messages that a person remembers 20 years later, but John Garlock has a knack and an anointing for preaching "rememberable" sermons. Others, of course, have a similar gift of preaching very forgettable messages. I've heard lots of them, and even preached my share.

Brother Garlock mentioned the story found in 2 Samuel 23:8–12 about three of David's mighty men: Shammah, Adino and Eleazar. Shammah had tenacity in the face of a humble assignment, defending a small plot of lentils from a bunch of Philistines. Adino personified tenacity in the face of overwhelming odds as he killed 800 Philistines single-handedly. Eleazar pictured tenacity in the face of incredible overwhelming fatigue as, after fighting for several hours, his hand had to be pried from his sword.

Thanks, Professor Garlock, for teaching me through three men and a frog the importance of perseverance and endurance. I rank it near the top of my list of most important spiritual traits. And the longer I live, the higher it rises. "Hang in there" didn't make it into the Ten Commandments, but it did into the nine fruits of the Spirit.

The word *makrothumia*, translated "long-suffering" in Galatians 5:22 (KJV), is defined by *Strong's Concordance* as "longanimity or fortitude."[1] That's what I said, "Hang in there."

In this day of instant everything—from "fast foods" to "get-rich-quick" schemes to "how to have the biggest church in town overnight" conferences to "four easy steps to answered prayer" seminars—we are rapidly losing the character trait of hanging in there. We cook faster, travel faster, produce faster and spend faster . . . and we expect God to keep pace with us, especially in prayer.

Dick Eastman, in his book *No Easy Road*, states:

> Much of society has forgotten to persevere. . . . Few have a striving spirit like the artist Raphael. Once he was questioned, "What is your greatest painting?" He smiled, saying, "My next one." One finds Raphael always striving to do better. This is what we need in prayer, an attitude of persistence.[2]

We are much like the African cheetah that must run down its prey to eat. It is well suited for the task, as it can run at speeds of 70 miles per hour. The cheetah has only one problem, however, in that it has a disproportionately small heart, which causes it to tire quickly. If it doesn't catch its prey quickly, it must end the chase.

How often we have the cheetah's approach in prayer. We speed into our closets with great energy, we speed to the front of the church, or we speed to someone else for prayer. But lacking the heart for a sustained effort, we often falter before we accomplish what is needed. For our next prayer excursion, we decide to pray harder and faster, when what is needed may not be more explosive power, but more staying power—stamina that comes only from a bigger prayer heart.[3]

George Müller was a "stayer." One example of his persistence is related by Dick Eastman in the previously mentioned book:

> "The great point is never to give up until the answer comes. I have been praying for sixty-three years and eight months for one man's conversion. He is not saved yet, but he will be. How

can it be otherwise. . . . I am praying." The day came when Müller's friend received Christ. It did not come until Müller's casket was lowered in the ground. There, near an open grave, this friend gave his heart to God. Prayers of perseverance had won another battle. Müller's success may be summarized in four powerful words: He did not quit.[4]

Easy Doesn't Do It in Prayer

The very Son of God spent many entire nights praying in order to fulfill His ministry. It took Him three arduous hours in Gethsemane to find strength to face the cross: "He offered up both prayers and supplications with loud crying and tears" (Heb. 5:7).

We, on the other hand, have mastered the art of one-liners in prayer, and think if we give God a two-hour service once a week we're fairly spiritual. "Easy does it" might be good advice in a few situations, but for most of life, including prayer, easy *doesn't* do it.

A pilot early in a flight went to the back of the plane to check on the reason for a warning light. The problem was a door ajar, which flew open as he approached it. The pilot was immediately sucked from the aircraft.

The copilot, seeing by his panel that a door was open, turned back toward the airport immediately and radioed for a helicopter to search the area. "I believe I have a pilot sucked from the plane," he said. After landing the plane, everyone was astonished to find the pilot holding on to the rung of a ladder, which he had miraculously managed to grab. He had held on for 15 minutes and, still more amazing, had managed to keep his head from hitting the runway, though it was only six inches away!

Upon finding the pilot, they had to pry his fingers from the ladder! That's perseverance![5]

Anyone long associated with the Church of this century, especially in America, knows that our problems do not result from a lack of information or material strength. If we fail in achieving what God asks from us as we run our race, it will be a failure of heart and spirit.

Like the frog, I have kicked and swum my way over time to more victories than I have accomplished quickly and easily. I have fought until my hand clove to the sword. I have found that a tenacious endurance is often the key to victory in prayer.

But WHY?

Why is persistence required in prayer? This I have labored about for years. Does God have a certain amount of prayers required for certain situations? Do we talk Him into things? Does God ever "finally decide" to do something? Do we earn answers through hard work or perseverance?

The answer to all these questions is no.

"What about the prayer of importunity in Luke 11:5–13?" some will ask. "Doesn't it teach that we importune or persist with God until He decides to give us what we need?"

The answer is an emphatic no! We don't persist against God.

The word "importunity" in Luke 11:8 (KJV) is an unfortunate translation of the word *anaideia*, which actually means "shamelessness"[6] or "bold unashamedness."[7] *Aidos*, the root word, means "modesty or shame"[8] and is translated as such in 1 Timothy 2:9. Here in Luke 11, it is in its negative form, making it "without modesty or shame."

The point of this story is the same as Hebrews 4:16, which is to approach the throne of grace boldly, not with a sense of unworthiness or shame. As the petitioner in the story, we can approach our friend, God, at any time knowing we are accepted.

Is God using the waiting period to teach us? I think at times this is certainly the case, and yet, if this is the reason for a delay, we shouldn't need to pray for the same thing again and again—once and then a waiting in faith would be adequate.

In other situations the delay might be that God has the right time for an answer to prayer. "And let us not lose heart in doing good, for in due time we shall reap if we do not grow weary" (Gal. 6:9). But, again, if this is the reason, asking once and waiting in faith should be sufficient.

So why is a persistence or perseverance necessary in prayer? Why did it take me 30 hours of praying to get the cyst dissolved on my wife's ovary? Why did it take a year to obtain a miracle for the little girl in the coma? Why does it sometimes demand several years of intercession to see someone saved? Why did Elijah have to pray seven times before the rain came? Why did Daniel have to pray 21 days before the angel broke through with his answer?

His Throne in Our Hearts

There are probably reasons I am not aware of for the need for persistence in prayer. I certainly don't have all the prayer answers, but I want to submit one explanation for your consideration. I believe our prayers do more than simply motivate the Father to action. I have become convinced of something Gordon Lindsay, a great man of prayer and the founder of Christ for the Nations, called the "substance" of prayer.[9] In fairness, I must say I don't believe it can be conclusively proven, but there is great weight of evidence suggesting it, and I have embraced it as truth.

The concept is that our prayers do more than just motivate the Father to action. They actually release the power of the Holy Spirit from us to accomplish things. Certain types of praying would of course do this more than others.

For example, in our chapter on travail we spoke of this happening as we pray in the Spirit. Another powerful way this occurs would be through speaking the Word of God as a sword into situations (see Eph. 6:17). General declarations or commands are other activities that release the power of the Holy Spirit (see Matt. 17:20; Mark 11:23). The practice of the laying on of hands is another scriptural method of imparting power (see Mark 16:18; Heb. 6:2).

That there is literal power from the Holy Spirit that can be released from us is absolute. The power of God that brings life, healing and wholeness to the earth flows out from us—the Church.

Please don't picture some throne in heaven and feel like it's all there. He has now made His throne in our hearts and we are the temple of the Holy Spirit. We are the *naos* of God. In 1 Corinthians 3:16 and 6:19, this word means "holy of holies."[10] We are now the holy of holies, the dwelling place of God upon the earth. When He moves to release power upon the earth, it doesn't have to shoot out of the sky somewhere—it comes from His people where His Spirit dwells upon the earth.

The Church, God's Womb Upon the Earth

Whether through speaking, touching, laying hands on the sick, declaration or worship, when God's power starts flowing upon the earth, it is flowing through human vessels. We, the Body of Christ, are God's womb from which His life is birthed or released upon the earth. The life that Christ produces flows from the womb of the Church.

In John 7:38, Jesus said, "He who believes in Me, as the Scripture said, 'From his innermost being shall flow rivers of living water.'" The innermost being, or belly (KJV), is the word *koilia*, which literally means "womb." Translating it literally, we would say, "Out of his womb shall flow rivers of living water." The word "womb" speaks of reproduction. It speaks of birthing. It speaks of the bringing forth of life.

A similar phrase is found in Revelation 22:1–2:

Then he showed me a river of the water of life, clear as crystal, coming from the throne of God and of the Lamb, in the middle of its street. And on either side of the river was the tree of life, bearing twelve kinds of fruit, yielding its fruit every month; and the leaves of the tree were for the healing of the nations.

The picture here is of Jesus as the source of life. Out of Him flows the river with trees on either side. Leaves are produced by the trees, which are fed by the river, which is fed by Jesus. People—the nations—eat the leaves and are made whole.

What I want to point out is that the phrase "river of the water of life" in this passage is the same phrase in Greek as the "rivers of living water" in John 7. There is no difference between the river of life flowing out of the Lamb bringing healing and wholeness to the earth, and the rivers of living water that are to be flowing from the womb of the Church. We are His birthing vessels, His incubation chambers. Why should that surprise us? Is it not supposed to be the very life of Jesus in us that we are ministering to the earth?

John 7:39 tells us, "But this He spoke of the Spirit." It is the Spirit of God flowing from us. He doesn't lay hands on the sick—we lay hands on the sick. He doesn't lay hands on a person and ordain—He tells us to do it for Him. He, inside of us, releases a river to flow into that person, and they are now anointed and appointed by God. When He wants to bring forth the gospel, which is the power of God unto salvation and life, He does not echo it from the heavens. He speaks it through us. God's life, the literal power and energy of God, flows out of our mouths and penetrates the hearts of unbelievers, and they are born again.

We are the ones who wield the sword of the Spirit—the spoken Word of God. When the Spirit of God wants to cut and bring judgment into situations, He doesn't just speak from the clouds. He speaks from His people—out of our spirits. When I speak His Word into a situation at the direction of the Holy Spirit, it is as if the Lamb of God Himself spoke the Word. It releases God's life! We are the womb of God from which the river is supposed to flow.

Measurable Power

It is important to realize that this power is measurable. There are cumulative amounts of it. That there are measurable levels of almost any spiritual substance is easily proven.

There are measurable levels of faith. Romans 12:3 says, "as God has allotted to each a measure of faith." The word "measure" here is *metron* from which we get the word "meter." In other words, God has "metered out" to each a portion of faith; from there it must grow. There are levels of faith. There are measurable portions of righteousness. There are even measurable portions or degrees of sin.

In Genesis 15:16, God told Abraham He was going to give the land to his descendants in four generations. The reason He could not give it to him yet was because "the iniquity of the Amorite is not yet complete."

There are measurable levels of grace. Second Corinthians 9:8 says, "And God is able to make all grace abound to you." In fact, in Acts 4:33, we are told that "with great power gave the apostles witness of the resurrection of the Lord Jesus, and great grace was upon them all" (KJV). The Greek word for "great" is *megas*, from which we get "mega." There is grace, there is mega grace and there is all grace!

There are measurable degrees of love. John 15:13 speaks of greater love. Matthew 24:12 talks of love that has grown cold. Philippians 1:9 refers to love abounding more and more.

There are measurable degrees of the power of God. In Mark 6:5, there was a measurable degree of the power of God missing. The verse says that because of the unbelief of the people in Nazareth, "He could do no miracle there." The Greek does not say, "He chose not to" or "He didn't." It says literally, "He could not" because their level of faith or unbelief had hindered the flow of the power of God. Although He was able to heal a few sick people, He could not work a miracle.

The same verse that talks about a "mega" grace talks about "mega" power (see Acts 4:33 KJV). They had mega power because they had mega grace! My point is simply that the aspects of the spirit realm are very tangible and real. The anointing is real. Power is real. We do not see it, but it is there. There are measurable, cumulative amounts that exist in the realm of the spirit.

Certain amounts of this power or river or life must be released in the realm of the spirit to accomplish certain things. Different amounts are required for different things. Just as in the natural you need different levels of power for different things, so it is in the spirit realm. It is like the difference between the amount of power it takes to light a flashlight versus a building, or a building as opposed to a city. The same thing is true in the spirit. Different amounts of God's power are needed to accomplish certain things.

Differing Measures of Power

Let's look again at Mark 6, where Jesus could not get enough power flowing in Nazareth to work a miracle. Enough power was flowing to get some healings, the implication being that they were minor, because the verse differentiates between the healings and miracles. Enough power was flowing for one, but not the other. This implies that differing amounts are needed for different things. Jesus could release enough to get a few healings, but He couldn't get enough flowing, because of their unbelief, to work a miracle.

The disciples in Matthew 17:14–21 had been casting out demons and healing the sick because Jesus had given them authority and power to do so. A lunatic boy was brought to them, however, and they couldn't get the job done. Jesus came along, and it was no problem for Him to exorcise the demon causing the lunacy.

The disciples had enough power flowing in their ministry to deal with most demons and diseases, but they came up against one that required more faith and power—and they didn't have enough to overcome that one! Again, the obvious implication is that different measurable levels are needed to accomplish different things.

I'm thoroughly convinced this principle is a reason it takes awhile to get most prayers answered. Receiving an instant miracle is far and away the exception. Usually it is not just a matter of asking the Father to do something, but rather a matter of releasing enough power in the spirit to get the job done. Most Christians are not aware of this. After asking, we tend to sit back and wait on God when He is often waiting on us. We have failed to understand that there are prayers that do more than just ask Him.

Sometimes, when it appears God has finally "gotten around to it" or when we think something just suddenly happened, the truth is that enough power has finally been released through prayer to accomplish it.

Prophets Who Persevered for the Power

When the prophet Elijah came to the widow's son who had died, he spread himself out on the corpse face to face and prayed three times (see 1 Kings 17:21). Why did it take three times? Because the man of God wasn't where he needed to be spiritually? Because he didn't have enough faith? Because he didn't do it right the first two times?

We are not told the reason, nor is it insinuated that any of those things are true. I believe the reason was that he was releasing a little more life out of his spiritual womb or spirit each time. It takes a good bit of life to raise the dead!

In previous chapters we have looked at 1 Kings 18, where Elijah prayed for rain, and discussed the significance of God choosing to work through man and man travailing to bring forth God's will. Let's look at this passage again.

In 1 Kings 18:1, the Lord said to Elijah, "Go, show yourself to Ahab, and I will send rain on the face of the earth." God didn't say, "I might." He didn't say, "If you pray hard enough." He didn't say, "I'm thinking about it." He just said, "I'm going to do it." It was God's timing, God's idea, God's will.

Yet, we are told at the end of this chapter that Elijah labored in prayer diligently seven times in the posture of a woman in travail before clouds appeared and the rain came. He didn't casually walk to the top of the mountain and say, "Lord, send the rain," and immediately it was done. That's not the "effectual fervent prayer" James 5:16–18 KJV tells us Elijah did to first stop and then bring the rain.

The question we must ask ourselves is: If it was God's will, timing and idea, then why did Elijah have to pray seven different times until the rain came? The most reasonable explanation to me is that it was necessary to persevere until he had completed enough prayer—until enough power had been released through his intercession to go up into the heavens and get the job done.

Why did it take Daniel 21 days to get his answer when God sent an angel to him the very first day he started praying? I would think if God wanted to send an angelic messenger, He could get it through immediately if He wanted. He has enough power, doesn't He? Then why was this angel detained for 21 days?

I believe Daniel's faithful praying every day was releasing power into the realm of the spirit. Not until enough power was released to break through the demonic opposition in the spirit could God get the angel through with the answer!

Please understand that I am not limiting God's power. I am fully aware that one word from God could rout every demon in hell. What must be factored in is God's decision to work on the earth through man. It seems reasonable to me that if a man's prayers were responsible for the angel being dispatched, they would also be the key to breaking through with the message. As Billheimer said, "Although the answer to his prayer was granted and already on the way, if Daniel had given up it presumably would never have arrived."[11]

Releasing the River of Power

Why did it take Jesus three hours in the Garden of Gethsemane to break through? Why didn't the angels come immediately and comfort Him? Surely God was not holding out on this righteous, sinless man! Power was being released in the spirit to cause the breakthrough.

I am not speaking to you about vain repetition. I am not talking about asking God again and again and again. I am talking about understanding the ways and principles of God enough to know how to release the river in order to give birth to things out of your spiritual womb. When we intercede, cooperating with the Spirit of God, it releases Him to go out from us and hover over a situation, releasing His life-birthing energies until that which we are asking for comes forth.

Why did it take a month to get rid of the cyst on my wife's ovary? What was I doing as I prayed for her an hour every day during that time? I was releasing the river from my womb!

Some would say that God finally did it after I had persevered enough. No. Throughout the entire month, her pain was decreasing, which according to our doctor had to mean the cyst was shrinking. It didn't just suddenly happen. Power being released in the realm of the spirit was accomplishing something physically inside of her. Every day when that power was released, it was destroying the cyst just a little bit more . . . and more . . . and more.

Why did I have to pray for more than a year for the comatose young lady I told you about at the beginning of this book? I went to see her at least once a week for a year, speaking the Word of God, weeping, calling forth a new brain inside of her head and fighting the good fight of faith. Why did it take a year? Because it takes a lot of power to form a new brain. Why didn't God do it instantly? I don't know. I tried everything I knew to get Him to do so.

I said, "Damsel, I say unto you, 'Arise!'" She arose not! I did all the things I'd read about the heroes of faith doing. In faith, I even sat her up in the bed and commanded her to wake up, but like a limp rag doll she flopped back down on her pillow. I do not know why God chose not to do it as an instant miracle, but because He didn't I'm relatively certain of this: A measurable amount of the river had to flow until there was enough of it to produce that miracle.

Ephesians 3:20–21 says:

> Now to Him who is able to do exceeding abundantly beyond all that we ask or think, according to the power that works within us, to Him be the glory in the church and in Christ Jesus to all generations forever and forever. Amen.

The word for "exceeding abundantly beyond" is the same word for the abundant grace of God in Romans 5:20. The word is *huperperissos*. *Perissos* means "superabundant";[12] *huper* means "beyond" or "more than."[13] Together, they would mean superabundantly with more added to that. That's like saying more than more than.

Ephesians 3:20 says He has enough power to do more than we can ask or think with more added to that—more than more than.

So, why are we often deficient?

Operative Power

The power source is not the problem. The rest of Ephesians 3:20 gives us a clue. It tells us He is going to do this more than more than enough "according to the power that works within us." Wuest translates the phrase "in the measure of the power which is operative in us." The word "measure" is *kata*, which not only has this implication of that which is measured in us, but Strong says it is also used at times with the connotation of "distribution."[14] He is going to do this superabundantly more than we can ask or think in the measure of the power that is distributed from us. Are you distributing power? Are you distributing the river?

Please don't think you are releasing enough power to accomplish the miraculous by sporadic or casual praying. You are not! You must release the power of God inside of you on a consistent basis. James 5:16 says, "The *effectual fervent* prayer of a righteous man availeth much" (KJV, emphasis added). Wuest translates it this way: "A prayer of a righteous person is able to do much as it operates." Notice the verse doesn't say, "A prayer of a righteous person is able to do much because it causes God to operate."

It certainly does this, but that's not what this verse is telling us. It says, "A prayer of a righteous person is able to do much as it [*the prayer*] operates." The Amplified translation reads, "The earnest (heartfelt, continued) prayer of a righteous man makes tremendous power available [dynamic in its working]." Wow! Our prayers go to work. Notice the word "continued." The Amplified captures the present tense meaning of the verb. We have the power inside of us that created the world. We have the same power in us that went into the depths of the earth and took the keys from the kingdom of darkness. We must release it. Release the river! Release the power! Release it and release it and release it and release it some more! Again and again and again!

Tipping the Prayer Bowls of Heaven

As we do, the Scriptures indicate that our prayers accumulate. There are bowls in heaven in which our prayers are stored. Not one bowl for all of them but "bowls." We don't know how many but I think it very likely that each of us has our own bowl in heaven. I don't know if it's literal or symbolic. It doesn't matter. The principle is still the same. God has something in which He stores our prayers for use at the proper time:

> "And when He had taken the book, the four living creatures and the twenty-four elders fell down before the Lamb, having each one a harp, and golden bowls full of incense which are the prayers of the saints."
>
> Revelation 5:8

> "And another angel came and stood at the altar, holding a golden censer; and much incense was given to him, that he might add it to the prayers of all the saints upon the golden altar which was before the throne. And the smoke of the incense, with the prayers of the saints, went up before God out of the angel's

hand. And the angel took the censer; and he filled it with the fire of the altar and threw it to the earth; and there followed peals of thunder and sounds and flashes of lightning and an earthquake."

Revelation 8:3–5

According to these verses, either when He knows it is the right time to do something or when enough prayer has accumulated to get the job done, He releases power. He takes the bowl and mixes it with fire from the altar.

I want you to picture this. He takes the same fire that fell on Sinai, the same fire that burned the sacrifice consuming the rocks and water and everything else when Elijah was on the mountain, the same fire that fell at Pentecost, the same fire that destroys His enemies, the very fire of almighty God, and He mixes your bowl of prayers with His fire! Then He pours it upon the earth . . . lightning starts to flash, thunder crashes, the earth quakes. Something awesome happens in the realm of the spirit, which then affects the natural realm.

This must be what happened when Paul and Silas were in jail and began to sing praises late in the night. Worship started ascending, God was anointing it, the bowls filled and God poured it out. The earth literally started quaking, the jail door opened and their shackles fell off. As a result, the first convert in Asia was born again in Philippi. The gospel made its first penetration into a new continent on Earth.

Recently, I believe the Lord showed me what sometimes happens when we come to Him with a need, asking Him to accomplish what He says in His Word. In answer to our requests, He sends His angels to get our bowls of prayer to mix with the fire of the altar. *But there isn't enough in our bowls to meet the need!* We might blame God or think it's not His will or that His Word must not really mean what it says. The reality of it is that sometimes He cannot do what we've asked because we have not given Him enough power in our prayer times to get it done. He has poured out all there was to pour and it wasn't enough! It's not just a faith issue, but also a power issue.

I hope this doesn't alarm you. I get excited when I think about it. I didn't know it at the time, but when I was standing over the comatose girl, every time I spoke the name above every name, every time I prayed in the Spirit, every time I laid hold of His Word and promises, every tear I shed was put in a bottle (see Ps. 56:8)—or a bowl—and God was just watching until finally it was full.

Get Radical—Pour on the Power

And on a Saturday morning in 1986, the Almighty looked over at one of the angels and said, "See the little girl over there whose brain is no longer functioning that has to be fed through her stomach and breathe through a hole in her throat and is lying there like a living dead person and the doctors say there's no hope and that she's going to die? Do you see her? Take this bowl that's been filled, mix it with My fire, and go dump it on her head." The rest is history.

Go into your child's room if he or she is not born again and, preferably when they're not there, put prayer power—substance—in everything they touch. This power can go into clothing or handkerchiefs and minister to people. Enough anointing and power from the river flowed out of Paul's innermost being and went into his handkerchief that notable miracles took place when people touched those handkerchiefs. Enough of it was in Jesus' clothes that when they reached out and grabbed the very bottom edge of it, something flashed out of Him.

You will recall the testimony of Polly Simchen who came to me with a handkerchief and said, "Would you pray over this? We're going to cut it up and put a piece everywhere our son goes. We're going to hide it everywhere we can." As she shared earlier, Polly would come to me every once in a while and say, "I've run out of them. I need another one." So we would pray and douse another one in the anointing of God.

She hid one piece under the insole in her son Jonathan's shoe and he loaned his shoes to a friend. This was the most radical, drunk, burned-out freak I'd seen in a long time. The friend made a mistake! He wore the wrong person's shoes! No, actually his life was saved—radically saved, filled with the Spirit of God and turned on for Jesus. Jonathan lost a rowdy friend because the friend became so filled with the presence of God that Jonathan couldn't stand to be around him anymore. As we mentioned earlier, Jonathan is now also living for the Lord.

Smear everything your children have with the anointing! The Old Testament word "anoint" means "to pour or smear with oil." It's okay to get a bit radical. Jesus liked it when people tore roofs off, crawled on hands and knees pressing through crowds, climbed trees, shouted obnoxiously crying out for mercy, bathed His feet with tears and hair—He simply loves wholeheartedness.

John Killinger tells about an interesting method used in the past to break a wild steed by harnessing it to a burro. The powerful steed would take off across the range, twisting and bucking, causing the burro to be tossed about wildly. What a sight! The steed would run away, pulling the burro alongside, and they would drop out of sight—sometimes for days. Then they would return, with the proud little burro in charge. The steed had worn himself out, fighting the presence of the burro. When he became too tired to fight anymore, the burro assumed the position of leader. And that's the way it is many times with prayer. Victory goes to the persistent, not to the angry; to the dedicated, not to those who can provide great demonstrations of emotion and energy. We need committed, determined, systematic prayer, not once in a while fireworks.[15]

Forgive Us, Father

Father, why is the thing we need the most, the thing we do the least? Why are most of us so busy we don't have time? You must have many frustrated days when Your eyes roam to and fro throughout the earth in search of someone whose heart is completely Yours. You must weep often when You seek for a man or woman to stand in the gap to fill the breech and find no one. Your heart must ache at times for us, Your people, to rise up and be what You've called us to be.

We humble ourselves before Your throne and ask You to forgive us for our lack of prayer. And forgive us as leaders, Lord, who have not told Your people the truth. Forgive us as a church—the Body of Christ—for allowing evil to rule in this land when You have more than enough power in our wombs to change it.

Forgive us, for it is not Your fault that we have a generation marked X. It is not Your will that we kill the next generation before it takes its first breath. It is not Your plan that we still have not overcome the principality of hatred that divides this land.

Forgive us, Lord. Cleanse us now and break the curses we have allowed to rule over us. Forgive us and cleanse us from the sin of apathy, complacency, ignorance and unbelief. Wash us with the water of Your Word. Break off of us this lethargic prayerlessness, which we justify a thousand different ways. It really boils down to disobedience, unbelief and sin.

Father, please forgive us and deliver us. Set us free from being hearers of the Word only, and not doers. Give us homes and churches that are founded on the rock of obedience to Your Word. Rise up in Your people with the stubborn tenacity that Jesus had, that the Early Church walked in. Cause us to cast off everything that would oppose Your Spirit, and move us into a realm that pays a price and lays hold of the kingdom of God.

Fill us with Your Spirit. Baptize us in fire. Let there be an impartation of the Spirit of grace and supplication. Let there be an anointing that comes from Your throne to hungry people who are tired of status quo, of mediocrity, of death and destruction. We are tired of it, God. We are tired of being defeated by a defeated enemy. We are tired of being held back from our destiny, both individually and as a nation. We are tired of lack and disease. We are tired of sin. We are hungry for something—the God of the Bible!

Questions for Reflection

1. Can you explain the real lesson being taught by the story in Luke 11:5–13? Is "the prayer of importunity" a good phrase to use in summarizing this passage?

2. What is meant by "the substance" of prayer? How does this relate to perseverance?

3. Provide some Scriptures demonstrating that spiritual things are measurable. Now apply this truth to prayer using Ephesians 3:20–21 and James 5:16.

4. Can you think of any situations where you may have stopped praying before your "bowl" was filled? Are there any current situations in your life that might need more power released to receive an answer?

5. Do you love Jesus?

13

Actions That Speak
and Words That Perform

A Most Amazing Prayer Meeting

In 1988 I was invited to England with a dear friend of mine, Michael Massa, to teach for a week. Two intercessor friends of ours from England, Derek Brant and Lew Sunderland, had invited us to minister to a group of about 40, representing the four British Isles (England, Scotland, Wales and Ireland).

I didn't realize several things going into that week. First, I didn't factor in the combined *years* of intercession represented by the group—Lew alone had been interceding for England nearly 30 years. This small, insignificant detail meant simply that *anything could happen.*

Second, I didn't know the Holy Spirit was going to show up with such intensity that on the final evening I wouldn't be able to finish my message. When I paused and said, "The presence of God is so strong, I just cannot continue," a spirit of

239

repentance and intercession for England came upon everyone and lasted all night.

Without question, it became one of the most amazing prayer experiences of my life. The prophetic actions and declarations that went forth—terms that I'll explain shortly—were incredible. We spoke Ezekiel 37:1–10 over the land in the same way Ezekiel himself prophesied to the dry bones of Israel and to the breath of God. We sat silently for over an hour—no one moving or uttering a word—in deep repentance and the fear of the Lord. The men among us walked the grounds all night in repentance and prophetic intercession, standing in the gap for the men of the land. It was truly an amazing night.

Third, I wasn't aware at the time that God was calling me to and giving me spiritual authority for the nation of England. I had received prophetic words and Scriptures from individuals speaking of a call to the nations. And I had certainly felt this was true, but I wasn't aware of a particular call for England, nor of the divine authority accompanying it.

I had been given Jeremiah 1:10 on more than one occasion: "See, I have appointed you this day over the nations and over the kingdoms, to pluck up and to break down, to destroy and to overthrow, to build and to plant." However, I wasn't sure I wanted such a calling, and must admit I didn't fully embrace it.

England's Call to a Reluctant Prophet

In May 1994 this same group invited me back to England, along with a worship team from the States, led by a close friend and associate, David Morris.

"It is time to follow up our last meeting by marrying the Spirit and the Word through anointed prophetic worship, followed by you, Dutch, speaking a prophetic message over the nation," they told me. "We're going to rent some of the old

240

cathedrals around England and have the services in them. We feel this will release some things in the spirit and further pave the way for God to move."

"I don't have a prophetic message for England and besides, I'm too busy" was my response. I maintained this position for months, up until several weeks before the meetings were to take place. At that time three different intercessors told me within the span of one week that I had missed God's leading and was supposed to go to England.

Oh, they were nice about it and very respectful, but the Holy Spirit was a little more blunt in interpreting for them: *Wake up, Sheets!*

Being the spiritually astute man that I am, three independent words of correction were enough. After the last one, I immediately picked up the phone and instructed my secretary to call England, informing them that I had missed God and would come if they had no one else.

"No, we don't have anyone else," they told her. "We knew he was supposed to do it. We've just been waiting for him to hear."

It makes you feel terribly unspiritual when everyone in the world knows God's will for your life, but you!

Lest you begin to mistake this book for an autobiography, I'll get to the point. In the last of our meetings in England, all of which were very powerful, we were ministering in Westminster Chapel.

As I was preparing myself to preach in this well-known church laced with a rich and wonderful heritage, located just a block or two from Buckingham Palace, I heard these words deep in my spirit (I trust you're ready for this. You probably know by now that I can be a bit on the radical side.): *You are not preaching to the people in attendance tonight. You are preaching to this nation. You are to declare My Word to it, calling it back to righteousness, to holiness, to repentance,*

241

to Me. Call forth My anointing, My fire and My presence to this land again.

Not wanting my hosts to think me too strange, I informed them as to what I intended to do. Then I did it!

I preached to the air.

I preached to the government.

I preached to the sinners of England.

I preached to the entire Body of Christ of England.

And I've never worked harder in my life. I felt as though I was warring against and trying to push through hordes of demons. At the conclusion of my message, I sat down behind the platform totally exhausted, drenched with perspiration and almost in a daze. I had no sense of victory or defeat, only of exhaustion from the battle.

Lew Sunderland, the matriarchal intercessor responsible for inviting and praying me there, a true mother in the faith, approached me with a sweet and understanding smile. Placing my cheeks in her hands, she assured me, "It's all right, darling, you made it through. You accomplished what was needed." She then said to me later, "You have accepted now, haven't you, darling"—to Lew everyone is darling—"that God has called you to this nation and has given you authority here?"

"Yes, ma'am," I said meekly and submissively, as would a small child to its mother after having just learned a valuable lesson.

"You won't question it any longer, now, will you?"

"No, ma'am."

"That's good. We'll just have you back when the Lord says it's time. Okay?"

"Yes, ma'am."

I returned the next month!

We received a call from England the week following our ministry. The message was, "Revival has broken out in London."

Renewal had, indeed, hit the nation, with many people coming to Christ and thousands receiving a renewing touch of the Holy Spirit.

The Boomerang Anointing: Action and Declaration

I would never presume that revival came solely because of our ministry. The years of intercession by many and the countless hours of selfless labor by hundreds of godly men and women had much more to do with it than anything our team ever could have done. What part did we play? Prophetic worship—declaring through pageantry and song the splendor, greatness, rule and authority of God, and prophetic declaration—proclaiming the will and Word of the Lord into the spirit realm.

There is an interesting aspect of intercession few people understand and still fewer do. It is *prophetic action and declaration*. What do we mean by this? When we say something is "prophetic," we mean it's foretelling (speaking about or predicting future things) or forthtelling (actions or words that declare something for God). In the latter case it may not be futuristic at all. Something that is prophetic in nature can be one or both—foretelling or forthtelling.

Either of them can have a forerunning or preparatory purpose. Prophetic words or actions prepare a way, in the same sense that John the Baptist, the prophet, prepared the way with his words and actions for the Messiah to come and for the glory of the Lord to be revealed (see Isa. 40:1–5). Prophetic ministry releases the way for the glory of the Lord and the ministry of Jesus to follow. Prophetic actions and declarations prepare the way for God to work upon the earth.

In a sense, they release God to do something, as they become the implemented means or method through which He has chosen to work. They do not release Him in the sense that

He is bound—God obviously is not bound. But they release Him in the sense that:

1. Obedience to God brings a response from God. As we shall see later in the chapter, prophetic actions and declarations mean nothing if they are not directed by God. In the same sense, when He gives instruction, it must be obeyed. He chooses to do things a certain way and when that way is implemented, it releases God to do what He wants to do. He doesn't always explain why we must do it a particular way. Being God, He has that right. But when His chosen way is implemented, He does what He needs to do.

2. Faith releases God. When He says, "Do this," faith and obedience release Him.

3. They release Him in the sense that His creative and effectual Word is released upon the earth. God's creative power, energy and ability that come forth through His Words are released upon the earth through prophetic declaration! If you are not open to revelation, you'll never be able to embrace this. Open your heart to enlightenment.

A more complete definition would be: Prophetic action or declaration is something said or done in the natural realm at the direction of God that prepares the way for Him to move in the spiritual realm, which then consequently effects change in the natural realm. How's that for God and man partnering? God says to do or say something. We obey. Our words or actions impact the heavenly realm, which then impacts the natural realm. Maybe this is the "boomerang anointing"!

I'm sure by now you could use some biblical examples of this, so let me give you several. First, I want to give you biblical examples of prophetic action that preceded and/or released literal action in the earth. Then we'll examine some prophetic declarations.

Prophetic Action

Moses stretching forth his rod over the Red Sea is an example of prophetic action (see Exod. 14:21). Why did he have to stretch forth his rod? Because God said to. He wanted the symbolic rod of authority to be stretched over the Red Sea. If there had been no extending of the rod over the sea, there would not have been a rolling back of the sea. God essentially said, "I want a prophetic act to release Me to do this!"

Another example of prophetic action is Moses' holding up the rod of authority at Rephidim where Israel was battling with Amalek (see Exod. 17:9–13). I shared the story in chapter 9 to point out the difference between authority and power, but it is also a vivid demonstration of prophetic action.

Moses was up on the mountain with the rod of authority lifted. When he held it up, Israel prevailed. When he let it down because of fatigue, Amalek prevailed. Morale wasn't the issue. Do you think those soldiers on the battlefield, instead of fighting, were watching Moses? It had nothing to do with morale—they probably didn't even see the rod going up and down.

It had to do with something happening in the realm of the spirit. This prophetic action was releasing something in the heavenlies. As it did, the authority of God was bouncing back to Earth and giving victory to the Israelites. I can't explain it any more than that. Some things, when dealing with God, simply cannot be explained.

God's Way, Even When It Makes No Sense

Moses' hitting the rock in Exodus 17:6 is another example of prophetic action. He took the rod of authority, struck the rock and water came out. Why? Because God wanted it done that way. We could elaborate on all the symbolism of these actions and possibly understand why God did them, but the bottom line is: When He chose to do it a certain way, someone had to perform an act upon the earth that often made no sense, but when performed, released something in the spirit, which released something upon Earth. A person doesn't normally get water out of rocks when he or she hits them with a rod . . . unless God says to do it. Again, when He tells us to act, it impacts the spirit, affects the earth and produces results—like bringing water out of rocks. That's prophetic action!

Many of these examples appear in Scripture. In 2 Kings 13:14–19, Elisha was about to die and King Joash came to him for advice. The Assyrians were camped around Israel and he wanted some instruction from the prophet. Elisha said, "Take your arrow and shoot it out the window toward the enemy camp!" It was a declaration of war. The king and the prophet put their hands on the bow together, shooting the arrow. Elisha then said, "That's the arrow of the Lord's deliverance, King. Now take these arrows and strike the ground."

The king was about to be tested. His actions were going to be prophetic. Not knowing what the prophet was up to, he took the arrows and struck the ground three times.

The prophet was grieved and angry. "Three times you will have victory over your enemies, and then they will conquer you," he said. "You should have struck with the arrows at least five or six times, then you would have conquered them!"

This story doesn't seem fair to me. How was the king supposed to know he should keep striking? I think the point is that if God says to hit it three times, then you hit it three times. But if God simply says hit it, you hit it until He says stop! God was after prophetic action, but He didn't get what He wanted. Neither did the king!

People were healed in Scripture through prophetic action. Jesus made clay with saliva, rubbed it in a blind man's eyes and told him to go wash in the pool of Siloam (see John 9:6–7).

Naaman the leper had to dip in the Jordan River seven times (see 2 Kings 5:10–14).

"I don't want to," he said.

"Then you won't get healed," replied Naaman's servants. Why? Because God chose to work in that way. And when God chooses to do it by a certain method, no other means will work.

Cindy Jacobs describes prophetic acts in her book *The Voice of God*:

> At other times, God would ask His people as a whole to do something that not only was prophetic, but also had great power as a form of intercession to bring profound change when obeyed. . . . In 1990, a team from Women's Aglow went to Russia to intercede for that nation. We were led to perform several prophetic acts. Our trip came before the fall of Soviet communism and several things happened that led us to believe we were being monitored. Before we left, my friend Beth Alves had a dream that we had actually buried the Word of God in the ground. This was to result in a critical prophetic act later in the trip.
>
> One strategy we used for intercession was to take a bus tour around the city. City tours are great because they take the visitors to all the historical sites. One place the tour visited was Moscow State University, a bastion of communist teaching. As we sat on a wall near the school, I suddenly remembered Beth's dream and thought of the "Four Spiritual Laws" tract I had in my purse. In a flash, I knew this was the place to do what Beth had dreamed about.
>
> I quickly jumped up (we had just a few minutes before the bus was leaving) and said, "Come on, let's plant the Word in the ground!" Several of the ladies came after me. Huffing and puffing as we ran, I reminded them of Beth's dream and told them of the tract. I glanced around to find the shelter of some trees in which to do the prophetic act. (We had encountered a person in Red Square that day whom we were pretty sure was a KGB agent, and since we weren't interested in a premature prison ministry we had to be careful!)

247

Finding a sheltered place, I knelt and started to dig. This was a dismal failure as I only succeeded in breaking my fingernails. Finally, I found a stick and dug a hole. Dropping the tract into the ground, I quickly covered it up while the ladies prayed. Pointing toward the university, I began to prophesy, "The seed from this tract will grow schools of evangelism, and theology will be taught here."

Later on, after the fall of Russian communism, Billy Graham did start schools of evangelism there. Sister Violet Kitely, a friend of mine, told me that a church has been planted in Moscow State University by Shiloh Christian Center (a large church in Oakland, California).

What happens through these prophetic acts? They are intercessory in nature. In fact, they might be called intercessory acts. Certain aspects of what happens might seem speculative in nature. We cannot prove a correlation between obedience in doing a prophetic act and, say, the starting of schools of evangelism. Time and time again in Scripture, however, we see where God spoke to His children to perform an intercessory, prophetic act, and He powerfully moved as a result.[1]

Prophetic Declaration

Let's look at some biblical examples of prophetic words that precede God's doing something. In Jeremiah 6:18–19, Jeremiah prophesied and said, "Therefore hear, O nations . . . Hear, O earth." Similarly, in Jeremiah 22:29, he again prophesied, saying, "O earth, earth, earth, hear the word of the LORD" (KJV).

Many would think I was an utter fool if I walked out of my house and said, "All the earth, hear me now! And all the nations, I'm speaking to you." But that's what Jeremiah did. It was prophetic declaration that made no sense naturally.

We must understand that it is not an issue of what our words would normally do. It is rather speaking *for God*, which releases His power to accomplish something. Isn't this what happens as we preach or declare the gospel, which is the power of God for salvation (see Rom. 1:16)?

Our mouths, speaking God's Word, release the power of those words. Is this not also what occurs when we speak His Word as a sword in spiritual warfare? He infuses our words with divine power. Why then would He not in other situations allow us to be His voice? When Jeremiah said, "O Earth! Earth! Earth! Hear the Word of the LORD!" it was exactly the same as if God Himself were saying, "O Earth! Earth! Earth! Hear My Words!"

God told Jeremiah earlier that He was going to use him "to pluck up and to break down, to destroy and to overthrow, to build and to plant" (Jer. 1:10). Notice, then, in Jeremiah 31:28 He says He has done just that: plucked up, broken down, overthrown and destroyed. It is imperative to see that God did these things through the words of His prophet.

In Micah 1:2, the prophet said, "Hear, O peoples, all of you; listen, O earth and all it contains."

Wouldn't you feel rather foolish saying, "O earth and everything in it, God wants me to talk to you. Are you listening?" Micah did just that, however. Obviously all the earth didn't hear him . . . no more than the storm heard Jesus tell it to be still or the fig tree heard Him command it to die. Whether anything hears us isn't the point. What we are to understand is the power of Holy Spirit-inspired declaration—it releases the power of God into situations.

We Become His Voice

"But those were the prophets and Jesus," some might argue. Yes, but after rebuking the storm, Jesus rebuked the disciples for their fear and unbelief, implying that they should have rebuked it. He also followed up His cursing of the fig tree with a promise that we could speak to mountains and cast them into the sea.

He is describing the power of Holy Spirit-inspired declaration. We become the voice of God upon the earth.

In her book *The Praying Church*, Sue Curran quotes S. D. Gordon:

> Prayer surely does influence God. It does not influence His *purpose*. It does influence His *action*. Everything that ever has been prayed for, of course I mean every right thing, God has already purposed to do. But He does nothing without our consent. He has been hindered in His purposes by our lack of willingness. When we learn His purposes and make them our prayers we are giving Him the opportunity to act.[2]

Hosea 6:5 is a powerful verse about God bringing judgment: "Therefore I have hewn them in pieces by the prophets; I have slain them by the words of My mouth." How did He do this? Through His words spoken by the prophets. God's words, released for Him by humans.

It is important to state clearly that to be effective, declarations must be the words or actions God commands. "So shall *My* word be which goes forth from *My* mouth; it shall not return to Me empty, without accomplishing what *I* desire, and without succeeding in the matter for which *I* sent it" (Isa. 55:11, emphasis added).

Please realize that when God said this, He was not talking about speaking from the clouds. He was referring to what He had been saying and was still saying to them through the prophet Isaiah. In essence He was declaring, "This man's words are My words. He is My voice. The words won't return to Me void, but will do exactly what I send them to do through this man!" That's pretty awesome!

Of course, there are some who say God doesn't speak anything directly to us today—He only uses the Bible—which would mean the only thing we can declare for Him is Scripture. I have great respect for my brothers and sisters who believe this, and would encourage them to speak the words of the Bible into situations. To others of you who believe the Holy Spirit does speak in our spirits, listen for His direction as you pray and, when so led, boldly speak and do as He instructs. Of course, all that we do must be judged by and never violate the Scriptures.

Beth Alves, in her outstanding prayer guide, *Becoming a Prayer Warrior*, gives excellent and thorough instruction about hearing the voice of God.[3] It would be wise to study this or a similar book to ensure accuracy in learning to hear God's voice. Also, check with godly and mature leaders before doing anything of a public nature or something that seems extremely strange. Don't take your cue from the prophet Isaiah and run around town naked (he probably wore a loincloth). Use wisdom and, when in doubt, always check it out. If that isn't possible, when in doubt, don't. Never do anything that contradicts Scripture or might bring a reproach on the name of the Lord.

Saying What God Says

The word in the New Testament for "confession" is *homologia*, which means "say the same thing."[4] Biblical confession is saying what God says—no more, no less. If it isn't what God is saying about a situation, it does nothing. But if it is what He says, it accomplishes much.

The Word of God is called a "seed" in the Scriptures. The root word in Greek is *speiro*. *Spora* and *sperma* are variations of the word, both of which are translated "seed" in the New Testament. It is easy to see the English words "spore" and "sperm" in them.

God's method of reproducing or bringing forth life is His Word by which we are born again (see 1 Pet. 1:23), cleansed (see John 15:3), matured (see Matt. 13:23), freed (see John 8:31–32), healed (see Ps. 107:20)—as well as many other results. When God speaks His word, He is sprinkling seeds that will bring forth. The Word of God is never ineffective; it will always produce. When we speak God's Words into situations, as the Holy Spirit directs, we are sprinkling the seeds of God, which then give Him the ability to cause life to come forth!

Job 22:28 declares, "You will also decree a thing, and it will be established for you." The word "decree" means literally "decide and decree"[5]—determine something and then decree it. The actual meaning of *omer*, the word translated "thing" is "a word; a command; a promise."[6]

A more precise wording would be, "You shall decree or declare a word." Then He says it will be established for you. "Establish" is the word *qum*, meaning not only to establish, but also to "arise or stand up."[7] Here's what I believe God is saying: "You shall decree a word and it will rise up. You shall sprinkle My seed. It will arise (grow) and establish something in the earth."

Why don't you establish some salvation upon the earth by decreeing salvation seeds? Establish freedom for someone by declaring freedom seeds. Establish unity over your church or city by commanding unity seeds. Establish God's destiny over your children by sowing destiny seeds. Plant your own personal garden. Tend it well. See if God's Word won't produce a harvest. Re-present the victory of Calvary from your mouth!

Job 6:25 reads: "How forcible are right words!" (KJV). "Forcible" is the word *marats*, which also means "to press."[8] As the signet ring of a king presses a document with his seal, our words also seal things. They seal our salvation, the promises of God, our destinies and many other things.[9]

Ecclesiastes 12:11 tells us, "The words of the wise are as goads, and as nails fastened by the masters of assemblies" (KJV). Our words act as nails constructing things in the spirit. Just as a nail is used to keep a board in place, words are used to keep

God's promises in place, allowing them to build or construct things in the spirit.[10]

Prophesying to Bones and Breath

Ezekiel and the Valley of Dry Bones is another example of prophetic declaration. "Speak to the bones!" God said to the prophet.

Can you imagine what Ezekiel thought? *Speak to them? God, if You want something said to skeletons, why don't You just do it?* But Ezekiel obeyed and said, "O dry bones, hear the word of the Lord." And they did! Bone came to bone, flesh came on them.

There was no life in them, however, and Ezekiel's next assignment amazes me more than prophesying to the bones. The Lord said, "Prophesy to the breath." Later in the passage we're told that the breath he was prophesying to was the Holy Spirit. God didn't say, "Prophesy *by* the Holy Spirit," nor did He say, "Prophesy *for* the Holy Spirit." God said, "I want you to prophesy *to* the Holy Spirit." Ezekiel did and the Spirit of God did what a man told Him to. Incredible!

Did the prophet actually command the Holy Spirit? Not really. He wasn't commanding God; He was commanding *for* God. As has been God's plan and heart from the Creation, He was partnering with man. Father and Sons, Inc. managing the planet! God working through the prophetic declaration of a human being. Who can fully understand such a thing?

Talking to the Wall

Several years ago the Lord sent Dick Eastman, president of Every Home for Christ, to Berlin. How would you like to get this assignment from God? The Berlin Wall was still up, and Dick felt the Holy Spirit prompting him with these instructions: *I want you to get on an airplane, fly to Germany, go to the Berlin Wall, lay your hands upon it and say five words to it: "In Jesus' name, come down!"* That was it—end of assignment! Five words and he could go home.[11]

How would you like to go to your spouse and say, "Uh, honey, the Lord has told me to do something."

"Yes, what is it?"

"Well, He wants me to go to Germany."

"Okay, what are you going to do over there?"

"Go to the Berlin Wall."

"Oh? What are you going to do at the Wall?"

"I'm going to put my hands on it and say, 'In Jesus' name, come down!' and then I'm going to come home."

Wouldn't that make for an interesting discussion?

That's exactly what Dick did, because he understood the power of prophetic action and declaration. Dick would never claim to be the only person used by God to bring down the Berlin Wall. However, shortly thereafter the Wall was torn down.

A Vision for the Youth

A few years ago I was in Washington, D.C., for the National Day of Prayer with the Master's Commission, a group of young people from Spokane, Washington. My wife, Ceci, and I accompanied them because, while I had been ministering to them a couple of months prior, I had an incredible picture—I believe it was a vision. The picture was of a stadium filled with young people who were radically committed to God. As I watched, this multitude of young people filed out of the stadium and flooded the nation, taking revival with them. I shared the picture with these young people and a spirit of intercession came upon us that lasted for about 30 minutes. It was truly an awesome time of prayer for the youth of America. As we finished praying, I felt I was to join these youths on their upcoming trip to Washington, D.C.

Shortly after we arrived in Washington, D.C., I sensed the Lord speak to me: *I'm going to confirm to you on this trip that I am sending revival to this nation. I'm also going to demonstrate to you that the youth will play a major role in it.*

The Vision Confirmed

My first confirmation came on The National Day of Prayer. There were probably 400 to 500 people gathered for the primary prayer meeting that morning—senators, congressmen, statesmen and spiritual leaders of the nation. I wasn't part of the program but was there to agree in prayer, as were most of the attendees. The Master's Commission had somehow received permission to be in the program, which was a miracle in itself. When these young people were invited up for their 15 minutes, they walked down the aisle singing, "Heal Our Land."

As they sang, the Spirit of God fell over the room like a blanket. Perhaps hovered would be a better way to phrase it. At no other point was the presence of God felt as strongly. I didn't see anyone present who wasn't weeping. Dr. James Dobson, who spoke after the Master's Commission, commented through tears that it is not often we get to witness history in the making. I'm sure everyone in attendance believed that day impacted the history of our nation.

These young people then rendezvoused with Norm Stone, a man from their church, Harvest Christian Fellowship. God called Norm several years ago to walk across America seven times as a prophetic act of repentance and intercession for the babies murdered in America through abortion. That is prophetic action! The Master's Commission, most of whom were from the same church, walked behind him, 20 miles a day for two weeks, praying.

The night before these young people were to join Norm, I heard these words from the Lord: *This is a prophetic declaration by Me that the generation that Satan tried to annihilate through* abortion—*My next generation of warriors in the earth—have not and will not be destroyed. I'm sending these young people to march behind Norm as a prophetic message saying, "No! This is My generation, Satan, and you will not have them!"*

Later that evening I heard the words, *I'm going to confirm to you once more that I'm sending revival to this nation in which the youth will have a major role. I'll do it through the Bible reading you're to do tonight.*

I was scheduled to be part of a three-day read-a-thon, the entire Bible being read by individuals while facing the Capitol building. Each person participating was allowed to read for 15 minutes, no more. We were required to read from wherever the progression happened to be in the Bible when our turn came. I didn't pick my reading time—someone else had signed me up the previous day and informed me I was supposed to be there at midnight the following night.

Due to the nature of the Lord's dealings with me at that time, I told Him, "Lord, there is only one way I could know of a certainty that You are confirming these things to me through my Bible reading. When I arrive, they must tell me that I can either read the book of Habakkuk or Haggai." This was not a fleece, nor was I testing God. It was because of the things I had already sensed Him saying to me through these two books.

Do you know the size of these books? They consist of *eight pages* in my Bible. What would the odds be, when not choosing my own reading—nor even the time of my reading, of my showing up and being told, "Here, read from these eight pages."

I walked up to the lady in charge.

"Are you Dutch Sheets?"

"Yes, I am."

"You are on in 15 minutes, after this person. You have your choice. You can either read the book of Haggai or the book of Habakkuk."

I nearly passed out! You can believe I read the Word of the Lord with authority, making prophetic declaration over the government of this nation with absolute faith that revival is coming.

Whatever He Says, Do It!

God is calling the Church to a new understanding of prophetic action and declaration, functioning as His voice and Body upon the earth. When He speaks His plan to us, however foolish it may seem—to hold up a rod, speak to the spiritually dead, walk our neighborhoods, march through our streets, hit rocks, decree to the earth, lay hands on and speak to oppressive walls, walk across America, read the Bible toward the Capitol, speak to a nation that isn't listening—He needs us to DO IT!

The Lord may lead you to go to the bedroom of a rebellious child and anoint things with oil, pray over clothing, speak over the child's bed, or some other symbolic act. Others of you will be called to make declarations over your cities and governments. Some will be told to march on land, claiming it for the kingdom of God. Whatever He says to you, do it. Be bold to declare the Word of the Lord over and into situations. Sprinkle the seed of His Word into the earth and expect a harvest. It will be established. It will arise! Life will come!

"You do know now that you're called to do this, don't you, darling?"

Questions for Reflection

1. Define prophetic action and declaration. Explain how they "release" God. Now give some biblical examples.

2. Can you explain the connection between God's Word, seeds and our Holy Spirit-inspired declarations?

3. Can you find some verses of Scripture that would be good to decree for an individual's salvation? . . . Healing? How about Scriptures to decree over your city?

4. Isn't God good?

14

The Watchman Anointing

The Genetic Plague

The only thing worse than shopping is watching someone shop. Except for my wife, of course. I don't mind at all following her around a mall for two or three hours. I show my interest periodically with pleasant little grunts—"Umph"; "Un-huh"; "Ahh-hum." Sometimes I get downright wordy—"Yes"; "No"; "Sure"; "HOW MUCH?!" I've gotten pretty quick at correcting that one: "Wow, what a deal!" I hastily add. About the closest thing I can compare "shopper watching" to would be watching a sewing match.

Which is why I'm sitting in the food court writing while my wife and youngest daughter, Hannah, shop. It's one of those outlet malls where they sell you the flawed stuff "on sale." My oldest daughter, Sarah, is with me, reading. She doesn't like shopping, either—yet. I informed her on the way to our "food court refuge" of the gene in her—which God gave all women—that simply hasn't kicked in yet. Told her not to worry, it'll happen.

In my studies of this genetic plague—most of them done through conversing with other men in food courts—I have discovered that no one knows for sure when the gene kicks in or what triggers it. It can hit anytime between the ages of 6 and 13. Sometimes it happens in the middle of the night; they just wake up with the shakes—flu-like symptoms. When it happened with Hannah, I was ready to anoint her with oil, until Ceci informed me it wouldn't help.

"What do you mean it won't help?" I asked in surprise. "Of course it will."

"No," she said, "it's her shopping gene kicking in. We've got to get her to a mall—fast."

Mom was right, of course. She usually is. Hannah came home proudly holding her shopping bag, looking like she'd just caught her first fish. Women! Who can figure?

To prove my point, I just counted the men and women in the food court and surrounding stores—26 females and 9 males. Half the males were kids that had been dragged there against their wills. Another was writing—yours truly—and the rest were grunting, "Uh-huh." I felt sorry for one guy; he actually looked like a zombie. I think he finally cracked under the stress.

Ceci and Hannah are back now, getting something to drink and showing us their "deals." I'm grunting. Ceci is merely dropping Hannah off so that she can run back for one more thing. Seven-year-olds—apprentice shoppers—can't always keep up with the pros. They haven't had enough aerobics classes, for which the real motivation is shopping conditioning.

Watching What You Watch

Why couldn't God have made women to like normal things, such as sitting in a woods for days in sub-zero weather, waiting for a deer or elk to walk by? Now that's my idea of exciting watching! . . . Or watching a football game! I'm not into TV too much—unless it's a good sporting event. Ceci doesn't always understand me in this area, but she is kind about it. "Who are you rooting for?" she sometimes asks.

"I don't care who wins," I often reply.

"Are these any of your favorite teams?"

"No, not really."

"A favorite player or two, perhaps?"

"Naw, I don't know much about these guys at all."

"Then why are you watching the game?" she asks with a quizzical expression.

"Because it's football," I reply as patiently as I possibly can. Sometimes people can't figure out the obvious. I'll tell you what puzzles me—why she and my two daughters like to watch stuff that makes them cry. Go figure!

Many kinds of watching take place: TV watching, parade watching, watching the clock, stock market watching, bird watching (ranks right up there with sewing matches to me), and a thousand other things. I like to watch kids laugh. I hate to watch people cry. I've watched individuals born; I've watched others die.

I once watched a lady in San Pedro, Guatemala, look for a watch. It was her husband's—he died in the earthquake of 1976. So did three of her kids. All she and her surviving infant had left were the clothes on their backs. Their small adobe home was a mound of dirt.

When our interpreter asked her what she was digging for, she replied, "A bag of beans we had and my husband's watch. He was sleeping about here when he was killed," she said, pointing at an area of approximately 10 square feet. "It would mean so much to me if I could find his watch."

We started digging.

Although it was like looking for a needle in a haystack, we asked God to help us and waded into the three-feet-deep dirt.

Right then I'd have charged hell for that watch. We found it an hour or so later.

"*Muchas gracias*," she repeated through tears, as she clutched the watch to her breast.

"Treasure" is such a relative term, I thought as I wiped my eyes. *I wish the world could see this. Maybe some priorities would change.*

I watched another lady, holding her three-year-old daughter, walk away from a food line in which I was serving. She was the last in line for the soup. As she held out the jar she had found, we looked at her and said, "*No mas*" (which means "No more"). Then I watched her walk away, holding her hungry child.

Things got all messed up at that point in my life. Neat little lists of needs disappeared. Certain important goals became strangely irrelevant. Things that mattered suddenly didn't. Bank accounts were looked at differently; success was redefined. Funny how one glance into four eyes can bring such chaos. In many ways, order has never been restored.

Be careful what you watch.

Be on the Alert

The Bible talks about watching—in various ways and for different reasons, not the least of which is watching in prayer. This chapter is about the "watchman anointing"—our calling and equipping as intercessors to be forewarned of and to pray against Satan's schemes and plans. It is a vital aspect of our intercession. Ephesians 6:18 says, "With all prayer and petition pray at all times in the Spirit, and with this in view, *be on the alert* with all perseverance and petition for all the saints" (emphasis added). The KJV version uses the word "watching" for the phrase "be on the alert."

First Peter 5:8, in warning us about our enemy, says, "Be of sober spirit, *be on the alert.* Your adversary, the devil, prowls about like a roaring lion, seeking someone to devour" (emphasis added). Again, other translations use the word "watchful." The context of both verses is spiritual warfare. Each mentions our adversary and challenges us to alertness or watchfulness, both for ourselves and for our brothers and sisters in Christ.

Another related verse, which we discussed in great detail in chapter 9, is 2 Corinthians 2:11: "In order that no advantage be taken of us by Satan; for we are not ignorant of his schemes." So as not to duplicate the material, I will simply summarize the deducted meaning we gave of the verse based on the Greek words used: "To the degree that we are ignorant of the way our adversary thinks and operates—of his plans, plots, schemes and devices—to that degree he will gain on us, prey on us, defraud us of what is ours and have or hold the greater portion."

I want to draw four conclusions from these three verses—Ephesians 6:18, 1 Peter 5:8 and 2 Corinthians 2:11—as an introduction for this teaching:

1. *Protection from the attacks of our enemy—even for believers—is not automatic.* There is a part for us to play. Though God is sovereign, this does not mean He is in control of everything that happens. He has left much to the decisions and actions of humankind. If God were going to protect or safeguard us from Satan's attacks regardless of what we did, these verses would be totally irrelevant to Christians. Somewhere in our theology, we must find a place for human responsibility. At some point we must begin to believe that we matter, that we're relevant, for ourselves and for others.

2. *God's plan is to warn or alert us to Satan's tactics.* This is deduced from the simple fact that since God says not to

263

be unaware of Satan's tactics, He must be willing to make us aware of them. If He says to be on the alert, this must mean that if we are, He will alert us. God wouldn't ask of us something that He wasn't also enabling us to accomplish.

3. *We must be alert—remain watchful—or we won't pick up on God's attempts to warn us of Satan's attacks and plans.* If these attacks were always going to be obvious, alertness wouldn't be necessary. Isaiah 56:10 speaks of blind watchmen. What a picture! I'm afraid it has been a fairly good description of many of us in our watching roles. We're often like the disciples of old: We have eyes, but we do not see (see Mark 8:18). It's time we do more than gaze; we must alertly watch!

4. *If we are not alert and watchful, if we are ignorant of Satan's schemes, he will take the bigger portion.* He will gain on us, taking advantage of our ignorance. Contrary to popular belief, we really can be destroyed due to ignorance (see Hos. 4:6). We may not like to admit it, but Satan really has gained a lot of territory in America. Don't be like the desert nomad who awakened hungrily one night and decided he'd have a midnight snack. Lighting a candle, he grabbed a date and took a bite. Holding the date to the candle, he saw a worm, whereupon he threw the date out of the tent. Biting into the second date, he found another worm and threw it away, also. Deciding he might not get anything to eat if this continued, he blew out the candle and ate the dates.[1]

Sometimes we, too, prefer the darkness of denial to the light of truth. Though the truth really does hurt at times, it is still truth. Denial doesn't change it. Where Satan has made gains, let's admit it and determine to take them back!

Two New Testament words for "watching" make the connection to the Old Testament concept of watchmen: *gregoreuo* and *agrupneo*. Both mean essentially to stay awake, in the sense that a sentry would need to refrain from sleep. Some of the verses where they're found are the following:

> Devote yourselves to prayer, keeping alert in it with an attitude of thanksgiving.
>
> Col. 4:2

> And He said to them, "My soul is deeply grieved to the point of death; remain here and keep watch. . . . Keep watching and praying, that you may not come into temptation; the spirit is willing, but the flesh is weak."
>
> Mark 14:34, 38

> Be of sober spirit, be on the alert. Your adversary, the devil, prowls about like a roaring lion, seeking someone to devour.
>
> 1 Pet. 5:8

> Be on the alert, stand firm in the faith, act like men, be strong.
>
> 1 Cor. 16:13

> With all prayer and petition pray at all times in the Spirit, and with this in view, be on the alert with all perseverance and petition for all the saints.
>
> Eph. 6:18

> But keep on the alert at all times, praying in order that you may have strength to escape all these things that are about to take place, and to stand before the Son of Man.
>
> Luke 21:36

The last two verses combine *agrupneo* with *kairos*, the strategic time (discussed in chapter 6), challenging us to be on the alert for the *kairos* times and pray accordingly. Again, so as not to be repetitive, we won't repeat the teaching. However, another look at the full definitions of *paga* and *kairos* in chapter 6 will enable you to make the obvious connection between the watchmen and setting boundaries of protection.

The Trophies of Intercession

I will share one story, however, to illustrate. Cindy Jacobs, in her book *Possessing the Gates of the Enemy*, tells of walking in the watchman anointing at a *kairos* time. While attending a prayer gathering in 1990, she was awakened one night at 2:00 A.M. with a sense of alarm. As she waited on the Lord, He brought to her mind the picture of a couple and their three children, a family she knew was traveling in their van to the meeting. In this vision she saw a wheel on their van come off, causing a terrible accident.

Cindy began to pray fervently for their safety and continued throughout the night. Upon their arrival the following day, she asked if they had had any problems with the right wheel. Though they had not, Cindy insisted they go to a garage and get it checked. The mechanic who inspected the van was amazed. He said there was no way they should have been able to drive the van without the wheel coming off.

Upon returning from the mechanic, Cindy's husband, Mike, who had accompanied the brother to the garage, held up a bag and declared, "The trophies of intercession." It held the old bearings from the right front wheel.[2]

That is the watchman anointing in operation, sensing the danger at a *kairos* time and establishing boundaries (*paga*) of protection through intercession.

Biblical Watchmen

Let's broaden our understanding of biblical watchmen. What was their purpose? The term "watchmen" comes from the Old

Testament and was used to describe what we would today call "sentries," "guards" or "lookouts." These individuals were responsible for protecting primarily two things: vineyards or fields from thieves and animals, and cities from invading forces.

Those watching crops were stationed on rocks, buildings or towers to provide a better range of vision. Towers or outposts in the fields usually had sleeping quarters because it was necessary to keep watch day and night during harvest. The watchmen would take shifts—one working, one sleeping—and thereby watch 24 hours a day.

This has great symbolism for us. In seasons of harvest, there is a more urgent need for watchmen, as the "thief" is going to do all he can to steal it, keeping the greater portion. It is little wonder that God has preceded the greatest harvest of souls the world has ever known—which is now happening—with the greatest prayer awakening in history. The Lord of the harvest is wise. I can assure you He has 24-hour sentries "watching" the harvest. May we be able to say with our Lord: Of those You have given me, not one of them perished (see John 17:12).

These watchmen were also posted on the city walls, where they would function as sentries. The following are a few Old Testament references:

> For thus the Lord says to me, "Go, station the lookout, let him report what he sees. When he sees riders, horsemen in pairs, a train of donkeys, a train of camels, let him pay close attention, very close attention." Then the lookout called, "O Lord, I stand continually by day on the watchtower, and I am stationed every night at my guard post."
>
> Isa. 21:6–8

> Lift up a signal against the walls of Babylon; post a strong guard, station sentries, place men in ambush! For the LORD has

both purposed and performed what He spoke concerning the inhabitants of Babylon.

Jer. 51:12

On your walls, O Jerusalem, I have appointed watchmen; all day and all night they will never keep silent. You who remind the LORD, take no rest for yourselves.

Isa. 62:6

From the walls of the cities they would watch for two things: messengers and enemies.

Watching for Messengers

They watched for messengers to inform the gatekeepers about when to open the gates and when not to. In those days runners were used to carry messages from city to city, and the watchmen would cry out when a friendly messenger was coming. Skilled watchmen could sometimes even recognize the runners by their stride before ever seeing their faces. In 2 Samuel 18:27, the watchman said, "The running . . . is like the running of Ahimaaz." Do you see any important symbolism here?

Seasoned watchmen are often alerted by the Holy Spirit, before they ever have any concrete evidence, that certain "messengers" are not to be trusted. They recognize "wolves" sent to devour the flock, or "hirelings" with improper motives. They bring warnings to those in leadership. They recognize them "by their stride," as it were—something just doesn't seem right. They sense and discern. To be sure, we must guard against human suspicion and judging after the flesh. But I have learned to listen to my trusted watchmen (one of whom is my wife) when they tell me they are uneasy about so and so. They are usually right.

At times, they are unable to give me specific reasons, which is difficult for my analytical mind, but I have learned to trust them. Most false doctrine, division and general destruction in the Body of Christ could be averted if the watchmen would watch and the leaders would listen! Peter speaks of this need in 2 Peter 2:1–2:

> But false prophets also arose among the people, just as there will also be false teachers among you, who will secretly introduce destructive heresies, even denying the Master who bought them, bringing swift destruction upon themselves. And many will follow their sensuality, and because of them the way of the truth will be maligned.

Paul warned the Ephesians of it in Acts 20:28–31:

> Be on the guard for yourselves and for all the flock, among which the Holy Spirit has made you overseers, to shepherd the church of God which He purchased with His own blood. I know that after my departure savage wolves will come in among you, not sparing the flock; and from among your own selves men will arise, speaking perverse things, to draw away the disciples after them. Therefore be on the alert, remembering that night and day for a period of three years I did not cease to admonish each one with tears.

Evidently they heeded Paul's advice, for the Lord commended them in Revelation 2:2:

> I know your deeds and your toil and perseverance, and that you cannot endure evil men, and you put to the test those who call themselves apostles, and they are not, and you found them to be false.

Watching for the Enemy

The watchmen on the wall also looked for the enemy. When they saw the potential danger approaching, they sounded an alarm, either by a shout or a trumpet blast. Soldiers could then prepare themselves for battle and defend the city. Watchmen do this today, in a spiritual sense. They alert the Body of Christ to attacks of the enemy, sounding the alarm. When the watchmen are functioning properly, we need never be caught off-guard by Satan and his forces.

As watchmen we do not live in fear of our adversary, nor do we live in "ignore - ance" of him. Contrary to what some would teach, alertness and vigilance are not synonymous with preoccupation. I must warn you, it is a common tactic of the enemy to dissuade Christians from watching for him by accusing them of a wrong emphasis.

Sadly enough, this message is often purported by well-meaning Christians. They teach that Satan is to be ignored or that little attention is to be paid him. No passage in the Bible supports this. Certainly we are not to become infatuated with Satan, but a good soldier is a well-informed soldier concerning his enemy. Be infatuated with and in awe of Jesus—be aware of the enemy. Love worship, not warfare, but when necessary, go to war.

In their book *How to Pray for Your Family and Friends*, Quin Sherrer and Ruthanne Garlock tell of a friend's pastor who had this attitude. "I don't think you should teach on spiritual warfare," the pastor told Hilda one day. "Concentrate on Jesus and not the devil."

Her response showed her wisdom and experience. "'Pastor, I do concentrate on Jesus and his victory,' she answered respectfully. 'Jesus taught that we have authority over the evil one. Until I began to use Christ's authority in spiritual warfare, I had four children going to hell. I've learned to bind the enemy's work in my family members' lives. Today *all* my children and grandchildren serve the Lord. I've seen the results of spiritual warfare, and I want to help others.'"[3]

The Watchman Looks Ahead

Watchmen did not only guard cities and fields in Scripture. The Hebrew words translated "watchman" are *natsar, shamar* and *tsaphah*. They mean to guard or protect by watching over, but also by "hedging around something"[4] as with thorns. They even have the connotation of hiding or concealing something.[5] The watchman—through intercession—creates the secret place of protection (see Ps. 91).

Another interesting meaning of *tsaphah* is to "lean forward and peer into the distance." The connection to prayer should be obvious. The watchman looks ahead, "peering into the distance,"[6] to foresee the attacks of the enemy. He is pro-active, not re-active. This is prophetic intercession!

Let's look at several references where these words are used, with each usage referring to guarding or protecting something different. The first is in Genesis 2:15, which also happens to be the first time one of these words is used in the Bible. "Then the LORD God took the man and put him into the garden of Eden to cultivate it and *keep* it" (emphasis added).

Theologians have what is known as "the law of first mention." This refers to the general rule that the first time a major subject is mentioned in the Bible, significant facts are given concerning it that will remain consistent and relevant throughout the Scriptures.

For example, the first mention of the serpent—Satan—is in Genesis 3:1: "Now the serpent was more crafty than any beast of the field which the LORD God had made. And he said to the woman, 'Indeed, has God said, "You shall not eat from any tree of the garden"?'" It is easy to see this law at work here, as the verse speaks of Satan's subtlety or craftiness. God is informing us of one of the most important things we must remember about Satan: He is far more dangerous to us as the crafty serpent than as a roaring lion.

Be Defensive—Keep the Serpent Out!

Adam was told in Genesis 2:15 to guard or "keep" the garden. From what? It had to be the serpent! I assert this because first of all, it is much in keeping with the nature of God to have warned him. To have done otherwise would not have been consistent with God's character. Second, neither Adam nor Eve seemed shocked when a snake talked to them. It evidently didn't come as a total surprise. Third, what else could there have been (before the Fall) to guard, keep or protect from in the garden? Only the serpent.

I want to emphasize an important point—the first mention of this term in Scripture gives us one of the primary responsibilities of the watchman: *Keep the serpent out!* Guard or protect that which God has entrusted to your care from the subtle encroachment of the serpent. Keep him out of your garden! . . . your home, family, church, city, nation! . . . Keep him out!

The word is used again in Genesis 3:24 when God stationed a cherubim at the entrance of the garden to keep man from the tree of life. Adam didn't keep the serpent out, so an angel had to keep man out.

In Genesis 30:31, the watchman concept is used in guarding a flock. It doesn't take much insight to see the correlation here. We can guard the flock of God through intercession. Ecclesiastes 12:3 refers to protecting a house. Psalm 127:1 uses the concept in reference to guarding a city. And 1 Samuel 26:15 and 28:2 speak of doing it for a person. Proverbs 4:23 instructs us to do it for our hearts.

These three Hebrew words are also translated in several other ways. I'm going to list a few of them, elaborating briefly, to provide a more well-rounded understanding of the concept. As you will plainly see, pages could be written commenting on the symbolism and connection to prayer. For brevity's sake I have not done so, but I would encourage you to think and meditate on each one, allowing the Holy Spirit to bring insight to you personally.

1. Keep or Keeper

This is by far the most frequent usage of these words—at least 250 times. Watchmen keep things, places and individuals safe. They ensure against loss, theft or damage. They keep things intact, in possession.

2. Guard

Watchmen are guards. This word is obviously similar to the next one.

3. Bodyguard

Watchmen guard individuals, protecting them from danger and harm. They are shields—the secret service agents of the kingdom, guarding and protecting others. Watchmen represent Jesus by watching over others.

Often, intercessors in our fellowship inform me of times they have spent covering me in prayer. More than once I've been told, "Pastor, I was up most of the night praying for you." Occasionally they ask, "Was something wrong?"

"No," I usually respond, "and that's probably why." Often my problems and distractions are "laid upon" others and they "carry them away from me." I am grateful and wise enough to realize that much of my success is due to their faithfulness. What a comfort to know I have bodyguards in the spirit! There would be fewer casualties in our ranks if we had more faithful watchmen.

Peter Wagner, in his book *Prayer Shield*, offers five reasons pastors and other Christian leaders are in such great need of watchmen interceding for them:

1. *Pastors Have More Responsibility and Accountability.* James 3:1, "My brethren, let not many of you become teachers, knowing that we shall receive a stricter judgment."

273

2. *Pastors Are More Subject to Temptation.* Make no mistake about it, the higher up you go on the ladder of Christian leadership, the higher you go on Satan's hit list.

3. *Pastors Are More Targeted by Spiritual Warfare.* It has now become known that over the last several years, satanists, witches, New Agers, occult practitioners, shamans, spiritists and other servants of darkness have entered into an evil covenant to pray to Satan for the breakdown of marriages of pastors and Christian leaders. The spiritual warfare has intensified.

4. *Pastors Have More Influence on Others.* The fourth reason why pastors need intercession more than other Christians is that by the very nature of their ministry they have more influence on others.

5. *Pastors Have More Visibility.* Because pastors are up front, they are constantly subject to gossip and criticism.[7]

In the book, Wagner elaborates more thoroughly on each reason. Elsewhere he says, "To the degree the intercessors pray, the leaders gain protection against the fiery darts of the wicked one, over and above the whole armor of God they are responsible for using."[8] This excellent book provides outstanding guidance about intercession for Christian leaders.

In the excellent training resource *Becoming a Prayer Warrior*, Beth Alves offers a suggested daily guide to praying for spiritual leaders, which Wagner summarized as follows:

Sunday:	Favor with God (spiritual revelation, anointing, holiness).
Monday:	Favor with others (congregations, ministry staff, unsaved).
Tuesday:	Increased vision (wisdom and enlightenment, motives, guidance).
Wednesday:	Spirit, Soul, Body (health, appearance, attitudes, spiritual and physical wholeness).
Thursday:	Protection (temptation, deception, enemies).

Friday: Finances (priorities, blessings).
Saturday: Family (general, spouse, children).[9]

4. Doorkeeper

Obviously similar to the next, so I will comment on both of them together.

5. Gatekeeper

Watchmen have the ability spiritually—in the prayer closet— to determine who or what goes in and out of their homes, their families' lives, their churches, their cities, etc. They discern by the Holy Spirit what to allow in, and through prayer, open and close the door. They invite in the work of the Holy Spirit and reject the works of darkness. They set boundaries, keeping enemies out. At times, when informed or confronted by an intercessor with the information that something improper has crept into our fellowship, I respond by asking, "What happened? Weren't you on the job?" I would simply say to the Body of Christ, "Don't blame it all on the pastors. You, too, are responsible for gatekeeping."

6. Preserve or Preserver

Watchmen preserve or keep things from ruin and destruction. They preserve lives, anointings, moves of God and a host of other things by covering them in prayer. Sherrer and Garlock tell of four ladies who functioned as watchmen for their farms. These women walked the perimeters of the fields while the husbands worked, sometimes covering as much as six miles in a day.

They prayed for protection from insects, crop diseases, hail and drought. They asked God to give their husbands wisdom in farming and marketing and prayed for angels to be assigned to the efforts.

The results were amazing. It turned out to be one of their better years. No storm or insect damage, no unwise decisions and a good profit—while others around them had a difficult year with little profit. We simply aren't practical enough at times with our intercession tactics. These ladies, watching in intercession, opened the way for God's blessing upon their families' financial endeavors.[10]

7. Pay attention

Watchmen must be on the alert. They must pay attention. Though obvious, it is important enough to emphasize. As soldiers, God "calls us to attention." Lives are at stake. The harvest must be guarded. Pay attention, watchmen!

8. Observe

This embodies the same concept as paying attention, yet adds the emphasis of contemplativeness and sharpness. Don't just look—see. Be observant. Quite simply, watchmen watch! They observe what others fail to see. We can observe much in prayer, often even before it happens.

9. Behold

This one is similar to observe, of course, but I list it because it reemphasizes the need for seeing clearly.

10. Beware

Watchmen must be vigilant, aware, on the alert. Again, 1 Peter 5:8 warns us to be of sober spirit. Always beware, intercessor! Watch for the lion and when you see him at work immediately "meet" him, enforcing Calvary's victory with the "bear anointing."

11. *Protect*

In the same sense as guarding and keeping, watchmen protect. They build walls or boundaries of protection from the attacks of the devil. They distribute this blessing of the Lord.

12. *Maintain*

Watchmen maintain things for the Lord. They are maintenance people. They may not set vision, build or plant in the way that some do, but they maintain. They keep things working well and prevent breakdowns. They maintain the anointing, integrity, health and many other necessary blessings of the kingdom.

In summary, God is raising up prophetic intercessors— watchmen—*to keep the serpent out!* Men and women who will "lean forward, peering into the distance," watching for the enemy's attacks. Sentries, bodyguards, gatekeepers, boundary setters and preservers in His kingdom. It is, indeed, a high calling!

Be Offensive—Lay Siege!

There is another facet to this type of prayer, however, that I now want us to consider. One of the most interesting and surprising things I discovered as I studied these words is that they embody not only protective or defensive meanings, but offensive as well.

The words mean "to besiege or lay siege to a city,"[11] the idea being to watch it to keep people and supplies from coming or going. One definition was "to spy on" or "lie in wait for someone to ambush the person."[12] They are actually translated this way in 2 Samuel 11:16, Isaiah 1:8, Jeremiah 4:16–17, Jeremiah 51:12 and Judges 1:24.

In 1989 when the Lord gave me this teaching, He clearly spoke in my heart that He was releasing the watchman anointing, which would enable individuals to "lay siege to" cities and nations through prayer. Where Satan had taken advantage and held the greater portion, the people of God would be given instruction about how to lay siege to these situations, cutting off his supply lines and removing that which had given him place. They would take back from him people, cities and nations.

This was before there was talk (at least in a broad degree) of reconciliation ceremonies, identificational repentance, spiritual mapping, prayer walks, marches and journeys—all of which are terms associated with systematically removing from Satan his hold on places and people to take them for Christ. These and other strategies are all a part of the watchman anointing God has released to the Church.

The Body of Christ is learning to *systematically* pull down the strongholds of darkness. God is giving us the ability—by His Spirit—to discern the enemy's plans, strengths, weaknesses and points of entry—to cut him off and take nations, cities and individuals through prayer. The strongholds of darkness are being torn down. Those imprisoned in satanic fortresses are being freed. Sieges are being laid in the spirit. God is showing us what to bind and loose, as well as how to do it. There is opposition, of course.

One of the things that keep some from this kind of prayer is the time element. The very concept of laying siege implies a duration of time. It may take days, weeks or years of daily intercession to receive the breakthrough. I certainly believe this can be sped up by more intelligent and informed praying, as well as by the multiplication of power that takes place through agreement.

However, nothing can change the fact that some situations require a degree of time. I laid siege to the cyst in my wife for 30 days. Polly Simchen, whom we spoke of in chapter 10, laid siege to the bondages in her son for 4 years. God gave her and her friends much strategy as they prayed, enlightening them on what to cut off and what to call forth. That is a siege. They discerned Satan's strategies, "spying out" his plans. Was it worth the effort and wait? Absolutely. They gained the greater portion.

This concept of laying siege is well-illustrated in a story about Theresa Mulligan, editor of a newsletter for intercessors called *Breakthrough*, related by Sherrer and Garlock in *How to Pray for Your Family and Friends*. Theresa and a friend had prayer-walked their neighborhood for a season, stopping in front of each house, taking hands and agreeing in prayer for the occupants' salvation.

Soon reports started coming in: A colonel's wife accepted Christ, the teenage daughter of a Jewish family met Jesus, an arthritic woman made a commitment to Christ and a college-age daughter of another family came to the Lord. Even after she moved away, Theresa continued to hear of these former neighbors coming to Christ.[13]

That is laying siege! It is the watchman anointing at its best and anyone can do it.

Taking Cities and Nations for God

I have focused most of my attention in this book on intercession for individuals. I would now like to comment briefly on intercession for cities and nations, especially as it relates to the watchman aspect of laying siege.

Scripture clearly shows that God deals with—relates to—not only individuals, but also groups of people. Because of the principles of authority, responsibility, free will, sowing and reaping, etc., which operate not only on an individual level, but also on the corporate level at which individuals join, God relates to people *groups*. Why?

Many of the decisions we make, the rights and privileges we enjoy, are not individualistic, but are jointly made with the people to whom we relate. For example, I make many decisions privately regarding my personal life. But for our household—our children, finances, home, time, and so on, my wife and I make the decisions together.

The same principle of shared authority can be incrementally expanded all the way up to a national level—from organizations to cities to counties to states to nations. These groupings could be secular or religious. In whatever way a group of people can be said to have rights, decision-making power and freedoms, there is reciprocal responsibility. As the decisions on laws, leaders, morals, interests, tolerances and intolerances are shared, so are the ramifications.

For example, I do not favor abortion, but I cannot escape the effects, though they may be indirect, of God's judgments on this nation due to this tragic holocaust. If God brings drought or inclement weather that affects our crops, I, too, will pay higher prices. As He turns us over to our degraded and perverted desires, accidents and illnesses increase, which raise my insurance rates, also. If the judgment happens to be war, I, too, pay for it in higher taxes and share in the grief of lost American lives. Numerous other examples could be given.

Although we may not like it, none can live as an island. Though we as believers can enjoy a certain degree of protection from these judgments—God might increase my prosperity to help me pay higher prices or taxes, for example—there is no way to totally avoid the principle of shared responsibility.

The Corporate Dealings of God

Having given the reason, I want to validate it by listing several ways in which God dealt with cities or regions in Scripture on a corporate level:

1. Cities were addressed or prophesied to: Jonah 1:2; Nahum 3:1; Micah 6:9; Revelation 2 and 3.

2. Cities and nations were judged: Nineveh, Sodom, Gomorrah, Tyre, Sidon, Bethsaida, Capernaum, Jericho, Jerusalem, and others. The nation Israel was judged as a whole on many occasions in Scripture, as were other nations.

3. Cities and nations were forgiven or spared judgment: Nineveh; Sodom could have been, had there been enough righteous people; the nation Israel was forgiven as a whole, as were others.

4. Cities and nations had divine purposes or callings: Israel, Jerusalem, the seven cities of refuge, and many others.

5. Cities were spoken of as being kept or preserved by God: Psalm 127:1.

6. Cities and nations had principalities ruling them: Tyre (see Ezek. 28:12); Persia (see Dan. 10:13); Ephesus (see Acts 19:28); Pergamum (see Rev. 2:12).

7. People groups have a corporate righteousness or sin level: Any nation (see Prov. 14:34); Sodom and Gomorrah (see Gen. 18:20–21); the Amorites (see Gen. 15:16).

8. Cities have a corporate faith or unbelief level: Nazareth (see Mark 6:5–6).

9. Cities have a corporate peace or welfare (see Jer. 29:7).

10. Cities can have revival: Nineveh (see Jon. 3:5–10).

11. Cities can miss revival: Jerusalem (see Luke 19:41–44).

I gave this entire list and the preceding explanation primarily to substantiate one thing: *God deals with people as groups, not just as individuals.* This fact is what also substantiates our intercession for people as groups.

Abraham successfully interceded for a city (see Gen. 18:22–33); Moses interceded for a nation (see Exod. 32:9–14). Exiles from Jerusalem were told to intercede for the cities they now lived in (see Jer. 29:7). We are told in 2 Chronicles 7:14 that our prayers and lifestyles can cause healing for a nation. Ecclesiastes 9:15 and Proverbs 21:22 inform us that wisdom can deliver a city and bring down strongholds.

Without question, God is releasing an anointing to lay siege to cities and nations to take them for Him! He is equipping us to "spy out" the enemy's plans and strongholds, "ambushing" him in the spirit. We are the Melchizedek order of priesthood prophesied in Psalm 110. We're a priestly army, stretching forth the scepter of our conquering hero, ruling in the midst of our enemies. Come on, join us!

For those who are serious about city taking, Peter Wagner's book *Breaking Strongholds in Your City* contains a wealth of information. In it, Victor Lorenzo tells of the three-year plan to evangelize the city of Resistencia, Argentina. One of the key elements of the effort was the spiritual mapping of the city by Lorenzo. Through this mapping he discovered four spiritual powers influencing the city. Lorenzo tells of praying to tear down these powers and the ensuing results:

> The next day our team went out to the plaza with the pastors of the Resistencia churches, a group of trained intercessors and Cindy Jacobs. We battled fiercely against the invisible powers over the city for four hours. We attacked them in what we sensed was their hierarchical order, from bottom to top. First came Pombero, then Curupi, then San La Muerte, then spirit of Freemasonry, then Queen of Heaven, then the Python spirit whom we suspected functioned as the coordinator of all the forces of evil in the city. When we finished, an almost tangible sense of peace and freedom came

over all who had participated. We were confident that this first battle had been won and that the city could be claimed for the Lord.

After this, the church in Resistencia was ready for full-scale evangelization. Unbelievers began to respond to the gospel as never before. As a result of our three-year outreach, church attendance increased by 102 percent. The effect was felt in all social strata of the city. We could undertake community projects such as providing drinking water for the poor. The public image of the evangelical church improved greatly by gaining respect and approval from political and social leaders. We were invited to use the media to spread our message. The spiritual warfare and mapping we were able to do opened new doors in Resistencia for evangelism, social improvement and reaping of the spiritual harvest.[14]

That is the watchman anointing! *We can impact our cities and nations through intercession.* We can lay siege to them, taking them for God. Strongholds of darkness can become strongholds of light.

Cities Transformed

Canaan, a cursed land (see Gen. 9:25), became the Promised Land of blessing.

Jerusalem, once a stronghold of evil giants, became the city of peace.

Seven cities, once ruled by idolaters and wicked giants, became cities of refuge where people who had accidentally taken a life fled for safety and protection. Hebron, the most famous of the seven, was formerly called Kiriath-Arba, which means the city of Arba. Arba was the greatest of the Anakim, or giants (see Josh. 14:15). Hebron, its new name, means "association, friendship, fellowship, communion."[15] Fittingly, Abraham, the friend of God, is buried there. Caleb, a man of faith and courage, was used to transform the stronghold of the greatest giant to a place where people ran to find safety and sweet fellowship or communion with God. This can happen to our cities!

Also, as a city of refuge, Hebron was a picture or type of Christ. One who killed accidentally could find safety in one of two places: in a city of refuge (for long-term protection) or holding on to the horns of the altar in the Holy Place (for short-term protection).

In Hebrews 6:18, the Lord draws from both of these pictures in one phrase: "In order that by two unchangeable things, in which it is impossible for God to lie, we may have strong encouragement, we who have fled for *refuge* in *laying hold* of the hope set before us" (emphasis added). Interestingly, individuals who were there for safety had to remain in a city of refuge until the death of the current high priest (see Num. 35:28), after which they were free to go safely. What a picture of our great High Priest who died so that we could go free from judgment and penalty.

My point for this story, other than just to enjoy a beautiful picture of Jesus, is to demonstrate that a former stronghold of giants was transformed into such a place of protection, refuge and fellowship with God that it became a picture of Christ Himself.

Can God do this again today? Can our cities and nations be so thoroughly transformed? Yes, unless God has changed in the last 3,000 years! That is, if He can find some Calebs. . . . If He can find some giant killers. . . . If He can find some "We're well able" attitudes.

He is asking us, as He did Ezekiel, to look on the dry bones of our nation—the men and women, the young and old, the rich and poor, the hurting and those who think they're healthy—and answer the same question he asked the prophet: "Can these bones live?" I say they can. What do you say?

Are You Ready?

We need to be like Sam and Jed. Hearing that a $5,000 bounty had been offered for the capture or killing of wolves, they became bounty hunters. Waking up one night, Sam saw that they were surrounded by 50 pairs of gleaming eyes—ravenous wolves licking hungry chops. "Jed, wake up," he whispered to his sleeping partner. "We're rich!"[16]

We need to see the multitude of unbelievers around us not as threats, but as opportunities. Our task would be overwhelming were it not for the fact that we are relying on God's strength and ability, not ours. Though a host should encamp against us, we can still be confident (see Ps. 27:3). Gideon's 300 were more than enough to defeat 135,000 with God on their side. If He is for us, who can successfully be against us (see Rom. 8:31)?

Let's do it! Let's let God arise and His enemies be scattered. Let's fill our bag with the stones of victory and run to meet Goliath. Let's take Kiriath-Arba. Let's run through some troops and leap over some walls.

Let's demonstrate the awesomeness of our God. Let's growl! Let's roar! Let's let Jesus live through us.

He is ready—are you?

Are you ready to walk in your calling as an intercessor? . . . To re-present Jesus as the reconciler and the warrior? . . . To distribute His benefits and victory? . . . To meet, to carry away, to set boundaries?

285

Are you ready to birth, to liberate, to strike the mark? . . . To fill some bowls, to make some declarations, to watch and pray? Are you ready?

Remember: "Life is fragile, handle with *PAGA!*"

Questions for Reflection

1. Can you summarize the four conclusions drawn from Ephesians 6:18, 1 Peter 5:8 and 2 Corinthians 2:11? Using the verses themselves, give reasons for these conclusions.

2. Describe the functions and responsibilities of Old Testament watchmen. How do they symbolize watching intercession?

3. Where is the first usage of the Hebrew word for "watchman" in the Scriptures? What significant insight can be drawn from this?

4. Based on the definitions and usages of the three words for "watchman," can you give some summary statements about the defensive aspect of the watchman anointing? How can you apply this to your family? . . . Pastor? . . . Church?

5. Describe the offensive aspect of the watchman anointing. Can you relate it to intercession for an individual? . . . How about a city?

6. Can you give the reason God deals with groups of people, not just with individuals? List three or four biblical examples.

7. Think of ways you and your prayer group can lay siege to your city. Do it!

Discussion Leader's Guide

The purpose of this book is to ignite and empower the prayer lives of those who read it. As the group grows in faith and unity, you may want to implement some of the prayer tactics mentioned in the book, such as using prayer cloths, prayer-walking and engaging in spiritual warfare for each other.

As a leader, it is important to be sensitive to the maturity level of the group. It is also important that you do not impose your beliefs on those who differ in the way they worship the Lord.

The optimum-sized discussion group is 10 to 15 people. A smaller group can make continuity a problem when too few members attend. A larger group will require strong leadership skills to create a sense of belonging and meaningful participation for each person.

If you are leading a group that already meets regularly, such as a Sunday school class or weekly home group, decide how many weeks to spend on the series. Be sure to plan for any holidays that may occur during your scheduled meetings.

Use creativity. This book's 14 chapters will fit a regular 13-week quarter if a couple of chapters are paired to provide time for personal sharing.

The first session would provide a perfect time for an open forum to create a sense of unity as you begin the series. A time for introduction followed by nonthreatening questions is often helpful for building close ties within the group. Chapter 1 can be used as the introduction. Consider one or more of the following questions:

1. Are you satisfied with your prayer life? If not, where are you struggling?
2. Why do you think prayer is such a lacking discipline in the Body of Christ?
3. What do you hope to gain from studying this book?
4. After reading chapter 1, do you think we should pray only once or do you think we need to be persistent? Why?
5. If you could ask God one question about prayer, what would it be?

Such questions will create a sense of identity among the class members and help them to discover their similarities.

Many individual questions may arise that will significantly contribute to the group's understanding of the subject. Group members should be encouraged to maintain lists of their questions. Suggest that they be submitted anonymously and combine them together to eliminate repetition. Many questions may be answered by the time the series reaches its conclusion. It is, therefore, a good idea to wait until your last session to discuss them.

Enlist a co-leader to assist with calling class members to remind them of meeting dates, times and places. Your co-leader can also make arrangements for refreshments and child care.

People will have a greater appreciation for their books if they are responsible for paying for them. They will also be more apt to finish the course if they have invested in their own materials. Be sure to have several extra Bibles available. *The Living Bible* is often helpful for people who have little or no Bible background; however, it is important to explain that the NASB differs considerably and will be the main version used in this book.

Be aware of the basic principles for group dynamics, such as:

1. Arrange seating in a semicircle with the leader included rather than standing in front. This setting invites participation.

2. Create a discussion-friendly atmosphere. The following tips are helpful for guiding discussions:

   a. Receive statements from group members without judgmentalism, even if you disagree with them. If they are clearly unbiblical or unfair, you can ask questions that clarify the issue; but outright rejection of comments will stifle open participation.

   b. If a question or comment deviates from the subject, either suggest that it be dealt with at another time or ask the group if they want to pursue the new issue now.

   c. If one person monopolizes the discussion, direct a few questions specifically to someone else. Or, tactfully interrupt the dominator by saying, "Excuse me, that's a good thought, and I wonder what the rest of us think about that." Talk with the person privately and enlist that person's help in drawing others into the discussion.

   d. Make it easy and comfortable for everyone to share or ask questions, but don't insist that anyone do so. Reluctant participants can warm to the idea of sharing by being asked to read a passage from the book. Pair a shy person with someone else for a discussion apart from the main group, and ask reluctant participants to write down a comment to be shared with the larger group.

  e. If someone asks you a question and you don't know the answer, admit it and move on. If the question calls for insight from personal experience, invite others to comment on it; however, be careful that this sharing is limited. If it requires special knowledge, offer to look for an answer in the library or from a theologian or minister, and report your findings later.

3. Guard against rescuing. The purpose of this group is to learn to pray for others, not fix them. This doesn't mean that poignant moments won't come up or unhappy problems won't be shared, but the group is for sharing and prayer—not fixing others. The leader should be open and honest about wanting to grow with the group instead of coming across as an authority about the subject.

4. Start and stop on time, according to the schedule agreed upon before the series begins. This is especially important for those who have to hire a baby-sitter or arise early for work the next morning.

5. During each session, lead group members in discussing the questions and exercises at the end of each chapter. If you have more than 8 or 10 class members, consider dividing into small groups, then invite each group to share one or two insights with the larger group.

6. Be sensitive. Some people may feel comfortable praying for others, but don't force those who don't. It is necessary to set aside a time either at the beginning or end of the meeting to pray for those in need.

7. Encourage members of the group to pray daily for each other. This will perpetuate a sense of unity and love.

8. As a leader, pray regularly for the sessions and the participants, asking the Holy Spirit to hover over each person throughout the week. The Lord will honor your willingness to guide His people toward a more intimate relationship with Him.

Notes

Chapter 1: The Question Is . . .

1. John L. Mason, *An Enemy Called Average* (Tulsa, OK: Harrison House, 1990), p. 20.

2. Craig Brian Larson, *Illustrations for Preaching and Teaching* (Grand Rapids, MI: Baker Books, 1993), p. 128.

3. Ibid., p. 75.

Chapter 2: The Necessity of Prayer

1. Paul E. Billheimer, *Destined for the Throne* (Fort Washington, PA: Christian Literature Crusade, 1975), p. 51.

2. Ibid.

3. James Strong, *The New Strong's Exhaustive Concordance of the Bible* (Nashville, TN: Thomas Nelson Publishers, 1990), ref. no. 120.

4. William Wilson, *Old Testament Word Studies* (Grand Rapids, MI: Kregel Publications, 1978), p. 236.

5. *The Consolidated Webster Encyclopedic Dictionary* (Chicago: Consolidated Book Publishers, 1954), p. 615.

6. Ibid.

7. Spiros Zodhiates, *Hebrew-Greek Key Study Bible—New American Standard* (Chattanooga, TN: AMG Publishers, 1984; revised edition, 1990), p. 1768.

8. Strong, *The New Strong's Exhaustive Concordance*, ref. no. 1819.

9. R. Laird Harris, Gleason L. Archer Jr., and Bruce K. Waltke, *Theological Wordbook of the Old Testament* (Chicago: Moody Press, 1980; Grand Rapids: William B. Eerdmans Publishing Co., revised edition, 1991), p. 426.

10. Zodhiates, *Hebrew-Greek Key Study Bible*, p. 1826.

11. Andrew Murray, *The Ministry of Intercessory Prayer* (Minneapolis, MN: Bethany House Publishers, 1981), pp. 22–23.
12. Billheimer, *Destined for the Throne*, p. 107.
13. C. Peter Wagner, *Confronting the Powers* (Ventura, CA: Regal Books, 1996), p. 242.
14. Jack W. Hayford, *Prayer Is Invading the Impossible* (South Plainfield, NJ: Logos International, 1977; revised edition, Bridge Publishing, 1995), p. 92, 1977 edition.

Chapter 3: Re-Presenting Jesus

1. *The Consolidated Webster Encyclopedic Dictionary* (Chicago: Consolidated Book Publishers, 1954), p. 384.
2. Ibid., p. 450.
3. James Strong, *The New Strong's Exhaustive Concordance of the Bible* (Nashville, TN: Thomas Nelson Publishers, 1990), ref. no. 1834.
4. Jack Canfield and Mark Victor Hansen, *Chicken Soup for the Soul* (Deerfield Beach, FL: Health Communications, Inc., 1993), p. 74.
5. R. Arthur Mathews, *Born for Battle* (Robesonia, PA: OMF Books, 1978), p. 106.
6. I have used the phrase "enforcing the victory of Calvary" throughout this book. Though not a direct quote, the seed thought was planted in my mind by Paul Billheimer, *Destined for the Throne* (Fort Washington, PA: Christian Literature Crusade, 1975), p. 17.
7. Mathews, *Born for Battle*, p. 160.

Chapter 4: Meetings: The Good, the Bad and the Ugly

1. Francis Brown, S. R. Driver, and Charles A. Briggs, *The New Brown-Driver, Briggs-Gesenius Hebrew and English Lexicon* (Peabody, MA: Hendrickson Publishers, 1979), p. 803.
2. Spiros Zodhiates, *The Complete Word Study Dictionary* (Iowa Falls, IA: Word Bible Publishers, 1992), p. 1375.
3. Ibid.
4. William Wilson, *Old Testament Word Studies* (Grand Rapids, MI: Kregel Publications, 1978), p. 263.
5. Spiros Zodhiates, *Hebrew-Greek Key Study Bible—New American Standard* (Chattanooga, TN: AMG Publishers, 1984; revised edition, 1990), p. 1583.
6. Ibid.
7. Jack Canfield and Mark Victor Hansen, *Chicken Soup for the Soul* (Deerfield Beach, FL: Health Communications, Inc., 1993), p. 74.

Chapter 5: Cheek to Cheek

1. Joseph Henry Thayer, *A Greek-English Lexicon of the New Testament* (Grand Rapids, MI: Baker Book House, 1977), p. 45.
2. Craig Brian Larson, *Illustrations for Preaching and Teaching* (Grand Rapids, MI: Baker Book House, 1993), p. 144.

3. Ibid., p. 99.

4. Francis Brown, S. R. Driver, and Charles A. Briggs, *The New Brown-Driver, Briggs-Gesenius Hebrew and English Lexicon* (Peabody, MA: Hendrickson Publishers, 1979), p. 671.

5. F. F. Bosworth, *Christ the Healer* (Grand Rapids, MI: Baker Book House/Revell, 1973), p. 26.

6. S. D. Gordon, *What It Will Take to Change the World* (Grand Rapids, MI: Baker Book House, 1979), pp. 17–21, adapted.

7. *New American Standard Exhaustive Concordance of the Bible* (Nashville, TN: Holman Bible Publishers, 1981), ref. no. 2428.

8. R. Laird Harris, Gleason L. Archer Jr., and Bruce K. Waltke, *Theological Wordbook of the Old Testament* (Chicago: Moody Press, 1980; Grand Rapids: William B. Eerdmans Publishing Co., revised edition, 1991), p. 453.

9. Spiros Zodhiates, *The Complete Word Study Dictionary* (Iowa Falls, IA: Word Bible Publishers, 1992), p. 1128.

10. Harris, Archer, Waltke, *Theological Wordbook*, p. 453.

11. Words by Julia Ward Howe, America melody attributed to William Steffe.

12. Larson, *Illustrations for Preaching*, p. 26.

Chapter 6: No Trespassing

1. *The Spirit-Filled Bible* (Nashville, TN: Thomas Nelson Publishers, 1991), p. 1097.

2. I first heard the phrase "prayer that sets boundaries" in a live message by Jack Hayford in Dallas, Texas, in 1976. He has since written about this in one of his books.

3. James Strong, *The New Strong's Exhaustive Concordance of the Bible* (Nashville, TN: Thomas Nelson Publishers, 1990), ref. no. 3427.

4. Francis Brown, S. R. Driver, and Charles A. Briggs, *The New Brown-Driver, Briggs-Gesenius Hebrew and English Lexicon* (Peabody, MA: Hendrickson Publishers, 1979), p. 533.

5. Ethelbert W. Bullinger, *A Critical Lexicon and Concordance to the English and Greek New Testament* (Grand Rapids, MI: Zondervan Publishing House, 1975), p. 804.

6. Ibid.

Chapter 7: Butterflies, Mice, Elephants and Bull's-Eyes

1. Francis Brown, S. R. Driver, and Charles A. Briggs, *The New Brown-Driver, Briggs-Gesenius Hebrew and English Lexicon* (Peabody, MA: Hendrickson Publishers, 1979), p. 803.

2. W. E. Vine, *The Expanded Vine's Expository Dictionary of New Testament Words* (Minneapolis, MN: Bethany House Publishers, 1984), p. 200.

3. Spiros Zodhiates, *Hebrew-Greek Key Study Bible—New American Standard* (Chattanooga, TN: AMG Publishers, 1984; revised edition, 1990), p. 1812.

4. Spiros Zodhiates, *The Complete Word Study Dictionary* (Iowa Falls, IA: Word Bible Publishers, 1992), p. 400.

5. The connection between Genesis 28:11–22 and Romans 8:26–28 along with several of the related thoughts, including the butterfly illustration, I first heard in a live message by Jack Hayford in Dallas, Texas, in 1976. He has since written about this in one of his books.

6. Communicated to me by Israeli student Avi Mizrachi at Christ for the Nations Institute in Dallas, Texas.

7. James Strong, *The New Strong's Exhaustive Concordance of the Bible* (Nashville, TN: Thomas Nelson Publishers, 1990), ref. no. 4878.

Chapter 8: Supernatural Childbirth

1. *The Consolidated Webster Encyclopedic Dictionary* (Chicago: Consolidated Book Publishers, 1954), p. 749.

2. W. E. Vine, *The Expanded Vine's Expository Dictionary of New Testament Words* (Minneapolis, MN: Bethany House Publishers, 1984), p. 110.

3. James Strong, *The New Strong's Exhaustive Concordance of the Bible* (Nashville, TN: Thomas Nelson Publishers, 1990), ref. no. 8414.

4. Spiros Zodhiates, *Hebrew-Greek Key Study Bible—New American Standard* (Chattanooga, TN: AMG Publishers, 1984; revised edition, 1990), p. 1790.

5. C. F. Keil and F. Delitzsch, *Commentary on the Old Testament*, Volume 1 (Grand Rapids, MI: William B. Eerdmans Publishing Co., reprinted 1991), p. 48.

6. William Wilson, *Old Testament Word Studies* (Grand Rapids, MI: Kregel Publications, 1978), p. 175.

7. *The Consolidated Webster Encyclopedic Dictionary* (Chicago: Consolidated Book Publishers, 1954), p. 89.

8. Francis Brown, S. R. Driver, and Charles A. Briggs, *The New Brown-Driver, Briggs-Gesenius Hebrew and English Lexicon* (Peabody, MA: Hendrickson Publishers, 1979), p. 934.

9. Strong, *The New Strong's Exhaustive Concordance*, ref. no. 3205.

10. Ibid., ref. no. 2342.

11. Ibid., ref. no. 1411.

12. Ibid., ref. no. 1982.

13. Joseph Henry Thayer, *A Greek-English Lexicon of the New Testament* (Grand Rapids, MI: Baker Book House, 1977), p. 242.

14. Spiros Zodhiates, *The Complete Word Study Dictionary* (Iowa Falls, IA: Word Bible Publishers, 1992), p. 1366.

15. Vine, *The Expanded Vine's Expository Dictionary*, p. 268.

16. Craig Brian Larson, *Illustrations for Preaching and Teaching* (Grand Rapids, MI: Baker Books, 1993), p. 165, adapted.

Chapter 9: Pro Wrestlers

1. R. Arthur Mathews, *Born for Battle* (Robesonia, PA: OMF Books, 1978), p. 113.

2. Jack W. Hayford, *Prayer Is Invading the Impossible* (South Plainfield, NJ: Logos International, 1977; revised edition, Bridge Publishing, 1995), p. 45, 1977 edition.

Notes

3. R. Laird Harris, Gleason L. Archer Jr. and Bruce K. Waltke, *Theological Wordbook of the Old Testament* (Chicago: Moody Press, 1980; Grand Rapids: William B. Eerdmans Publishing Co., revised edition, 1991), p. 715.

4. Hayford, *Prayer Is Invading the Impossible*, p. 5.

5. Ethelbert W. Bullinger, *A Critical Lexicon and Concordance to the English and Greek New Testament* (Grand Rapids, MI: Zondervan Publishing House, 1975), p. 400.

6. Spiros Zodhiates, *Hebrew-Greek Key Study Bible—New American Standard* (Chattanooga, TN: AMG Publishers, 1984; revised edition, 1990), p. 1797.

7. Spiros Zodhiates, *The Complete Word Study Dictionary* (Iowa Falls, IA: Word Bible Publishers, 1992), p. 1173.

8. James Strong, *The New Strong's Exhaustive Concordance of the Bible* (Nashville, TN: Thomas Nelson Publishers, 1990), ref. no. 4122.

9. Bullinger, *A Critical Lexicon and Concordance*, p. 28.

10. Geoffrey W. Bromiley, *Theological Dictionary of the New Testament Abridged* (Grand Rapids, MI: William B. Eerdmans Publishing Co., 1985), p. 935.

11. Strong, *The New Strong's Exhaustive Concordance*, ref. no. 4314.

12. Ibid., ref. no. 1747.

13. Ibid., ref. no. 2442.

14. Harris, Archer, Waltke, *Theological Wordbook*, p. 791.

15. Strong, *The New Strong's Exhaustive Concordance*, ref. no. 6960.

16. Zodhiates, *Hebrew-Greek Key Study Bible*, p. 1733.

17. Strong, *The New Strong's Exhaustive Concordance*, ref. no. 4049.

18. Zodhiates, *Hebrew-Greek Key Study Bible*, p. 1796.

19. Ibid.

20. Gordon Lindsay, *The New John G. Lake Sermons* (Dallas: Christ for the Nations, Inc., 1979), pp. 29–30.

21. Strong, *The New Strong's Exhaustive Concordance*, ref. no. 7218.

22. Joseph Henry Thayer, *A Greek-English Lexicon of the New Testament* (Grand Rapids, MI: Baker Book House, 1977), p. 240.

23. Hayford, *Prayer Is Invading the Impossible*, p. 140.

24. Bullinger, *A Critical Lexicon and Concordance*, p. 731.

Chapter 10: Most High Man

1. Spiros Zodhiates, *The Complete Word Study Dictionary* (Iowa Falls, IA: Word Bible Publishers, 1992), p. 816.

2. James Strong, *The New Strong's Exhaustive Concordance of the Bible* (Nashville, TN: Thomas Nelson Publishers, 1990), ref. no. 575.

3. Craig Brian Larson, *Illustrations for Preaching and Teaching* (Grand Rapids, MI: Baker Books, 1993), p. 98.

4. Zodhiates, *The Complete Word Study Dictionary*, p. 1464.

5. Ibid., p. 1463.

6. Strong, *The New Strong's Exhaustive Concordance*, ref. no. 1994.

7. Ibid., ref. no. 1124.

8. Ibid., ref. no. 3056.

9. Spiros Zodhiates, *Hebrew-Greek Key Study Bible—New American Standard* (Chattanooga, TN: AMG Publishers, 1984; revised edition, 1990), p. 1718.

10. W. E. Vine, *The Expanded Vine's Expository Dictionary of New Testament Words* (Minneapolis, MN: Bethany House Publishers, 1984), p. 125.

11. Strong, *The New Strong's Exhaustive Concordance*, ref. no. 5188.

12. Ibid., ref. no. 5187.

13. Larson, *Illustrations for Preaching*, p. 134.

14. Strong, *The New Strong's Exhaustive Concordance*, ref. no. 1415.

15. Ibid., ref. no. 2507.

16. Walter Bauer, *A Greek-English Lexicon of the New Testament* (Chicago: The University of Chicago Press, 1979), p. 386.

17. Strong, *The New Strong's Exhaustive Concordance*, ref. no. 2192.

18. Zodhiates, *The Complete Word Study Dictionary*, p. 923.

19. Strong, *The New Strong's Exhaustive Concordance*, ref. no. 5313.

20. Bauer, *A Greek-English Lexicon*, p. 851.

Chapter 11: The Lightning of God

1. Spiros Zodhiates, *Hebrew-Greek Key Study Bible—New American Standard* (Chattanooga, TN: AMG Publishers, 1984; revised edition, 1990), p. 1846.

2. Craig Brian Larson, *Illustrations for Preaching and Teaching* (Grand Rapids, MI: Baker Books, 1993), p. 133.

3. Ibid., p. 72, adapted.

4. Joseph Henry Thayer, *A Greek-English Lexicon of the New Testament* (Grand Rapids, MI: Baker Book House, 1977), p. 422.

5. James Strong, *The New Strong's Exhaustive Concordance of the Bible* (Nashville, TN: Thomas Nelson Publishers, 1990), ref. no. 7931.

Chapter 12: The Substance of Prayer

1. James Strong, *The New Strong's Exhaustive Concordance of the Bible* (Nashville, TN: Thomas Nelson Publishers, 1990), ref. no. 3115.

2. Dick Eastman, *No Easy Road* (Grand Rapids, MI: Baker Book House, 1971), pp. 96–97.

3. Craig Brian Larson, *Illustrations for Preaching and Teaching* (Grand Rapids, MI: Baker Books, 1993), p. 245, adapted.

4. Eastman, *No Easy Road*, pp. 97–98.

5. Larson, *Illustrations for Preaching*, p. 114.

6. Joseph Henry Thayer, *A Greek-English Lexicon of the New Testament* (Grand Rapids, MI: Baker Book House, 1977), p. 38.

7. Jack W. Hayford, *Prayer Is Invading the Impossible* (South Plainfield, NJ: Logos International, 1977; revised edition, Bridge Publishing, 1995), p. 55, 1977 edition.

8. Thayer, *A Greek-English Lexicon*, p. 14.

9. Gordon Lindsay, *Prayer That Moves Mountains* (Dallas: Christ for the Nations, Inc., revised 1994), p. 43.

10. Thayer, *A Greek-English Lexicon*, p. 422.

11. Paul E. Billheimer, *Destined for the Throne* (Fort Washington, PA: Christian Literature Crusade, 1975), p. 107.

12. Strong, *The New Strong's Exhaustive Concordance*, ref. no. 4057.

13. Ibid., ref. no. 5228.

14. Ibid., ref. no. 2596.

15. Larson, *Illustrations for Preaching*, p. 177, adapted.

Chapter 13: Actions That Speak and Words That Perform

1. Cindy Jacobs, *The Voice of God* (Ventura, CA: Regal Books, 1995), pp. 251–253.

2. Sue Curran, *The Praying Church* (Blountville, TN: Shekinah Publishing Company, 1987), p. 140.

3. Elizabeth Alves, *Becoming a Prayer Warrior* (Ventura, CA: Renew Books, 1998), pp. 167–210.

4. Spiros Zodhiates, *Hebrew-Greek Key Study Bible—New American Standard* (Chattanooga, TN: AMG Publishers, 1984; revised edition, 1990), p. 1861.

5. R. Laird Harris, Gleason L. Archer Jr., and Bruce K. Waltke, *Theological Wordbook of the Old Testament* (Chicago: Moody Press, 1980; Grand Rapids: William B. Eerdmans Publishing Co., revised edition, 1991), p. 158.

6. Ibid., p. 118.

7. Ibid., p. 793.

8. James Strong, *The New Strong's Exhaustive Concordance of the Bible* (Nashville, TN: Thomas Nelson Publishers, 1990), ref. no. 4834.

9. Adapted from a message by Pastor Tim Sheets, Middletown, Ohio.

10. Ibid.

11. Dick Eastman, *The Jericho Hour* (Orlando, FL: Creation House, 1994), pp. 10–11, adapted.

Chapter 14: The Watchman Anointing

1. Craig Brian Larson, *Illustrations for Preaching and Teaching* (Grand Rapids, MI: Baker Books, 1993), p. 59, adapted.

2. Cindy Jacobs, *Possessing the Gates of the Enemy* (Grand Rapids, MI: Chosen Books, 1991), pp. 21–22, adapted.

3. Quin Sherrer with Ruthanne Garlock, *How to Pray for Your Family and Friends* (Ann Arbor, MI: Servant Publications, 1990), p. 127.

4. James Strong, *The New Strong's Exhaustive Concordance of the Bible* (Nashville, TN: Thomas Nelson Publishers, 1990), ref. no. 8104.

5. Ibid., ref. no. 5341.

6. Ibid., ref. no. 6822.

7. C. Peter Wagner, *Prayer Shield* (Ventura, CA: Regal Books, 1992), pp. 66–73.

8. Ibid., p. 180.

9. Ibid., p. 177.

10. Sherrer with Garlock, *How to Pray for Your Family*, pp. 152–153, adapted.

11. Spiros Zodhiates, *Hebrew-Greek Key Study Bible—New American Standard* (Chattanooga, TN: AMG Publishers, 1984; revised edition, 1990), p. 1752.

12. Ibid., p. 1787.
13. Sherrer with Garlock, *How to Pray for Your Family*, p. 95, adapted.
14. C. Peter Wagner, *Breaking Strongholds in Your City* (Ventura, CA: Regal Books, 1993), pp. 176–177.
15. Strong, *The New Strong's Exhaustive Concordance*, ref. no. 2275.
16. Larson, *Illustrations for Preaching*, p. 12, adapted.

Bibliography

Alves, Elizabeth. *Becoming a Prayer Warrior*. Minneapolis, MN: Chosen Books, 1998, reissued 2016.

Bauer, Walter. *A Greek-English Lexicon of the New Testament*. Chicago, IL: The University of Chicago Press, 1979.

Billheimer, Paul. *Destined for the Throne*. Minneapolis, MN: Bethany House, 1975, revised edition 1996.

Bosworth, F. F. *Christ the Healer*. Minneapolis, MN: Chosen Books, 1973, revised edition 2008.

Bromiley, Geoffrey W. *Theological Dictionary of the New Testament, Abridged*. Grand Rapids, MI: William B. Eerdmans Publishing Co., 1985.

Brown, Francis, S. R. Driver, and Charles A. Briggs. *The New Brown-Driver, Briggs-Gesenius Hebrew and English Lexicon*. Peabody, MA: Hendrickson Publishers, 1979.

Bullinger, Ethelbert. *A Critical Lexicon and Concordance to the English and Greek New Testament*. Grand Rapids, MI: Zondervan Publishing House, 1975.

Canfield, Jack, and Mark Victor Hansen. *Chicken Soup for the Soul*. Deerfield Beach, FL: Health Communications, Inc., 1993.

The Consolidated Webster Encyclopedic Dictionary. Chicago, IL: Consolidated Book Publishers, 1954.

Curran, Sue. *The Praying Church*. Blountville, TN: Shekinah Publishing Company, 1987.

Eastman, Dick. *The Jericho Hour*. Orlando, FL: Creation House, 1994.

———. *No Easy Road*. Minneapolis, MN: Chosen Books, 1971, 30th anniversary edition, 2003.

Gordon, S. D. *What It Will Take to Change the World*. Grand Rapids, MI: Baker Book House, 1979.

Harris, R. Laird, Gleason L. Archer Jr., and Bruce K. Waltke. *Theological Wordbook of the Old Testament*. Chicago, IL: Moody Press, 1980; Grand Rapids, MI: William B. Eerdmans Publishing Co., revised edition, 1991.

Hayford, Jack. *Prayer Is Invading the Impossible*. South Plainfield, NJ: Logos International, 1977; revised edition, Bridge Publishing, 1995.

Jacobs, Cindy. *Possessing the Gates of the Enemy*. Minneapolis, MN: Chosen Books, 1991, 3rd edition, 2009.

———. *The Voice of God*. Minneapolis, MN: Chosen Books, 1995, 2004.

Keil, C. F., and F. Delitzsch. *Commentary on the Old Testament, Volume 1*. Grand Rapids, MI: William B. Eerdmans Publishing Co., reprinted 1991.

Larson, Craig Brian. *Illustrations for Preaching and Teaching*. Grand Rapids, MI: Baker Books, 1993.

Lindsay, Gordon. *The New John G. Lake Sermons*. Dallas, TX: Christ for the Nations, Inc., 1979.

———. *Prayer That Moves Mountains*. Dallas, TX: Christ for the Nations, Inc., revised 1994.

Mason, John L. *An Enemy Called Average*. Tulsa, OK: 1990.

Mathews, R. Arthur. *Born for Battle*. Robesonia, PA: OMF Books, 1978.

Murray, Andrew. *The Ministry of Intercessory Prayer*. Minneapolis, MN: Bethany House, 1981, revised 2003.

New American Standard Exhaustive Concordance of the Bible. Nashville, TN: Holman Bible Publishers, 1981.

Sherrer, Quin, and Ruthanne Garlock. *How to Pray for Your Family and Friends*. Ann Arbor, MI: Servant Publications, 1990.

The Spirit-Filled Bible. Nashville, TN: Thomas Nelson Publishers, 1991.

Strong, James. *The New Strong's Exhaustive Concordance of the Bible*. Nashville, TN: Thomas Nelson Publishers, 1990.

Thayer, Joseph Henry. *A Greek-English Lexicon of the New Testament*. Grand Rapids, MI: Baker Book House, 1977.

Vine, W. E. *The Expanded Vine's Expository Dictionary of New Testament Words*. Minneapolis, MN: Bethany House, 1984.

Wagner, C. Peter. *Breaking Strongholds in Your City*. Shippensburg, PA: Destiny Image, 1993, reissued 2015.

———. *Prayer Shield*. Minneapolis, MN: Chosen Books, 1992, reissued 2014.

Wilson, William. *Old Testament Word Studies*. Grand Rapids, MI: Kregel Publications, 1978.

Zodhiates, Spiros. *The Complete Word Study Dictionary*. Iowa Falls, IA: Word Bible Publishers, 1992.

———. *Hebrew-Greek Key Study Bible—New American Standard*. Chattanooga, TN: AMG Publishers, 1984; revised edition, 1990.

Scripture Index

Genesis

1 66, 136, 138–39, 141
1:1–2 137, 150
1:26 33
1:26–28 31
1:27 32
2:7 136
2:15 32, 271, 272
3:1 271
3:5 195
3:15 67, 169
3:24 272
9:25 283
15:16 225, 281
18:20–21 281
18:22–33 281
28:10–17 113, 121
30:31 272
32:22–32 173
32:27 174

Exodus

14:21 245
17:6 245
17:8–13 173
17:9–13 245
19:16 204
32:9–14 281–82

Numbers

10:35 167, 214
35:28 284

Deuteronomy

6:7 92
32:10–18 140, 150
32:18 139–140
32:41 205

Joshua

1:3 85
6 164
6:6 214
6:16 167
9–10 81
10:22–27 82, 87
14:15 284
19 89–90

Judges

1:24 277
7:20 167
8:21 66, 154
15:12 66

1 Samuel

4:4 214
13:8–14 164–65

22:11–19 154
22:17–18 66
26:15 272
28:2 272

2 Samuel

1:11–16 154
1:15 66
5:24 164
6:12–19 214
11:16 277
18:27 268
23:8–12 218

1 Kings

2:25–46 66
17:21 228
18 37, 41, 149, 228
18:1 37, 228
18:41–45 134
18:45 144

2 Kings

5:10–14 247
13:14–19 168, 246

2 Chronicles

7:14 282
20:1–30 165
32:21 174

Nehemiah
4:14 198

Job
6:25 252
9:32–33 47
15:7 139
22:28 252
36:32 202
39:1 139
41:11 39

Psalm
2:4 66
2:8 124
2:9 169
3:7 59
8:3–8 31
8:5 33
18:13–14 205, 209
18:14 206
22:3 165
22:31 66
23:4 78
27:1 206
27:3 285
27:14 161
29:3 209
29:7 205
33:20 161
37:7, 9, 34 162
42:2 161
46:6 203
50:10–12 39
56:8 234
62:1–2 161
63:1 161
68:1 167, 214
68:2 203
77:17–18 206
78:48 206
85:10 61
87 143
90:2 138–139
91 92, 271
91:1 94
91:3 101
97:3–4 206
97:5 203
103:12 73

107:20 252
110 83–84, 87, 282
110:1 84
110:2 168
110:2–3 84
115:16 32
119:18 182
126:5–6 135
127:1 272, 281
144:6 206
149:5–9 165

Proverbs
3:5–6 96
4:23 272
14:34 281
17:12 65
21:22 282
22:6 92

Ecclesiastes
9:15 282
12:3 272
12:11 252

Isaiah
1:8 277
1:19 91
21:6–8 267
28:6 175
40:1–5 243
40:31 162
53 73
53:5 67
53:6, 12 73
53:11 146
55:11 250
56:10 254
60:1–3 209, 214
61:1 67
62:6 268
63:3 85
66:7–8 135, 137, 143
66:8 141
66:8 139

Jeremiah
1:10 240, 249
2:13 78

4:16–17 277
6:18–19 248
8:22 78
17:13 78
22:29 248
29:7 281
31:28 249
51:12 268, 277

Ezekiel
1:14 204
21:9–10, 15, 28 205
22:30–31 40
28:12 281
33:11 40
37:1–10 240, 253, 285
37:9–10, 14 136–137

Daniel
9 38
9:3 39
10:12 39
10:13 281

Hosea
4:6 264
6:5 250

Joel
3:16 80

Amos
1:2 80

Jonah
1:2 281
3:5–10 281

Micah
1:2 249
6:9 281

Nahum
3:1 281

Habakkuk
3:4 202

Zechariah

4:6 117
4:7 167

Malachi

3:8–12 91

Matthew

6:6 94
6:10 36
6:11 36
7:5 184
9:38 36, 124
13:23 251
14:17–19 50
16:18 175
16:18–19 170
16:19 68, 158
16:24–26 174
17:5 141
17:14–21 227
17:20 91, 223
21:21 91
24:12 225
26:36–39 135
26:38 146
27:3–5 128
27:50 167
27:51 66
27:52–53 67
27:54 66–67
28:18 67

Mark

6 226
6:5 226
6:5–6 281
8:18 264
11:22–24 91
11:23 223
11:25–26 92
14:34, 38 265
16:15–18 213
16:17 158
16:18 223

Luke

1:34–35 136
1:35 141, 150

2:9 204
4:6–7 35
4:13 95
4:14, 18 136
4:18 193
8:13 95
9:23–25 174
9:29, 32 204
10:18–20 207
10:19 83, 158, 172
10:40 162
10:42 163
11 221
11:5–13 221, 237
11:8 221
13:16 112
18:1 112
19:41–44 281
21:36 265
22:31–32 96

John

1:1–3 138
1:4–5 208
1:5 210
1:18 47
3:3–8 136
5 126
5:39 182
6:63 183
7 224
7:38 131, 223
7:39 224
8:31–32 251
9:6–7 246
11:33–44 135, 145
12:31 35
14:1–4 127
14:10 51
14:26 110
14:30 35
15:3 251
15:7 92
15:13 225
16:11 35
16:26 48
17:12 267
19:30 66
20:21 51

Acts

1:8 136
2:1–4 137
4:33 225–226
5:15 141, 144
10:38 136
12:1 96
16:16–36 165
17:24–25 39
19:23 96
19:28 281
20:28–31 269
26:18 181, 198
27:41 67

Romans

1:16 249
5:20 231
6:4, 6 76
8 119
8:22–25 136
8:26 112, 117
8:26–27 121, 135
8:26–28 110, 114, 296
8:31 285
10:17 92
12:3 225
12:15 71
15:1–3 73, 77–78
16:20 83, 158

1 Corinthians

2:14 183
3:16 213, 223
6:19 223
10:6, 11 85
11:7 33
15:27 83
16:13 265

2 Corinthians

2:11 155, 175, 263, 286
3:6 79
3:7 204
3:18 34
4:3 198
4:3–4 178–179, 181, 195

4:4 179, 180, 185, 187
4:6–7 214
5:7 25
5:18–19 50, 62
5:21 73
6:1 175
9:8 225
10:3–5 187, 195
10:4 85, 96, 158, 179
10:5 193, 196
11:3 160–161
12:9 118

Galatians
4:19 136–137, 144, 148
5:22 218
6:2 24, 71, 73, 77–78
6:9 22, 222

Ephesians
1:18 1801:22 83
2:6 83
3:20 231
3:20–21 230, 237
3:21 210
4:2 72, 77
5:8 209
5:31–32 59
6 158–159, 176
6:10–20 158
6:12 96, 155, 158
6:13–18 92
6:16 172
6:17 204, 223
6:18 96, 104, 262–263, 265, 286

Philippians
1:9 225

Colossians
1:13 172
1:16 138

1:24 77
2:15 82, 172
3:13 72, 77
4:2 265

1 Thessalonians
2:18 156

2 Thessalonians
3:1 36

1 Timothy
2:5 48–49
2:9 221
6:12 169
6:16 204

2 Timothy
2:3–4 158

Hebrews
1:3 203
3:1 47
4:12 205
4:15 78
4:16 174, 221
5:7 220
6:2 223
6:12 91
6:18 284
9:22 146
10:12 77
11:11 140
12:12 143
12:24 78
12:29 203

James
1:5 24
1:6–7 91
1:17 204

3:1 273
3:15 194
4:7 92, 152, 158
5:16 135, 231, 237
5:16–18 228
5:17–18 37, 38

1 Peter
1:23 251
2:4–10 143
2:9 210
2:24 67
3:19 67
4:6 67
5:8 92, 172, 263, 265, 276, 286
5:9 158

2 Peter
2:1–2 269
3:10, 12 67

1 John
1:5 203
2:1 48
3:8 67
5:14 175
5:19 198

Revelation
2–3 281
2:2 269
2:12 281
2:16 205
4:5 204
5:8 232
8:3–5 233
8:5 206
11:19 206
16:18 206
19:15 85, 205
21:23 204
22:1–2 224

Subject Index

abide, 92, 94, 182, 214
abortion, 255–256, 280
Abraham, 112, 114, 140–141, 147, 225, 281, 284
Acapulco, 107
adam, 30–31
Adam, 30–35, 41, 46–47, 146, 172, 181, 195, 202, 272
  first, 47, 60
  last, 47, 60
Advocate, 48, 110
Africa, 116–117, 160, 219
agathos, 163–164
agnoeo, 155
agnostic, 155
agrupneo, 265
Ahab, 37, 134, 164, 228
Ahimaaz, 268
Alaska, 179
Alves, Beth, 247, 251, 274, 299
Amalek, 173, 245
ambassador(s), 41, 51–52, 55
Amorites, 281
anaideia, 116, 221
Anderson, Mike, 79
Anderson, Pam, 80
Anderson, Toby, 79–80
anechomai, 72, 74, 82

angel(s), 39, 113, 134, 141, 173–174, 191, 204, 206, 222, 228–229, 232–234, 272, 275
angel of light, 209
anoint(ing), 80, 129, 132, 142, 145, 162, 164, 218, 224, 226, 233–235, 242–244, 257
  bear, 65–66
  boomerang, 243–244
  butterfly, 115–122
  lightning, 209–212
  Thomas, 126–127
  watchman, 259–286
apathy, 93, 236
apekduomai, 172
apokalupsis, 178
apostle, 24, 47, 213, 225, 269
Ark of the Covenant, 167, 214–215
armor, 92, 172, 197, 274
army, 81–84, 103, 167, 173–174, 282
asah, 66
Astaire, Fred, 22
astheneia, 111
attorney(s), 46, 47
awesomites, 54–55

baseball, 58, 60, 70, 72
bastazo, 72–74, 78, 80, 82, 84
Battle Hymn of the Republic, The, 85

bear (noun), 65
bear(ing) (verb), 71–77
Becoming a Prayer Warrior (Alves), 251, 274, 299
bending the bow, 84
Berlin, 253
Berlin Wall, 142, 253–254
Bethel(s), 113–114, 120–121
Bethsaida, 281
Bible college, 57, 156
Billheimer, Paul E., 229, 293–294, 299, 301
birth(ing), 129–135, 138, 143, 149, 183, 224, 229
  agent, 136–142
  prayer, 37, 124, 130, 135–136, 145
bodybuilder, 160
bodyguard, 273, 277
boomerang, 243–244
boundary(ies), 90
  building, 277
  prayer, 96, 102
  protective, 96, 102
Bounds, E. M., 30
bounty hunters, 285
Bourbon Street, 165, 211
bowls (of prayers), 232–234, 286
Brant, Derek, 239
Breaking Strongholds in Your City (Wagner), 300, 303
Breakthrough (Mulligan), 279
bring(ing) forth, 114, 130, 135, 138–139, 144, 147
brood(ing), 138, 140–143
Brooks, Hap, 103
Brother Wonderful, 151–152
Brown, Charlie, 71
Buckingham Palace, 241
bull's-eye, 114
Bullinger, 156, 295, 297, 301
butterfly, 115–117, 121, 210, 212, 296

Caleb, 284
Calvary, 51, 60, 65–66, 69–70, 147, 153, 168, 210, 252, 276, 294
Canaanite, 81
Capernaum, 281
Capitol building, 256–257

captain, 164, 185, 186
Carlsbad Caverns, 208
Carter, Gary, 211
cast(ing) down, 193, 197, 207
cast(ing) out, 118, 158, 170, 213, 227
cause and effect, 91, 157
cesarean section, 177
chakah, 161
chayil, 84
cheetah, 219
childbirth
  natural, 124
  supernatural, 124–149
Christ for the Nations, 101, 211, 218, 222, 297
chronos, 95–96, 105
chuwl, 138–139
Cincinnati, Ohio, 191
cities of refuge, 281, 283–284
Clemens, Roger, 210–211
Cleveland, Tennessee, 115
coma(tose), 19–21, 29, 222, 230, 234
Comforter, 110
conception of Christ, 144
confession, 47, 169, 174, 251
Confluence Park, 166
Cross, the, 58–61, 66–68, 73, 76, 84, 115, 147, 167, 169, 208–209, 215, 220
Curran, Sue, 250, 299, 302
Curupi, 282
cyst, 29, 118–120, 222, 230, 278

daily bread, 36, 94
Dallas Morning News, The, 99
Dallas, Texas, 99–100, 189, 295–298, 302
damah, 33
Daniel, 38–39, 41, 222, 228–229
darak, 84–85
David, 161–162, 164, 218
Dayton Daily News, 20
dei, 112, 116
demonic, 67–68, 153–154, 158, 229
demon(s), 96, 153, 155, 157–158, 167, 171, 179, 190, 194, 207, 211–213, 227, 229, 242
demuwth, 33
Denver, Colorado, 166

Diane, 19–22, 29
Dobson, Dr. James, 255
doorkeeper, 275
Doty, Sue, 170
doxa, 33
dream, 55, 64, 101, 109, 191, 247
dumiyah, 161
dunamis, 171–172
dunatos, 188

earthquake, 29, 52, 104, 206, 233, 261
Eastman, Dick, 219, 253, 298–299, 302
Eaton, Ohio, 94
echo, 156, 192, 224
Elijah, 37–39, 41, 134, 137, 144, 149–
    150, 227–228, 233
Emmanuel, 165
England, 239–242
English class, 43
enlighten(ed)(ment), 156, 170, 177, 180–
    181, 188, 197–198, 244, 274, 278
Ephesus, 281
epilambanomai, 169
episkiazo, 141, 149
epistrepho, 181
Esau, 113, 174
Europe, 22, 142, 166
Eve, 195, 272
Every Home for Christ, 253
exegeomai, 47
exousia, 172
Ezekiel, 295, 240, 253, 285

Fall, the, 44–46, 48, 56, 181–182, 186,
    194–195, 198, 272
fig tree, 249
food court, 259
Fort Worth, Texas, 93
fortresses, 179, 187, 189, 278
free will, 91, 157, 279
Freemasonry, 282
frogs, 217

Gabriel, 39, 50
galah, 182
Garden of Eden, 32, 60, 271–272
Garden of Gethsemane, 60, 135,
    146–147, 229

Garlock, John, 218
Garlock, Ruthanne, 270, 275, 279,
    299–300, 302
gatekeeper, 268, 275, 277
Germany, 143, 253–254
Gibeonites, 81–82
Gideon, 167, 285
go(ing) between (noun), 32, 47
    (verb), 45–46, 48–49
God-man, 47
Goliath, 211–213, 285
Gomorrah, 281
Gooden, Dwight, 211
Gordon, S. D., 29, 75, 250, 295, 302
governing principles, 91–93
graphe, 182
greater portion, 156, 263, 267, 278–279
gregoreuo, 264
Guatemala, 51–52, 54, 62–63, 68, 102–
    103, 151, 153, 261
Guatemala City, 103–104
Guatemalan airlines, 103

Haiti, 213
Harvest Christian Fellowship, 255
Hayford, Jack, 41, 153–154, 170, 294–
    298, 302
headship, 49, 169, 171–172, 192, 210
Hebron, 283–284
Helper, 110, 114, 121
hematidrosis, 146
High Priest, 47, 74, 78, 284
high thing, 195
high-minded, 185
holy of holies, 213–214, 216, 223
homologia, 251
Hoshea, 82
How to Pray for Your Family and
    Friends (Sherrer & Garlock), 270,
    279, 299–300, 302
huperperissos, 231
hupsoma, 195, 197

identificational repentance, 278
Incarnation, 35
innermost being, 131, 223, 234
intercessory work, 45, 49–50, 54, 77, 87,
    146, 153, 169, 210

Isaiah, 146, 250–251
Israel, 18, 39, 41, 81–82, 85, 87, 90, 114,
    140–141, 144, 147, 149, 167–169,
    173–174, 214–215, 240, 245–246,
    281, 296

Jacob, 23, 113–114, 173–174, 247, 266,
    282, 289, 302
Jacobs, Cindy, 247, 266, 282, 299, 302
Jamaica, 79
Jed, 285
Jehoshaphat, 165
Jeremiah, 38, 249
Jericho, 94, 164, 167, 281, 299, 302
Jerusalem, 268, 281–283
Joash, 168, 246
John the Baptist, 243
Joshua, 81–82, 85, 164, 173, 175

kabowd, 33
kairos, 95–105, 171, 265–266
kalos, 163–164
kalupsis, 178
kata, 208, 231
katalambano, 208
kathairesis, 189, 192
Kevin, 139–140, 196–197
Killinger, John, 235
Kingdom Enterprises, 54
Kiriath-Arba, 284–285
koilia, 131, 223

Lake, John G., 166–167, 297, 302
Lancaster, Texas, 97
Last Days Newsletter, The, 22
law of first mention, 271
lay siege, 277–279, 282–283, 286
lay(ing) on, 83–84, 120
Lazarus, 135–136, 145, 147
Liberator, 55
lighthouse, 186
lightning, 85, 171, 201–216, 233, 298
Lindsay, Gordon, 229, 297–298, 302
Lion of Judah, 80, 86
logic, 193–194
logismos, 190–195
logos, 182
long-suffering, 218

lookouts, 267
lordship, 183, 185, 192
Lorenzo, Victor, 282
lost, the, 23, 40, 124, 128, 140, 142, 175,
    178, 187, 193, 197
Love and Faith Christian Fellowship, 191
lovingkindness, 61
lunatic, 227
luo, 67–70, 89
luwn, 94

magnifying glass, 201–202, 212
makrothumia, 218
Maple Valley, Washington, 139
marats, 252
Mardi Gras, 165, 211
Mary, 141, 191–192
Mary (nursing home), 190–192
Mary (and Martha), 162–164, 175
mashal, 31–32
Massa, Michael, 239
Master's Commission, 254–255
Mathews, Arthur, 153, 294, 296, 302
McGee, Bob, 165
mediate(d)(ing)(tion)(or), 32, 39, 45–51,
    55, 69, 77, 80, 102, 132, 146, 149,
    168, 171, 174, 178, 182, 185, 208,
    220, 228–229, 241, 275
meet(s)(ing), 46, 57–70, 79–80, 101, 104,
    114–115, 121, 128–129, 133, 141, 166,
    171, 182, 211, 233, 239–241, 255–256,
    276, 285, 287–288, 290, 294
mega, 225–226
megas, 225
Melchizedek, 282
Merchant, Celia, 57
mercy, 40, 49, 59, 61–62, 235
Messiah, 36, 243
metanoia, 181
milagro, 64
Millspaugh, Carol, 143
mindset(s), 130, 193–195
ministry of intercession, 50, 74, 78, 294,
    302
ministry of Jesus, 50–51, 62, 78, 145,
    220, 243
ministry of reconciliation, 62, 166
missionary(ies), 79, 116, 166

moaning, 144
Moffatt, 169, 194, 208
moria, 183
moron, 183
Morris, David, 240
Moses, 85, 140, 173, 245, 281
Müller, George, 219–220
Mulligan, Theresa, 279
Mummert, Gail, 97–99
Mummert, Gene, 97–99
Murray, Andrew, 24, 38, 294, 302
Murray, Pastor Mike, 191

Naaman the leper, 247
nails, 252–253
naos, 213, 223
nasa, 73, 78, 80, 84, 101
nathan, 32
National Day of Prayer, 254–255
natsar, 271
Nazareth, 226, 281
new birth, 136–137
new creation(s), 66, 137, 139
Nineveh, 281
No Easy Road (Eastman), 219, 298, 302
noema, 155, 191–192, 196–197
nomad, 264
nursing home, 20–22, 190–192

O'Hern, Marlena, 139, 196
ochuroma, 192
offense(ive), 92, 111, 159, 277, 286
Ohio, 74, 94, 104, 142, 151, 190–191,
     213, 299
Oklahoma, 89, 157
omer, 252
ovary, 29, 118, 222, 230
overshadow, 141

paga, 60, 62, 65–66, 68, 70, 73, 78,
     80, 82, 84, 87, 89–90, 93, 95–97,
     100–102, 105, 110, 113–114, 117,
     120–121, 132, 154, 165, 168–169,
     175, 190, 192, 202, 207, 212–213,
     215, 266, 286
paid in full, 66
paradoxes, 59
Parakletos, 110

paralyze(d),73, 75, 80, 82, 84, 87, 89–90,
     93, 95–97, 100–102, 105, 110, 113–
     114, 117, 120–121, 132, 154, 165,
     168–169, 175, 190, 192, 202, 207,
     212–213, 215, 266, 286
partnership, 41, 82–83, 87
Passion River, 102–109
pateo, 84
Paul, 24, 36, 67, 137, 144, 148, 156–157,
     165, 181, 213–214, 233–234, 269
people groups, 166, 193, 281, 286
Pergamum, 281
perispao, 163
Persia, 281
Peten Jungle, 102
Peter, 96, 135, 141, 144, 147, 204, 269
phantom, 33
Pharisees, 182
Philippi, 233
philosophy(ies), 194
photismos, 180
photizo, 180
photo(graph), 180–181, 198
pilot, 103, 220
pleon, 156
pleonekteo, 156
policemen, 46
Pombero, 282
pool of Bethesda, 126
pool of Siloam, 246
Popham, Eva, 190
Possessing the Gates of the Enemy (Ja-
     cobs), 266, 299
power of Christ, 54, 226–237
powers of darkness, 60, 67–69, 160, 176,
     198, 208, 210–213, 215
Prayer Is Invading the Impossible (Hay-
     ford), 153, 294, 296–298, 302
Prayer Shield (Wagner), 273, 299
prayer(s)
     cloths, 132–133
     fervent, 37, 135, 228, 231–232
     journey, 23
     meeting(s), 60, 65, 70, 133, 266, 286
     of importunity, 221, 237
     that births, 124, 130–137, 145, 149
     travailing, 37, 125, 129, 134, 144–145
prayer-walk(ing), 62, 170, 287

Praying Church, The (Curran), 250, 299
pray(ing) in the Spirit, 96–97, 111, 113,
    115–116, 118–119, 121, 149, 170
pregnant, 144
present(ing) again, 32–34, 43–56, 60, 64,
    77–78, 80, 169, 210, 252, 285, 294
present participator, 55
present participle, 43–44
pro(s), 159
pro athlete, 159
prophetic, 82, 124, 133, 241, 256, 272,
    277
    action, 240, 243–248, 254–255, 257
    declaration, 240, 243–244, 248,
        253–255, 257
    worship, 240, 243
prophets, 36–37, 227–229, 249–250, 269
protective boundaries, 89–101, 266, 275,
    277, 285, 295
pull(ing) down, 188–189, 193, 195, 278
Pulpit Digest (Woods), 208
Python spirit, 282

qavah, 161
Queen of Heaven, 282
qum, 252

rachaph, 138, 140–141, 149–150
Raphael, 219
rattlesnake, 93–94, 97
Ravenhill, Leonard, 22
re-defeat, 169
re-present(s)(ing)(ation), 31–33, 43–56,
    60, 77–78, 80, 169, 210, 252, 285, 294
read-a-thon, 256
realm
    natural, 128, 233, 244
    spiritual, 128–129, 166, 207, 226, 229,
        230, 233, 243–245
reconciliation, 45, 50, 61–62, 165–166,
    278
Reconciliation Coalition, 166
Red Sea, 245
Red Square, 247
redemption, 48–49, 146–147
Reese, Pee Wee, 72
repentance, 128, 181, 183, 198, 240–241,
    255, 278

Rephidim, 245
Resistencia, Argentina, 282–283
revival, 29–30, 38, 64, 142, 242–243,
    254–257, 281
river, 224–226, 229–232, 234
Robinson, Jackie, 72
rosh, 169
royal priesthood, 210
Russia, 247–248

Salzburg, Austria, 192
Sam, 285
Samuel, 164–165
San La Muerte, 282
San Pedro, Guatemala, 261
Sarah (Abraham's), 140–141, 147
Sarah (fictitious name), 183–185
Satan, 23, 35, 49, 51, 58, 66–69, 73,
    80, 82–83, 89, 92, 95–97, 101, 112,
    130, 153, 155–158, 161, 164–165,
    171–173, 175, 185, 189, 191–193,
    195–197, 207–210, 255–256, 262–
    264, 270–271, 274, 278–279
Saul, 164–165
scapegoat, 75, 87
schemes, 155–158, 162, 196, 219,
    262–264
seed, 135, 182, 195, 248, 251, 257–258,
    294
seize, 162, 169–170
self-conceit, 185
send(er), 37, 47, 51, 110, 116, 135, 185,
    194, 206, 215, 228–229, 233, 250,
    255–256
sent one(s), 51–56
sentry(ies), 265, 267, 277
separate(ing), 49, 56, 63, 84, 152, 154,
    198
serpent, 34, 58, 60, 83, 121, 160, 165,
    169, 172, 192, 271–272, 277
shadow(s), 33, 85, 94, 102, 105, 141
shakan, 214
shamar, 32, 271
shamelessness, 221
shatter(ing), 59, 98, 169
Sheets, Ceci, 107, 118–120, 123–134,
    254, 260–261
Sheets, Dean, 213

Subject Index

Sheets, Dutch, 44, 48, 57, 79, 81, 119, 123, 131–134, 171, 179, 211, 240, 256
Sheets, Hannah, 123, 259–260
Sheets, Sarah, 123, 259
Sheets, Tim, 74
shekinah, 214, 299, 302
Sherrer, Quin, 270, 275, 279, 299–300, 302
ship, 95, 185
shop(ping), 179, 259–260
Sidon, 281
Silas, 165
Simchen, David and Polly, 131, 234, 278
Simchen, Jonathan, 131–134, 235
Sims, Sandra, 190–192
sin(ned)(s)(ners), 33, 38, 40, 48–49, 59, 61, 73–78, 80, 108, 132, 145–147, 180, 184–185, 203, 208, 225, 236–237, 242, 281
Skywalker, Luke, 205
slain in the Spirit, 128, 250
smoke screen, 185
Sodom, 281
soldier(s), 82, 158, 212, 214, 245, 270
Son, 31, 48, 55, 61, 66–67, 172, 182, 202, 205, 215, 220, 253, 265
South Africa, 166
sovereign(ty)(ly), 28, 30, 35, 40, 62, 90, 98, 113–114, 263
sowing and reaping, 91, 157, 252, 279
speiro, 251
spinal cord, 64
Spirit-Filled Bible, The, 295, 302
spiritual
  attributes, 22
  authority, 240
  experiences, 127–129
  explanation, 102, 228
  giant, 16
  happening, 129–130
  Israel, 141, 147
  jargon, 24
  Laws, 247
  leaders, 255
  life, 124, 136, 147
  mapping, 278, 282–283
  person, 45
  power(s), 129, 167, 182, 282

principles, 118
realm, 207, 243
reproduction, 136
traits, 218
travail, 128–129, 144
warfare, 23, 61, 68, 84, 96, 119, 124, 133, 153–154, 158–159, 163, 167–168, 176, 178, 187, 195, 249, 263, 270, 274, 283, 287
weapons, 169, 189
womb, 228–229
Spokane, Washington, 254
Spurgeon, Charles, 22
Star Wars, 205
Stephenson, Jean, 166
sterility, 137
Steven, 75–76
steward, 32
sting of death, 59
Stone, Norm, 255
storm, 67, 151, 175, 209, 249, 276
Straarup, Al, 163
strike down, 154
strike the mark, 201–202, 207, 286
strongholds, 30, 145, 166, 179, 187–189, 193, 195–198, 278, 282–283, 300, 303
suicidal, 148
sunantilambanomai, 117
Sunderland, Lew, 239, 242
superabundant, 231
surgery, 19, 64, 118
sword, 85, 168, 204–205, 212, 216, 218, 221, 223–224, 249
  lightning, 210–211, 215
symbol(ic)(ize)(ism), 37, 74, 80, 85, 149, 159, 207–208, 232, 245, 257, 267–268, 286

taking hold of together with against, 117–121
tarasso, 145
teenagers, 30
temple, 213–214, 223
tetelestai, 66
thanatos, 146–147
theater, 170
theology, 24, 33, 54, 125, 130, 151, 203, 248, 263

theories, 194
Thomas, 126–127
Tibet, 49
tied to tree(s), 52–53, 55–56, 68
Timothy, 169
tithe, 91
tohuw, 137, 140, 147
tongues, 111, 117
tornado, 98–99
tracheostomy, 19
Transfiguration, 141
travail(ed)(ing), 37, 124–130, 134–140,
    143–150, 222, 228
tread(s)(ing) upon, 27, 82–85, 158, 163,
    172, 205
trespassers, 89
tsaphah, 271
tselem, 33
tuberculosis, 63
Tulsa, Oklahoma, 157, 293
tuphloo, 185
tupho, 185
Tyre, 281

uncovering, 178
uniting, 49, 61, 153
unveiling, 178–179, 181

vain repetition, 229
Valley of Dry Bones, 253
veil, 177–184
victory of Calvary (Cross), 51, 65, 69,
    153, 252, 294
violent(ce), 58, 66–67, 69, 84, 154,
    166–168, 189–190, 192
Voice of God, The (Jacobs), 247

Wagner, Peter, 40, 273–274, 282, 294,
    299–300, 303
wait(ed)(ing), 22, 38, 40, 50, 63, 77,
    83–84, 86, 96, 99, 121, 126, 133, 150,
    160–165, 175, 213, 215, 221–222,
    227, 241, 260, 266, 277, 279, 288
walls of protection, 94, 99, 277

war, 66, 84–85, 94–96, 154, 156, 158,
    170, 187, 189, 192–193, 198, 205,
    207–208, 213, 270, 280
warfare, 23, 39, 61, 68, 84–85, 96,
    119, 124, 133, 153–154, 158–160,
    162–168, 170–171, 173, 175–178,
    187–189, 195, 214, 249, 263, 270,
    274, 283, 287
Washington, D.C., 254–255
watchman(men), 32, 34, 259–286, 299
weakness(es), 73, 77–78, 82, 86, 101,
    110–111, 113, 116–118, 121, 135, 278
weapons, 85, 96, 101, 158, 160, 169,
    187–189, 192–193, 196, 198
Webster's Dictionary, 138
Wesley, John, 29
Westminster Chapel, 241
What It Will Take to Change the World
    (Gordon), 295
wheelchair, 68
widow's son, 227
window of opportunity, 95
witch doctor, 69
without form, 137
wolves, 268–269
womb, 84, 131, 141, 223–225, 228–230,
    236
Women's Aglow, 247
Woods, Bob, 208
word
    living, 182
    written, 182
work of intercession, 45, 49–50, 54, 68,
    77, 87, 146, 153, 169, 210
wrestle(d), 96, 154–155, 158, 176
wrestler, 151, 153, 155, 157, 159–160,
    173, 175
Wuest, 169, 204, 208, 231

yalad, 138–140
yaresh, 162
yashab, 94

Zerubbabel, 167
Zion, 80, 84, 135, 139, 143, 168

AUTHORITY
IN
PRAYER

PRAYING WITH

POWER AND PURPOSE

"We live in perilous times! The vigilant parent, pastor, or politician is aware that God's purposes in their lives will be challenged over and over again. Praying with authority is a necessary part of your dominion tool kit. More than a manual for effective prayer, Dutch Sheets distills a lifetime of experience and scholarship into the essentials of high-impact prayer. I began using the breakthrough concepts unveiled in this book the same day I read it. My results have been amazing—yours will be, too."

—Harry R. Jackson, Jr.
Senior Pastor, Hope Christian Church
Chairman, High Impact Leadership Coalition

"In this book, Dutch Sheets brings to the surface something that most of us will readily admit, namely that a good bit of the time we pray, we pray like wimps! Long before I came to the end of the book, I decided that I'm not going to pray like a wimp anymore—I'm going to pray like a winner! I'm thankful for this huge upgrade to my prayer life, and I know that you will be just as thrilled when you read *Authority in Prayer*."

—C. Peter Wagner
Chancellor, Wagner Leadership Institute

"This is a fantastic, funny, and life-changing book on prayer. It is one of Dutch's best. I highly recommend it."

—Ché Ahn
Pastor, Harvest Rock Church
Founder and President,
Harvest International Ministry

Contents

1. The Question   323
2. The Author   335
3. The Poet   347
4. The Assignment   359
5. The Contest   371
6. The Ekklesia   381
7. The Dynasty   397
8. The Voice   411
9. The Sword   423
10. The Heavens   435
11. The Room   447
12. The Interruption   461
13. The Levels   477
14. The Degrees   489

Epilogue: The Gains   501
Notes   513

1

The Question

A few years ago I was given a double-billed cap with one bill pointing to the left, the other to the right. The words on the front of the cap, "I'm the leader, which way did they go?" are intended to prompt the obvious question, "Who, really, is in charge?" I loved the humor in spite of the not-so-subtle and obviously asinine aspersion it cast on my leadership skills.

That question in one form or another is asked throughout the world millions of times a day. I recall the day our dog, Mercedes—she's a Boxer, so ugly she needed a classy name—tried to assert her dominance over me. She was young, and the two of us were in a season of trying to establish who would rule our house. I was lying on the floor watching a football game, and she, very ceremoniously I might add, sauntered over and sat right on my chest. She then stuck her chest out, head up, and looked disdainfully at me out of the corner of her eye, glancing proudly at everyone else in the room. Easy to interpret: *I'm in charge here; you will submit to me.* (Maybe it was because I was wearing the cap.)

Mercedes is quite large, and at that time she was already full grown. Having her plop down on me was uncomfortable, not to mention humiliating. The guffaws of my wife and daughters didn't help matters much. Of course, girls do stick together. I took authority over the situation immediately, commanding Mercedes to get off of me. As I'm sure you'd assume, she obeyed her master—and within two or three minutes promptly removed herself! I won that power struggle and have been in charge ever since.

But it is not only people and their dogs that struggle with the "Who's in charge?" question. It is at the heart of all conflict on earth. The question was born in the heart of Lucifer when he tried to sit on God's chest in heaven, and it spread to earth when he passed the question on to Adam and Eve in the Garden of Eden. Satan spewed his poisonous deception, and our foreparents also tried to sit on God's chest. We humans have been wearing a double-billed cap ever since, thinking we're in charge, all the while stumbling around, wondering which way to go. It seems that at every level and in every arena of life, power struggles occur:

- Men and women wrestle over control of relationships.
- Parents and children struggle with who will rule the house.
- Siblings quarrel over toys, clothing, TV, and a host of other issues.
- Businesses connive to corner various consumer and investment markets.
- Sports teams vie for first place.

- Democrats and Republicans strive for the domination of America.
- Leaders of nations war over control of lands, people, and wealth.

Everybody wants to be in charge! Who is ruling your world? I'm not referring to the big one, as in planet earth. At least not yet. I'm talking about the world you live in every day, your *personal* world. I'm speaking of your home, family, job, health, dog—well, okay, maybe not your dog. God doesn't intend that *any* outside force dominate you. He has given you jurisdiction over your life.

God began dealing with me a few years back about governing my world. And He wasn't referring to Washington, D.C. He was talking about the gray matter in my cranium—my thoughts as well as my house, my finances, my health, and so on. In ever-expanding circles He began to teach me about governing the world around me. God did actually want to use me to influence cities, states, and nations, and has since sent me to Washington dozens of times, to all fifty states on an amazing prayer assignment, and on numerous other prayer journeys.

I want to share with you what He has taught me. I'm certainly not implying that I have full understanding of this or any other aspect of truth. In fact, much of my learning has come through paradigm-stretching assignments and frustration-prompted questions. Desperation often births inspiration, like the day at the airport . . .

I was about to break out in hives I was so tense. It was during a prayer tour to all fifty states that Chuck Pierce and I conducted in 2003–2004.[1] I left my home early, as I frequently did, to fly to another state where I would speak and lead large prayer gatherings that evening and the following morning. That day I wasn't flying my normal airline with which I had special "go to the short line, receive preferential treatment, and get your upgrade" status.

As I stood in the long "NO preferential treatment and NO upgrade" line of this other airline, things became more chaotic by the minute. I don't know if the employees were learning a new system, their computers were malfunctioning, or just what was happening. But everything was in total confusion. I wanted to pass out double-billed caps to all the workers and sit on somebody's chest!

I was already running a bit late, and after waiting twenty minutes with the line not moving, I was getting pretty uptight. My stomach was knotting up, and my anxiety level was rapidly increasing.

I wasn't the only one.

People started pushing their way to the front. Others were shouting from where they stood about not wanting to miss their flight, for the workers to hurry up, etc. And, believe it or not, the workers were beginning to become unnerved and belligerent also! I had never seen anything like it. One lady began to shout about not missing her plane and then began pushing others out of the way as she bullied her way toward the counter.

I remembered a story about my friend and Bible teacher John Dawson, who once had a frustrated and obnoxious lady behind him in an airport line. He decided to witness God's love to her by giving her his place in line. I prayed to receive the "John Dawson anointing" but it didn't work. By this time the "Dutch Sheets anointing" was too strong—she wasn't getting my position! (I'm just as Christlike as John, it's just that God has given me a more intense personality.)

My next thought was to beat her up, but I could see the headlines: "Preacher on Way to Prayer Meeting Pummels Lady in Airport." Then I took a closer look and decided I couldn't have whipped her anyway. She was big and mean—looked like someone from the WWE! We all backed out of her way as she marched forward.

By this time I had decided I would miss my flight and Chuck would have to do the meeting alone. Then in great desperation but no real faith, I decided to pray. "Lord, do something to stop this chaos and get me on my flight," I whispered.

As clearly as I have ever heard Him, the Holy Spirit responded, "You know this is all about you, don't you?"

"I didn't do anything," I replied in surprise. "Don't blame me!"

"This is all about Satan trying to hinder your assignment," I heard.

Remembering 1 Thessalonians 2:18: "We wanted to come to you—I, Paul, more than once—and yet Satan hindered us," I realized the possibility. *All this confusion and anxiety is about me and my assignment?* I thought. *No way.*

Yet I knew I was hearing the Spirit as He said, *Yes, it is.*

"Well, do something about it," I quietly whispered.

But He was trying to teach me something. *No, you do something about it. Move in the authority I have given you and command the demonic hindrances of your assignment to be ineffective. Declare that you have favor and will get to your meeting on time.*

I did as instructed and then heard, "Now, go over to your right, to the end of the counter, and wait." This ticket counter was on the end of a row next to a wide thoroughfare. I stood at the end of the counter which, naturally, ticketing agents didn't even use.

Almost immediately, though, an agent walked over and said kindly, "Can I help you, sir?"

"Yes, I'm on flight number so and so." I handed her my driver's license, she checked my luggage, gave me a boarding pass, and I was off to my gate—where I was immediately upgraded to first class!

I was pretty pumped. "Whatever you're teaching me, I sure do want to learn it," I told the Lord. "This is nice."

God has given you jurisdiction over your world—under His authority, of course. He wants you, not sin, demonic powers, negative circumstances, or any other outside force to govern it. I realize this was an extraordinary experience, and I, like Paul, have been successfully hindered a few times. Even so, God *doesn't* want the devil or any of his agents ever to sit on our chests.

The question of who's in control is a governmental issue. We often think of government only in its civil sense, but *Webster's* defines *govern* as "to direct and control; to regulate by authority; to influence; to direct; to restrain; to steer or regulate the course of; to exercise authority; to maintain the superiority."[2] *To exercise authority is to govern.* Praying with authority, therefore, is "governmental intercession." So in essence, this is a book about government—not politics, but prayer! Politicians and government officials legislate through man-made laws and rulings. We legislate through spiritual laws, principles, and activities.

One of Scripture's primary themes is governmental authority. The primary biblical struggle is over the questions "Who will rule humankind?" and "Who will rule the world?" We will see as we progress that the answer to the first determines the answer to the second—yes, in many ways the war is about you and me and who we listen to—*we* are going to help answer the question of who is in charge of the earth. In this earthly war over who is going to rule it, you and your double-billed cap are caught right in the middle!

God and the devil, opposing forces of good and evil, life and death, truth and deception, seek to govern the earth, beginning with you. The more you learn to govern your world the way God intends, the more His cause prospers. God and good will ultimately win, of course. We're promised this in Revelation 20:10: "The devil who deceived them was thrown into the lake of fire and brimstone, where the beast and the false prophet are also; and they will be tormented day and night forever and ever." But God wants to enable each of us to win over evil, governing our personal world *in the now,*

> *God and the devil, opposing forces of good and evil, life and death, truth and deception, seek to govern the earth, beginning with you.*

every day, and in every circumstance. As we learn to do this, He then needs us to join Him in His overall governing of the earth, becoming active participants in His war against evil and His fight for life. What an exciting adventure life can be!

You were actually created with a nature to rule, to govern, to exercise authority. Using *Webster's* definition of governing, you were created "to direct and control; to maintain the superiority," not be lorded over by other people, evil forces, or even unfortunate circumstances. You're an overcomer, a conqueror. Though this God-given propensity lost most of its purity at the fall, becoming infected with pride and selfish ambition (Genesis 3), nonetheless, the desire in humankind to govern its world was placed there by God.

We are descended from a king, Jesus, Creator and Lord over all, so it logically follows that deep in our DNA we have a desire and ability to rule. God speaks of this motivation in Romans 5:17: "If by the transgression of the one [Adam], death reigned through the one, much more those who receive the abundance of grace and of the gift of righteousness will *reign in life* through the One, Jesus Christ."[3]

This word *reign* means to rule as a king or queen.[4] It refers to our royal nature as sons and daughters of the Most High God. The same word is used in 1 Peter 2:9, where we're called a *"royal* priesthood,"* again referring to our ruling nature. Children of the King are always to rule and reign in the world and overcome in life. To do so, we must learn to pray with authority and govern through intercession.

In the *Pentecostal Evangel,* J. K. Gressett writes about Samuel S. Scull, who settled on a farm in the Arizona desert with his wife and children:

> One night a fierce desert storm struck with rain, hail, and high wind. At daybreak, feeling sick and fearing what he might find, Samuel went to survey their loss.
>
> The hail had beaten the garden and truck patch into the ground; the house was partially unroofed, the henhouse had blown away and dead chickens were scattered about. Destruction and devastation were everywhere.
>
> While standing dazed, evaluating the mess and wondering about the future, he heard a stirring in the lumber pile that was the remains of the henhouse. A rooster was climbing up

through the debris and he didn't stop climbing until he had mounted the highest board in the pile. That old rooster was dripping wet, and most of his feathers were blown away. But as the sun came over the eastern horizon, he flapped his bony wings and proudly crowed.[5]

Why did this emaciated rooster insist on rising above the debris to crow? Because it was his nature. His DNA was programmed to announce the beginning of a new day. True to his nature, he stuck out his bare chest and declared, "Wake up, world—a new day awaits!"

And so it is with us. Deep in our DNA is the nature of a King. He speaks to us from within our inner nature, and sometimes when we're under mounds of circumstantial rubble, "in all these things we overwhelmingly conquer" (Romans 8:37). We were made to rule!

I must say at this point, however, that I don't want this book to take on an air of religiosity. There are many religious clichés thrown around in the church, especially in charismatic circles, about "ruling and reigning," being "more than conquerors," etc. Though these expressions are biblical, and we *will* use them in this book, for many Christians they are not reality, but wishful thinking. This—words or actions without the power or substance that should accompany them—describes one meaning of *religiosity* (see 2 Timothy 3:5).

Expressions like these are often only heartwarming phrases of religious denial among Christians—stemming from a mentality that spouts slogans and verses about "overcoming," while people are actually being beaten up by circumstances and walked on by the adversary at every turn. For many believers it seems enough to simply be called an overcomer or to think of themselves as one. Christ's abundant life is for them an appealing hope, perhaps even an intent, but not actual. The tragic reality is:

- Their minds are controlled by sin and compromising thoughts.
- Their marriages fail along with those of the world around them.
- Their children grow up questioning God's reality or relevancy.
- Their businesses fail alongside those whose owners don't know God.
- They walk in very little true peace or joy, experiencing the same stressed-out lifestyle as unbelievers. (No wonder most unsaved Americans see no need for God. What difference would He make? they question.)
- They speak of prayer's power, but rarely pray; even less frequently do they see answers.
- They speak of an all-powerful God, who is "in charge" but who seems to be losing control of our nation—our schools, government, and culture as a whole.
- They glibly sing, "Come on, let's take this city . . ." but they haven't taken even one yet, at least in the U.S.

Yet off we go to our church services, week after week, learning our lingo and getting our denial fix, all the while wondering why the rest of society—and many of our children—think we live in a make-believe world of religion without reality, performance without power. Talk about a double-billed cap! *What's wrong with this picture?!*

Something has to change, and it can. Our God *is* all-powerful, and everything He has said of us is true. His promises are indeed "yea, and in him Amen" (2 Corinthians 1:20 KJV). We absolutely can reign in life and be the overcomer He intends us to be, taking charge of our personal world and changing the world around us. We don't have to allow sin, Satan, or life's circumstances to sit on our chest.

Beginning with your *private* world—your thoughts, body, actions, and ultimately your God-ordained destiny—you can take charge. Authority is yours.

Then because God established and so honors the principle of authority, He will back you as you walk in the government He has delegated to you regarding your *extended* world—your home, family, business, and possessions.

You have been offered the great privilege of helping to answer the "Who's in charge?" question for the earth.

Finally, God's plan is for you to partner with Him on the earth in broader realms of influence and authority—your *universal* world. Jesus, the sovereign King over the earth, wants to rule institutions, cultures, societies, and governments through you and your prayers. He needs you: Your choice matters and your involvement is crucial. You have been offered the great privilege of helping to answer the "Who's in charge?" question for the earth.

I want to help you take off the double-billed cap, answer the question clearly and emphatically . . . and sit on the devil's chest!

2

The Author

I don't remember her real name, but it doesn't matter because I just called her "Idiot." She was stubborn, stupid, and strong. To this day I can't forgive her. Don't judge me too severely—she was a horse.

I don't have anyone else to blame for this weeklong test of self-control—which you can already tell I passed with flying colors. The delusional idea of renting the horses for that year's elk hunt was mine. Yes, I said renting: I paid $300 for my misguided, romantic decision to relive the Old West on our annual attempt to "feed the family." I had probably just watched *City Slickers* or some great movie about taming the frontier. Anyway, back to Idiot.

"Do you have enough experience with horses to do this?" the man asked when dropping off the animals.

"Sure," I replied confidently. "All I need is for you to show me how to do that fancy little knot with those straps that hold the saddle on. It's been a while." He gave a big smile, showed me how, and was on his way. *What a friendly guy,* I thought.

The next morning we had our early coffee, dressed in our warmest clothes—it was very cold—took thirty minutes to do the fancy saddle-strap-knot, and we were off for the mountaintop. Idiot was nice on the way up.

But everything changed when we returned to the horses after several hours of hunting. With my incredible knowledge of horses, I had known we couldn't shoot from their backs; they weren't used to it and would have reacted violently. So we tied them to some bushes and wandered off. I don't think horses like being tied to bushes for several hours with nothing to eat or drink, because when we came back to ride them down the hill, they were really mad.

Idiot wouldn't stand still so I could load my gear, then she wouldn't stand still while I mounted up. Also, we were on such a steep slope that when standing on the downhill side it was hard to reach up and over her back to tie things on. And she kept moving up close to the bush, keeping it on her uphill side. Oh, she knew what she was doing, all right.

Like I said, Idiot wouldn't be still. To make matters worse, I had already untied her because the reins were so long I couldn't have reached far enough to untie them from her back. Then the real problem became evident. From the downhill side and with my thick hunting clothes hindering my mobility, I couldn't hike my leg high enough to reach the stirrup—I couldn't get on.

And Idiot was ready to go!

I was fighting her, trying to hold her long enough to mount up, when finally my brother, Tim, succeeded in climbing on

Idiot's co-worker. (For a few minutes we looked like Laurel and Hardy—or rodeo square dancers.) When Tim finally made it, his horse decided she'd had enough and took off for camp.

Idiot was not about to be left behind. So there I was, hanging on to the side of a moving Idiot, trying to climb aboard from the downhill side of Hell Mountain. One hand on the stirrup, the other holding the reins; one foot hopping off the ground, the other reaching for the stirrup.

"Stop your horse!" I yelled. "I can't get mine to stop with yours trotting."

"She won't stop!" Tim yelled back. "You're on your own."

So Idiot and I did the mountainside do-si-do for a couple hundred yards until we finally reached a level-enough grade for me to jump on. It's a good thing I'm as athletic as I am. In fact, if not for my amazing combination of intelligence and athleticism, I don't think I would have survived the ordeal.

When we finally caught up with Tim, he looked at me and said, "What an idiot."

"She sure is," I said.

He mumbled something that sounded like "not the horse." The animals were moving so fast I couldn't hear him, so I just agreed. We never could get them to slow down—they ran all the way down.

It was a humorous sight when we came crashing into camp. Guys started diving out of the way as equipment flew everywhere. "You idiot!" one of them shouted.

"I know!" I yelled back.

Nonetheless, I had the last word where Idiot was concerned. I made her stay in camp the rest of the week—wouldn't let her go hunting with me. Tim did the same with Idiot's sister. Each time we fed and watered them, Tim gave me a disgusted look and said, "Idiot."

"I know," was always my quick response. "She sure is."

He later gave me a T-shirt with the word *Idiot* on the front in big letters. "Why would I want a shirt with that horse's name on it?" I asked him.

He just rolled his eyes.

The "Who's in charge?" question centers around the concepts of power and authority. Many people don't know the difference. I do, as I demonstrated with Idiot. She had the power, but I had the authority. She exerted her power for a while, but I used my authority when I made her stay in camp.

Though many dictionaries and lexicons include "power" in their definitions for authority, strictly speaking, authority and power are not the same. Power is the "strength or force" needed to rule; authority is the "right" to do so. They are governmental twins and must operate in tandem; authority without the power to enforce it is meaningless; power exercised without authority—the right to use that power—is usurpation and is morally wrong.

Where God and Satan are concerned, the issue has never been power; it is always and only a question of authority.

Where God and Satan are concerned, the issue has never been power, including control of the earth. God is all-powerful. When Satan tried to pull off a coup in heaven, there was a flash of lightning and Satan was gone (see Luke 10:18). No battle, no time delay, no sweat or exertion on God's part—just a release of His power and glory. It is always and only a question of authority.

The same is true with us and our struggle against the kingdom of darkness. Satan didn't gain any power at the fall and didn't lose any at the cross. His power or ability didn't change at either event; his authority, or the right to use that power, *did*. In fact, though Christians often state otherwise, Scripture nowhere says that Christ delivered us from or dealt with Satan's power at Calvary. *He dealt with Satan's authority.*

The King James Version uses the Greek words *dunamis* (power) and *exousia* (authority) interchangeably, which is unfortunate and creates confusion. In Colossians 1:13, for example, it translates *exousia* as *power:* "Who hath delivered us from the power of darkness, and hath translated us into the kingdom of his dear Son." The verse should read that Christ has delivered us from the *authority* of darkness, as most other translations actually do. Likewise, in Matthew 28:18, Jesus didn't say He had been given "all power," as the KJV renders—He already had that. Christ used *exousia:* He was stating that He had taken back the authority for us that Adam had lost.

This is more than a mere technicality. If Jesus stripped Satan of his power, as some teach, then we no longer need to concern ourselves with him—he becomes a nonissue. Or if we Christians have been delivered from Satan's power, as some teach, then he can no longer affect or control us. We would be able to ignore him completely, which is precisely what many Christians do.

If on the other hand, Jesus dealt with Satan's authority— the right to use his power or abilities—then we would need to deal with him as a usurper, a rebel, a thief that has no *right* to steal, kill, and destroy but *will* if not stopped (see John 10:10). If we have been delivered from Satan's authority and given a higher authority in Christ's name, then we must exercise that authority over the devil's works and power. When we do, God's awesome power will back up our authority. Luke 10:19 refers to this—using our *authority* over Satan's *power:* "Behold, I have given you authority *[exousia]* to tread upon serpents and scorpions, and over all the power *[dunamis]* of the enemy, and nothing shall injure you."

My problem with Idiot was her power, not her authority. She was a rebellious horse, using her greater power to resist me. Though I ended up wasting my money, I really did use my authority to pen her up and keep her from harming me or further interrupting my hunt. Likewise, Jesus said we have authority ("keys") to "bind" the forces of hell (see Matthew 16:19). The term is *deo,* and means to "fasten or tie, as with a chain or cord,"[1] just as I did with the horse. The word is also used in legal circles to mean "legally or contractually binding," which obviously conveys the idea of authority. We can pray with authority, binding or tying Satan legally, and God will back us with His power. So again, what will determine victory for us is understanding and exercising authority.

Will Ford tells how the Lord used him and his wife, Michelle, to move in the authority God gave them and see death averted for Michelle's uncle:

> My wife, Michelle, had an elderly uncle who had been ill and suddenly taken a turn for the worse. The family was called in to meet with the doctor and was informed that her uncle wouldn't live to see the morning. His vital signs were shutting down. He even had the familiar "death rattle" in his voice, and it appeared to everyone that he wasn't going to be with us much longer.

My wife and I were praying at home, and just when we were about to accept what was happening to him due to his age, we both heard the Holy Spirit say her uncle's time on earth was not yet finished. We believed the Lord was instructing us to take authority over the spirit of death, and speak life to her uncle. When the two of us prayed in this manner, we felt the presence of God and His authority released through us in a powerful way. It was the first time we had experienced praying and using a clear word of knowledge from the Holy Spirit.

The next morning, to everyone's surprise, her uncle was very much alive, and totally turning around! Within three days, he was released from the hospital and eventually made a full recovery! You see, his time was not up. When he recovered, he reconciled with family members and was allowed to catch up on time he had missed out on with his daughters. Two years later, he went home to be with the Lord, but not until closure was brought into these important relationships.

This is using God-given authority to rule or legislate in prayer—here, actually stopping premature death. I know Will and Michelle very well and can attest to their understanding of spiritual authority. God has used them often in governmental intercession, not only in this situation involving their family but also in many extraordinary adventures of intercession.[2]

Before we endeavor to move forward in understanding our personal authority in Christ, however, we must first look at His ultimate authority over the earth as Creator. This is the foundation all of our governmental prayers must be built upon. I was somewhat surprised when I looked up the word *authority* in my older *Webster's* dictionary, a huge ancient one passed down from my dad—so big that I think it doubled as a weapon. At first I couldn't find *authority* in it. Puzzled, I kept looking. Then I saw it, tucked away under the various derivatives and definitions of the word *author*. The root concept behind authority is authorship, not as in writing but as in origination or creation. One has authority over what one authors. A creator determines the purpose of his creation and holds all rights to it.

God, of course, is creative—it is His nature. And how can a creator not create? So the great Creator went to work, and the first two chapters of Genesis describe the results. One verse in particular describes His pleasure over the outcome: "God saw all that He had made, and behold, it was very good" (1:31).

> *The root concept behind authority is authorship, not as in writing but as in origination or creation. One has authority over what one authors.*

That God is Author and Creator of the earth and all it contains settles the issue of ultimate authority over it. Jesus has always maintained His ownership and authority. (Again, the authority He won back at Calvary was what Adam lost, not His own.) Little wonder that Satan, through theories of macro-evolution and other forms of humanist thinking, wants to dispel belief in God as Creator, for if He is the *author* of all creation, then He has *authority* over all creation, including humankind. If He is not the creator, then authority over the earth and all it contains is up for grabs.

Bible-believing Christians know that Jesus is Author and Creator of everything and therefore has authority over all. The following New Testament verses, as well as Genesis 1–2, make clear His claims:

All things were made and came into existence through Him; and without Him was not even one thing made that has come into being. (John 1:3 AMP)

From Him and through Him and to Him are all things. [For all things originate with Him and come from Him; all things live through Him, and all things center in and tend to consummate and to end in Him.] To Him be glory forever! Amen (so be it). (Romans 11:36 AMP)

By Him all things were created, both in the heavens and on earth, visible and invisible, whether thrones or dominions or rulers or authorities—all things have been created by Him and for Him. And He is before all things, and in Him all things hold together. (Colossians 1:16–17)

Kings, dictators, other forms of human government, organizations, and even individuals may think they own the earth and therefore have complete authority over parts of it. But they do not; they are simply stewards. The earth is the Lord's and all it contains (see Psalm 24:1). Psalm 75:7 says, "God is the Judge; He puts down one and exalts another." Even the authority in which Satan operates is a limited amount conferred upon him by the decisions and actions of human beings. Like ours, in a sense, his has been delegated to him— not by God, but by the actions of people.

As already stated, Satan, through deception and man-centered thinking, has tried to convince the world that there is no Creator and, accordingly, that ownership and authority over the earth really is up for grabs.

- Educators who buy into this reasoning believe they have the right to dictate God's place and role in the process of teaching.

- Some government officials believe they have more authority than God over their jurisdiction, and that they even possess the right to dictate His role in government. (What an asinine thought. America's founding fathers knew better and stated emphatically that their authority was derived from God.)
- Entertainers and artists often believe their gifts are theirs to use as they please.
- Many individuals believe they have the right to rule their lives independent of God's authority.

The Author—the Alpha and Omega, the Beginning and End—knows He has ultimate authority over all creation. *Every aspect of every form of life on all of planet earth is owned by God, giving Him all rights of ownership.* The choice not to submit to Him, though permitted at this point in time, is rebellion. This is why God reminds us that He is the Judge who one day will hold every person who has ever lived accountable for his or her deeds (Revelation 20:11–15).

Establishing this fact that Christ is Creator and Owner—and, therefore, the ultimate authority—of all is critical if we are to truly pray with authority and legislate through intercession. Why? There are probably more, but I want to mention four reasons, then expound on each:

1. Only those who have authority can delegate it. If Christ doesn't have complete dominion over the earth, He can't give it to us.
2. Understanding Christ's ownership and authority over all the earth brings great faith to fulfill our callings and assignments, including, of course, our personal world.

3. Without Christ's true ownership of and authority over the earth, the final outcome of this battle for earth could be in doubt.
4. We must submit to Christ's authority before He will delegate His authority to us.

In the next chapter we will look at each of these individually. As we do, you will see that the great Author has written His plan for your life before you were even born. His plans for you are good (Jeremiah 29:11), He wants to relate to you as a loving Father (Romans 8:15), and He desires that you partner with Him in the greatest family enterprise history has ever known.

3

The Poet

Nikola Tesla is the scientist who invented the method of generating electricity in what we call alternating current. Many people regard him as a greater scientific genius than the better-known Alexander Graham Bell.

Philip Yancey tells an interesting anecdote about Tesla. During storms Tesla would sit on a black mohair couch by a window. When lightning struck, he would applaud—one genius recognizing the work of another.[1]

In chapter 2 we stated the importance of knowing that Christ, by rights of creation and ownership, has all authority over the earth and all it contains. We ended by listing four ways in which this understanding affects our ability to pray with authority. Let's look at these four points.

You Can't Give What You Don't Have

First, only those who have authority can delegate it. I know this is a "duh" statement, but sometimes the obvious remains hidden. If Christ doesn't truly possess all authority, then He cannot give you the absolute right to rule your world. That would mean, of course, that at times you can only be a victim. It implies that Satan, other people, or circumstances can have the right to trump your authority, dictating whether or not you'll be an overcomer in any given situation. You might believe, for example:

- Satan has the right "to steal, and kill, and destroy" you and/or yours (see John 10:10).
- You can never overcome drugs, alcohol, or another addiction that has held you captive.
- You have to endure or put up with negative circumstances or "bad luck."
- You are powerless to deal with rebellion in your children.
- Your God-given destiny is up for grabs—that other forces have the right to steal yours from you.

The reality? None of these is true. Neither you nor your family, possessions, or destiny are at the mercy of Satan, circumstances, or the world. The Author wrote the ending to your story, and no one but you has the authority to alter it. This doesn't mean everything that happens to you was planned by God. You may have indeed been victimized through abuse or other misfortune. Pain in one form or another may have entered your life. But God is not behind your misfortune. He didn't author it. He *is* the Author and Perfecter of your faith (Hebrews 12:2) and the Author of your destiny—one that

includes overcoming *every* single devastation and making
you more than a conqueror in the process (Romans 8:35–39).
However, you must agree with Him. You can change His
ending if you like, for the Author authorized *you* to write as
well. He gave you and only you the right to rewrite the ending
to your story, changing it from His to yours.

That God has authored a secure destiny for you can be seen
in one of the New Testament words translated *purpose* (see
2 Timothy 1:9; Romans 8:28). It comes from the Greek term
prothesis, which means to set forth the purpose of something
in advance. "Exposition" is a good meaning for it, as is *thesis*
(a word found in the original term). God wrote His plan—an
exposition, a thesis—about you before you were even born.
Psalm 139:16 bears this out: "Your eyes saw my substance,
being yet unformed. And in Your book they all were written,
the days fashioned for me, when as yet there were none of
them" (NKJV). You have the right to experience this destiny—
the authority to insist on it—but you must understand that
He has given you this right.

The following testimony illustrates God's ability to heal
us from the wounds of devastating circumstances:

I went through a period of my life where I wasn't sure exactly
where I fit in. My parents were divorced when I was a little girl.
No one could fully explain the who, why or when to me. All
I knew was I didn't live with Daddy or my sisters anymore.
For a long time, people told me it had nothing to do with
me. I now know that even though it really had nothing to do
with me, it still affected my life a great deal.

I searched and searched for relief from my pain. I searched
in the bottle and then I tried drugs. Still I had no relief. Yes,
the alcohol and drugs numbed my pain. But when the effects

wore off, I still had pain. Then finally on a cold Sunday afternoon in Germany in a small army chapel, I heard the voice of God say, "It's time." I remember looking around thinking someone had whispered in my ear. Then I heard the voice again and I knew in my heart that it was time to give my life to God. That was eleven years ago.

What happened to the pain? I gave it all to Jesus. The Bible says, "Cast all your cares upon him, for he cares for you" (1 Peter 5:7). He took away the deep and festering wounds of my childhood. That little lost girl is no longer; a saved and healed woman emerged out of the ashes. "Weeping may endure for a night, but joy comes in the morning" (Psalm 30:5). People often ask me why I praise the Lord the way I do. To put it simply: He gave me "beauty for ashes."[2]

What a beautiful story of God's faithfulness. For every evil intent of the destroyer of lives, God has a restorative process already planned. We have the right to receive that plan and take charge of our private world. We need not remain a victim.

Another verse confirms God having written our destiny in advance: "We are His workmanship, created in Christ Jesus for good works, which God *prepared beforehand*, that we should walk in them" (Ephesians 2:10, emphasis added). The works He prepared for you to walk in were planned "beforehand," and they are "good." The word *workmanship* is the Greek *poiéma*, which here means an end product or that which is made. From this same term come the English words *poet* and *poem*: God is the Poet, and you are the poem. Though difficult times may cause you to feel otherwise, the Poet has rhyme and reason for your life. The Author had a plan for you before you took your first breath, and no other being, human or otherwise, has the authority to steal it from you.

Even if you've made some bad decisions that have set you back, or others have done things that seem like they could rob you of your destiny, God already has a plan to remedy the situation and get you back on His course. Our English word *prosthesis* also comes from *prothesis* ("purpose"); a prosthesis is an artificial body part, intended to restore lost usefulness. The Creator has already determined how He will restore every aspect of your purpose that Satan or others have tried to destroy, even using the bad as building

The Author had a plan for you before you took your first breath, and no other being, human or otherwise, has the authority to steal it from you.

blocks. And, unlike our human prostheses, God's are not limited in their perfection or ability. This is what Romans 8:28 is speaking about: "We know that God causes all things to work together for good to those who love God, to those who are called according to His purpose."

If you're a believer in Jesus and understand this truth, you know you're never at the mercy of circumstances, fate, luck, or any negative event. Again, this doesn't mean things won't hurt us in life, and I would never minimize the very real pain you may have experienced. I'm only saying that before life dealt you the destructive blow, God had a plan to heal and restore.

At the Royal Palace of Tehran, in Iran, you can see one of the most beautiful mosaic works in the world. The ceilings and walls flash like diamonds in multifaceted reflections. Originally, when the palace was designed, the architect specified huge sheets of mirrors on the walls. When the first shipment arrived from Paris, they found to their horror that the mirrors were shattered. The contractor threw them in the trash and brought the sad news to the architect.

Amazingly, the architect ordered all of the broken pieces collected, then smashed them into tiny pieces and glued them to the walls to become a mosaic of silvery, shimmering, mirrored bits of glass.[3]

As a Christian, just like these mirrors, you can't be broken beyond God's creative ability to restore. For you, there is no such thing as irreparable damage. You can rise up in the authority He has given you and say, "No one and nothing is going to rule my life but Jesus. I may have lost a battle, but I will win the war. God sees the end result and has already written about my ultimate victory!"

- God told the Israelites they could choose life or death (Deuteronomy 30:19). So can you.
- He told New Testament believers that we could triumph through Christ (2 Corinthians 2:14).
- We are promised that we can always overcome sin and the world around us through faith in Him (1 John 5:1–5).
- Our Creator has said that he can meet our every need (Philippians 4:19).

Don't ever accept defeat again. Yes, there are conditions to each of these promises, but only we have the authority to determine whether or not we will meet those conditions. Therefore, only we have the right to determine whether or not we receive the fulfillment of every promise.

My dear friend Will Ford tells how God delivered him from an injustice. But Will had to use his authority and take charge of his private world.

Several years ago, I was in a situation where I was being forced to pay $70,000.00 that I didn't owe. I couldn't prove it due to poor record keeping, the details of which would take too long to explain. The other company was pressuring me with threats, knowing I didn't owe the money, and that I couldn't prove otherwise. It was a situation where I had all the responsibility and no authority, or so it seemed.

Depressed and fighting back suicidal thoughts and scenarios the enemy was throwing at me, I forced myself to attend a midweek revival service at a local church in town. I cried myself through praise and fought my way through worship. Having been discouraged and depressed beyond description for months, I sat in the middle of 2,000 people feeling all alone. But when the speaker came forward to speak, something unusual happened.

The evangelist walked to the pulpit but before he spoke, he peered over the crowd. Suddenly he made eye contact with me in the middle of the audience. He then leaped forward from the platform and began walking briskly toward me, without breaking eye contact. I thought, *Is he coming toward me?*

About that time, a lady sitting in front of me stood and threw up her hands, thinking he was coming to pray for her. I, too, thought he was coming to pray for her. But he politely excused her out of my way and said, "I'm sorry, but not you, Ma'am. You, Sir, step out into the aisle." He laid hands on me and prayed, and I went "out in the spirit" for about 30 or 40 minutes. It was the first time I'd experienced anything like this.

While lying on the ground I felt Christ's love coursing through me in a powerful way. With tears of joy streaming down my face, I asked the Lord why He had the evangelist single me out of the crowd. I'll never forget His response.

"William, I'll part a Red Sea to make a way for you, and I'll part a crowd of people to let you know how much I love you."

That night, my nightmare of depression, suicide and despair was broken. The moment I heard Him say this, I knew He was making a way out of "no way" for me. I've never felt that sense of hopelessness or struggled with suicide again.

And with the newfound faith and assurance God had given me regarding this matter, I found that I did have authority over this situation—in prayer! Over the next few weeks and months, I prayed and took authority over this unjust circumstance. What did God do? Eventually, the other company was investigated, audited and exposed for corruption. They later went out of business, and my "debt" was cancelled!

That is governmental prayer. God gave Will the assurance he needed, then Will had to use his faith and pray, exercising his authority. Authority released God's power, which caused the situation to change. This is how we rule our world. God will work on your behalf too as you release what He has given you and take charge of your world.

Belief and Faith Are the Same

A *second* reason we must be absolutely convinced that Christ has all authority is that if we don't, we will experience trouble walking in faith.

I recall the prayer assignment the Lord gave me in January 2000. For three years I had been going in and out of D.C. to pray. Before this visit, however, God began to show me that we, the body of Christ, had made great progress in our prayers for America. "I am now going to begin a new phase of changing the spiritual climate over America," He said to me.

It was in this meeting, in fact, that God gave me a powerful new revelation and teaching I called "The Divine Shift."[4] *This* time, I was not only praying but also speaking in a conference. Before my session, I again heard the Spirit speak: "I want you to change the atmosphere for Me, over this city and nation. Command it to shift!" I was somewhat stunned. I remember the intimidation I felt standing to the side, waiting to be introduced. Finally, in my insecurity, I said to the Lord, "I sure hope I don't mess this up."

As clearly as I have ever heard God speak, I heard Him that day. "You would have to try real hard to mess this up. Unless you totally rebel against My leadership and refuse to do what I've instructed you, *I'm going to do this!* You don't have to say or do things perfectly. Just do what I've asked you to and I'll do the rest. I need your voice, not your perfection."

Those were some of the most comforting words I've ever heard. I knew God had full authority to do this, and I knew He was authorizing me to be His instrument. I told those present what God had said, made the decree, and what happened next is impossible to fully grasp if you weren't there. God's power *filled* the room! None of the six-to-seven-hundred present doubted it. *And we could literally feel the atmosphere around us change!* It was one of the most profound experiences of my life.

Did things in D.C. and the nation subsequently change? Absolutely! Not long after, we actually heard a police officer on capitol hill say, "The atmosphere here on the hill has completely changed." A few months later The Call took place—a gathering under Lou Engle of at least four hundred thousand young people on the Washington mall to fast and pray for

America, which brought further change. Then George W. Bush was elected president, restoring righteousness—not perfection—to the White House. Everyone with any spiritual discernment knew that things began to shift spiritually over America in 2000.

We must be convinced that Christ has all authority over the earth and can use us to release it through governmental intercession! This will release us into a dimension of prayer that most of us have never dreamed of.

The End Is Certain

A *third* reason we must understand Christ's complete authority over all the earth is that otherwise we might think His opponents could ultimately win the battle for the earth. This is laughable. Humanists won't defeat Him, nor will other religions, anti-God liberals, or any other group. Psalm 2:4 says God laughs mockingly at them. As far as He is concerned, the war has never been about who will win ultimate control of the earth—it's about who will be on the winning side with Him. Revelation 11:15 gives the final outcome: "Then the seventh angel sounded; and there were loud voices in heaven, saying, 'The kingdom of the world has become the kingdom of our Lord and of His Christ; and He will reign forever and ever.'"

Those who walk in this revelation have a victorious mindset and walk in greater authority, rejecting a defeatist mindset that believes we must simply hold on as best we can while everything around us falls apart. To know in advance you're on the winning side breeds confidence, vision, and even energetic action.

Lyle Arakaki shares this insight:

In Hawaii, because of the time difference with the continental U.S., the NFL Monday Night Football game is played in midafternoon, so the local TV station delays its telecast until 6:30 in the evening.

When my favorite team plays, I'm too excited to wait for television, so I'll listen to the game on the radio, which broadcasts it live. Then, because they're my favorite team, I'll watch the game on television, too.

If I know my team has won the game, it influences how I watch it on television. If my team fumbles the ball or throws an interception, it's not a problem. I think, *That's bad, but it's okay. In the end, we'll win!*

"In this world you will have trouble," said Jesus. "But take heart! I have overcome the world" (John 16:33).

As intercessors, knowing the final outcome makes all the difference.[5]

Power Comes From Submission

A *fourth* and final reason we must understand Christ's ultimate authority is that we can never take charge of our personal world in a way God can *bless* until we do so under His lordship or authority. Most people, and far too many Christians, believe they can do as they please and still expect God to take care of them. This is a great deception. It's like trying to sit on His chest.

Scripture tells us that if we "consent and obey" we "will eat the best of the land." Listen to this verse in its full context from *The Message*:

"I'm sick of your religion, religion, religion, while you go right on sinning. When you put on your next prayer-performance,

I'll be looking the other way. No matter how long or loud or often you pray, I'll not be listening. And do you know why? Because you've been tearing people to pieces and your hands are bloody. Go home and wash up. Clean up your act. Sweep your lives clean of your evildoings so I don't have to look at them any longer. Say no to wrong. Learn to do good. Work for justice. Help the down-and-out. Stand up for the homeless. Go to bat for the defenseless.

"Come. Sit down. Let's argue this out." This is God's Message: "If your sins are blood-red, they'll be snow-white. If they're red like crimson, they'll be like wool. If you'll willingly obey, you'll feast like kings. But if you're willful and stubborn, you'll die like dogs." That's right. God says so. (Isaiah 1:14–20)

Strong, isn't it? God makes it pretty clear: Choose to obey Him, walk under His authority, and you'll receive the good and avoid the bad. Author-God loves to bless and doesn't like to condemn. Walk in His ways and "feast like kings."

Your story is waiting to jump from the pages of "God's Destiny Book" to the pages of your heart. Believe in His authority and believe in His plan. He is waiting to move you to higher authority than you ever dreamed possible, enabling you to take charge of situations through authoritative prayer.

Let's take a closer look at what the Author planned for us "in the beginning." This will give us an even firmer foundation for our authority.

4

The Assignment

We've all heard the cliché "If it ain't broke, don't fix it." But sometimes we don't fix it because we don't know it's broken. In some cases the bar has been lowered for so long that mediocre has become standard and normal has become relative. Take, for example, my life in regard to Mercedes. Normal was one thing before she came into it. It is quite another now. I am often asked if things I've written about her are true. Yes, she TP'd my yard.[1] Yes, I had to chase her around my roof one day.[2] Yes, she sat on my chest. Such things are now normal for me. Normal will never be normal again.

- She crawled into my lap the other day—was jealous of the little dogs and wanted some comfort. "Oh, how sweet," my wife, Ceci, said. Sweet? Hardly. She's ninety pounds!

- She eats me out of house and home. The other day she ate a whole cake. She has eaten steaks, burgers, chips, candy, and just about anything else you can think of that's been left below five feet.
- She drools. Let me make myself clear—she drooooooools!
- She goes to the bathroom—big time. I clean it up. She watches me . . . and laughs. No, I can't prove it, but I know she does.
- And she costs me lots of money. It started with surgery when she broke her toe. Yes, she broke her toe. Yes, the vet amputated it. Yes, I paid for it. Then she tore a tendon in her knee.

"Dogs don't tear tendons," I said to the vet. "Football players do."

"Oh yes, dogs do," he said.

"I guess it'll take a while to heal?" I said.

"It'll never heal on its own. She needs surgery" was his matter-of-fact reply.

"We'll just have to put her down," I told the family later that night. I seriously thought they were going to hurt me. "Well, maybe I could take a few more meetings, write a few more books," I offered.

She healed up nicely after surgery and has returned to "normal." I'm writing another book.

Like I said, normal is relative. So is restoration. We cannot return to normalcy until we know what it was. We, the body of Christ, speak often of restored authority, but we will never fully understand what Jesus restored to us if we don't know what we lost. Let's go back so you can move forward—*let's go back to the future* to experience what God intended as the norm for us.

God never does anything without purpose or intent. Since He knows the end from the beginning, He never has to ad-lib or figure things out as He moves along. You'll never find Him saying He is trying to "come up with" a plan for us; rather, you find Him saying, "I know the plans that I *have* for you . . . to give you a future and a hope" (Jeremiah 29:11). He starts with purpose—the end result—and backs up to design, which is the way something must be made in order to fulfill His desired purpose.

God starts with purpose—the end result—and backs up to design, which is the way something must be made in order to fulfill His desired purpose.

The prophet Isaiah actually speaks of God declaring "the end from the beginning" (Isaiah 46:10). *End* is the same Hebrew word as *future* in Jeremiah 29:11; at times it is also translated *destiny*. God knows and declares—from the beginning—what the end, future, destiny, or purpose of a person or thing will be. In Isaiah 44 and 45, the Lord declared the name and purpose of a pagan king, Cyrus, one hundred fifty years before he was even born!

Consistent with this truth, God didn't create the earth and then decide what He might do with it. From its inception He knew its purpose—*us!* We, the human race, are the reason God made the earth. It was created to be our home and domain. The Architect of the universe designed the most incredible home for us, made it, placed us on it, and put us in charge of it.

The Creator was so excited about all this that after six days of creation He planned a day of celebration. The word translated *rested* in Genesis 2:2 also means "celebrate" and could be translated as such. Have you ever wondered why God needed to rest? I don't believe He ever grows tired, and on the seventh day I believe He celebrated! He was a proud and elated Father, and He just couldn't help but celebrate this "very good" creation (1:31).

Then came our assignment. God's original intent was that this creation would be governed through humans. That's actually what the Hebrew word and name *Adam* means: "a human being (an individual or the species, mankind)";[3] it "usually refers to mankind in a collective sense."[4] Interestingly, the Hebrew term for dirt or soil is *adamah,* from the same root as Adam. God formed *adam* (humans) out of dust from the *adamah* (ground—see 2:7). We are made from the same material as our home!

So God made *adam*—humankind—and named the first one "Adam." I know, that's like naming your dog, Dog, or your daughter, Daughter. It's not that the Creator wasn't feeling quite as creative when naming the man. He was making the point that this first *adam* was the beginning of an entire race of *adams.* He was the prototype, representing all of us. We would trace our ancestry to him and receive from him our nature and inheritance. *What God intended for Adam He intended for all adams, including authority over the earthly realm.*

This is why Genesis 1:26 says God made "man" (*adam*) in His image and then said "Let *them* rule." All *adams,* the entire human race, were given authority over the earth. That's exciting! Look out, Mercedes, here I come! (Okay, I'll let it go—it's just such a big world.)

Psalm 115:16 confirms God's original intent concerning humankind's dominion mandate: "The heavens are the heavens of the Lord, but the earth He has given to the sons of men [*adam*]." This verse's "given" comes from a Hebrew word that can mean ownership but also means "to give in the sense of an assignment"; it means "to put in charge of."⁵ God was saying to us adamites, "I'll take care of the stars, planets, and galaxies; but the earth is yours—you're in charge of it." That is why James Moffat, in his translation of Scripture, renders this portion, "the earth he has assigned to men." God didn't give away ownership of the earth, but He did assign humans the responsibility of governing or stewarding it, starting with our private world and continuing to our extended and universal ones.

Why would He do such a thing? Because He wanted a family, born of His very nature, made in His image and likeness, filled with His own breath, with whom He could share His plans. God was saying, in essence, "I want a family. I'm going to create for them an incredible home—the earth—and put them in charge of it. They will manage it for Me and, of course, for themselves. All that I do down there, I will involve them in it."

What a bold and daring plan! This is unquestionably the story of the Bible: God and humans working together, for better or worse.

- See Him negotiating with a human over whether or not He'll judge a city (see Genesis 18:16–33).
- See Him waiting for a man to pray so he could send rain (see 1 Kings 18:41–46).
- See Him telling a nation they will determine whether He can bless them or whether they will receive curses instead (see Deuteronomy 27–28).
- See Him anguishing because He wants to spare a people from judgment but is unable to do so because He can't

find an intercessor to ask Him. (See Ezekiel 22:30–31; talk about honoring partnership and delegated authority!)

• See Him asking a prophet to prophesy to a nation in order that He might restore them (see Ezekiel 37:1–14).

• See Him wanting to redeem the human race but knowing that doing so while honoring His initial decision means He'll have to become one of them! (see John 1:14).

It's obvious from Scripture that God works on the earth *through humans,* not independently of them. For example, this is why, in spite of God's sovereignty, things get so messed up on earth and why at times it takes God a while to bring about the changes He wants. Also, lack of understanding of this truth is why we grow disillusioned at times, wondering why God isn't doing a particular thing He promised to do. The answer often is that He is waiting on us to do something! Understanding God's plan of partnership with us answers so many questions.

For example, I was ministering with Chuck Pierce in D.C. in October 2002, when the two snipers were indiscriminately shooting people. Over a several-week period they shot thirteen, fatally wounding ten. The trauma was overwhelming. It was pitiful to see people run to their cars, pump gas while kneeling, and, generally speaking, living lives filled with terror.

In one of our services, God gave Chuck a prophetic word that if the church would pray diligently for seventeen days, the snipers would be found.

Though many people were already praying, the prayer became more diligent and coordinated. Elements of Christ's body began to pray together and with great diligence as the Lord had instructed. *On the seventeenth day* from the prophecy, the snipers were caught. What an example of God waiting for the church to do our part to see breakthrough in the earth!

Looking at a few more definitions will reinforce God's plan of partnership with humankind. God told Adam in Genesis 2:15 to "keep"[6] the garden. This word is elsewhere translated as *watchman* and means "to guard or protect."[7] Adam, as God's government on earth, was responsible to protect it—no doubt from the serpent, since as yet there was nothing else to protect it from. Adam failed in this, and the serpent gained influence.

As Chuck and I ministered in New Jersey on the Fifty-State Tour, I was led by the Holy Spirit to minister on being watchmen. The Spirit kept saying to me that New Jersey was a "watchman state," called to keep the serpent out of their garden. I referred to their state and the nation as "the garden" and repeatedly said, "You must keep the serpent out of the garden."

The people began to chuckle and nudge one another as I spoke. I became somewhat self-conscious and thought for a moment I had made some sort of blunder. Finally someone shouted, "Do you realize we are called the Garden State?" I had known this, but had completely forgotten, which made it all the more powerful to them.

At this point, Chuck came to the microphone and began to prophesy, much as he did in D.C. As he spoke of their watchman calling, he called the state to twenty-one days of prayer and fasting, with actual prayer meetings taking place from three to six in the morning. (I was glad I live in Colorado!) The Spirit had said that if they would do this, the "vipers" trying to come into their state would be exposed. We knew, of course, that the vipers symbolized the evil plans of Satan.

The New Jersey prayer leaders believed the word was from God and took action, organizing early-morning prayer meetings all across the state for twenty-one days. Many fasted. Imagine the encouragement and confirmation of their calling these intercessors felt when toward the end of the three weeks a plan to smuggle missile launchers into the nation through their port was exposed!

We are God's methods. He governs and protects the earth through us. That is what governmental intercession is all about. The concept of authority or government over the earth could not be clearer than in these two passages:

Then God said, "Let Us make man in Our image, according to Our likeness; and let them rule over the fish of the sea and over the birds of the sky and over the cattle and over all the earth, and over every creeping thing that creeps on the earth."

And God created man in His own image, in the image of God He created him; male and female He created them.

And God blessed them; and God said to them, "Be fruitful and multiply, and fill the earth, and subdue it; and rule over the fish of the sea and over the birds of the sky, and over every living thing that moves on the earth" (Genesis 1:26–28).

When I consider Your heavens, the work of Your
    fingers,
    The moon and the stars, which You have ordained;
What is man that You are mindful of him,
    And the son of man that that You visit him?
For You have made him a little lower than the angels,
    And You have crowned him with glory and honor.

You have made him to have dominion over the works
of Your hands;
You have put all things under his feet.

Psalm 8:3–6 NKJV

These passages use two different Hebrew words for *rule,*
both of which convey the ideas of authority and government.
Radah, used in Genesis, means "to subjugate, to subdue, to
cause to rule, to reign or to take possession of."[8] That's what
we humans are to do on earth! God's
ultimate intention is for you to rule your
personal world and to partner with His
other kids in ruling the world around
you. You are a government official!

The term translated *rule* in Psalm
8:6 is *mashal,* meaning "to govern or
manage."[9] This same word is actually
translated *govern* in Genesis 1:16 and
1:18, the context being the sun governing the day and the moon the night. The
sun and moon do a pretty good job; it's you and me I'm
concerned about! How are we doing at governing or taking
charge of our world?

> *God's ultimate
> intention is for you
> to rule your personal
> world and to partner
> with His other
> kids in ruling the
> world around you.*

In 2001, God sent me, Will Ford, Lou Engle, Jim and Faith
Chosa, and a thirty-to-forty-member (fluctuating) team of
intercessors on a prayer journey to the nation's Northeast.
Our purpose was to experience breakthrough over the region
and begin the process of turning it spiritually back to Christ.

We went to all the New England states, many of the nation's original cities and settlements, most of the Ivy League
colleges and universities, and dozens of other places. It was

grueling, but amazing! God did more than we ever dreamed. I won't share the details now—Will Ford and I do that in *History Makers*.[10] What is relevant here are the Lord's instructions to me when He led us on this journey: "Go and command breakthrough for Me in the Northeast; open the Northeast gate of the nation to Me." (See Psalm 24:7–10.)

Shocked and intimidated, I replied, "Well, Sir, we'll give it our best shot."

I'll never forget His answer to me. When I say He spoke to me, I don't mean I heard His audible voice. It was the Lord's small voice in my heart: "I didn't tell you to give it your best shot. I told you to do it. When I told John [the Baptist] to go prepare the way for My Son, turning the people [see Luke 1:16] back to Me, I didn't ask him to 'give it his best shot.' I told him to do it.

"This isn't about you, your abilities, or how perfectly you pray. It is about obeying Me. There has been enough prayer, fasting, and repentance on the part of My church for Me to do this, and it is time for it to begin. Now, go declare it for Me!"

That is *radah* and *mashal*, managing and governing the earth for God. I was amazed by the simplicity of what the Lord had spoken. I realized more than ever before that it isn't about our strength but His. He simply needed some individuals to understand delegated authority and release His kingdom government on earth. We did just that, and the results were astonishing.

God's assignment to us *adamites* took a nasty turn, however, early in our history. So complete and final was God's decision to give Adam this authority on the earth that Adam had the right to give it away. God didn't give Satan authority on earth—Adam did. When Adam decided to submit to Satan instead of God, much of our forefather's delegated authority was forfeited to Satan, who gained great governmental control over all the earth. Our ability to govern our world was dealt a crippling blow. God acknowledges this authority on several occasions in Scripture. Let's take a closer look at how Satan ended up with such influence and what it means for us.

5

The Contest

I was a great quarterback in high school—at least that's what Mom always told me. And Mom always told me the truth. According to her, if everyone else had been as good as me, we would never have been defeated. Sure, I threw a few interceptions, but they were from my receivers' mistakes, not mine.

I was a pretty good runner, too. Mom said my brother, Tim, and I were the best on the team. We scored our share of touchdowns—would have made many more if our blockers had been better.

I remember when we played one of our arch rivals, Talawanda (no, I didn't make that up). I had no TD passes that game; my receivers weren't playing well, but we were doing okay anyway. The score was tied, and Talawanda had the ball with time for one more play. I played defense also, and I was covering their speedster superstar. As fate would have it, he caught the winning TD on the final play. *This* wasn't my fault either. One of our guys got in my way and "picked" me off my assignment. Mom confirmed this when I arrived home later. She's pretty sharp.

Though the final outcome in the game of life has never been in question, it has nevertheless presented some changes of possession and shifts in momentum. In Genesis 3, Adam fumbled. He blamed Eve, she blamed the serpent, and all of us humans have been blaming one another ever since. Satan recovered the ball, and headship of the earth saw a change of possession. Demons took the field; all "adamites" went on defense.

God, the adamites' coach and, thankfully, the official crew chief *and* chairman of the rules committee, made an important declaration at this point. To the serpent He said, "I will put enmity between you and the woman, and between your seed and her seed; he shall bruise you on the *head*, and you shall bruise him on the *heel*" (v. 15, emphasis added).

When God said He would crush Satan's head, He was not referring to his physical head but to his *headship* or authority. The Hebrew word *rosh*—also translated elsewhere in Scripture as *chief, leader, captain,* and *ruler*—can refer to a literal head, but it also means first in rank or authority, in much the same way we use it today in regard to a head of state or the head of a corporation. God was acknowledging what had just occurred—Satan had succeeded in taking earth's headship from Adam. But God was also stating that He already had a plan to take it back. "I will win!" He was declaring.

Jesus acknowledged Satan's earthly authority by calling him "the ruler of this world" (see John 12:31; 14:30; 16:11).

Ruler is the Greek term *archon* and, like *rosh*, also means "first in rank or order." It even means "to govern" and so is elsewhere translated *prince, chief,* and *magistrate*. Christ was reiterating what was known thousands of years earlier in the garden—Satan was at that time the head over the earth. Satan, during his temptation of Jesus in the wilderness, boasted of this. The worship-hungry serpent took Him to a mountain and showed Him the world's kingdoms, then stated, "I will give You all this domain and its glory; for it has been handed over to me, and I give it to whomever I wish. Therefore if You worship before me, it shall all be Yours" (Luke 4:6–7).

Satan's reference to his "domain" contains the word *exousia*, which we noted (in chapter 2) as the basic New Testament word for authority. "It has been handed over to me," Satan bragged. It was true; Jesus knew it, and He also knew the devil had been sitting on the chest of the human race ever since the turnover was committed.

But this was also why Jesus came. Though He wouldn't accomplish it Satan's way, Christ came to take over the game and set us free. He came to regain the headship Adam had lost. Listen to His words in Luke 4:18–19: "God's Spirit is on me; he's chosen me to preach the Message of good news to the poor, sent me to announce pardon to prisoners and recovery of sight to the blind, to set the burdened and battered free, to announce, 'This is God's year to act!'" (THE MESSAGE).

And act He did.

There was an instant momentum switch when Jesus tucked away the ball. His crushing of the serpent's head was awesome. It began with His earthly ministry: "He went about

373

doing good, and healing all who were oppressed by the devil"
(Acts 10:38).

- He forgave sinners, giving them a new lease on life.
- He delivered the demonized, giving them freedom from captivity—even from insanity. Demons cried out in terror as the warrior-Christ entered the scene.
- He healed multitudes of sick, diseased, and physically challenged people.
- He exposed false religion for what it is—giving all people hope that real relationship with the father God is indeed possible.
- He spoke truth with such clarity and authority that even his enemies were overwhelmed by it.

Jesus wreaked overarching havoc on the sidelines of hell! The kingdom of darkness began to lose momentum—no play worked, no demon was safe, and no human seemed off-limits from the Lord's loving mercy and redemptive power. Satan remembered being kicked out of heaven by this very being, and no doubt he remembered the Genesis promise about his headship being crushed. Unquestionably, he was terrified.

Hell called a time-out and huddled for a strategy session; Satan tried one last power play at the cross. Just when he thought the scheme had worked and he had put away the game, all hell broke loose—literally! In sudden-death overtime, Jesus crossed the goal line, and Adam's race was redeemed. Christ, a flesh-and-blood *adam,* a full-fledged member of the human race and thus legally qualified to take our place, saved the day for all adamites who would accept His victory.

In *Planet in Rebellion,* George Vandeman writes:

It was May 21, 1946. The place: Los Alamos. A young and daring scientist was carrying out a necessary experiment in preparation for the atomic test to be conducted in the waters of the South Pacific atoll at Bikini.

He had successfully performed such an experiment many times before. In his effort to determine the amount of U-235 necessary for a chain reaction—scientists call it the critical mass—he would push two hemispheres of uranium together. Then, just as the mass became critical, he would push them apart with his screwdriver, thus instantly stopping the chain reaction.

But that day, just as the material became critical, the screwdriver slipped. The hemispheres of uranium came too close together. Instantly the room was filled with a dazzling bluish haze. Young Louis Slotin, instead of ducking and thereby possibly saving himself, tore the two hemispheres apart with his hands and thus interrupted the chain reaction.

By this instant, self-forgetful daring, he saved the lives of the seven other persons in the room. . . . As he waited for the car that was to take them to the hospital, he said quietly to his companion, "You'll come through all right. But I haven't the faintest chance myself." It was only too true. Nine days later he died in agony.

Nineteen centuries ago the Son of the living God walked directly into sin's most concentrated radiation, allowed himself to be touched by its curse, and let it take His life. . . . But by that act He broke the chain reaction. He broke the power of sin.[1]

The difference between Christ and Slotin is that Christ not only took our place in death but He also conquered it. He entered the arena of death, took its keys, and became the forever antidote for its sting. And a fact of utmost importance not generally understood is this: *He became the new human head over the earth.* Authority over earth was now safe in the hands of a human that could never lose it again—the God-man, Jesus. Ephesians 1:22 says all things have been placed in subjection to Him who is the "head over all things." Colossians 2:10 says, "He is the head over all rule and authority."

At this point, remember what this does and doesn't mean. Once more: This act dealt with Satan's authority, not his power. You might consider rereading what we said about this in chapter 2. If you're like me, though, you'd rather not have to flip back and find it, so I'll quote it here.

Where God and Satan are concerned, the issue has never been power, including over control of the earth. God is all-powerful. When Satan tried to pull off a coup in heaven, there was a flash of lightning and Satan was gone (see Luke 10:18). No battle, no time delay, no sweat or exertion on God's part—just a release of His power and glory. It is always and only a question of authority.

The same is true with us and our struggle against the kingdom of darkness. Satan didn't gain any power at the fall and didn't lose any at the cross. His power or ability didn't change at either event; his authority, or the right to use that power, *did.* In fact, though Christians often state otherwise, Scripture nowhere says that Christ delivered us from or dealt with Satan's power at Calvary. *He dealt with Satan's authority.*

The King James Version uses the Greek words *dunamis* (power) and *exousia* (authority) interchangeably, which is unfortunate and creates confusion. In Colossians 1:13, for example, it translates *exousia* as *power:* "Who hath delivered us from the power of darkness, and hath translated us into the kingdom of his dear Son." The verse should read that Christ has delivered us from the *authority* of darkness, as most other translations actually do. Likewise, in Matthew 28:18, Jesus didn't say He had been given "all power," as the KJV renders—He already had that. Christ used *exousia:* He was stating that He had taken back the authority for us that Adam had lost.

This is more than a mere technicality. If Jesus stripped Satan of his power, as some teach, then we no longer need to concern ourselves with him—he becomes a nonissue. Or if we Christians have been delivered from Satan's power, as some teach, then he can no longer affect or control us. We would be able to ignore him completely, which is precisely what many Christians do.

If on the other hand, Jesus dealt with Satan's authority—the right to use his power or abilities—then we would need to deal with him as a usurper, a rebel, a thief that has no *right* to steal, kill, and destroy but *will* if not stopped (see John 10:10). If we have been delivered from Satan's authority and given a higher authority in Christ's name, then we must exercise that authority over the devil's works and power. When we do, God's awesome power will back up our authority. Luke 10:19 refers to this—using our *authority* over Satan's *power:* "Behold, I have given you authority *[exousia]* to tread upon serpents and scorpions, and over all the power *[dunamis]* of the enemy, and nothing shall injure you."

My problem with Idiot was her power not her authority. She was a rebellious horse, using her greater power to resist me. Though I ended up wasting my money, I really did use my authority to pen her up and keep her from harming me or further interrupting my hunt. Likewise, Jesus said we have authority ("keys") to "bind" the forces of hell (see Matthew 16:19). The term is *deo,* and means to "fasten or tie, as with a chain or cord" (Zodhiates, *Hebrew-Greek Key Word Study Bible*, NASB), just as I did with the horse. The word was also used in legal circles to mean "legally or contractually binding," which obviously conveys the idea of authority. We can pray with authority, binding or tying Satan legally, and God will back us with His power. So again, what will determine victory for us is understanding and exercising authority.

Jim and Faith Chosa, Native American prayer leaders from Montana, understand these truths in a way few people do, which is why they could be used in the following example of governmental intercession.

In the early spring of 2004, we received notice of the plans of the Dalai Lama to travel to Toronto, Canada, and release 722 occult Tibetan spirits into the Great Lakes Northern Gate of our country. The Spirit of God raised up a great army to prevent this from happening. He inspired us to gather a team at Sault Ste. Marie, Canada, equip them in the ways of territorial warfare and deliverance, and as one Body begin the process of dismantling the defilements in this gateway. We then bound the local demonic spirits thus negating their ability to invite the 722 demonic spirits into the spiritual landscape of this region.

The result was immediate: the Dalai Lama himself said, "Toronto is a very hard place; I could not accomplish what I planned to do." In other words, he could not release the 722 occult spirits into this very important northern gateway, and had to take them home with him.

That is praying with authority! It pleases our Captain when we take the authority He has won back for us and enforce His victory. We should never waste what His heroic efforts achieved.

I love Christ's trophy acceptance speech in Matthew 28:16–20, after the cross and the resurrection. The disciples had been told to go "to the mountain which Jesus had designated" (v. 16), and there He made His great declaration of victory: "All authority has been given to Me in heaven *and on earth*" (v. 18, emphasis added). Again, *authority* is *exousia*, the same word translated *domain* at Christ's temptation when Satan used it regarding his authority. Jesus was proclaiming, once and for all, "Satan doesn't have it anymore! I took it back, and *I* have all authority—not only in heaven, but on earth as well."

Here is something that can't be proven, but I sometimes wonder about. Jesus "designated" a mountain upon which He would make this declaration. Remember that Satan took Jesus to a mountain, where he boasted of his authority and tempted Christ with it—could this be the very mountain Satan had taken Him to? Was Jesus doing one more "in your face" to the devil? One thing I know for certain: The contest had been decided; victory had been won.

The Father's original plan is now reinstated— He is governing the earth through His kids.

Though he still fights, Satan's doom is sure, his fate sealed; Adam's lost authority is now safe in the hands of the last Adam (see Romans 5). Now we can pray with true authority, knowing that Christ our Head wants to release His kingdom rule through us. The Father's original plan is now reinstated—He is governing the earth through His kids. Lynnie Walker, an intercessor in Nevada, demonstrated this:

At the beginning of 2004, I was awakened with the urgent thought, "A bomb is about to go off somewhere in the world, and you need to get up and pray that it be averted." I began to question if this was my imagination, and besides, I was too tired to get up. But the message came again, stronger as an "inner audible voice." So I got up, went to the closet and knelt and prayed that the plot would be exposed and that nothing would happen. I continued to pray as the Spirit led me, and then I heard, "It's done. You can go back to bed now."

I got up to go to bed, but then I knelt down and added a quick request. "Lord, it would be really nice to hear about this on the news tomorrow, even though 'a bomb that didn't go off' wouldn't normally make the news." Then I went to bed.

The next morning after I awoke, I told Dennis about what I had heard during the night. He said, "Well, let's turn the TV on and see what's on the news."

We turned CNN on and there was the breaking news: "A large bomb was found on the tracks in Spain." It proceeded to explain that a railway worker had found the bomb. It was rigged and ready to blow, but whoever had the detonator must have gotten scared off somehow! There had been a previous bomb that had exploded some days before, killing hundreds of people. The news of the bomb greatly overshadowed the installation ceremony of the newly elected leaders. Wow! It really did make the news!

I came to a humbling and awesome understanding of God's ways. On earth, He has given authority to mankind. He has chosen to work through His people. He woke me up, and perhaps many others, to release His power in this event. All I had to do was say what He was telling me to say, and He responded! How could it get any easier?

6

The Ekklesia

When Jesus showed up on the fallen world scene, He left no doubt as to His ownership of it:

- He established authority over the laws of nature, walking on water (Matthew 14:25).
- He controlled the forces of nature, altering weather patterns (Mark 4:39).
- He trumped the laws of physics, multiplying food, turning water into wine, translating his physical body from one place to another, and destroying trees simply by speaking to them (Matthew 15:36; John 2:9; 6:21; Mark 11:13–14, 20).
- He demonstrated authority over the animal world, using a fish to collect money needed for a tax (Matthew 17:27).
- He had dominion over disease, healing multitudes (Acts 10:38).

- He even displayed power over death, bringing dead people back to life (John 11:43–44).

In a plan so daring, bold, and staggering in its ramifications that no one, including Satan's kingdom and even the angels, could guess what it was, God had become an *adam*—a human being—and thereby qualified himself to redeem humankind and win back their lost authority. As established earlier, ownership of the earth wasn't the issue, nor was Christ's authority—He had never lost His. This issue was authority for the human race, whether or not they would re-inherit their governmental rights to earth.

When the God-man, Jesus, paid our penalty and restored us to God, in the process He won back Adam's lost authority. It is now safe in the hands of a human being who will never lose it again. God's original plan was restored: *There is now a race of humans on the earth filled with God's life and nature, capable of relating to Him as Father and managing this incredible home He made for them.*

If they only realized it!

When we are born again, we are no longer simply humans—*adamites*—we are a new race of supernatural beings called Christians (or "little Christs"). In his first letter to Corinth, Paul chastised the believers for acting like "mere men" (3:3). We are not merely human; we are supernatural daughters and sons of the Most High God, filled with His Spirit and anointed to rule. God has His family back and can now get on with His plan of carrying out the great family enterprise of governing the earth.

On a wall near the main entrance to The Alamo in San Antonio, Texas, is a portrait with the following inscription:

James Butler Bonham—no picture of him exists. This portrait is of his nephew, Major James Bonham, deceased, who greatly resembled his uncle. It is placed here by the family that people may know the appearance of the man who died for freedom.[1]

No literal picture of Jesus exists either. But He can be seen in the lives of His followers, the church. The big question now centers around whether or not we will take on our role of revealing and partnering with God on the earth. Will we allow God to move us back into His original plan, or do we think we are saved just to get to heaven someday? Let's seek a better understanding of what Jesus meant when He said He would build His church. The church is mentioned for the first time in Matthew 16:18–19:

> I also say to you that you are Peter, and upon this rock I will build My church; and the gates of Hades will not overpower it. I will give you the keys of the kingdom of heaven; and whatever you shall bind on earth shall be bound in heaven, and whatever you shall loose on earth shall be loosed in heaven.

When Jesus used the word *church* (Greek: *ekklesia*), the disciples weren't hindered by our contemporary preconceived ideas as to what it meant. Their paradigm of an *ekklesia* differed greatly from what it has become. To us today it is (1) a worship service; (2) a building used by Christians; (3) a local congregation of Christians; or (4) for those who tend toward a more literal meaning, the people of God, "called out" from the world. The last concept is the most accurate, according to a strict translation, but it still falls far short of communicating what an *ekklesia* was when Christ made His stunning announcement.

To the Greeks in Christ's day an *ekklesia* was an assembly of people set apart to govern the affairs of a state or nation—in essence, a parliament or congress. To the Romans, it was a group of people sent into a conquered region to alter the culture until it became like Rome. Realizing this was the ideal way to control their empire, they infiltrated government, social structure, language, schools, etc., until the people talked, thought, and acted like Romans.

When Jesus said He would build His church, He was without question speaking of a body of people that would legislate spiritually for Him, extending His kingdom government (rule) over the earth. His statement that "the gates of Hades will not overpower it" makes much more sense when we understand this. These "gates" are not physical gates, but rather the governmental plans of hell. Biblical gates were often where judges sat to rule or governing councils met to make decisions, and therefore they often symbolized government (for example, see 2 Samuel 19:8; Proverbs 22:22–23). In Ruth 4:10–11, the Hebrew word for gate is actually translated *court*.

In this first decree about the church, Jesus is saying that the kingdom government (rule, decrees, councils) of hell won't prevail over His kingdom government on earth—the church. He follows this declaration by saying He would give to His *ekklesia* "keys" (Matthew 16:19), which also bring to mind authority. Keys lock or unlock, in order to close or open, doors and gates. Christ's church would have keys (authority) to lock the gates (government) of hell and release the gates (government) of heaven.

What a statement!

In *World Vision* magazine, John Robb writes:

Seven years ago, a giant tree stood on the banks of the Awash River, in an arid valley about two hours' drive southeast of Addis Ababa, Ethiopia. It had stood there for generations, seemingly eternal.

For years, the people who lived in the surrounding district had suffered through famines. . . . In their suffering, the people looked to the tree for help. Believing a spirit gave it divine powers, they worshipped the towering giant. Adults would kiss the great trunk when they passed by, and they spoke of the tree in hushed, reverential tones. Children said, "This tree saved us."

In 1989, World Vision began a development project there, including an irrigation system. . . . But even as they labored to build the system, the great tree stood like a forbidding sentinel of the old order, presiding over the community, enslaving the people through fear. Spirits needed to be propitiated with animal sacrifices and strict observance of taboos.

When World Vision workers saw how the villagers worshipped the tree, they knew it was an idolatrous barrier to the entrance of God's kingdom and transformation of the community.

One morning as the staff prayed together, one of Jesus' promises struck them: "If you have faith, you can say to this tree, 'Be taken up and removed' . . . and it will obey you." In faith, they began to pray that God would bring down the menacing goliath.

Soon the whole community knew the Christians were praying about the tree. Six months later, the tree began to dry up, its leafy foliage disappeared, and finally it collapsed like a stricken giant into the river.

The people of the community were astonished, proclaiming, "Your God has done this! Your God has dried up the tree!" In the days and weeks afterwards, approximately 100 members of the community received Jesus Christ because they saw His power displayed in answer to the Christians' prayers.[2]

That's what I'm talking about! Where have we been in our thinking? How have we missed this truth? The church of Christ is not supposed to be a group of harmless, irrelevant, mind-your-own-business worshipers who gather once a week, tucked away from anything public, just to practice their particular mode of religion. This is, of course, what many unbelievers think is appropriate. I frequently hear statements from the media, political leaders, and others that religious beliefs should be kept "private" or that they "have no place in the public arena," and especially that they "have no place in government."

> *If I were Satan and wanted to stop evangelism, the spread of biblical morality, or the rule of God into the earth . . . My first priority would be to keep the church from truly being the church.*

Nothing could be more unbiblical. The purpose behind this satanically inspired dogma is to keep the church from being the church—the *ekklesia*. The Bible brims with examples of God and godly individuals involved in government and other public arenas, intentionally representing God and His will while doing so. The Scriptures are filled with admonitions to minister and promote Christ outside the walls of the gathering place.

If I were Satan and wanted to stop evangelism, the spread of biblical morality, or the rule of God into the earth, I couldn't think of a better way than convincing Christians NOT to be the *ekklesia*—in other words, leave God in the closet, tucked away in their own private world. My first priority would be to keep the church from truly being the church. *My goal would be to leave God without a government on earth.* Then, even though I had lost my authority, I could still rule.

While we certainly are not to spread our faith or God's rule on earth by physical force or domination, as some religions teach, implying that we are not supposed to spread our faith and His rule at all is just as ludicrous. We are to invade our culture, workplace, city, nation, etc., with the might of God's kingdom and spread His life and rule *everywhere.* That is what praying with authority is all about. Jesus told us to "make disciples of all the nations" (Matthew 28:19) and to preach or declare the good news of Him "to all creation" (Mark 16:15). The Acts church turned their world "upside down" (17:6 AMPLIFIED). They upset status quo everywhere they went—and so should we. If a society or culture remains the same after Christ's church shows up, then the church is not being the church.

Bill Johnson doesn't believe in the church staying in the closet, as you will see from the following report. The ministry that took place on an outreach to Tijuana, Mexico, was so powerful it's almost hard to believe. But I know Bill, and I can assure you of his integrity. The report is somewhat lengthy, but so exciting I couldn't decide what to cut out. Enjoy.

The team met at 6:00 p.m. on a stage set near the most desperate part of the street, which houses prostitutes, gangs and a rampant drug trade. After a time of prayer together during which the team got completely filled with His presence, the surrounding people were being drawn to the spectacle, as in the book of Acts when people gathered around the people of God to see what was happening in the Spirit. However, the rain that had been threatening to pour all day, started to fall shortly after ministry began. Bobby Brown, one of the Third Year leaders, ran up to the microphone, knowing that if the rain continued, it would take away from what God wanted to accomplish that night. He told the crowd that God was going to stop the rain. As he spoke, and then prayed a quick prayer, the rain stopped, leaving all amazed and wondering how it could have possibly happened! News of the miracle spread and even more people came out of restaurants and shops to see what was happening. People couldn't help but be drawn in. One look at the nationals' faces revealed their desire for His presence and a deep longing for a revelation of His love.

For six hours the team preached, received words of knowledge, led people to the Lord, and saw numerous miracles of healing. It was as if what was happening had a momentum of its own because it was beyond comprehension. The team was co-laboring with God; the Kingdom was coming and the team was simply a piece of letting the Gospel come to life. There were at least six altar calls, but even between asking people if they wanted to receive Jesus, the team connected with people surrounding the stage. Over one hundred people received Christ into their hearts, including five prostitutes, an immigrant from Iran, and a man whose eye had been gouged out in a fight! Many experienced healing in their bodies. A few of the healings are as follows: a man who had been using crutches walked away with the crutches on his shoulder; an older woman could barely walk due to the arthritis in her wrists, knees and hips, but by the time the team finished praying for her, she could walk freely and quickly without pain! Another woman, sick with the flu, was healed and actually felt the "heat" of the fever leave her. A man got saved and healed in his knee. One girl had a tumor in her throat that completely dissolved. An alleged hit-man fell to his knees and repented of murdering people and trading drugs.

For several hours during the night, one young woman, who was obviously demonized, kept trying to access the stage. Many students prayed for her, but she still seemed to act crazily. Dale, one of the students, asked to pray for her and pleaded the blood of Jesus over her. She responded and became completely calm and secure. Her mentor, a known witch, kept trying to disrupt the event as well, yet when she got close enough to one of the speakers on stage, a leader turned and told her to "Be gone!" She ran away and was not seen again.

Another woman, who had been listening from her fifth-story window across from the stage, cried out for Jesus when one of the leaders pointed her out from the stage, asking her if she wanted to know Him.

Another miraculous event occurred during this time that mirrors the story of the feeding of the five thousand in Matthew. A section of the team was commissioned to find Bibles for the newly saved. They went into a nearby hotel thinking, *Most hotels have Bibles on their bedside tables.* After finding out that the hotel had none, they were not willing to give up.

"Can you check, please?"

The manager opened up a closet behind the desk and saw 15 Bibles sitting inside. The team passed them out, but came back for more a little while later.

"We really don't have any more Bibles," the same manager repeated.

"Please check in the closet again." He opened the closet and found half a box of Bibles on the floor! They came back a while later, realizing that they still did not have enough.

"I didn't even know we had the other box; I really don't have any more, I'm sure."

One of the team asked, "What's that box on the floor in front of you?"

He looked down, opened the box and found it was completely full of new Bibles!

"I cannot believe this!" he stated excitedly. Altogether the team passed out about 70 Bibles.[3]

I am fully convinced that this should be the norm for Christ's church. We should leave the mark of changed lives everywhere we go. However, since we (1) have not understood what it means to be an *ekklesia*, (2) don't understand our spiritual weapons and the invisible spirit realm where they operate, and (3) know we cannot force Christ and His ways on people, our conclusion often has been to assume that we can make very little difference in our world. The prevailing mindset has been to simply place all hope for change in God's sovereignty—a belief that when He wants and chooses to, He will change a particular problem or situation to be in accord with His will. I don't believe we think through this viewpoint well enough to see its complete ramifications. If this concept of God's sovereignty were true, it would mean that places, cultures, and lives are messed up, that suffering is occurring and that people are going to hell simply because God isn't yet motivated enough to do anything about it. I don't blame most unbelievers for not wanting the God that many Christians preach and teach. I wouldn't want to love and follow a god like that.

We will later address the invisible realm of the spirit and our weapons that impact it. We must begin by realizing that we are God's governing force on the earth and that the government of hell can't stop us when we use the authority Christ has given us, becoming true governmental intercessors.

There is another governmental word—used in Acts 13:36—that pictures our role of being God's government on earth. "David, after he had served the purpose of God in his own generation, fell asleep, and was laid among his fathers, and underwent decay." Here, *purpose* is *boule*, meaning counsel, decree, aim, or intention. Zodhiates says it also means "the assembly of the council. In modern Greek, parliament is called *boule*."[4] Let's place that definition back into the verse: "David . . . served the *parliament* of God in his own generation." David knew that in his role as king, he was representing and serving God's government and thus carried God's authority and was answerable to God. Would that government leaders today understood this!

All of them should recognize that they are to represent God's will and purpose in their position of authority. I can assure you that every single one someday will stand before Him and answer for every action and decision. Neither ignorance nor the "will of the people" will serve as an excuse. All pompous arrogance will disappear before the blazing eyes of the Ancient of Days, the true Judge of the universe, who knows the ones who flaunted their rule in His face and mocked His Word and ways. Their prestigious black robes and "honorable" titles will mean nothing to Him. Psalm 2—in its entirety, but especially verses 10–12—is a sobering and appropriate warning:

> Now therefore, O kings, show discernment; take warning, O judges of the earth. Worship the Lord with reverence, and rejoice with trembling. Do homage to the Son, lest He become angry, and you perish in the way, for His wrath may soon be kindled. How blessed are all who take refuge in Him!

But while the rulers of this world are meant to represent God in the natural realm, we, the *ekklesia,* are the spiritual council or parliament of God on earth. We ascertain what His will is, then see that it is implemented by operating in the spiritual realm through prayer and other spiritual weapons. The word *served*—*(huperetes)* in Acts 13:36—is also revealing. Literally "under rower," it was used of the several rowers in a ship's galley. The key to their success was the synergy created by rowing together or simultaneously; to take turns rowing would have accomplished little. David, in his day, led a nation of "under rowers"—notice that he was one also—enabling them to row in sync with God's cadence. That's how all government leaders should serve, and when they do, they produce a righteousness that "exalts a nation" (Proverbs 14:34) and enables its people to "lead a tranquil and quiet life in all godliness and dignity" (1 Timothy 2:2).

Jesus truly is building His church: a government headquarters, a parliament, discerning and insisting on God's will over the earth.

Jesus truly is building His church, but it is not what we have thought of as the church—a social club, a building on the corner, or even a teaching center or place of worship. It is a government headquarters, a parliament, discerning and insisting on God's will over the earth. We row together, creating an unstoppable thrust of kingdom life into every sector of society: religion, government, education, the arts, media, business, and family. As the true church continues to arise, heaven gains increasing influence on earth, while hell's influence decreases.

Richard Brink, pastor and state coordinator for the U.S. Strategic Prayer Network in Maine, shares the following story that illustrates this kind of authority:

> In 1997, reports came out of New Brunswick, Canada, that the tenth teenager had just committed suicide at Big Cove, a Micmac First Nation reserve. Over the next five years, our church did various outreaches and prayer projects there. We found that besides unemployment and substance abuse, there was something more sinister behind some of the suicides. A local witch doctor was leading many of the teens into the sweat lodges and teaching them how to talk to the "spirits." The suicides increased soon afterward.
>
> We had the opportunity to share Jesus with this witch doctor and also to go on the reservation and pray against this situation.
>
> When we returned last year, we found that there had been no documented suicides since 1997 and that the government was no longer funding the witch doctor's sweat lodges. God showed His mighty power and love to the wonderful Micmac people.

He did so through the church, His *ekklesia*. That was His plan two thousand years ago, and it is still His plan today!

We have seen that when Jesus spoke of building His *ekklesia*, He said He would give them keys to lock the government (gates) of hell and unlock the kingdom government of heaven. In 2000, God began making this real to me in a very personal way.

On a cross-country flight I happened to notice that my departure time was 2:22. I was then seated in row number 22, and the total travel time was 2 hours and 22 minutes. My first thought was what a strange coincidence! Then the Lord reminded me that He had been speaking to me from Isaiah 22:22 about the upcoming presidential election: "Then I will set the key of the house of David on his shoulder, when he opens no one will shut, when he shuts no one will open." *Would God do something like this to bring me confirmation?* I wondered. I knew that keys symbolize authority and that the shoulder symbolizes government (see Isaiah 9:6).

A couple of days later I received a phone call from Sam Brassfield, a spiritual father in my life. While in prayer, Sam had felt the Lord prompt him to call and give me Isaiah 22:22, emphasizing the phrase *the key of the house of David*. He said, "Dutch, God is giving you a key of governmental authority in this nation."

Soon afterward I went to D.C. on a ministry trip, and there a trusted intercessor friend gave me a gift after the meeting. She said the Lord had impressed on her months earlier to buy it for me, with the instruction that He would let her know when to give it to me. It was a beautiful silver key; her words to me were "This is the key to the city!" I knew it represented the key spoken of in Isaiah 22:22.

Another man, knowing nothing about this, came to me after that meeting with three keys and said, "This morning I felt impressed to bring you these three keys." He too realized they symbolized spiritual authority. Again, I knew they pictured Isaiah 22:22. Matthew 16:19 came to mind, "I will give you the keys of the kingdom of heaven; and whatever you shall bind on earth shall be bound in heaven, and whatever you shall loose on earth shall be loosed in heaven." This had never happened to me before—no one had ever given me keys to symbolize anything.

A week later I was in San Diego with Chuck Pierce, who told me that God had led him to give me a key. He had been given this key in New York by people who said it represented a revival anointing for America. Chuck said, "The Lord impressed me to give it to you."

After that service, another man gave me three more keys, saying he had been impressed by the Lord to do so. Incredibly, the number "222," and no other number, was on each of these keys!

A couple of weeks later I was in California again to meet and pray with my friend Lou Engle. Lou said, "God has been speaking to me about Isaiah 22:22. I've even had dreams about the number 22 and this verse. And at a meeting I did recently, the number of my hotel room was 222."

I came home from that meeting, shared this with our church, and a young man in our congregation said to me, "Just today God directed me to Isaiah 22:22. I felt it was a verse for our church."

Another lady in the service had been awakened from a dream at 2:22 a.m., and she shared her experience with me.

Still another lady in the service, a visiting pastor's wife from New England, had also had a dream the previous night. In her dream there was a man with an old set of keys. She asked him, "What are you doing with those?" He replied that he was going to throw them away because they were just old keys. In the dream she said to the man, "Please don't throw them away. They are precious. May I have them?" He then gave her the keys.

Over the course of two weeks, I had no fewer than twenty-five remarkable confirmations that God was speaking to me about keys of authority and relating this to Isaiah 22:22. He was clearly saying, "I am giving you authority—keys—to impact the nation."

Though the occurrences were happening to me, I realized the message was for the entire body of Christ. We truly have been given keys of authority from God to legislate from the heavenlies (in the realm of the spirit), opening doors that can't be closed by Satan or any person, and closing doors through which evil and destruction might otherwise enter.[5]

I began to trumpet this message around the nation, calling people to pray as never before for the upcoming presidential election. Others, in their own way, did as well. And probably like no other time in America's history, God's *ekklesia*—the governmental intercessors and saints of the Lord Jesus Christ—prayed for a presidential election with such fervency and diligence that it turned the tide. God's will was done, and again, righteousness (not perfection) was restored to the White House.

I have used Isaiah 22:22 many times as a source of inspiration and authority as I have prayed. It has become a life verse for me. Though it is often impossible to measure immediately the effectiveness of intercession, since the fruit often takes time to materialize, consider the following confirmation God gave to assure me of the reality of this verse. . . .

7

The Dynasty

Then I will set the key of the house of David on his shoulder,
when he opens no one will shut, when he shuts no one will
open.

Isaiah 22:22

"Go to the White House and, using Isaiah 22:22, close the door
to the counsel currently coming to the president that is not My
will. Then open the door for My counsel to come to him."

These were the words I heard the Lord speak to me in
January 2003. I was in D.C. for a prayer gathering, and on
this particular morning we were scheduled to tour the State
Department. The actual purpose of the tour was to pray for
the State Department as we walked through the building.
When I awoke, however, I had the clear impression, *Don't*

go to the State Department; go to the White House instead, followed by the above instructions. I prayed about this for a few minutes and also called Ceci, looking for confirmation. She, too, felt this new assignment was from the Lord, and I determined to obey the prompting. The rest of the group headed for the State Department, while I hailed a taxi and left for the White House.

It was a cold and windy day, and I would be praying outside. Not a good day to forget my overcoat! The more I prayed, the colder I got, which was affecting my attitude. In addition, lots of people were milling around taking pictures, and a group of protestors was shouting one-liners and singing antiwar songs. On top of that, security was strong—I felt that every move I made as I paced in front of the fence was being scrutinized. This made me very nervous, which I'm sure caused me to look suspicious. As I prayed quietly, I was almost sure the entire Secret Service was watching this strange man— me—pacing and obviously alone but speaking to someone. I could imagine that they pictured a hidden microphone or walkie-talkie that enabled me to communicate with someone waiting to detonate a bomb or commit some other act of terrorism.

Suffice it to say that after about half an hour of this, I'd had enough. I felt nothing but cold and frustration—no anointing, feeling of peace, or any other confirmation in my heart that I was accomplishing anything. My self-conversation went something like this: *Sheets, who do you think you are? You're not accomplishing a thing. God gives you a verse a couple of years ago, uses it in your life, and you then think you can do anything you want with it. You're moving in presumption, not obedience. You should be over at the State Department with the rest of the team. You might as well go back to your room and get out of this bitter cold.*

As I turned to go, tail tucked between my legs, a young woman with a baby stroller next to her approached me from behind. When I turned around, she was so close I almost ran into her.

"Excuse me, sir," she said. My first thought was that she was going to ask me for money—D.C. has many panhandlers. But was I ever wrong!

"I hope you don't think I'm weird," she went on, "but is your name something like Dutch Pierce?"

After getting over my initial shock, I had to deal with the incredible offense of being confused with Chuck Pierce! (Actually, Chuck is a close friend, and we frequently minister together.) That this lady wasn't even sure of who I am made what was about to happen much more believable and impactful.

"My name is Dutch Sheets," I said, "and I minister some with a guy named Chuck Pierce. Do I know you?"

"Oh, yeah, that's right—Dutch Sheets. No, you don't know me. I hope you don't think I'm weird," she repeated, "but I heard you speak a couple of years ago, and you talked about a verse in Isaiah—2:22 or 22:2—something like that."

She was getting my attention!

"It was 22:22," I said.

"Yeah, that's right—22:22, the verse about keys to open and close doors. Well, this morning the Lord awakened me early, reminded me of that verse and your message, told me to go to the White House, and said, 'I'll show you what to do when you get there.'"

"I've never done anything like this," she said, "and I don't come here regularly to pray. But the impression was so strong that I bundled up my baby and came to see what would happen. I have really struggled with what I'm doing. It's cold, my baby is probably cold [her baby was well bundled and covered; I've since learned who she is, and I'm sure she's a wonderful mother], and I've been questioning if I really heard the Lord. Then I saw you and thought, *Is that the man who preached about this verse in Isaiah?* I've been watching you for the last thirty minutes, asking God if I'm supposed to approach you, and if so, wondering what to say. I even called my husband, asking him if I should speak to you. He told me that I must! So here I am.

"I know you already know this, and I feel really strange telling you, but the only thing coming to me is that the Lord wants to remind you of that verse in Isaiah and tell you, 'you really do have the keys to open and close doors in the Spirit.'"

I was blown away! And deeply embarrassed.

"Ma'am," I replied, "I've been praying and decreeing some things, using that verse, for the last thirty minutes—in complete unbelief. You have fulfilled your assignment. Now get your baby home where it is warm. I'm going to go back and complete my assignment, this time in faith."

I did. Later, I signaled a taxi and headed toward my hotel. On the way, I got one of the hardest spankings from the Lord I've ever received. It went something like this: "Don't you ever make Me get mama and her baby out of bed again and send them into the cold to teach you 'Faith and Obedience 101,' especially after I've already given you so many confirmations relating to the situation."

Ouch!

This authority for the church to use our spiritual keys, opening and closing spiritual doors, is an aspect of prayer I sometimes refer to as *kingly intercession*. My understanding of this facet of prayer, which I also call governmental intercession, began with an unusual comment made to me by a prophet in the late 1980s and culminated with a statement the Lord made to me in 2002. That's right—it took about fifteen years for me to fully grasp it. Talk about slow! I'm so embarrassed writing this that I've now put my double-billed cap back on. . . .

I knew the prophet's remark was Spirit-inspired, and I asked him what it meant. He said he didn't know. Prophets can be strange like that, saying things they don't even understand. Some of them are downright weird. Those in the Bible were often different than the average person—a camel-haired wardrobe here (John the Baptist), fed by ravens there (Elijah). But perhaps the strangest thing about them, at least to us today, is that they claim to hear from and speak for God! What a bizarre thought: God might speak and a human being made in His image might be able to hear it.

I'm being facetious, of course. I do believe God speaks today, and true prophets are not weird. But many people don't believe the Lord speaks verbally to us today. Beyond unbelievers, even some theologians and denominations warn against prophets and prophetic giftings. And I've actually heard media people mock the possibility of someone hearing God speak, both while interviewing a Christian and when simply referring to one.

I guess I can see how some unbelievers, ignorant of Scripture and having no relationship with God, might think people who believe they hear from the Lord are strange. They've probably met some of the ones I've also run into, the ones who approach me with a sort of spaced-out, super-spiritual, I'm-from-another-planet look and give me a message "from God" (a message usually as bizarre as their expression). However, I do get a little puzzled by Christians who reject the possibility of God speaking to a person's heart, mind, or spirit. Most of these believe He spoke in Old Testament times and then stopped after He gave us the Bible. I'm not criticizing them or belittling their position, but it does seem strange to me that God would suddenly lose His desire or ability to communicate verbally, especially to His kids. I don't carry on a running conversation with God, and I've never heard His voice audibly, but I confess to being one of the "nut cases" that believes God talks to him at times. And I believe in prophets.

Back to the statement from the late '80s. I was having a fairly normal phone conversation with this brother when he began speaking to me prophetically. I don't remember much of it, but one phrase I have never forgotten was so unique, it stood out to me. He said God was going to bring forth "the fresh age of the Melchizedek order" and that I would be a part of it.

"What is that?" I asked when he concluded.

"I don't know," he said somewhat humorously. "But when you find out, let me know."

Fast-forward approximately fifteen years to October 2002. I was praying for America, primarily concerning the judicial system, when I heard the Holy Spirit clearly say, "You will fully shift the government of America when the prayer movement fully shifts from priestly intercession to kingly intercession as well." I suddenly remembered what the prophet had long ago said to me, the dots connected in my mind, and at last I understood "the fresh age of the Melchizedek order." Grasping this revelation will expand our understanding of governmental intercession.

There is rich and powerful revelation connected to Melchizedek in the Scriptures, but for our subject I'll skip over much of it. He is first mentioned in Genesis 14, again in Psalm 110, and then in the New Testament book of Hebrews. Some theologians think he was an Old Testament-era appearance of Jesus, others that he only symbolically pictured Christ. Of the latter we are certain as, indeed, it was said of Jesus that He is a priest "according to the order of Melchizedek" (see Psalm 110:4; Hebrews 5:6–10).

As high priest, Jesus represents us to God. As king, He represents and releases the rule or authority of God from heaven to earth.

One fascinating fact about Melchizedek is that he was both a *king* and a *priest;* this was one of the ways in which he imaged Jesus, our King and High Priest. Zechariah 6:13 refers to this, stating, "It is He who will build the temple of the Lord, and He who will bear the honor and sit and rule on His throne. Thus, He will be a *priest* on His *throne,* and the counsel of peace will be between the two offices" (emphasis added).

It is important for us to understand the differences between these two functions. As our High Priest, Jesus represents us *to God.* For example, through Him we have forgiveness; it is through Him that we have access to the Father; He is the guarantee in heaven that we receive all the benefits He secured for us; and, being human himself, He can relate to and sympathize with our human weaknesses and temptations, thereby coming to our aid.

On the other hand, as King, Christ represents and releases the rule or authority of God from heaven *to earth*. In Psalm 2 the Father says, "I have installed My King upon Zion" (v. 6), then goes on to describe Christ's awesome power and authority. Jesus is not only King over the church but also over all the earth.

Here is a further summary of the differences between these functions:

- As king He represents the rule and will of God; as priest He represents the needs and desires of people.
- His kingly role is downward, from heaven to earth; His priestly role is upward, from earth to heaven.
- His kingly activity is God-centered, his priestly activity is human-centered.
- His kingly function requires authority and power; His priestly role requires love, mercy, and grace.
- Kings have a scepter that symbolizes authority; priests use a censer that symbolizes worship. One releases power, the other a fragrance.

While we must comprehend these functions of Christ, we must also realize that as His body on earth He fulfills them through us. We are His voice, His hands, His feet. We are Christ's church, His legislature and, as such, partners in His mission and partakers of His anointing. What He is, He is through us; what He does, He does through us. It's not really complicated—we're partners, a team, a unit. Not equal partners, of course. As the Head, He's in charge; as the body, we serve the will of the Head.

Keeping this partnering and representational relationship with Christ in mind, we can grasp the fresh age of the Melchizedek order, in which we have become extensions of His King-Priest role. We too are called priests, and, as such, we're an extension of Christ in His priestly role, representing the needs of people *upward* to heaven. Just as Christ "*offered up* both prayers and supplications" while on earth (Hebrews 5:7, emphasis added), we also as priests "*offer up* spiritual sacrifices" (1 Peter 2:5, emphasis added).

Jeremy was Miriam's teenage son who worked at a car wash. One Wednesday night Miriam had been driving home from a prayer meeting at her church, and as she drove she was fervently praying for her children. She was so engrossed in prayer that she didn't even look up when she passed the car wash to see if Jeremy was there.

Shortly afterward, Jeremy came home, badly shaken. "Mom," he said, "I saw you pass by while I was at the car wash."

"I'm sorry, Jeremy. I should have stopped."

"No, let me tell you what happened. At the very moment you passed by, a man had a gun at my head. It was a holdup. He said, 'Give me your keys and your money.' I said, 'Man, don't do this.' That's when I looked up and saw you pass by.

"When I looked back at the man, he was looking at me strangely, but not really at me. He was sort of looking past me, and it was as though he saw something or someone at my shoulder. All at once he turned and ran."

"Jeremy," said Miriam. "I was praying for you at that very moment."

"I believe you, Mom," said Jeremy. "I believe you."[1]

What an incredible example of timely, priestly intercession. Who knows what would have happened had Jeremy's mother not been praying for him at that dangerous moment.

Most Christians, though they may or may not think of it as priestly activity, realize that we send worship and prayer from earth to heaven. But most of us completely miss God's plan concerning our kingly anointing of representing Christ. We are not only priests, we're a "*royal* priesthood" (1 Peter 2:9, emphasis added).

Symbolically, we are seated with Christ on His throne (Ephesians 1:20; 2:6), told to reign in life (Romans 5:17); we are instructed to extend His scepter (Psalm 110:2) and are given keys of kingdom authority with which to bind and loose, forbid and allow (Matthew 16:19). We are kings and queens—royalty. And whereas priests "offer up" to heaven, kings "proclaim" downward to earth. Just as Christ decreed the will of the Father in situations—pronouncing blessings and curses, casting out demons, healing the sick, even raising the dead—we are told as royal priests to "*proclaim* the excellencies" of God (1 Peter 2:9, emphasis added).

What do we proclaim? "Excellencies" is the Greek word *arête,* also meaning "manliness, valor, superiority." One lexicon calls it "virtue as a force or energy of the Holy Spirit accompanying the preaching of the glorious gospel."[2] As representatives of King Jesus, we are called to proclaim the "superiority" of God. We have the privilege of releasing the "force or energy of the Holy Spirit" as we proclaim the good news of Christ.

I intentionally used the word *decreeing* to describe my actions in front of the White House. I was not so much asking God to do something, I was decreeing for Him His will. In the next two chapters we'll discuss this declarative facet of governmental intercession in detail. For now, I am simply highlighting that this is one of the ways we release kingly intercession.

Both the priestly and kingly dimensions of prayer can be seen through what we call "the Lord's Prayer" (Matthew 6:9–13 NKJV):

- The prayer begins with praise, an obvious example of priestly intercession: "Our Father in heaven, Hallowed be Your name."
- The prayer then shifts to kingly intercession with imperatives: "Your kingdom come. Your will be done, on earth as it is in heaven." The verbs "come" and "be" are both in command form (imperative) in Greek. In other words, we are not only to request His kingdom rule and will—we are to decree them into situations for Him. Kingly, governmental intercession, bringing heaven to earth.

- The prayer then shifts back to priestly petitioning, asking for provision, forgiveness, and freedom from temptation.

This pattern can also be seen in several of the psalms, Psalm 24 being a prime example. Beginning with priestly language, the psalmist starts with praise, then speaks about ascending into God's presence with clean hands and a pure heart, seeking His face (vv. 1–6)—all priestly activities.

Notice, however, the shift in verse 7: "Lift up your heads, O gates, and be lifted up, O ancient doors, that the King of glory may come in!" The direction changes from upward to downward as the activity shifts from priestly to kingly. Decrees and commands replace praise and communion. The psalmist commands gates to open so "the King of glory" can enter. He is representing "the Lord strong and mighty, the Lord mighty in battle" (v. 8), and in so doing he has shifted from humble praise to bold proclamations.

Dick Eastman, president of Every Home for Christ, tells of a prayer that exemplifies just such a shift from priestly to kingly intercession. He and others were praying for the sale of their California headquarters building so they could move the organization to Colorado Springs. In Dick's own words:

What happened next prompted me to look at my watch. It was 9:55 a.m. The intercessor who had been petitioning God for His intervention had completely changed the tone of his praying.

He had been rehearsing in prayer certain factors God was certainly well aware of: the declining economic conditions of the city; recent articles in the local newspaper explaining how few, if any, office buildings were selling in the Los Angeles area; and the fact that our small street was lined with buildings for sale, some perhaps better and even cheaper than ours. What a faith-building prayer!

But then came the change. The prayer seemed to take a quantum spiritual leap in boldness. It began with a simple phrase, "God, no matter the circumstance, You have just the right buyer for this building." Next came, "In fact, I believe You can see that buyer even now. You know his name. You can see where he is—what he's doing right now."

What happened next I believe was a divinely initiated transition into the arena of prophetic prayer. The intercessor suddenly spoke directly to the would-be buyer, "I believe that even now God sees you driving along the streets near the EHC office, looking for just the right building for your business." An even more startling directive followed, *"I command you to come forth now. Not tomorrow, not next week, not next month, but today."*

Remarkably, an older man with a young couple walked through the front door a few minutes after 10:00 a.m. Theirs would be the only offer on the property. The purchase was finalized exactly on time for that summer's move to Colorado Springs. And it had all begun with a prophetic prayer.[3]

What Dick calls "prophetic prayer" was also kingly intercession. It is God's royal priesthood reigning in life through the authority of Christ. As you intercede for individuals, places, or situations, the Holy Spirit will at times lead you to move into this type of prayer. When He does, be bold and respond in faith. Don't waver as I did at the White House. You do have kingly authority.

8

The Voice

How forcible are right words!

Job 6:25 KJV

Traveling to all fifty states with Chuck Pierce was a lesson in
flexibility. In San Antonio, he ran to the platform, interrupted
my message—yes, he interrupted my message—took the microphone, and began to prophesy.

The first time he did this was in our first state on the tour,
New Mexico. There he didn't come to the platform, didn't
say "excuse me," didn't wave to get my attention, didn't even
stand up. They had given him his own mic, so when he decided it was time to prophesy, he just flipped it on and, right
from his seat, took off.

Scared me half to death!

"Just give me a little warning, next time," I pleaded. "Wave, stand up, anything at all. Just give a little warning." So Chuck started coming to the platform when he felt led to interrupt my messages.

We actually operated this way often. Our purpose on this tour was not to teach, but rather to discern what God was saying, pray it, and decree it. Therefore, it was never truly an interruption, but a welcome accomplishment of our mission. Sometimes I would continue my message after he finished; other times we moved into prayers and declarations based on what he prophesied.

On this particular night in Texas, Chuck began to speak and in the course of the prophecy said that if we prayed, Saddam Hussein would be captured within seven days. Then he turned around and handed me the mic with an "I can't believe I just said that, you'd better do something" expression.

My first thought was, *Why are you handing me the mic? You got us into this situation, you get us out.* But it was too late—I had the mic and everyone was looking at me. I did the only thing I knew to do—pray. As I prayed, I began to move from priestly to kingly intercession. I discerned the Spirit leading me to command and decree that the demonic activity keeping Hussein hidden be broken. Other leaders came to the platform and offered similar prayers and decrees.

Saddam Hussein was captured three days later!

Kingly intercession is released through decrees. With them we "legislate" God's will on earth, in much the same way an earthly king would enact his. Chuck says the following about prophetic revelation and decrees:

> God has chosen us as the necessary link to bring His will from heaven to earth. He wants us to commune with Him, listen

carefully to His voice, gain prophetic revelation, and decree that revelation into the earth. This will unlock miracles and release His blessings. Once we hear God, we can intercede, but we can also prophesy. Prophesying is declaring His mind and His heart. As we speak, He forms His will in the earth. We should always be willing to say "yes and amen" to His promises. When we receive prophetic revelation, we need to decree the prophetic revelation. This was the pattern that we operated in, once we gathered together in our meetings from state to state.[1]

There are two types of prophetic activity, and here Chuck alludes to both. Prophesying is more than *foretelling*—predicting the future. It is also *forthtelling*—speaking forth the plans and will of God for the present and the future. This is still classified biblically as prophetic because of the discernment required for us to know His plans and will. John the Baptist was called a prophet, yet as far as we know he did no foretelling or predicting future events. He *did*, however, discern the times and *speak forth* what God was saying about the present. Accordingly, this forthtelling aspect of the prophetic is also referred to as "prophetic intercession."

When Chuck and I met with intercessors and other church leaders in all fifty states in 2003–2004, our purposes were:

(1) To gather God's people for agreement and the resulting synergy;

(2) To discern Satan's strongholds over a given region and what caused them;

(3) To discern the Lord's strategies in order to break those strongholds, and also His strategy for how He intended to move the church forward toward revival;

(4) To release priestly intercession through corporate repentance and prayer;

(5) To release kingly, governmental intercession through prophetic decrees.

We never released the same prophetic words, decrees, or strategies for any two states.[2] In the Texas gathering where we decreed Saddam's capture, God had given me a word about the state's prophetic calling and destiny. When I said this meant God's purposes for America will sometimes be declared, launched, or pictured from there, Chuck began to receive a prophetic download. He heard the Spirit say, "Go to the platform and prophesy what I give you—and don't think about it." He knew later that he probably wouldn't have said it (about Saddam) had he thought about it first.

Prophesying is more than foretelling— predicting the future. It is also forthtelling—speaking forth the plans and will of God for the present and the future.

What prophetic dynamics occurred in the meeting that night? (1) *Prophetic discernment* of one of God's overall purposes for a state; (2) this prepared the way for a *prophetic word* concerning His specific desire at that moment; (3) the word prompted me to seek *prophetic instructions*; (4) these led us to release *prophetic decrees,* a type of governmental intercession, that is, legislating from the heavens. All of this worked together to become kingly intercession made by the *ekklesia,* the legislative body of Christ, ruling for Him on earth. It was kingdom authority releasing kingdom power, just as Jesus instructed us to do: "Your kingdom come, Your will be done!"

We and an army of intercessors moved in every state in this prophetic, kingly intercession; you need to do this from room to room in your house! You can and should release this type of intercession, not only for the world at large but also for your private and immediate world. Do it for individuals, your family, business, church, and city. Sit on the devil's chest!

What are decrees, declarations, and proclamations? Chuck says:

> A *decree* is an official order, edict, or decision. A decree is something that seems to be foreordained. This is what makes a decree prophetic. *Decree* can also mean to order, decide, or officially appoint a group or person to accomplish something. A decree is linked with setting apart or ordaining something or someone. A *declaration* is an announcement, a formal statement. . . . This statement is what a plaintiff sometimes releases in his complaint, which results in a court action. A *proclamation* actually brings something into a more official realm. A proclamation can ban, outlaw, or restrict. This is linked with the process of binding and loosing.[3]

Words, in general, are amazing. James, in chapter 3 of his letter, notes that with them we bless and curse. He goes on to compare the power of words to a forest fire, a fountain of life, a world of iniquity, and deadly poison. Strong words about the power of words!

Our opening verse from Job calls words "forcible." The Hebrew *morat* means "to press." One of its biblical uses describes a king pressing his seal of authority onto a decree or legal document with his signet ring, making it legally binding (the law of the land). Words seal deals and decree laws. They are powerful, even unto life and death (see Proverbs 18:20–21).

The New Testament says we are justified or condemned by them (see Matthew 12:37).

- Wars are started with words.
- Love is communicated through words.
- Instruction and education are shared by words.
- Deception and confusion are propagated with words.
- Kingdoms are built with words.
- People are controlled by words.
- Lives are shattered and healed through words.
- Worlds are created by words—the earth was and so is our personal world.

That last one is pretty heavy, isn't it? But it's true. Words may very well be the most powerful conduit of authority and power in the world. God's *Let there be . . .* created the world and everything in it.

Ecclesiastes 12:11 says, "The words of the wise are as goads, and as nails fastened by the masters of assemblies" (KJV). Nails help us build, construct, assemble, and hold things together. So do words. The Master Craftsman used them to build the earth, the seas, the mountains, and all the other amazing elements and dimensions of creation. Hebrews 1:3 tells us He holds it all together by the power of His words and decrees!

Luke's gospel says that even the incarnation—God becoming human—was caused by a combination of God's words and Spirit. When Mary asked how she, a virgin, could have a child, the angel informed her that the power of the Holy Spirit would overshadow her and impregnate her with Jesus (1:35). Then he said, "Nothing will be impossible with God" (1:37).

This translation doesn't do justice to the strength of what the angel actually said. The most literal and accurate rendering is: "No word spoken by God is without power." What a claim this is, and what ramifications it carries for us. *Our all-powerful God infuses transcendent power into His words.* They become the carriers of His awesome strength.

In the Scriptures, God issues myriad decrees or declarations. Zodhiates says, "The Ten Commandments are actually ten declarations."[4] They are not the Ten Suggestions. When God issues a command or decree, it is earth's law. To violate one is rebellion against His authority and invites certain judgment.

God also calls His Word a sword with which He rules and judges. His declarations not only create and build but they also judge and destroy. They are both *constructive* and *destructive.* Consider the following: "Out of His mouth came a sharp two-edged sword; and His face was like the sun shining in its strength" (Revelation 1:16); "Repent therefore; or else I am coming to you quickly, and I will make war . . . with the sword of My mouth" (2:16; see also 19:15, 21).

Some of God's decrees are to create or perform something in the present; others are declarations about the future. In Isaiah 46:9–10, God says of himself,

> I am God, and there is no one like Me, *declaring the end from the beginning* and from ancient times things which have not been done, saying, "My purpose will be established, and I will accomplish all My good pleasure" (emphasis added).

What an amazing God! He stands outside of time and looks ahead, declares the future, and eventually time catches up to His decree. How preposterous the fools who think they will outwit or overpower Him! Chuck shares the following story that illustrates God's ability to declare the future:

When my son Daniel was seven years old he came to his mother and me with a question: "What is anthrax?" We both were astonished that a seven-year-old boy would ask such a question. My stepfather (Daniel's grandfather) had cows and land, so I assumed that he had mentioned the issue of anthrax occurring in a natural context. However, when my wife and I questioned Daniel over where he had heard the word "anthrax" he said, "The Lord spoke it to me and said it is coming to America." I explained to him what anthrax was. We have always been honest with our kids, so I just laid it all out on the line. This caused him to fear that it might come upon him. When he would touch something, he would immediately wash his hands. This threw us into a crisis as a family.

In my quiet time one morning I began to seek the Lord, asking Him how He would pull us out of this awkward situation and bring freedom and confidence to Daniel. The Spirit of God said: "This will not be an issue in Daniel's life until he is 20 years old." At breakfast that morning when he began to obsessively discuss anthrax with us, I told him what the Lord had said. Pam gave me that look that said "Why in the world would you say this so I have to live with his obsessive fear for the next 13 years?" Nothing really changed, except that I had heard God.

When I do not know what to do, I either worship or ask God what I can give. I find that I can begin to hear Him when I begin to worship, and He will always tell me where to give. Then I can hear Him on the issues that burden my heart. That night when I put Daniel to bed, I said to him, "Let's worship." We listened to an audiocassette and sang along. At the end of the music, I said to Daniel, "You know how much

418

Mom and I love you. We have tried every way we know to help you get through the fear of what God has shown you. Perfect love casts out all fear. God does not give you the spirit of fear. Therefore, ask the Lord to show you how much He loves you. Since we've worshiped, is there anything you want to ask the Lord?" Daniel replied, "I've been trying to catch a butterfly all week, and I've not been able to."

As any good parent, I wanted to go out and find every butterfly I could and put them all in his room so that when he awakened, they would be surrounding him. However, I knew I could not do that. I had to trust the Lord. The next morning, when he got up and we were sitting outside, he still feared anthrax. While I was praying for him before I left for work, an interesting thing happened. A butterfly flew into our yard and landed upon Daniel's shirt. He cupped his hands around the butterfly and looked up at the Lord and said, "Because You have shown me how much You love me, I'm just going to set this butterfly free." This was quite a moment.

On Daniel's 20th birthday, the headlines in the newspapers in America read "Anthrax Strikes America." I was traveling and called him on his birthday. Remembering God's word about anthrax, I asked Daniel how he was doing. He said, "Dad, since we worshiped that night and God revealed His love to me the next day, I have never questioned His love protecting me in the midst of this particular crisis." He had received faith that would last him the next 13 years of his life and extend into the future.[5]

Thirteen years before they happened, God declared that the anthrax attacks would occur. I want us to see what happens when time catches up to the decree God makes concerning the future. What does He do at that point? He involves us in its fulfillment. *We become the voice of God in the earth, decreeing His decrees for Him!* Job 22:28 says, "You will also decree a thing, and it will be established for you; and light will shine on your ways." The first part could be more literally rendered "You will decree a decree." We discern God's will and decree—what He has determined about a given situation—and decree His decree.

When time catches up to the decree God makes concerning the future, He involves us in its fulfillment. We become the voice of God in the earth, decreeing His decrees for Him!

The verse then says that when we decree the decree, it will be "established." This is the Hebrew word *quwm*, which means "to rise."[6] God's Word is called a seed (1 Peter 1:23), and when we sow it into a situation, we are sprinkling the seeds through which He causes His will to spring up. *Quwm* also describes a variety of other activities, including God's "creative, saving and judging action" rising up.[7] Our decreeing the Lord's Word releases His *creativity,* His *salvation,* and, yes, His *judgments!*

Now a twist to the anthrax story. Chuck said his son would not face anthrax until he was twenty. Time did catch up to the decree from thirteen years earlier; God's decree did not create these attacks, but He knew they were coming and told Chuck. When they arrived, He used His people to decree against and stop them. Jim and Faith Chosa, powerful Native American prayer leaders from Montana, with New Jersey Strategic Prayer Network coordinators John and Sheryl Price, relate the details.

Just after the WTC disaster on 9/11/01, unknown individuals began sending through the postal service, from somewhere in the city of Trenton, NJ, envelopes filled with anthrax. The effect on the nation, already in shock, was severe. And even more so in the state of New Jersey.

However, spiritual mappers [those who understand how to discern the spiritual cause of certain natural events] within the prayer networks in New Jersey, were able to link the current event with an ancient bio-terrorism event perpetrated in 1763 by William Trent, the namesake of Trenton, NJ, against the Ottawa Indians who at the time were laying siege to Fort Pitt. Inspired by a British commander, William Trent had sent into the Ottawa camp two blankets and several cloths which were inoculated with the smallpox virus. The effect on the Ottawa people was devastating. The surviving remnant packed up and headed into the Ohio Valley carrying smallpox with them, increasing the terror for all people they came in contact with.

This unrepented sin was allowing Satan to visit on America the same type of judgment. (A biblical precedent can be found in 2 Samuel 21.) The Chosas and Prices go on to say:

On November 1, 2002, we gathered in New Jersey with a united representation of the prayer networks of the state. Twelve Native believers participating in this event released the preemptive forgiveness of God to immigrant believers present, as they represented the immigrant bloodlines that perpetrated the act in 1763. We then removed from the spiritual landscape the defilements of bloodshed and broken covenants caused by this act and, united with the Body of Christ as one, broke the ancient curse of bio-terrorism in the landscape.

The Anglo-American Body of Christ gave the Chosas, as representatives of the Native Americans, two blankets, again inoculated, but this time with praise and worship to God! The Anglo-Americans then mailed these blankets through the postal system to our address in Montana, in order to cleanse this system from any lingering effects of the bio-curse. The impact was immediate, resulting with no more anthrax attacks through the postal system from Trenton, NJ.

That, my friend, is kingly intercession! The power of God's inspired words is extraordinary. *He rules through words—and so must we.* In fact, you will never truly rule your world until you learn the force of words. Thank God for leaders and intercessors who understand this spiritual authority and know how to pray!

You too are a part of God's government on the earth, and He desires to decree His will and purposes through you. You are a member of His church—the *ekklesia*—and as such have authority to insist on His will and stop the plans of hell.

9

The Sword

We have seen that awesome authority and power are released when God uses the church to decree His will over situations. This power releases both the Lord's salvation to His people and His judgments to His enemies. The following is one of the most amazing testimonies of this I have ever heard. God used Jay Swallow, Native American spiritual leader, and a team of intercessors to overthrow a spirit of suicide on the Sioux Standing Rock reservation. With Jay's permission, here is the story in his own words.

> Prior to my personal involvement in the recovery of the Sioux Standing Rock reservation to a more normal way of life, I had been keeping track of the percentage of suicides among the mostly younger generation of the members of the tribe. There had been dozens of suicides and attempted suicides over the past few years. Just in the last three months they

had had six suicides and 31 more attempts. I, being a long-time visitor of the Reservation since 1968, and [having] seen many forms of revivals in all of the Districts that make up the community population of the whole Reservation, was fairly well known for my efforts to bring relief to this needy area of Indian Country.

Back then as it is today, poverty is still the reason for the collapse of hope, especially among the younger generation. As we know, this leads to alcoholism, drug abuse, child abuse, and many other problems. When added up, the ultimate relief was "suicide."

The atmosphere on the reservation was saturated with panic, not only in homes that feared their own children would be the next to take their lives, but also in the Tribal Government itself. More and more Federal programs were called on to bring relief, totaling a million and a half dollars. Social programs, prevention programs, health programs, judicial programs, welfare programs and youth programs of every description were major players in trying to bring back social order to the reservation. Instead, the suicides escalated out of control.

In October of 2001, I was contacted by Pastor/Evangelist Antoine American Horse, Jr. He sounded desperate and tired as he explained the suicide situation that was, in his own words, "completely out of control."

He stated that he had talked with the Tribal Chairman and the elected officials as well as the Supreme Court Justice, and they gave him full permission and authority to contact me to see if I could come and help resolve the problem. After a lengthy talk on the phone and a three-day time frame of seeking the Lord for my personal direction, I answered with a definite "yes." All I required was the complete authority to do things my way after I sought God for direction.

After being allowed for two weeks before my journey there to use the Tribal radio station that services three surrounding reservations, I spoke to leaders of all faiths and organizations to join with me in a conference to end the reign of terror by the spirit of suicide. One hour a day for a week we sought the attention of those that would join with me in the conference beginning December 27–29, 2001. We called it "The Summit Meeting on Suicide."

Between October and December I started an intense spiritual preparation for this mission. Needless to say, the warfare at times was almost overwhelming.

After assembling my team of five including myself, we were anointed and prayed over by the Oklahoma Concert of Prayer to separate us for this mission (Acts 13:2). We left Oklahoma early morning of the 26th of December. At approximately 3:00 a.m. on the 27th, we arrived at the Reservation line on the south end, which was actually in South Dakota.

We stopped long enough to serve notice to the strongman residing over the Reservation. Larry Brown, a man of great reputation and authority of blowing the shofar, sounded the battle cry of the ancient instrument of history past.

I, Dutch, want to insert here that, true to his nature, Jay is being humble. The spiritual authority he walks in is truly amazing. The hair on the back of my neck stood up and I had chills all over when I heard him tell this story. In this written report, he mentions stopping at the border of this reservation and blowing the shofar. What he does not say is that he then made a powerful declaration over the entire reservation. Jay bound the strongman, forbidding him and his demons from causing any more suicides until he and the team received further strategy from God—they would then give the strongman and his demons their final orders. My friend, that is faith—and that is authority!

The summit meeting started at 8:00 a.m. with registration. I was overwhelmed to see that 110 concerned leaders had heard my plea and decided that what I was proposing was probably better than all the previous efforts. After addressing the clergy of the various Christian organizations, I boldly told them they were responsible for the takeover of their reservation by another spirit. They all humbly agreed, repented, and reconciled with one another in front of a large number of non-believers. This itself was historical and later proved to be effective.

The next two days were very intense and the resistance in the atmosphere was very challenging. I thought my intercessors and I were the only ones that actually knew what we were dealing with and what we were after. But I found out that the anointing given to me for this occasion was understood clearly by those in attendance. On the afternoon of the 29th at 3:30 p.m., the Lord said, "Now is the time," I asked for the shofar to be blown into the heavens, and the strength and courage came to me as I began to dismantle the strongman over the Reservation. We were totally immersed into an atmosphere that I had not experienced before. The whole room and the people there were affected by the spiritual visitation. The assurance came to me. I, and those in attendance, knew we had cleared the atmosphere over the Reservation from the grasp of the strongman. This began the two year and ten month total absence of suicide attempts and actual suicides. The Reservation and its people were free and normalcy came back to the homes.[1]

Awesome! That is kingly intercession at its highest level— using the sword of the Spirit (Ephesians 6:10–17) to war against the powers of darkness. Isaiah 48 also speaks of God's words and the creative power of this partnership between Him and His people. Look especially at verses 6–7:

> You have heard; look at all this. And you, will you not declare it? *I proclaim* to you new things from this time, even hidden things which you have not known. They are *created* now and not long ago; and before today you have not heard them, lest you should say, "Behold, I knew them" (emphasis added).

Now notice verse 7 in the *Amplified:* "They are created now *[called into being by the prophetic word],* and not long ago; and before today you never heard of them, lest you should say, Behold, I knew them!" God wills and proclaims His plan, then we are called to prophetically discern His will and timing and to prophetically decree it, which in turn releases His creative power to accomplish it.

Sandy Grady, an intercessor in Washington, D.C., was used in this way for the state of Virginia. She saw a situation that needed to change, then discerned God's plan and implemented it. Here is her story:

> In the early nineties, I noticed that a lot of focus was being drawn to the federal government for prayer and action, but very little attention was being given to the state governments.
>
> In working with the WallBuilders organization, I decided to use the state in which I live, Virginia, as a model for praying over state government. I knew very little about this state's government at the time, but after research, realized there was a desperate need of prayer for government leaders and for pro-family values in the Commonwealth. A majority of the legislative leaders were showing a great disrespect for the

sanctity of life, prayer in schools, and other values that I held dear.

After surveying the situation (using the Nehemiah pattern), I asked God for a prayer strategy. The Lord showed me to write a Proclamation over Virginia stating the present condition and what would happen when the citizens of Virginia prayed for His government to take over. This Proclamation went out all over Virginia, courtesy of many ministries. It seemed that everyone was in total agreement. At the first joint prayer meeting, the room was packed with intercessors from all over the state who had just been waiting for an invitation like this. The room we used in the Capitol was the very room where Patrick Henry and Thomas Jefferson had spoken in earlier years. Together we decreed this proclamation and continued to do so.

Within one election year, the legislative makeup began to change to a more pro-life and pro-family friendly Assembly. The new administration welcomed prayer regularly in the Capitol and in the Governor's Mansion. Prayer has continued each day on site during the General Assembly meetings since then, and we continue to add to the number of legislators who believe in and pass Godly legislation.

This is legislating for the legislature! It is God's kingdom government praying and decreeing into earthly government what is needed.

Ezekiel 37 is a striking biblical example of God ruling and creating through the decrees of a person. In this passage Israel's spiritual condition is seen in a vision as a valley filled with dry, scattered bones. In other words, Israel was spiritually dead. God's method of restoration was for Ezekiel to prophesy or decree to them:

> Again He said to me, "Prophesy over these bones and say to them, 'O dry bones, hear the word of the Lord.' Thus says

the Lord God to these bones, 'Behold, I will cause breath to enter you that you may come to life. I will put sinews on you, make flesh grow back on you, cover you with skin, and put breath in you that you may come alive; and you will know that I am the Lord.' So I prophesied as I was commanded; and as I prophesied, there was a noise, and behold, a rattling; and the bones came together, bone to its bone" (vv. 4–7).

At this point, even though the bodies were now whole, there was still no breath in them. Again the prophet was told to prophesy, this time to the breath or Spirit of God to enter them. It would seem that God needed or required the prophet's involvement at every step of the process:

Then He said to me, "Prophesy to the breath, prophesy, son of man, and say to the breath, 'Thus says the Lord God, "Come from the four winds, O breath, and breathe on these slain, that they come to life."'" So I prophesied as He commanded me, and the breath came into them, and they came to life and stood on their feet, an exceedingly great army. (vv. 9–10)

This is astounding—a human decreeing to and releasing the Holy Spirit! Note, however, that Ezekiel was not dictating *to* the Spirit but *for* Him. God was giving the orders. Ezekiel was partnering with Him, functioning as His voice on the earth. In verse 14, God says, "I, the Lord, have spoken and done it." He refers to the prophet's words as His own—and indeed they were, for they carried His authority and released His power. Several characteristics of God's Word that we examined in the last chapter are here in this powerful account. God's words through the prophet:

- Were forceful (Job 6:25 NKJV).
- Had the power of death and life (Proverbs 18:20–21).

- Were well-driven nails—(Ecclesiastes 12:11).
- Were not without power (Luke 1:37).
- Established God's will (Job 22:28).

Jeremiah's ministry is another vivid portrayal of God releasing His words through a person: "Then the Lord stretched out His hand and touched my mouth, and the Lord said to me, 'Behold, I have put My words in your mouth'" (1:9).

Next, God told him what they were going to do: "See, I have appointed you this day over the nations and over the kingdoms, to pluck up and to break down, to destroy and to overthrow, to build and to plant" (v. 10).

After this Jeremiah records, "Then the Lord said to me, 'You have seen well, for I am watching over My word to perform it'" (v. 12). Please don't miss this: God's words, which He intended to watch over and perform, were going to be those He spoke through a human being, as verses 16–17 bear out one more time. "I will pronounce My judgments on them. . . . Arise, and speak to them all which I command you."

The pattern could not be clearer: God's Word, but spoken through people. This has always been the way He has operated. Hosea 6:5 states: "Therefore I have hewn them [My people] in pieces by the prophets; I have slain them by the words of My mouth; and the judgments on you are like the light that goes forth." God's decrees and judgments, released by a person's words.

You may be thinking, "Yes, but that was all Old Testament." God's method of operation hasn't changed! The New Testament also speaks of God releasing His judgments through our declarations. Recall the passage in which Jesus speaks of His *ekklesia* (church), which we defined as His parliament or governing body on earth. Look at the *Amplified* Matthew 16:19:

> I will give you the keys of the kingdom of heaven, and whatever you bind—that is, *declare to be improper and unlawful*—on earth must be already bound in heaven; and whatever you loose on earth—*declare lawful*—must be what is already loosed in heaven (emphasis added).

(Incidentally, after this verse, the *Amplified* references Isaiah 22:22, which I used at the White House, about governmental authority to open and close doors.)

Here Jesus tells us, as His government on the earth, to declare—*based on God's will and Word*—what is lawful and unlawful, allowed and disallowed. Seemingly incredible, but also reasonable, for how could we govern on God's behalf without such authority?

The following account pictures both the Lord's judgments released against His enemies, as He did through Jeremiah's words, and the bringing forth of His plans and purposes. I want to stress that these "enemies" are the powers of darkness, not people.

I have prayed in and around various government buildings on numerous occasions. One of those was on June 16, 2005, at the Supreme Court. I had been given a five-point prayer assignment by a trusted friend and intercessor, Jay Comisky. Jay told me he had received five biblical declarations over the Court while praying and that he had envisioned me decreeing them there.

My schedule was extremely full, with no windows for a trip to D.C. However, I believe very much in Jay's credibility, in the power of Spirit-led decrees, and in God's calling on my life. So I rearranged my schedule and on my next ministry trip routed through D.C. in order to fulfill this assignment.

I felt that rather than going inside the Supreme Court building, I was to make these five decrees from the outside, once on all four sides. I did this and in a couple of hours was on my way. Decree number two was that God's shifting of the Court was changing from a "siege" to a "suddenly." I had no idea what this meant, I simply decreed it the way Jay received it.

In order to be effective, the content of our decrees must be what God desires.

This is an important point. We must not inject our understanding or wishes into an assignment from God. We must be very careful to do and say what He instructs. I'm not implying that we have to hear God's decree word for word and say it in exactly that form. But in order to be effective, the content of our decrees must be what *God* desires.

As I stated, I had no idea what the "suddenly" was, but two and a half weeks later Sandra Day O'Connor resigned. No one expected it—most (including me) thought Chief Justice William Rehnquist would be first. But the "suddenly" did come, and I knew it was from God.

My assignment for the "suddenly" wasn't over, though. Twice since, I have been back to D.C. to pray about this appointment (and will be going again soon). One of those trips was three days before President Bush nominated John Roberts.

Knowing that President Bush was under great pressure to appoint a moderate rather than a strong moral and constitutional conservative, I felt I was to go to the White House and pray for him. I did so with Lou Engle and Sandy Grady. We were there simply as "tourists," not by official invitation. We walked through the White House for approximately an hour, praying for God to lead the president in his decision and decreeing that only God's choice would be made.

During this time, something strange kept occurring. Sandy, one of the most tuned-in intercessors I know and an intercessor on D.C.'s behalf for thirty years, kept bringing up horses. She said she kept thinking about horses when she prayed, and then she kept being drawn to pictures and sculptures of horses in the White House.

We could not discern what this was about, but we knew God was trying to direct us. Again, it is not necessary to have exact words and phrases in order to speak for God. He is not legalistic. He requires our involvement, obedience, and prayer—not perfection in our verbal delivery.

Believing God was saying something but not knowing what it was, we offered a prayer that went something like this: "God, You are obviously drawing our attention to horses. We don't know why and it makes no sense to us. But we declare that Your plans and purposes concerning 'horses' and this Supreme Court decision will be fulfilled. We decree that Your kingdom will come and Your will be done." Then we continued praying for the president and various facets of his decision.

I must confess that it seemed very foolish praying about horses, but the three of us have learned to obey even when we don't understand. Imagine our pleasant surprise a few days later when we read the following teaser: "How a quartet of power brokers known as the Four Horsemen is shaping the future of the high court."[2] A portion of the article stated:

The men, who have been dialing in [to the White House] since 2003, have come to be known as the "Four Horsemen": C. Boyden Gray, Edwin Meese III, Jay Sekulow, and Leonard Leo. Hand-picked by the White House for their ties to disparate conservative groups, they have been instrumental in helping the president name strict constitutionalists to the federal bench—and now they hope to do the same on the nation's highest court. "We've been waiting for this for four years," says Sekulow of the American Center for Law and Justice. And so the Four Horsemen are galloping into this confirmation fight.

We didn't know the president's four advisors were called "the Four Horsemen." We simply prayed and decreed that God's purposes concerning the court decision would be fulfilled and that the "horse" part of it, whatever it was, would be taken care of. We now know we were praying for wisdom to be given to them and the president as they worked together on this issue. We believe that happened, and that Supreme Court Justice Roberts was the right choice.

We are God's plan! He is waiting for the church to be the *church*—functioning as His parliamentary council, legislating His will through Spirit-led decrees, frustrating the councils of hell. He is waiting for us to command His will over the lives of individuals and declare that they will not be destroyed by Satan's schemes. If you're a true Christian, you're a part of this great governing body. Don't wait any longer to begin extending God's rule into the earth.

10

The Heavens

Blessed be the God and Father of our Lord Jesus Christ, who has blessed us with every spiritual blessing in the heavenly places in Christ . . . which He brought about in Christ, when He raised Him from the dead, and seated Him at His right hand in the heavenly places . . . and raised us up with Him, and seated us with Him in the heavenly places, in Christ Jesus . . . so that the manifold wisdom of God might now be made known through the church to the rulers and the authorities in the heavenly places. . . . For our struggle is not against flesh and blood, but against the rulers, against the powers, against the world forces of this darkness, against the spiritual forces of wickedness in the heavenly places.

Ephesians 1:3, 20; 2:6; 3:10; 6:12

This sounds like one uninterrupted passage of Scripture, doesn't it? I became fascinated one day as I read these verses consecutively with none of the in-between sections. When I saw how well they flowed together, I realized they really do provide a continuity of thought. In summary, they tell us we have been given everything we need in order to operate in heavenly places; Christ has been given all authority in this realm; we have been seated there with Him in that position of authority; through us, from our position there with Christ, God intends to deal with the kingdom of darkness; finally, the last verse describes that evil kingdom, listing its various components.

What are "heavenly places"? This is not referring to heaven, God's home, but to the invisible atmosphere all around us. We must understand this relatively unknown dimension in order to fully partner with God and experience the fullness of His blessing. This is the unseen realm of the spirit—invisible yet real, hidden yet very active. Much of what happens on earth is influenced by it; certainly anything of eternal significance or regulating the destinies of people and nations is controlled within it. Most people, including Christians, give little thought to the unseen world governing the one we see. Many, especially in cultures that emphasize higher education and intellectualism, are actually cynical of this arena. But the Bible is filled with descriptions and accounts of it—in fact, this is the story of Scripture. Apart from it, there is no God, Satan, angels, demons, fall of humankind, birth of Christ, redemption through the cross, miracles, or resurrection of the dead. Yet again, surprisingly, most American Christians live their lives without weighing how much this realm affects us, let alone how we can influence it.

Here is a significant truth: *The more we learn to function in the invisible spiritual realm, recognizing and applying its governing principles, the more we can partner with God, positively impact our world, avoid the snares and influence of the evil one, and enjoy the blessings of our salvation.*[1] As I meditated on the Ephesians verses, God began revealing to me that I was not conscious enough of this realm. It was not a new subject to me. I have comprehended it for many years and realized that we can influence it through our prayers and actions. But the Holy Spirit began revealing to me that I was not as aware of this dimension as I needed to be.

I saw clearly that if I was going to be as effective as I could be in changing situations on earth, I had to understand how this heavenly realm affected it. Conversely, I also needed greater understanding of how I could influence the invisible world. And hopefully do all of this without becoming weird!

The more I meditated on this spiritual sphere, the more I realized it is the Bible's major theme—two invisible kingdoms warring for control of the world. If we could see what takes place around us in this realm, we would no doubt see a great kingdom clash—angelic and demonic forces engaged in phenomenal warfare. I don't know exactly what it looks like, but I know it goes on. The following vivid account of the unseen gives us a glimpse:

> When the attendant of the man of God had risen early and gone out, behold, an army with horses and chariots was circling the city. And his servant said to him, "Alas, my master! What shall we do?" So he answered, "Do not fear, for those who are with us are more than those who are with them." Then Elisha prayed and said, "O Lord, I pray, open his eyes that he may see." And the Lord opened the servant's eyes, and he saw; and behold, the mountain was full of horses and chariots of fire all around Elisha. And when they came down to him, Elisha prayed to the Lord and said, "Strike

this people with blindness, I pray." So He struck them with blindness according to the word of Elisha.

2 Kings 6:15–18

The invisible forces were there all along—it was just that Elisha's servant could not see them. And so it is with us. We live in a world filled with constant and tremendous angelic and demonic activity. Our natural eyes simply cannot perceive it.

It amazes me how many Christians, though they claim to believe the Bible and would say they believe in these "heavenly places," still have a problem consciously relating to it. Many, for example, take issue with any form of prayer dealing with demons, angels, or invisible strongholds.

The world, of course—those who do not profess to be Christians—has an even greater problem acknowledging the invisible spiritual realm. The very suggestion of an invisible sphere influencing the visible world elicits immediate skepticism (or mockery) and often an inference that anyone who believes in this realm is not in touch with reality.

What a boost for the devil's activities!

But at some point, if we are going to be truly effective in prayer, especially governmental intercession, we must acknowledge, understand, and learn to influence the spiritual realm. We must move beyond our fear of what others think, and agree with Scripture. Jesus is our example, and He frequently dealt with the invisible. He was always aware of it and consistently engaged unseen entities, stirring up demonic opposition everywhere He went.

The early church in Acts did so as well, confronting forces of darkness and dealing with them when appropriate. We are inconsistent if we confess to be Bible-believing followers of

Christ and yet refuse to acknowledge and deal with the invisible kingdom of darkness. Failure in this area has rendered us largely impotent.

This account, which demonstrates our need to become involved in the spiritual arena, also shows kingdom authority being dramatically released.

Some of our staff, along with students from our ministry school, have gone a number of times to a nearby university that is a major center of New Age spiritualism. The most popular religion on campus is witchcraft. My senior associate [Kris], a wonderfully anointed prophet of God, was invited to speak in a class on Christianity and the supernatural. He stood before the students and shared a brief testimony. At the end of the class a young lady who was tormented by demons began to manifest under their influence. Kris commanded them to leave, and she was delivered in front of many wide-eyed students! She was then filled with so much joy that they had to carry her out of the classroom into the parking lot so the next class could begin. The students from both classes looked on at what was happening, stunned and dumbfounded. My associate began to call people out, pointing at them and speaking strong prophetic words into their lives that touched the secret things of their hearts. Some dropped to the floor instantly as if they'd lost their strength. Others sat there with their mouths gaping. "I saw you being dedicated to God," he told one young man who was the only unbeliever in a large family. And on it went until those witches and warlocks who had devoted their lives to the powers of hell knew there was a mighty God in Israel, and in the Church![2]

This is the church being the church. We must grow in our boldness and skill, learning to partner with the Spirit to operate in and impact this realm.

Another Old Testament passage, Exodus 17, demonstrates this invisible war in Joshua's leading the Israelite troops into battle against the Amalekites. God told Moses to go up on the mountain overlooking the battlefield with the rod He had given him and to hold it aloft. This rod symbolized God's authority in much the same way a king's scepter represents his; it had been so throughout Israel's deliverance from Egypt, always representing His authority, which released His power. Raising the rod, Moses was exalting God's strength.

Scripture tells us that when Moses' arms became weary and he was no longer able to hold up the rod, the battle would turn against Israel. When his hands were held high with the rod extended, the battle would go in Israel's favor. This was obviously not an issue of morale. The soldiers were not watching Moses while engaged in conflict. The cause of the momentum swings was completely separate from their conscious minds. It was the invisible war in the heavens.

While there were *visible*, flesh-and-blood people fighting with tangible, physical weapons on a very real battlefield, the action of Moses on the mountain was releasing an *invisible* force determining the conflict's outcome. Notice that both realms were actually influencing the other: (1) Actions occurring in the *visible* realm [Moses lifting the staff] (2) activated God's *invisible* authority and power, (3) which in turn, determined the outcome in the *visible* realm (the battle). Each arena—natural and spiritual, seen and unseen—still affects the other today. Millions of good and bad events occur on earth every day due to this two-way cause and effect.[3]

Daniel 10 records an example of angels serving Daniel in an extraordinary angelic visitation with a remarkable message from God.

Behold, a hand touched me and set me trembling on my hands and knees. And he said to me, "O Daniel, man of high esteem, understand the words that I am about to tell you and stand upright, for I have now been sent to you." And when he had spoken this word to me, I stood up trembling. Then he said to me, "Do not be afraid, Daniel, for from the first day that you set your heart on understanding this and on humbling yourself before your God, your words were heard, and I have come in response to your words. But the prince of the kingdom of Persia was withstanding me for twenty-one days; then behold, Michael, one of the chief princes, came to help me, for I had been left there with the kings of Persia. . . ." Then he said, "Do you understand why I came to you? But I shall now return to fight against the prince of Persia; so I am going forth, and behold, the prince of Greece is about to come" (vv. 10–13, 20).

Daniel, a man of passionate prayer, had cried out to God for several things, one of which was Israel's restoration. As incredible as it sounds, the angel that appeared said to him, "I was sent to you the first day you began to pray, but I was opposed by a spirit called the prince of Persia."

In late October 2004, just a few days before the presidential election, I lived an experience somewhat similar to Daniel's. In fact, his story influenced mine. Unlike Daniel, I didn't see angels, but they were there. I should have known better than to try to take a vacation the week before an election. I'm usually engrossed in prayer at that time, but on this occasion I felt the election would go the way the Lord wanted.

A few days before the end of my vacation, however, I became very troubled. I sensed a great increase of spiritual warfare over this election. Satan must have brought in demonic reinforcements from all over the world to try to turn it toward his desired end. The burden on me was so great I knew I had to go to D.C. to pray. I have been there to pray just before every major election for the past eight years, so that in itself was nothing new. The suddenness and interruption was what made this trip unique.

Ceci and I decided she would go home to Colorado Springs and I would catch a flight to Washington. She knows the assignment on my life and knew the importance of this vote, so she was fully supportive. Later that night, an intercessor in Colorado Springs, Timmerle DeKeyser, called me. She said, "One of the other intercessors in the church had a dream about you last night, which I felt you should know about immediately. She dreamed she was attending a conference and went into an average-sized room for the first teaching session. There was a man standing up front, ready to begin teaching, with a large media screen behind him. As he started to teach, he turned to this intercessor and said, 'Tell Dutch Sheets he must go up to 11 and 12.' On the screen behind him, the numbers 11 and 12 appeared as he said this.

"In her dream the scene changed and she was in another room for another session. The same man was there to teach, and again he looked at her before he began and said, 'Tell Dutch Sheets he must go up to 11 and 12.' This ended the dream."

I took this call while in the lobby of a music hall; Ceci had gone in to get our seats. As I walked in, pondering, I saw Ceci waving, and I made my way over. Entering our row, I noticed it was row 12, but darkness kept me from seeing seat numbers. "What seats are we in?" I asked her.

"Row 12, seats 11 and 12," she said.

"I think God is talking to me!" I said and then related to her the dream. Indeed, He was.

I began to seek the Lord as to what these numbers meant. Why was He saying I must go up to 11 and 12? Why would this be given to me on the eve of my trip to Washington to pray for the upcoming elections? My first thought when seeking direction is always to look in Scripture, so I began to look up references with 11 and 12 in them.

I felt drawn to Matthew 11:12: "From the days of John the Baptist until now the kingdom of heaven suffers violence, and violent men take it by force." I contemplated this verse and discerned that God was indeed giving me prayer insight for the Washington assignment.

I also looked at Revelation 12 and realized it's all about spiritual warfare. God's angel Michael and other angels were warring against Satan, the dragon. I found verse 8 particularly interesting: No room was found any longer in the heavens for the dragon and his angels. I realized God was confirming to me that there was great warfare over D.C. and that I was definitely going there to participate in it.

What a way to end a vacation!

I was especially encouraged by verse 11—until I got to the last phrase, that is: "for they did not love and cling to life even when faced with death" (AMPLIFIED).

Meditating on Revelation 12, I received a call from a different Colorado intercessor, Jean Steffenson, who said, "I have been praying for you and felt strongly led by the Holy Spirit to ask you to read Daniel chapter 10. God wants to speak to you from there."

As I read and meditated, I realized the chapter also includes a story about Michael warring in the heavens, this time against a spirit called the Prince of Persia. Daniel had been praying and God had dispatched angels with an answer, but demonic forces in the spiritual realm were warring against the angels bringing him the answer. God sent Michael to help the other angels break through to Daniel.

While meditating on this, I suddenly remembered a prophetic exhortation given to me a few months earlier. Jane Hamon, while speaking in our church, prophesied that sometime in the near future God was going to send the archangel Michael to war over D.C. and I was going to go and partner with him.

I had forgotten this word. Probably on purpose! But after reading about Michael warring in the heavens in Revelation and Daniel, I remembered. God was telling me, "I have sent you here to Washington to war against Satan's strategies to control this election, and I am sending Michael to help you."

I am very grateful for the prophetic gifting God has placed in the church. If not for this dream about the numbers 11 and 12, I would not have been reading Revelation 12 and would not have remembered the prophecy about warring alongside Michael in D.C. Because of these occurrences, however, I and several others asked God to send Michael and a host of angels to help us in this battle. The result was immediate and incredible. In my life I have never been in a room where the atmosphere changed more quickly and dramatically. I knew Michael and his angelic force had come.

As one final encouragement for this assignment, the Lord led a member of Congress to call me just before I left for the White House. "How are you feeling about the elections?" he asked.

I explained what had transpired while on vacation, where I was, and what I was about to do. "Perhaps you're supposed to pray for me and with your governmental authority send me, in a spiritual sense, into this assignment," I suggested.

"I believe so," this legislator said, "because you just came to mind and I felt impressed to call you immediately." The prayer was powerful and added greatly to my confidence.

I and three others had a powerful prayer time at the White House for an hour or more. We bound the efforts of Satan to determine the election's outcome. With many petitions and decrees we released kingly, governmental intercession. We commanded God's kingdom rule to come and His will to be done in the upcoming days.

We believe our prayers were answered. Of course, there were thousands of believers around the nation also praying concerning these elections, and we are certainly not trying to take the credit. We were only a part of the efforts. But sometimes the Lord needs someone to go to the heart of the battle and make His decrees. When I do this, I see myself as the point of a spear or arrow, with all the prayers of God's people being the shaft and bow. All of it is necessary.

There is one further significant interpretation of the 11 and 12 dream, relating to biblical symbolism of the numbers 11 and 12. I should add at this point that I would never base doctrine on the interpretation of numbers, nor would I ever take action based only on it. However, God does use the symbolic meaning of numbers in Scripture. No serious biblical scholar questions this. I don't want to bore you with a lot of theology, so I'll simply give you enough reference to assure you of this pattern. The number three, for example, represents resurrection; five is the number of grace. Seven pictures completion and rest, as in the Sabbath; eight symbolizes new beginnings.

In this biblical numbering system, the number 11 refers to a change of paradigm or a transition from one place or way of thinking to another. It can also picture disorder, because there is often a temporary season of disarray or disorder during a transition. The number 12 is the number for kingdom order and government. For example, the crown in Revelation 12:1 had twelve stars, probably referring to the twelve tribes of Israel; 21:14 speaks of the wall of the New Jerusalem having twelve foundation stones, which had on them the names of the original twelve apostles of Christ.

Through these two numbers I felt God was saying to me, "You must go through the disorder (11) in the heavens and exercise My kingdom government or rule (12)." As you can imagine, with so much confirmation and orchestration by the Spirit, I fulfilled this assignment with great confidence, knowing I was obeying God's direction and moving in His authority.

11

The Room

"Dad, I had an interesting dream last night," said my youngest daughter, Hannah. Knowing she receives dreams from the Holy Spirit on occasion, I was anxious to hear the details. After I did, I knew it wasn't just for Hannah, but also for the body of Christ in general. And without any question, it was for me. Though some details are not pertinent to our subject, others are.

In her dream we were dropping her off at a college or university. The first thing she had to do was get new shoes. We went into a store named "Safeway," a supermarket chain in many parts of the country, and found the ones she needed. In her dream, she thought it was unusual that the shoes were found in a supermarket, so she looked back at it as we left. The name was no longer "Safeway" but "Other Things."

As we sought the Lord for interpretation, we felt the Spirit was saying there is a new phase or season coming (new shoes) and that on this journey we would not be able to go the "safe" and familiar way—He was about to do "other things." We would need to leave our comfort zones and be stretched into new methods and activities, all of which would require us to think differently.

When given her room assignment in the dream, Hannah was told she was in a particular building on "Gray Floor." That the name was a color was interesting and significant. "What do you think that means?" she asked.

Knowing that gray hair is biblically symbolic of the wisdom that comes from age—the same Hebrew word meaning "old age" and "gray hair" *(siyb)* is also translated "elder" (see Ezra 5:5, 9; 6:7–8, 14)—I knew immediately that the floor's name symbolized wisdom.

Then she said, "Dad, when they gave me my room it was number 601. I know that seems strange, but it was very clear in my dream—601."

Instantly I knew what this meant also. With my love of word studies, I have examined the Greek for "revelation" *(apokalupsis)* enough to remember its number in Strong's numbering system for New Testament words. The number of this term's verb form ("to reveal") is 601; 602 is the number of its noun form.

Fascinated and amazed, I replied, "I know what it represents, Hannah—revelation. You were assigned the room of Revelation on the floor of Wisdom." Immediately I thought of Ephesians 1:17, "that the God of our Lord Jesus Christ, the Father of glory, may give to you a spirit of wisdom and of revelation in the knowledge of Him."

Hannah continued. "Dad, when I opened the door you were inside. Surprised, I said, 'Sorry Dad, I thought this was my room.'"

"It is," I had said to her in the dream. "I've been staying here, but now I'm giving it to you."

This dream carried great significance for me. I knew it indicated a new work God was about to do in our nation and a new phase of ministry for me. I believe He is beginning something very new in Hannah's generation, a move of the Spirit that for some time I have known in my heart was coming. I am convinced there is an imminent revival for America, starting with Hannah's generation, then spreading to all age groups. Through the dream God was instructing me to help father her generation, giving wisdom and the revelation I have received.

The symbolic designations of her room and floor—which one was wisdom and which was revelation— were intriguing. The broader area (the floor) was wisdom, yet it wasn't complete without revelation (the room). Neither would be adequate or functional without the other. Revelation, spontaneous and specific understanding or strategy for current situations, must be interpreted in the larger context of wisdom, a general understanding of God's ways, purposes, and principles learned over time. *Every floor of wisdom must have a room of revelation; and every room of revelation must be found on the floor of wisdom.*

Revelation, spontaneous and specific understanding or strategy for current situations, must be interpreted in the larger context of wisdom, a general understanding of god's ways, purposes, and principles learned over time.

Most of the church focuses on one or the other—not a balance of the two—and I think it is fair to say that the greater portion of Christ's body focuses on the need for wisdom and knowledge. While I would never downplay the need for wisdom—in the dream it was the larger portion (an entire floor is obviously bigger than one room)—it is also true that wisdom without revelation is very detrimental to our cause.

What is revelation? It is more than simply gaining intellectual knowledge we didn't previously have. It is an understanding originating from the heart or spirit, revealed to us by the Holy Spirit. The following verses make this clear:

> [I pray] that the God of our Lord Jesus Christ, the Father of glory, may give to you a spirit of wisdom and of *revelation* in the knowledge of Him. I pray that the *eyes of your heart* may be enlightened, so that you may know what is the hope of His calling, what are the riches of the glory of His inheritance in the saints.
>
> Ephesians 1:17–18, emphasis added

> Even if our gospel is veiled, it is veiled to those who are perishing, in whose case the god of this world has blinded the minds of the unbelieving, that they might not see the light of the gospel of the glory of Christ, who is the image of God. For we do not preach ourselves but Christ Jesus as Lord, and ourselves as your bond-servants for Jesus' sake. For God, who said, "Light shall shine out of darkness," is the One who has shone *in our hearts* to give the light of the knowledge of the glory of God in the face of Christ.
>
> 2 Corinthians 4:3–6, emphasis added

It is inarguable that the biblical concept of revelation is not of the mind and does not originate with ourselves. The words *veiled (kalupto)* in the latter passage and *revelation (apokalupsis)* in the former come from the same root. The basic concept of *kalupto* is to hide or conceal something by covering or veiling it. Adding the prefix *apo* means to undo or reverse that process, giving us the concept of revelation. Simply stated, revelation is when God lifts the veil created by sin from our hearts and allows us to receive insight or understanding directly from Him.

> *Revelation is when God lifts the veil created by sin from our hearts and allows us to receive insight or understanding directly from Him.*

Highlighting some of the differences between wisdom and revelation will help us understand their different roles. Wisdom is formulated based upon truth learned in the *past*; revelation, on the other hand, produces *present* truth and makes our wisdom relevant. Revelation brings *current strategy for current situations*; wisdom enables the *implementation of that strategy with skill*. Wisdom generates *consistency and balance*; revelation *prohibits stagnation*.

Note several potential ramifications of emphasizing one without the other. If we operate in wisdom without current revelation, we might:

- Become an "old wineskin" (Matthew 9:17). (An old wineskin doesn't refer to a person without truth but to one without "present truth" [see 2 Peter 1:12]).
- Know right principles but fall short in their proper timing and application.
- Emphasize theology and doctrine while lacking power (truth over spirit).

- Emphasize intellect over gifts or power, formulas over the spirit's direction.
- Become religious—outwardly displaying Christianity without power, putting forward routine without relationship.

If on the other hand, we overemphasize revelation and/or underemphasize wisdom and understanding, we have the potential of:

- Not placing enough importance on sound doctrine.
- Becoming too subjective in our approach to life and spirituality.
- Misinterpreting and misapplying the revelation we receive.
- Prioritizing power over truth, spirit over word.

Since there is a far greater emphasis in the church on wisdom and learned knowledge, contrasted to what I believe is a great lack of revelation, I want to focus the remainder of my comments in this and the next chapter on the need for and benefits of revelation, *in the context of praying with authority.*

Kingly, governmental intercession is absolutely linked to revelation. We can never be confident we are operating in God-given authority if we are not certain we are functioning according to His will and strategy.

This is the confidence which we have before Him, that, if we ask anything according to His will, He hears us. And if we know that He hears us in whatever we ask, we know that we have the requests which we have asked from Him. (1 John 5:14–15)

My first thought when praying about any situation is usually *What Scripture applies to this?* or *Holy Spirit, what is Your will and strategy in this matter?* Our greatest lack in prayer is allowing the Spirit to help us. Jesus said it was to our "advantage" that He leave the earth, for if He did not, the "Helper" would not come (see John 16:7). *Helper* comes from a Greek word meaning "one who comes alongside to give aid." We don't press our advantage—the Holy Spirit—enough in prayer.

Jesus went on to say of the Spirit that He would "disclose" things to us (vv. 14–15). While not the same Greek word as revelation, the term used for disclose, *anaggello*, is equally important and revealing. The prefix *ana* means "back," and *aggello* means "to announce";[1] "possibly the *ana* carries the significance of upward, i.e., heavenly, as characteristic of the nature of the tidings. To tell in return, bring word back."[2]

The significance is obvious and cannot be overemphasized. The Spirit, our Helper, wants to bring us heavenly counsel and strategy, disclosing God's plans to us. It should be obvious that to whatever degree this occurs, to that degree we will have success. Proverbs 16:3 (AMPLIFIED) agrees: "Roll your works upon the Lord—commit and trust them wholly to Him; [He will cause your thoughts to become agreeable to His will, and] so shall your plans be established and succeed." The following story illustrates the role of our Helper and the success that comes when we allow Him to help us.

A young man named Brandon, who is a graduate of Bethel School of Supernatural Ministry, was visiting friends in Washington State. They were at a restaurant and the waitress came to take their order. Brandon began to perceive things in his heart about the woman, and he shared them with her. They pertained to her relationship with her mother. The waitress was amazed, and she became so emotional that she had to take a break.

While the waitress was away, Brandon noticed an Asian couple staring at him from across the room. The woman had wrist braces on because she suffered from carpal tunnel syndrome, and one of her hands was completely frozen in a fist. Brandon walked over and asked if he could pray for her. She said that they were Buddhists, but they were willing to receive prayer. He prayed for her and she was healed on the spot. The whole family was instantly overjoyed and began praising Jesus, right at their table. They said they had been praying to their ancestors for a long time for her hands to be healed, but the prayers hadn't worked. Brandon explained who Jesus is, and they received the gospel with wonder and thankfulness. He went back to his table and for the rest of the evening, the healed woman sat there opening and closing her hand in amazement.

About that time, the waitress came back and asked if she could talk with Brandon outside. She was understandably confused and yet eager, and wanted to know more about God. Brandon shared further insight that the Holy Spirit gave him about her life and told her about Jesus' love. She gave her heart to the Lord and was filled with the Holy Spirit right there. She was breathless with excitement and declared she was going to tell all of her friends what had happened.[3]

Without disclosure from the Spirit, neither the salvation of the waitress or the healing of the Buddhist would have occurred. Governmental intercession discerns the will of the King in heaven and insists on it being accomplished on earth. God loves the lost and desires to demonstrate that love. The Holy Spirit desperately wants to help us make the demonstration.

God speaks to us in many ways. Scripture is absolutely the primary and only infallible method He uses, the standard by which all other revelation must be judged. But God does speak to us by His Spirit, directly to our hearts and minds, and through supernatural methods such as dreams, visions, and prophecy. He also uses circumstances. Regardless of His chosen method, hearing from God is not optional if we are to be overcomers in life. The following testimony of Lou Engle's assistant and intercessor, Brian Kim, illustrates just how willing God is to disclose to us His direction and strategy.

Since July 2002, I have been on a Daniel-type fast, eating no meats or sweets (Daniel 8:1–16) for the ending of abortion and for justice and righteousness to be restored in America. After President Bush, who was clearly pro-life, was reelected in November, I wanted to end the fast and eat meats and sweets again. So the morning after it was official that President Bush had won the election, I prayed to the Lord and said, "Lord, I want to end this fast today, so if you don't give me an indication that I am to stay on this fast, I'm going to eat cake tonight."

Throughout the day, I continually prayed and asked God for confirmation if I was to continue on the fast. At 10:00 p.m. that night, I went to meet one of my college friends to study and when I arrived in the library I noticed a young man already studying with my friend. I walked up to the young man I did not know and introduced myself saying, "Hello, I am Brian Kim." The young man responded saying, "Hello. I am Daniel Fast."

How's that for divine revelation! In this situation, God chose not to speak directly to Brian's heart but rather to use an amazing set of circumstances. I know Brian personally. He continued the fast and now lives in the D.C. area, giving himself to prayer and fasting for the ending of abortion and the release of revival. Brian is a member of the emerging generation that will live on the floor of wisdom in the room of revelation.

Sometimes finding our personal room of revelation is a process, requiring time and great perseverance. After several years of tragedy, pain, and loss, the Smith family in my congregation shares their testimony of God's faithfulness and ultimate victory.

My husband, Steve, and I were married in 1984 and we have five beautiful children. Just before our son Zack turned eleven, he was diagnosed with a rare form of children's cancer and given a 20 percent chance of a five-year survival. He went through years of chemotherapy and radiation, had 32 surgeries and made it through a stem cell transplant. His leg was eventually amputated at the pelvis.

We all fought, none harder than Zack. At times I had such faith that things would be okay, at other times fear that they would not. On April 16, 2003, he went home to be with Jesus. At first Steve and I felt relief that his suffering was over, but then the guilt and depression set in. I felt so guilty, wondering if I prayed hard enough. A deep sadness came over me and I thought I was going to die from it at times.

We experienced depression and disappointment, anger, tormented sleep, and enough tears to drown in. Our hope, peace, and joy were all taken from us. Even our very identity was gone—our whole life had been wrapped up in Zack and his illness. Sometimes people would not even call me by my name but say, "Hey, are you Zack's mom?" It was the same for all of us.

Another problem became a complicating factor. Finances have always been a problem for us; it seemed like we were always going around the same old mountain. Making ends meet often seemed impossible. As is typical in situations like ours, Steve and I were even starting to grow apart, each in our own little corner dealing with things in our own way. After Zack passed away I started working to help make ends meet and even that did not seem to help. It seemed like there was always something coming along to steal from us so we could never get ahead.

Then in March of 2005 Steve lost his job. He carried so much guilt. He applied for several jobs, and one that looked promising was a welding job, something he had not done in years but was trained to do. To our great disappointment, however, he did not pass the test. He took a job at Wal-Mart, making much less than before and hating it.

I had finally had enough. I knew we had to do something. All the depression and hopelessness was getting the best of Steve and me. We were the picture perfect—*unhappy*—family. There was no joy, no hope—things I should have found joy in I did not. I wore a façade, but inside was miserable. We decided we needed help. Restoring the Foundations, a model of prayer and deliverance based on a combination of Scripture and Spirit-led prayer was suggested to us. I was afraid, because to do the program meant opening up and letting go of so many things, but I went ahead with it anyway. It is hard to let God do such a deep surgery. Healing often hurts, especially when things need to be cut out. Steve was also hesitant but went through the program as well.

Things began to change. Hope and peace were starting to come into our home. The atmosphere began to change as God was being put in His rightful place of authority and as Steve and I were willing to let God have the things that were separating us from Him. He had always been there but we had given other things and strongholds more authority than Him.

One week before we were to finish RTF Steve got a call from the welding place. They wanted him to try again, so three days after we finished RTF the test was scheduled. I had lost my position at work and was again stressing out a little, but Steve was different this time. He and the kids began to pray for me. My kids were prophesying and Steve was praying with more spiritual authority than I had seen in him in years. The next day Steve went for the weld test and told me not to worry, he was going to get the job. God and I talked a lot that morning and I was still unsure about my not working. I told God that if He wanted me to be a stay-at-home mom, that Steve not only needed the job but I also told Him what Steve needed to make! Not only did Steve get the job, he was hired at almost 20 percent more than I asked for!

When a shift took place in Steve and me, everything changed at home. It became a totally different place. Not only did God show himself to be our provider, He restored so many things. I have joy unspeakable. There is peace, laughter, and hope for each new day. Steve and I are praying together. Our kids are praying again and on fire for God. There is more worship in our home than television. Our healing is ongoing, of course. God gracefully and gently encourages us forward. We will always miss our son, but where there was a deep, bleeding wound, God has brought healing and given us a peace.

It is amazing that when God is given His rightful place of authority He comes running with open arms, wanting nothing more than to bless and restore all that was lost. The enemy still tries to defeat us but the Lord says all things are possible if we believe. Our new family motto is, "A problem is really not a problem at all; it is just an opportunity thrown in our path to give God praise and testify to His greatness." Our lives have truly been turned around. There are really no words to describe what I feel in my heart. The sun seems to shine brighter and there is no heaviness in my heart, only joy and peace.

The transformed Smith family is an amazing inspiration to me. Many elements came into play in their story of triumph over tragedy. Of course they went through an unavoidable grieving process, but they ultimately had to make a conscious decision to allow God to bring them out of it. And more was needed than just the decision—discernment and revelation were required for them to know how to break free from their pain and current lack of provision. This came through skillful discernment and prophetic insight. Wisdom was required to apply that revelation in an appropriate and healing way. As they stated, they had to rise up and place God "in His rightful place of authority."

God wants you also to find your room of revelation. No matter how difficult your situation, the Holy Spirit is willing to disclose heaven's strategy and insight to you, enabling you to get Satan and adverse circumstances off your chest. Your destiny is to be a kingly warrior, overcoming in life through the kingdom authority of Jesus Christ.

You can do it!

12

The Interruption

We were in Florida on the Fifty-State Tour when Chuck interrupted my message. As usual, something I said awakened the prophetic anointing in him. I don't know how he functions in meetings without me.

"There is a terrorist cell in Tampa," he said in the course of his prophecy.

Again he handed me the microphone with a do-something-about-it look. Almost as if he were saying, "I found it. Now you deal with it."

I did the only thing I knew to do—pray. I led, while those present joined with me in agreement. We decreed that the terrorists would be found. Two weeks later a professor at a Tampa university was exposed and arrested as the leader of a group that funded Islamic terrorists.

That is warring by interruption and revelation!

In Matthew 16:18, Jesus speaks of building and warring by revelation. The context is that Peter has just received a powerful revelation of Jesus as the Messiah, the Son of God. Jesus commended him and said, "Upon this rock I will build My church." *The Amplified Bible* makes it clear that Jesus (1) was talking about spiritual warfare and (2) was not saying He would build His church on Peter, but upon the rock of revelation:

> I tell you, you are Peter [Petros, masculine, a large piece of rock], and on this rock [petra, feminine, a huge rock like Gibraltar] I will build My church, and the gates of Hades (the powers of the infernal region) shall not overpower it—or be strong to its detriment, or hold out against it.

Regarding "the gates of Hades," I love Kenneth Wuest's Translation, "the counsels of the unseen world shall not overpower it." Jesus then made His famous promise of giving us the keys, or authority, with which to bind and loose in the invisible realm called "heavenly places."

Far too often we try to build the church and war against Satan's plans and counsels without revelation—the counsels of heaven. This is futile, and our lack of success in many areas is the fruit of it. God, however, has been restoring our understanding of the need for the prophetic anointing that brings discernment and revelation. This is changing everything.

One of my favorite verses relating to the need for and power of revelation is 1 Chronicles 12:32: "Of the sons of Issachar, *men who understood the times, with knowledge of what Israel should do,* their chiefs were two hundred; and all their kinsmen were at their command (emphasis added)."

Times in this verse is a Hebrew word meaning strategic or opportune times. (For those who enjoy word studies and know the Greek word *kairos*, this is the Hebrew equivalent.) These were men of revelation, and it was this revelation of the times that brought them knowledge of what to do.

We must realize this is a passage about war—the passage is often referenced, but that aspect is usually overlooked. Verse 1 introduces the upcoming list of David's mighty men with "they were among the mighty men who helped him in war." At the chapter's conclusion, we're again reminded that all these men were warriors (v. 38). Please don't miss the significance of this. This prophetic anointing—the ability to understand the times, which brought knowledge of what to do—had to do with war. This is instructional: For us to be effective in our *spiritual* war, we too must have an ability to discern the times. And like these men of old, from that revelation we can receive strategy.

This Hebrew word for "understanding" the times is also significant. This is more than a *learned,* intellectual knowledge or wisdom; it is *prophetic* revelation or discernment—a spiritually imparted knowledge. Several other passages where the same word is used will confirm this:

- In 1 Kings 3:9, Solomon asked God for an ability to "discern."
- In Daniel 1:17, 20, Daniel was given this kind of "understanding" to interpret visions and dreams.
- In 8:15–16, Daniel asked for "understanding" to interpret a vision.
- In 9:22, Daniel was given "instruction" and "insight with understanding" by an angel. (I find the phrase "insight with understanding" fascinating. I equate it to "wisdom

and revelation" in Ephesians 1:17, which we discussed in chapter 11.)

- In 10:1, Daniel received "understanding" to interpret a vision from God.
- And in Proverbs 3:5, God says, "Do not lean on your own understanding."

Proverbs 3:5 makes much more sense when understood in this light of prophetic revelation. God is not saying we should abandon wisdom or common sense. He is telling us not to rely on our own human discernment of what to do. "Receive revelation from Me," He is saying. Again, placing this understanding into the context of war (1 Chronicles 12) makes it especially significant. If we are to know what to do to overcome in spiritual warfare, we must receive spiritual revelation.

In October 2003, Chuck and I held our state meeting in Kansas. During this meeting, Chuck prophetically called the state to hold a worship gathering in Wichita, where worship would go forth to war against abortion. Wichita has become a leading national abortion center. Chuck said abortion is a sacrifice issue and the only thing that would successfully counteract it is worship.

Earl Pickard, U.S. State Strategic Prayer Network prayer coordinator, waited for the Lord to show him the right timing, and then in obedience to the God-given strategy, he conducted the worship gathering in Wichita. Here is the chronology of what occurred, along with the fruit, as reported by Jeff Kahrs.

On March 7, 2004, a twenty-four-hour worship service was held in Wichita, Kansas, to break the stronghold of abortion and death over Wichita. This time of worship was called by Chuck Pierce during the Fifty-State Tour held in Kansas last fall and was later organized by Earl Pickard.

On March 17, 2004, the noted serial killer BTK resurfaced for the first time in twenty-five years. (January 11, 2004, had marked the thirtieth anniversary of his first killings—the Otero family. He later went on to kill a total of ten people, but had not been heard of since 1979, and was assumed dead by most people—including the Wichita police department.)

Shortly after the BTK resurfaced the Lord revealed to me (and to my sister-in-law) that the enemy was very upset over the focused and intensified prayer and worship going out over Wichita in order to break the stronghold of abortion and death over our community . . . and thus brought the BTK out of hiding to instill fear throughout our community. Over the next eleven months the BTK began a series of bizarre and cryptic communications with the police department and the general public.

The Lord also impressed upon me the importance of prayer and that the local Christian community would have to "pray-in" the BTK before he was captured . . . that the powers keeping him concealed were very strong. I, along with others, I am sure, encouraged the believers to pray and press into the Lord for his capture. I took every opportunity I had to meet with area Christian leaders and preachers who loved the Lord and encouraged them to direct their congregations to pray for the capture of the BTK. I am quite sure many others were doing the same thing.

On January 11, 2005, a city-wide prayer meeting was called and organized by two prominent evangelical pastors in Wichita: Joe Wright of Central Christian Church and Terry Fox of

Immanuel Baptist Church. The purpose of the prayer meeting was to pray for the capture (or surrender) of the BTK, pray for the healing of the victims' families, and pray for the healing of the community. Between fifty and one hundred people attended, including a representative of the local city government, city police department, and family members of the victims.

On February 25, 2005, the BTK was captured by local police authorities. This is less than one year after he resurfaced but more than thirty-one years after he committed his first serial killing.

No one can prove that the worship gathering brought the BTK killer out of hiding or that the prayers of the saints caused him to be captured. To the skeptic it will all be co-incidental. But to those who believe in the power of prayer, the facts and chronology of the events speak for themselves. This was warring by revelation!

Paul told Timothy to "fight the good fight" by using "the prophecies previously made concerning you" (1 Timothy 1:18). David warred against the Philistines by receiving divine revelation (2 Samuel 5:23–25). Elijah overcame Jezebel through God-given revelation and strategy (1 Kings 17–18).

In 2 Chronicles 20, Israel defeated an invading army through receiving heavenly strategy. A prophet named Jahaziel gave them divine revelation for the battle (vv. 14–17). Listen to King Jehoshaphat's instructions to Israel before the battle: "Listen to me, O Judah and inhabitants of Jerusalem, put your trust in the Lord your God, and you will be established. Put your trust in His prophets and succeed" (v. 20).

If Israel had to listen for God's strategy from heaven in order to win their battles, isn't it reasonable that we will need to do the same in our spiritual warfare? To fail in this is to be defeated.

The Scriptures actually equate a lack of revelation to judgment. In Luke 12:54–56 and 19:41–44, Jesus rebuked the Pharisees and Jerusalem's religious community for not being able to understand or discern the times. Because this was caused by the hardness of their hearts, they received great judgment instead of blessing. He said to Jerusalem, in essence, "I wanted to send you a mighty visitation, but because you could not understand the times, you could not receive what I wanted to do" (see 19:44). Lack of revelation caused loss of God's visitation.

In verse 42, Christ also said that a part of their judgment was a further loss of revelation! His plans for them would be "hidden from [their] eyes." Because they refused to receive His current revelation, there was a greater inability to discern placed upon them. God began to intentionally hide things from them. What a terrifying thought.

Another similar judgment is pronounced in 13:35. Because the religious rulers had rejected the prophets, God said to them, "Your house is left to you desolate." This Greek phrase literally says, "Your house is left to you." In other words, God's judgment to them was, "You are now on your own. You rejected My prophetic anointing; you did not want My words. Therefore, that is exactly what you are going to get— you will be left with your own." Fearsome judgment!

There is an attitude within certain elements of the church that opposes the prophetic anointing, just as these early church leaders did. This is extremely dangerous. When we reject the prophetic anointing, we are rejecting a facet of Christ himself. He *is* our prophetic anointing. According to Revelation 19:10, the testimony of Jesus is the spirit of prophecy. Ephesians 4:7–12 tells us that the prophetic office and anointing is one of the five anointings of Christ.

When we reject the prophetic anointing, we are rejecting a facet of Christ himself. He is our prophetic anointing.

Not to belabor the point, but 1 Samuel 3:1 is still another verse that lets us know a lack of revelation can be God's judgment. "The boy Samuel was ministering to the Lord before Eli. And word from the Lord was rare in those days, visions were infrequent." Because of the apostasy and sin of the priesthood, God had refused to release revelation in Israel. Because Samuel was a true worshiper, however, this was all about to change. God was lifting the curse and rebirthing a season of fresh revelation.

A prayer effort the Lord called me to a few months ago is another good example of how He uses revelation to lead us in spiritual warfare. As you will see, God went to great lengths to get the revelation to me. The saga began with a dream a young friend of mine, Crystal Hamon, was given in the latter part of 2003. Here are the primary details.

Lou Engle and Dutch were together, in a building used for banquets and other gatherings. Lou was talking to people around him about prayer and fasting and was growing frustrated that they were not listening to him, but rather were just chattering and eating. Dutch, on the other hand, was talking to individuals and they were listening to him.

The scene changed and Dutch approached Lou, handed him something I could not yet see in the dream and said,

"Here, Lou, if you will strike this, they will listen to you."
Dutch also handed him a conductor's wand with which to
strike the unseen object. Lou did as instructed and a sound
reverberated through the room. When the sound was heard,
everyone began to pay close attention to him.

When Lou turned back around to Dutch in the dream,
what he was striking could be seen—it was "the scales of
justice." He then looked at him and said, "This will crescendo
on March the first."

As we, like Daniel, sought the Lord for insights concerning the dream, we received some we felt were significant. The
scales of justice obviously referred to the courts. That the
scales had to be struck evokes intercession (the Hebrew word
for intercession is *paga,* "to strike the mark.") The conductor's wand indicated agreement, since the Greek word for
agreement is *sumphoneô,* from which we get our word "sym-
phony." That Lou and I were together and I handed him these
things obviously indicated a need for our partnering in this.

In obedience to the revelation brought through this dream,
Lou and I sent a letter asking intercessors associated with
us in the prayer movement to fast and pray for a shift in the
Court for forty days. Interestingly, backing up forty days from
the day the dream said everything would crescendo—March
1—was Inauguration Day for President Bush's second term.
Many people responded and joined us in prayer.

Here is when things got really interesting. At the end of the
forty days, I was scheduled to minister in England. The night
before I was to leave, February 27, I looked at the expiration
date in my passport and realized I had been reading the date
wrong for the last few years. The date was written in two different languages, and it had confused me. My passport had

expired! I couldn't believe it. I felt foolish, embarrassed, and angry—and I was in a panic. I couldn't believe I was doing this to the people who had scheduled me for their conference. *I just have to get there,* I thought.

Both Ceci and Hannah had a different reaction. They told me from the very moment I realized my passport had expired that God was somehow in it. I did not accept this and said, "No, it's just my stupidity. I can't believe I did this. How could I be so stupid? I'm not a novice traveler. I should know how to read these things. How could I have misread this date for the last couple of years?"

"No," Hannah—who is very prophetic—said adamantly. "God is in this. You be alert to what He is doing."

I arose early the next morning, the day I was supposed to leave, and called the phone number I had for the U.S. Passport Agency. "How can I get a passport renewed quickly?" I asked.

"You will have to call one of the U.S. passport offices [she listed approximately ten cities], see if you can get an appointment, fly there, walk through the process, and if there are no problems, they will issue you a new passport," she told me. "But it is hard to get an appointment on short notice. Most of them are booked several days, sometimes even weeks, ahead."

Great, I thought.

I knew I would be at least a day or two late for this conference—if I made it at all. But since I was the keynote speaker for the latter half, I realized I might be able to get there for most of my teaching slots. If, that is, I could get an appointment in one of the passport-issuing cities, secure the necessary flights to it, and then get booked on new flights to England!

I then asked, "Of all of the passport office cities you have mentioned, which one would you recommend I try to get an appointment with?"

She thought for a moment and said, "I think you should try Philadelphia."

I hung up, called Philadelphia, and, to my surprise, they had an opening at nine the next morning. When calling them, there was no opportunity to talk to a person, so I could not plead my case or beg for a time slot. What was available on the computerized schedule is all that was offered, period.

I was able to route myself into Philadelphia late that night in order to be at the passport office the next morning. I was also able to get a new flight to England for the afternoon, should I be successful in renewing the passport. On the way to the office that morning I noticed, to my surprise, that it was only a block away from the Liberty Bell and Constitution Hall, where our government was formed. I have prayed there many times, and it is a very special place to me. As I rode in the taxi, I found myself thinking: *Wouldn't it be wonderful to spend some time praying here today?*

An hour or so later, while filling out my forms, suddenly I realized as I wrote the day's date that it was March 1, the last day of the forty days of prayer for the courts—Crescendo Day. In the panic of the last two days, I had completely forgotten. *What a shame,* I thought. *Here it is Crescendo Day and instead of praying, I'm distracted by this mess. Wouldn't it be great if I were here to pray instead of dealing with this situation?* Then I actually thought, *Wouldn't it be interesting if I ended up with time to go to Constitution Hall and pray? Could it be that Hannah was right and God wanted me to be here? No, I won't have any time to pray. This will take all morning, then I have to rush from here to the airport to catch the flight to London—if I even get my passport in time. No, I wish I were here for that reason, but it won't happen.*

After my forms were completed and I was called to the counter, the agent took all my information and said, "You have two hours now to wait. Go find something else to do for the next two hours."

"Don't I need to stay here?" I asked.

"We don't want you to stay here," she said. "Please go and return in two hours (at 11:00)."

As her words sank in, I began to sense God's presence in a strong way. Chills went up and down my spine as I sensed the Spirit's anointing coming upon me. Suddenly I knew in my heart all of this really was arranged by God. He had caused me to misread the date so He could get me to Philadelphia to pray on the Crescendo Day of this assignment. I still did not know, however, exactly what He wanted me to do.

First, I walked to the Liberty Bell and began to decree over America the verse written on it, Leviticus 25:10: "You shall thus consecrate the fiftieth year and proclaim a release through the land to all its inhabitants. It shall be a jubilee for you, and each of you shall return to his own property, and each of you shall return to his family." Then I went to Constitution Hall and signed up for a tour in order to go inside and pray through the building. When the tour ended, I knew my assignment still wasn't accomplished, but didn't know exactly what remained. I kept asking the Lord, "What do You want me to do?"

I continued to walk by myself around the outside of the hall, praying but not discerning what the Spirit wanted me to do. Finally, as I was about to leave the premises, I saw an adjacent building I had never entered. In all of the times I had been to this place, I had not even noticed it. While walking around praying, I had actually seen one or two people go in and out and wondered what it was, but there was no sign over the door and absolutely nothing to indicate its purpose. I felt the Spirit's prompting and kept hearing in my heart, *Go in there.*

I decided to obey, not even knowing if I actually was allowed to do so. Inside, I found a guard and a courtroom, which I could tell was very old and preserved in its original state. Inside, I again began to feel an incredible anointing and a great sense of destiny. (I have this hard-to-explain-feeling when on a strategic assignment from the Lord.) I asked the guard, "What is this place?"

"This is the original Supreme Court," he said, "where it all started."

I could not believe what I was hearing and replied in astonishment, "Are you telling me this is the birthplace of the Supreme Court of America?"

"Yes," he said, "this is where it began, in this very room."

I was speechless. I knew that at that very moment Lou Engle, my counterpart in the dream, was with a group of young people at the current Supreme Court building, "striking the scales of justice" through intercession. And here I was, the other man in the dream, standing in the original Supreme Court of America on Crescendo Day. In God's amazing sovereignty, He had orchestrated this series of events to get me to the place where our nation was born and our judicial branch was started. While Lou was decreeing God's will at the current Supreme Court, I was going to the root.

I realized I was on a very holy and important assignment. God had sent me there to "strike" the Supreme Court of America, decreeing His Word over it and commanding a return to its original intent. I knew I was there to call it back under God and to a fear of the Lord . . . to command it to become once again a government institution that would not try to expel God from public life in America but would welcome and honor Him. I was then to decree that it become again a court that would honor life and morality. Very quietly and while looking like nothing but a tourist I did these things, commanding God's kingdom to come, His will to be done, and a rebirth of His purposes for the Supreme Court of America.

Crescendo Day!

Do I really believe God orchestrated all of this and that my words made an impact? Absolutely! And we have now begun to see the changes. I realize it is not just because of my prayers but thousands of others as well. As is often the case, however, God needed someone to go and issue His divine decree.

God gave a young lady a dream. He gave Lou and me the interpretation of the dream. And then, in His sovereignty, He interrupted a trip overseas and motivated a passport agent who had no idea what was happening to advise me to go to Philadelphia. He opened a slot for me to be there at just the right time and led me to a building I did not even know existed—all in order that His purposes might be decreed over the place. Then He got me to my meeting on time—I never missed a session. What a God! And what evidence of His need and desire for us to represent Him in kingly governmental intercession.

Do not underestimate the importance of prophetic revelation. Your Helper is waiting to disclose God's will and strategies to you, and He will do whatever is necessary to make it happen. Ask for His help.

His "interrupting revelation" is waiting.

13

The Levels

I did pretty well in math—almost went into accounting. This was obviously an anomaly, because I can't seem to follow the simplest arithmetic when the three ladies in my life come home from a shopping excursion. Though I still do not understand the math, I am confident of the right question when they arrive: "How much money did you save me?"

I once made the idiotic mistake of asking, "How much did this cost me?" I received a quick lesson in protocol and Math 101.

So when Hannah (sixteen) came home last night from shopping with her mother, she started in immediately telling me how successful it was. "Great," I said. "How much money did this save me?" She rattled off the original price of each garment, then the sale price, announcing at the end of the list that she had just saved me $150.

I was ecstatic. So was she—and very proud of me. "You've made a lot of progress in understanding how this works, haven't you, Dad?"

"Absolutely."

Though I don't really understand this form of accounting, I realize that God made the female species with superior math skills. I am also very aware that my ignorance has caused an erosion of authority when it comes to shopping. There are other areas of our family life in which I do have great authority—the TV remote, the garage, and the trash, for example.

It is a common misconception that all Christians have the same amount of authority to operate in Christ's name. We do not. There are several principles that will determine the varying degrees of spiritual authority we operate in as followers of Jesus (none of which have anything to do with math or shopping, by the way). I want to mention seven principles in this chapter and the next. Grasping this won't solve the confusion surrounding the male-female shopping breach, but knowing them will eliminate some confusion about prayer.

We Are One in Christ Jesus

The first principle that determines our level of authority in prayer is simply *our relationship to Christ—our salvation.* While each believer moves in differing levels of authority for some activities, everyone has equal authority to access the Father in Jesus' name. No Christian has any more authority to go before the heavenly Father than you do. No one has more access to the provisions procured for us by Christ than you. God has no second-class children. We all stand on equal ground and have the exact same potential level of authority when it comes to petitioning the Father in Jesus' name and requesting of Him the biblical promises made to us.

Notice that I used the word *potential* in the previous sentence. While we all have equal access to our heavenly Father in Christ's name, there are factors that can alter this. They have to do with our obedience to His Word and our freedom from sin. These can and will affect our right to approach the Father for His blessings.

The Bible is filled with passages indicating that our level of authority and favor with God is linked to our level of purity. Psalm 24, a striking example, tells us that those who have clean hands and a pure heart can approach God and His throne (see also 1:1–3; 1 John 1:5–10). We must not be deceived into believing we can do as we please, live contrary to God's laws, and still be welcome before our Father, let alone move in significant intercessory authority for others.

In Revelation 2 God addressed the church at Thyatira about their compromise with the spirit of Jezebel. He was angry with them because they were tolerating this spirit; He challenged them to change this, then said in verses 26–27, "He who overcomes, and he who keeps My deeds until the end, to him I will give authority over the nations, and he shall rule." God unquestionably links our authority level to our purity level. If we choose to compromise or allow a particular evil spirit to operate in our life, it will diminish the level of authority we possess, both when petitioning the Father for ourselves and for others.

Samson, of course, is another good example. His compromise with Delilah eventually eroded his authority and power and cost him his ministry, his freedom, his eyesight, and yes, his destiny. Our obedience to the Lord absolutely determines our rights before Him.

Circles of Authority

The second principle regarding our level of authority is what I call the principle of concentric expansion. Picture a small circle with ever-expanding circles around it, much like a target with larger and larger circles around the bull's-eye. For our discussion, the inner circle would represent us as individuals. As the circles expand and grow larger, they include more people and greater territory. As this increases, our authority decreases, since we are sharing it with others. The second circle might represent an individual's family, the third their city, the next their nation, and so on. Again, as the circles expand outward, our personal authority decreases.

No one has more authority over your life than you do. No one has greater authority to pray for you than yourself.

No one has more authority over your life than you do. No one has greater authority to pray for you than yourself. We are born with a free will, the right to choose, and as we mature into adulthood this freedom increases. As far as God is concerned, no one can take it from us. With it, however, comes not only authority but also responsibility. Back in the late 1970s and early 1980s, I had numerous warts on my hands—as I recall, between thirty and forty. I had spoken with doctors, who were hesitant to remove them because several were next to my fingernails, some of them actually eating into the nail. On my right index finger I only had half a fingernail. Several cuticles were gone, having become one huge wart. They were irritating and embarrassing.

I had sought the Lord earnestly, asking Him to heal me, and I had fulfilled most if not all biblical procedures for healing. I had called the church elders to pray for me (James 5:14–15). I'd had hands laid on me according to Mark 16:18. I had other individuals who agreed in prayer with me (Matthew 18:19–20), I had been in services where the gifts of the Spirit, especially the gifts of healing, were manifesting in a pronounced way (1 Corinthians 12:9). I could never seem to receive my healing.

One day the Lord spoke to my heart very clearly: "I am never going to heal your hands based upon someone else's prayer or faith. You must fight the good fight of faith and lay hold of this healing yourself. I have taught you well—you have sat under tremendous teaching for years. To whom much is given, much is required, and I am requiring you to do this." This was not cruel or unkind. He was doing what any loving parent would do—helping me, even requiring me, to grow up. Our Father does not want us to remain spiritual babies.

I began to put into practice what God had taught me. Primarily I used Mark 11:23–24: We can speak to a mountain of adversity and command it to be removed. I did this for approximately thirty days, several times daily. I would look at my hands and say, "According to the Word of God, which tells me that Jesus bore stripes for my healing and that I have authority to rebuke these warts and command them to leave me, I now command you warts to leave my hands in Jesus' name." Did it seem foolish? Of course. Many spiritual practices and guidelines seem foolish to our natural minds

(1 Corinthians 2:14). But I did it anyway, and the outcome speaks for itself.

After approximately two weeks, I began to notice the warts shrinking. From that point on, they began quickly to decrease in size. Over the next two weeks—a total of four weeks of doing this—every wart was gone from my hands, and I had brand-new cuticles and fingernails. A creative miracle!

My point in sharing this story is simply to illustrate that no one has more authority to pray for you or lay hold of God's promises for you than *you*! And at times God will actually require us to use that authority, refusing to do some things for us based on another individual's prayers and faith.

Again, our authority decreases as we move outward to the next circle. Though our family members have individual authority as they relate to God, we also possess authority to pray for them. God has given me the responsibility to be a covering or protection for my wife and children and with this comes great authority to pray for them. I recall the testimony of a man in the late 1970s, illustrating the authority God has given us to pray for our children. His daughter had several dozen growths on her hands; I believe they also were warts. The Lord spoke powerfully to him one day, as he was praying, and said, "How long are you going to put up with those warts on your daughter's hands?" The gentleman was very surprised and even a little intimidated, as the Lord seemed upset with him. As he questioned, the Lord again spoke to him: "You have authority to cover and protect your daughter. You have the right to make the warts leave her hands. How long are you going to put up with them?"

The father of the young girl took this seriously and, just as I had done for myself, began daily—and several times a day—to command them to leave her hands. After many days of faithful obedience, his daughter received her healing. Hers did not happen gradually, however, as mine did. She received an instant miracle. One day, as she was hanging clothes in her closet, she hung up one garment and her hands were the same. She then reached down, grabbed another piece of clothing, and from the time she picked up the clothing until the time she reached the rod, her hands were completely transformed. Not one wart remained—beautiful skin like a baby's covered her hands. She screamed and ran to her father with the news, and the two of them rejoiced together. *We have authority to pray not only for ourselves but also for those for whom we are a covering!*

In 1985, God used my prayers to heal Ceci of an ovarian cyst. She'd had it for approximately a year and was told by a doctor that she would need surgery to remove it. He hoped to take only the cyst, but there was the possibility he would have to remove the affected ovary as well.

This doctor was a Christian, and I knew he believed in the power of prayer, so I asked if he could safely give us some time to pray for Ceci. I really believed we could get the cyst removed through the power of prayer. Since it was not malignant, he said, "Yes, I will give you two months, and if we don't get rid of it your way, we will get rid of it my way."

I sought the Lord, asking Him for the strategy I needed to lay hold of this healing for Ceci. I heard Him clearly say to me that if I spent an hour a day praying for her that she would receive this healing. I began to faithfully obey. I do not know why this was God's chosen plan nor do I care. He has His reasons.

After two weeks of prayer for her, the pain began to decrease. After four weeks the pain was completely gone and so was the cyst! This was then verified by the doctor's new tests.

Once more: As our circles expand, our influence and authority decreases. I have authority, for example, to pray for my city, but others in my city have just as much authority as I do. All of us have authority to pray for our nation, an even larger circle, but other believers in the nation have equal authority to do so. It becomes obvious that as the circles expand, our authority decreases.

Know and Believe

A third principle in connection with our level of authority in prayer is our understanding of God and His Word. Without knowledge of it we will not be aware of His provisions for us or of His ways through which they come. Hosea 4:6 says that we as God's people can be destroyed for lack of knowledge. Obviously, if we are ignorant of what is rightfully ours through Christ, we will not exercise authority to lay hold of those provisions by faith. Paul told his spiritual son Timothy to "take hold of the eternal life to which you were called" (1 Timothy 6:12). Timothy was already saved and therefore had received eternal life. Why, then, would he be told to "take hold" of it? The covenantal provisions promised to us in Christ do not automatically come to us just because we're Christians. We must learn to exercise our authority, release our faith, and *seize* these provisions—which is the literal meaning of the Greek word translated "take hold of."

This third principle also links authority to faith. Without a knowledge of God's Word we will not have faith (see Romans 10:17). To the degree we believe the Word, to that degree we will obey and act upon it with authority. After healing the lame man at the Beautiful Gate in Acts 3, Peter said, "On the basis of faith in His name, it is the name of Jesus which has strengthened this man whom you see and know; and the faith which comes through Him has given him this perfect health in the presence of you all" (v. 16). Peter made it clear that the authority releasing the power to perform this amazing miracle was through faith in Jesus' name.

Our authority level is connected to our faith level.

In Matthew 17:14–23 the disciples attempted and failed to deliver a young boy of an evil spirit. Christ delivered the boy, and when questioned by the disciples as to why they couldn't do it, He attributed it to a lack of faith on their part. They had already been given authority over demons and had delivered other individuals (see 10:1, 8), but their faith wasn't strong enough to exorcise this one. It is obvious that our authority level is connected to our faith level.

The following story, written by a doctor who worked in Central Africa, is one of the greatest examples of simple faith I have ever heard.

One night I had worked hard to help a mother in the labor ward; but in spite of all we could do, she died, leaving us with a tiny premature baby and a crying two-year-old daughter. We would have difficulty keeping the baby alive, as we had no incubator (we had no electricity to run an incubator). We also had no special feeding facilities. Although we lived on the equator, nights were often chilly with treacherous drafts. One student midwife went for the box we had for such babies and the cotton wool that the baby would be wrapped in. Another went to stoke up the fire and fill a hot water bottle. She came back shortly in distress to tell me that in filling the bottle, it had burst (rubber perishes easily in tropical climates). "And it is our last hot water bottle!" she exclaimed. As in the West it is no good crying over spilled milk, so in Central Africa it might be considered no good crying over burst water bottles. They do not grow on trees, and there are no drugstores down forest pathways. "All right," I said, "put the baby as near the fire as you safely can, and sleep between the baby and the door to keep it free from drafts. Your job is to keep the baby warm."

The following noon, as I did most days, I went to have prayers with any of the orphanage children who chose to gather with me. I gave the youngsters various suggestions of things to pray about and told them about the tiny baby. I explained our problem about keeping the baby warm enough, mentioning the hot water bottle, and that the baby could so easily die if it got chills. I also told them of the two-year-old sister, crying because her mother had died. During prayer time, one ten-year-old girl, Ruth, prayed with the usual blunt conciseness of our African children. "Please, God," she prayed, "send us a water bottle. It'll be no good tomorrow, God, as the baby will be dead, so please send it this afternoon."

While I gasped inwardly at the audacity of the prayer, she added, "And while You are about it, would You please send a dolly for the little girl so she'll know You really love her?" As often with children's prayers, I was put on the spot. Could I honestly say, "Amen." I just did not believe that God could do this. Oh, yes, I know that He can do everything, the Bible says so. But there are limits, aren't there? The only way God could answer this particular prayer would be by sending me a parcel from my homeland. I had been in Africa for almost four years at that time, and I had never, ever received a parcel from home. Anyway, if anyone did send me a parcel, who would put in a hot water bottle? I lived on the equator!

Halfway through the afternoon, while I was teaching in the nurses' training school, a message was sent that there was a car at my front door. By the time I reached home, the car had gone, but there, on the veranda, was a large twenty-two-pound parcel. I felt tears pricking my eyes. I could not open the parcel alone, so I sent for the orphanage children.

Together we pulled off the string, carefully undoing each knot. We folded the paper, taking care not to tear it unduly. Excitement was mounting. Some thirty or forty pairs of eyes were focused on the large cardboard box. From the top, I lifted out brightly colored knitted jerseys. Eyes sparkled as I gave them out. Then there were the knitted bandages for the leprosy patients, and the children looked a little bored. Then came a box of mixed raisins and sultanas—that would make a batch of buns for the weekend. Then, as I put my hand in again, I felt the . . . could it really be? I grasped it and pulled it out—yes, a brand-new rubber hot water bottle. I cried. I had not asked God to send it; I had not truly believed that He could. Ruth was in the front row of the children. She rushed forward, crying out, "If God has sent the bottle, He must have sent the dolly too!"

Rummaging down to the bottom of the box, she pulled out the small, beautifully dressed dolly. Her eyes shone! She had never doubted! Looking up at me, she asked: "Can I go over with you and give this dolly to that little girl, so she'll know that Jesus really loves her?"

That parcel had been on the way for five whole months. Packed up by my former Sunday school class, whose leader had heard and obeyed God's prompting to send a hot water bottle, even to the equator. And one of the girls had put in a dolly for an African child—five months before, in answer to the believing prayer of a ten-year-old to bring it "that afternoon."[1]

If you're like me, your eyes are wet after reading this. Perhaps God's are too. If you will spend time reading and meditating on God's Word, your faith and authority, like this little girl's, will grow. God is waiting to be able to use you to do the impossible.

14

The Degrees

Behold, I give you the authority.

Luke 10:19 NKJV

We have been looking at the various principles that determine our level of authority in prayer. Contrary to what some believe, all Christians are not given the same amount of spiritual authority. We listed three of these principles in the last chapter and will now discuss numbers four through seven.

Near to His Heart

The fourth principle that will determine our authority level is our connection to and identification with God's heart. This is often overlooked. God gives authority to those who think the way He thinks and want what He wants. When He began mantling me for my calling to America in 2000, first He allowed me to feel His heart for America. I had numerous experiences, one of them very profound, when I wept for hours over this nation's condition. The Lord was allowing me to feel what He felt and identify with it at an acute level. This gives Him the ability to trust a person. If He knows we will do what He wants, and not our own thing, He can trust us with more responsibility and greater authority.

Jesus said in John 8:29 (NKJV), "He who sent Me is with Me. The Father has not left Me alone, for I always do those things that please Him." Jesus always endeavored to find out what the Father wanted and then to fulfill His pleasure. We must do the same.

Before Nehemiah was given authority to rebuild the walls of Jerusalem, he first went through four months of grieving over the city's condition. We are told that he "sat down and wept and mourned for many days . . . fasting and praying" (Nehemiah 1:4 NKJV) to God on Jerusalem's behalf. The prerequisite to the Lord's conferring upon him the authority to change the situation was his allowing God to impart to him His heart for Jerusalem. Afterward, Nehemiah was given not only the assignment but also great favor and provision from the Persian king, Artaxerxes. *Favor, provision, and authority follow the receiving of God's heart.*

This has proven true in my life time and time again. In *Intercessory Prayer,*[1] I tell of praying for a young girl who had already been in a coma for a year and a half. I prayed for a year, spending one to two hours a week in her room interceding over her. After this year—making it two and a half years in the coma—God gave her an amazing miracle.

To the absolute amazement of the medical community, she was completely restored.

Why did this require a year of prayer on my part? Perhaps to allow God to work in my heart, just as He did with Nehemiah. I cannot tell you how much my heart was impacted over the course of that year. God was allowed to share with me His heart for suffering people. I was deeply "moved with compassion," just as Christ was over the sick and hurting during His earthly ministry. There came a point when He could trust me with this miracle—with not prostituting it for gain or self-promotion—and when this time came He released the necessary authority for me to make the decree. The authority we walk in is most definitely connected to possessing God's heart.

Hear and Understand

The fifth principle determining our level of authority is our ability to listen to God and discern His will. Delegated authority has everything to do with representation. We receive authority from the one we represent. Obviously, we must know what he/she expects or desires of us. "This is the confidence which we have before Him, that if we ask anything *according to His will*, He hears us. And if we know that He hears us in whatever we ask, we know that we have the requests which we have asked from Him" (1 John 5:14–15, emphasis added).

Jesus often mentioned that He was always and only doing the Father's will, His inference clearly being that this was what gave Him the ability to act with such authority (see John 4:34; 5:30–32; 6:38). Likewise, as His representatives, we derive our authority from carrying out His will and desires.

A story in Acts 16 from the life of the apostle Paul illustrates this. He was attempting to travel to Asia in order to preach the gospel there but was informed by the Lord that this was not His will. He then attempted to go into Bythinia with the same results. The Holy Spirit then made clear to Paul, through a dream, that He wanted him to go to the region of Macedonia.

In obedience, Paul traveled to Philippi, where tremendous ministry took place. He moved in great authority over a spirit of divination and cast it out of a person. This created a great controversy, and after being thrown in jail, Paul and Silas's worship brought about an earthquake that freed them. The jailer was born again, as was his family, and eventually the magistrates in Philippi humbled themselves before Paul, seeking his forgiveness.

The level of authority Paul operated in at Philippi was remarkable. He was able to do so because he discerned God's will and was where God wanted him to be, doing what He wanted him to do. Had he failed to discern God's will and gone to the other locations, we have every reason to believe he would not have been able to operate in the same level of authority. Our ability to discern God's will and operate therein really does have a major bearing on our level of authority.

The Impact of Choices

A sixth principle regarding our level of authority in prayer is the decisions of others. When I am praying about the situations of other individuals, their actions can determine the authority level I possess to accomplish a breakthrough. For example, sin in that person's life or an unresolved issue between him and God may affect how much authority I have to lay hold of a biblical promise for him.

Others' actions can even at times affect an answer to prayer for us personally. Second Samuel 21 tells of King David and national Israel undergoing judgment. When David sought the Lord as to why this was happening, he was told it was because of the sins of his predecessor, Saul. This sin had to be repented of and atoned for in order for the judgment to be stopped. Though David had great authority with God where Israel was concerned, he did not have the authority to accomplish a breakthrough for them until Saul's sin had been dealt with.

Another example of this can be seen in the life of Moses. In Numbers 14, Moses interceded for Israel after they had sinned against God, and the Lord essentially responded, "I have pardoned them according to your request, Moses." In that situation, God forgave them because of Moses' intercession. But on another occasion (Exodus 32:32–35 AMPLIFIED), when Moses asked God to forgive Israel, God said He would not do it:

> Yet now, if You will forgive their sin—and if not, blot me, I pray You, out of Your book which You have written! But the Lord said to Moses, Whoever has sinned against Me, I will blot him [not you] out of My book. But now go, lead the people to the place of which I have told you. Behold, My Angel shall go before you. Nevertheless, in the day when I punish I will visit their sin upon them! And the Lord sent a plague upon the people, because they made the calf which Aaron fashioned for them.

Awesomely strong words. Whereas before God had told Moses He would forgive the people just because he had asked Him to, this time God basically said, "I am not going to do it, and I don't want to hear any more about it." There are times when the sins or actions of others limit the authority God is willing to give us to accomplish something in prayer.

Marching Orders

The seventh and last principle determining our level of authority in prayer (or any spiritual activity, for that matter) is our assignment. This is the authority that comes from *representation*. Though we all have the same level of authority when it comes to accessing our heavenly Father and petitioning Him for our personal needs in Christ's name, we do not walk in the same level of authority when it comes to fulfilling spiritual assignments.

A good example is the scope of U.S. citizenship. Every U.S. citizen has the exact same constitutional rights, with the same freedoms, liberties, and protections. However, if a U.S. citizen is appointed as an ambassador to another nation, he will possess authority that the average U.S. citizen does not have. Both have the same rights as Americans, but they do not carry the same right of representation.

The same is true in the kingdom of God. Every Christian is a citizen with the exact same rights and privileges through Christ, as far as personal life is concerned. Every Christian does not, however, possess the same right of representation. When God gives an assignment, just as with any government, He delegates the necessary authority to fulfill that assignment.

There are numerous scriptural examples of this. Paul speaks of it in 2 Corinthians 10, regarding his authority to engage in spiritual warfare over their church:

> The weapons of our warfare are not of the flesh, but divinely powerful for the destruction of fortresses. We are destroying speculations and every lofty thing raised up against the knowledge of God, and we are taking every thought captive to the obedience of Christ. (vv. 4–5)

Though we often quote this in the context of doing so for ourselves, which I do believe is valid, Paul spoke here of doing it for others. He was saying, "I have authority to war over you and tear down strongholds in your mind that are holding you captive." In verse 6, he makes the bold statement that he was actually ready to punish any disobedience when he arrived. Paul was confident that he possessed much spiritual authority in Corinth.

When God gives an assignment, just as with any government, He delegates the necessary authority to fulfill that assignment.

He later referred to the parameters of this authority, speaking of the measure of authority that had been given him (see 10:13–18). The word he used for *measure* is *metron*, which means a limited portion, or, as translated here, a measure. (We derive our English word *meter* from this term.) He then spoke of his "sphere" of authority. This term, *kannon*, means a sphere of rule, a boundary, a sphere of activity. Paul acknowledged he did not possess the same authority elsewhere as he did at Corinth. Because of his assignment God had measured to him a higher portion of rule in Corinth.

Acts 15 also illustrates this principle. The early church was trying to solve a doctrinal dilemma relating to new Christians from the Gentile community. Even though many Jews had become Christians, at this point in time they were still under the assumption that they needed to carry out many traditions of the Jewish faith. When the Gentiles began receiving Christ, the obvious question was "Do we make them fulfill these Judaistic rites?"

After much discussion, James stood and basically said, "I have heard all of the reports and arguments; here is what we are going to do." He then made his declaration, and there was no further discussion. It is clear that each member present did not have the same level of authority—they did not have the same assignment. James had obviously been assigned by God to be the lead person in the Jerusalem church.

No one would argue with me that I have the highest level of authority in the congregation for which I am responsible. While this involves governmental authority to make decisions and implement policies, I am certain it is also true in the area of prayer. I have great authority to pray for and decree over my congregation. I do not possess more authority than the members when it comes to the right to approach the Father in prayer, but I do when it involves the congregation as a whole.

There is still another fascinating example of this in Exodus 32. Moses had been on the mountain receiving God's law for Israel, when God told him to return to the people because they were engaged in sin. This is where the Israelites fashioned a golden calf to worship as an idol. Look at the Lord's words concerning why this happened: "Moses saw that the people were out of control—for *Aaron had let them get out of control* to be a derision among their enemies" (v. 25).

This is a profound indication of how literal is the authority God gives to us for our assignment. The direct insinuation is that Aaron possessed the authority, had he chosen to exercise it, to stop this idolatry regardless of how many Israelites wanted to participate in it. If he had declared that Israel was not going to do this, God would have backed up his authority and somehow stopped it. We absolutely do have the authority to fulfill the assignment God gives us.

This has become obvious in my life. I have come to realize that God has given me a level of authority in America—to pray, make decrees, and perform certain activities for Him—that not all American believers possess. This is not because I know more spiritually or have more overall favor with God than others in the body of Christ. It is because of my assignment.

As I traveled around the nation with Chuck Pierce, praying for revival, there were many occasions when he would turn to me and say, "You need to decree such and such over this state." At the beginning of this time together I sometimes said to him, "Why don't you decree it?" He would usually answer something like "Because you have a great authority to decree over the nation."

I was a little confused at first, wondering about this, but I gradually came to realize and believe it was true. God has assigned certain responsibilities to me regarding America. It is a part of my assignment and therefore a part of my equipping, mantling, and authorization. Now when God sends me to make declarations over D.C. or other parts of the country, I no longer question whether I have the right. I often seek counsel in order to ensure that I am truly hearing from God, but once I have ascertained that I am, I go and obey.

There is, of course, a reciprocal level of humility that must accompany our confidence. No matter how much authority any of us possesses spiritually, we must always remember that it is delegated to us through Christ.

Alex Haley, author of *Roots*, has a picture in his office, showing a turtle sitting atop a fence. The picture is there to remind him of a lesson he learned long ago: "If you see a turtle on a fence post, you know he had some help."

Says Alex, "Any time I start thinking, *Wow, isn't this marvelous what I've done!* I look at that picture and remember how this turtle—me—got up on that post."[2]

We're all turtles when it comes to authority. Without Christ we're helpless and easy prey for sin, Satan, and life's negative circumstances. Nor do we have the means to fulfill any spiritual assignment to overcome evil and establish life and righteousness. However, with Christ as our Head and the Holy Spirit as our Helper, we're equipped to conquer evil and see the kingdom of God established in the earth.

In Daniel 7, Daniel was allowed to look into the future and glimpse amazing events concerning the end times. One thing he saw—though he probably didn't fully understand it—was Christ coming as the Son of Man to establish His kingdom or dominion on earth. Verses 13–14 tell us:

> I kept looking in the night visions, and behold, with the clouds of heaven One like a Son of Man was coming, and He came up to the Ancient of Days and was presented before Him. And to Him was given dominion, glory and a kingdom, that all the peoples, nations, and men of every language might serve Him.

His dominion is an everlasting dominion which will not pass away; and His kingdom is one which will not be destroyed.

Though Scripture promises that one day Christ will return to earth, rid it of all His enemies, and fully establish His kingdom here, there can be no doubt that this "everlasting" rule began at the cross. The effect of this kingdom rule is increasing—Jesus said His kingdom is like leaven that spreads until it overcomes all others (see Matthew 13:33)—and Isaiah said, "There will be no end to the increase of His government" (Isaiah 9:7).

We are a part of this increase. The influence of Christ's kingdom has reached exponential growth. The power of this divine, unstoppable leaven is conquering everything in its path. You are part of this. The church of Christ is moving from being congregational to being congressional—moving outside the walls of our gathering places and into the halls of kingdom legislation. We are dangerous to evil, we are unavoidable, and we are undefeatable.

The church of Christ is moving from being congregational to being congressional— moving outside the walls of our gathering places and into the halls of kingdom legislation.

You were created to be a part of God's government of the earth, and when you were born again that calling was ratified. Take the sword and the scepter and begin to govern your world. Serve notice on the powers of darkness that their chest-sitting days are over where you and yours are concerned. Beginning with your *private* world— conquer! Then in your *extended* world—overcome! And finally, in your *universal* world—rule!

To the victors belong the spoil.

Epilogue

The Gains

As you have no doubt deduced from many of this book's statements and stories, my heart and calling is very much to see the turning of our nation back to Christ. I live for this cause. Though the purpose of *Authority in Prayer* has been to apply its principles to our lives generally, here I want to encourage you concerning the spiritual progress we are making in America and to enlist you in the cause. Though we have far to go, we are making great gains—be encouraged!

> There is an appointed time for everything. And there is a time for every event under heaven. . . . A time for war, and a time for peace.
>
> Ecclesiastes 3:1, 8

"We are a generation called to war!" cried the young intercessor, with great passion.

Epilogue

I was leading a prayer meeting in D.C. for the Supreme Court. I have been part of many such gatherings of crying out to the Lord for the turning of this institution that in recent times has opposed so much that stands for life and morality.

I couldn't help but think of the young Israelite generation spoken of in Judges 3:1–2. The Lord had left enemies in Israel both to test the nation and "that the generations of the sons of Israel might be taught war, those who had not experienced it formerly." It was important to God that the generation coming up under Joshua and Caleb would learn how to fight. In that day, it was crucial for their survival. It is for us today too, even though our war is spiritual.

Another Old Testament verse about war, Psalm 78:9, has always intrigued me: "The sons of Ephraim were archers equipped with bows, yet they turned back in the day of battle." What a sad statement—equipped with the right training and weapons, this tribe retreated from conflict.

I have often asked myself concerning my generation, "Will we be as Ephraim—called, equipped, but no-shows in the battle for the soul of America?" The answer, much like for Israel of old, will determine whether our destiny in God survives or we spiritually become another has-been nation.

Our war is *not* physical. Though Satan uses people to advance his causes, the New Testament makes clear that we are not warring against flesh and blood. Unbelievers, atheists, and those who disagree theologically are not our enemies. They are all loved by God, and He wants each of them to be saved. Our real enemies are the powers of darkness waging war against God's kingdom, trying to hinder His purposes on the earth. Make no mistake: Our war with these forces is

Epilogue

a war for the soul of a nation and the destinies of millions of people.

The good news is that a generation of believers arising in America understands this. Certainly there are also those who do not, maintaining Jesus did all that needs to be done and relying solely on God's sovereignty to make needed gains. This breeds horrible complacency in the body of Christ. Fortunately, the rising generation knows that what God does on the earth He does through His people. They know we are called to use the spiritual weapons He has given us to extend His dominion into the earth.

I recall sitting with prayer leader Lou Engle several years ago as he was trying to "sell" the vision of The Call to a roomful of national spiritual leaders. If you're unfamiliar with them, The Call events were seven large twelve-hour gatherings of young people (initially Lou planned only one) for the purpose of praying and fasting to see America turn back to God. The first of them was in D.C., in summer 2000. Eventually, the momentum led to Call events in other cities and nations.

Many of these well-meaning leaders tried to discourage Lou from attempting the first event: "You don't have enough time." "This will cost too much money." "The kids won't come unless you have a lot of entertainment, bands, etc." It was very discouraging for Lou. After much prayer and fasting, however, he and his pastor, Che Ahn, felt that it was indeed God's will and moved forward with the vision.

The day before The Call I spoke with Lou. He was a bit nervous, wondering if perhaps there would be an embarrassingly small crowd on the Mall. Since there was no registration, he had no way of knowing. Would the youth come? When he showed up early the next morning, there were already tens of thousands gathered. Before the day was over, there were conservative estimates of 400,000 young people gathered for the sole purpose of a solemn assembly—praying, worshiping, fasting, and crying out to God for revival.

This astounded many people. But most surprising was the behavior of the young people. When the few well-known performers and speakers on the program were singing or sharing, many of the young people would disengage. When it was passionate worship or prayer, they would re-engage.

What an eye-opening revelation. It was almost as though this young generation had greater understanding than their fathers and mothers. Perhaps they understood America's desperate condition more than their leaders, and it certainly appeared that they were far more desperate.

I found myself remembering all of this as the young man in our recent D.C. prayer meeting cried out, "We are a generation called to war!" How accurate he is, and how necessary is the revelation.

Last year I was ministering in Florida, and at the end of my message I began praying with the spiritual leaders present. Many were discouraged and disillusioned. As I prayed in earnest for them, an amazing passion came over me. I found myself shouting, "We are warriors!" Something supernatural came over all of us at that moment. A great roar went up from these leaders as their hope deferred was transformed into a warrior spirit.

I want to enlist you in the war.

Judges 5:2, referring to a war led by Deborah and Barak, says, "The leaders led in Israel . . . the people volunteered, bless the Lord!" Psalm 110 also talks about God's volunteer army, in the context of the Melchizedek (king-priest) order we discussed in chapter 7. The word used for *volunteer* in these two passages is also used for *freewill offering*. That's what God is looking for—radical, spiritual warriors who are willing to become freewill, volunteer offerings to Him in this conflict over who will rule the earth.

I was a part of a conference call shortly after Sandra Day O'Connor resigned from the Supreme Court. She was called a moderate by the press but was in reality a liberal who often voted against life and morality. She voted to allow partial-birth abortion, the most appalling travesty of our day. Thousands of babies have been slaughtered because of her vote. Upon her resignation there was a great stirring in the body of Christ, just as there typically is when we have the opportunity to gain a vote for morality.

Fifty or sixty leaders from the most visible and powerful Christian organizations attempting to promote issues of life and morality in D.C. participated in The Call. The purpose was to determine our strategy in trying to influence the next Court appointment. I listened for an hour. There was great disunity, posturing for position and control, and through the entire time nothing was said about prayer, let alone fasting.

I was terrified. I couldn't help but think about the ground we've lost in the war for America's soul over the past few decades. *Little wonder,* I thought, *that up until recently we have made such little progress.* I have regained my footing and perspective, however. Encouraging news: There really is a generation of believers in America beginning to understand our call to spiritual war through prayer. And, at last, this generation is making great gains.

Epilogue

A friend of mine, Ken Malone, has an intercessor in his church to whom in 2002 God gave a significant dream about great gains. Though the context was a football game, it was obviously a spiritual dream. The intercessor is a woman, and in the dream she was a running back. Her jersey number was 22. The dream started at the beginning of the second half, and the quarterback said to her, "We are going to call your number [give you the ball], and the first play of the second half is going to be a double reverse."

When she was given the ball, she began to make great gains against the opponent, which quickly became demoralized. It was obvious they could not stop her, and the game would be won by her team. While the game was taking place, the Lord himself began to quote Matthew 3 over the PA system.

What is the interpretation? As we prayed about it, we felt the Holy Spirit was saying the second half represented the second term of President Bush. He had not yet been reelected, but we felt the Lord was saying he would be and that the bigger gains for life and morality would take place in his second term. We believe that the second half, beginning with a double reverse, was God saying to us there would be a multiplied anointing to reverse the gains the enemy has made in America and bring great gains to the Lord.

The female ball carrier in the dream represents the church, the bride of Christ. God has put the ball in the hands of the *ekklesia*. I am certain that the number being called in the second half, 22, refers to Isaiah 22:22, "Then I will set the key of the house of David on his shoulder, when he opens no one will shut, when he shuts no one will open." Again, this is the verse God gave me when He called me to pray for the

2000 elections and in front of the White House in 2003. (See chapters 6 and 7.)

The fact that the Lord was declaring Matthew 3 over this contest is extremely significant. Matthew 3 begins with the ministry of John the Baptist, the forerunner who was sent to prepare the way for the Messiah. It starts with John commanding the people to repent because the kingdom of heaven is at hand. He baptizes the people as they confess their sins, confronts the religious structure of his day, and calls all who came to hear his message to repentance. Then he begins to announce Messiah's coming, declaring in verse 12, "His winnowing fork is in His hand, and He will thoroughly clear His threshing floor; and He will gather His wheat into the barn, but He will burn up the chaff with unquenchable fire." All of John's ministry was to prepare the way for Christ's first coming.

At this point, the scene changes dramatically with the announcement, "Then Jesus arrived." How promising! The remainder of the chapter brings Christ into the narration, ending with the Father saying of Him, "This is My Beloved Son, in whom I am well-pleased" (v. 17).

What a passage for the Lord to be declaring while this "football game" was taking place. The way is being prepared, and the Lord is indeed coming to America. It makes no difference to God that many rulers of this nation have decided they don't want to serve Jesus, or that the principalities and powers have determined to try to stop Him. God has already made His decision, and the Lord is coming on the scene. The Father is saying once again, "This is My beloved Son, in whom I am well-pleased." We are in the second half, where great gains are being made, and we are preparing for another great visitation of the Lord.

Among other things, He is coming to restore justice and truth. God is all about justice; it is the very foundation of His throne (Psalm 89:14). America desperately needs this justice-restoring visitation. The words of Isaiah are descriptive of us: "We have made a covenant with death" (Isaiah 28:15); "[our] feet run to evil, and [we] hasten to shed innocent blood . . . justice is far from us . . . truth has stumbled in the street" (59:7, 9, 14).

Just as in this prophecy, though, we are not without hope. Later in Isaiah 59, the Lord declares that He is about to change the situation. He is telling America this also, and we, the church, will be His instrument. Micah 6:8 says, "He has told you, O man, what is good; and what does the Lord require of you but to do justice, to love kindness, and to walk humbly with your God?" The Hebrew word translated *do* in this verse is also the biblical word for *create*. The phrase could easily be translated "create justice." The Lord has shown us what is good—what He requires of us—and one of those things is to create justice. I say to you unequivocally that our prayers and the exercise of true biblical authority have the power to create justice in the earth. And our number is being called!

God has brought us to a strategic time in the history of our nation and of the world. As you may know, there are two New Testament Greek words for *time*. One, *kairos*, means "an appointed or opportune time." It has the concept of a window of opportunity when something must be done. The other, *chronos*, is simply a word for chronological time. Zodhiates says of *chronos* that it is "passing moments without any moral impact as to the opportunity and the accomplishments in that time."[1] Notice the phrase "without any moral impact." That is not where we are!

We are not in a *chronos* time but a *kairos* season that will have great moral implications. We have a window of opportunity to turn this nation, and we must not miss it. Daniel 7:25 warns us that Satan tries to "make alterations in times and in law." *Times* is one of the Old Testament words for an appointed time (similar to *kairos*), and the Hebrew word translated *law* means a royal decree. It is used twenty times in Esther referring to kingly decrees.

The context of Daniel 7:25 is that the Judge of all the earth, the Ancient of Days, has ruled in favor of the saints (v. 22). But Satan, ever deceived, makes one last attempt to alter God's decree and appointed time for victory. He always tries this. For every person, every people, every nation, and in every age, Satan tries to alter God's timing and plans.

How? Obviously not by changing God's mind. He does so by seeking to affect us in such a way that we are not able, or choose not, to cooperate with God's purposes. In this Daniel passage, the demonic strategy was to "wear down the saints," (v. 25). "Wear down" (Hebrew *bela*) doesn't refer to a physical weariness but rather a mental or emotional fatigue. Satan tries to discourage us, defer our hope (Proverbs 13:12), and elicit fear, unbelief, complacency, etc., to cause us to miss God's timing and plans for us.

Lest you think that God's sovereignty alone insures against this, remember that Satan succeeded in doing so with Israel in Christ's day. Jesus said of the religious community in Jerusalem that they did not have the ability to understand their *kairos* season (see Luke 19:44). He actually said, "You did not recognize the time *[kairos]* of your visitation." Visitation is the word *episcopé,* meaning to be an overseer, watcher, or bishop, implying watchful care. The Lord was saying to

Jerusalem, though they could not discern it, "I came to bishop you, to watch over you, to care for you." God is saying the same to Americans today. It is time—with great moral implications—for a visitation from heaven. Jesus wants to bishop our nation. He wants to heal us, cover us, and return us to "the Shepherd and Bishop of [our] souls" (1 Peter 2:25 KJV). But He must have our involvement. My good friend, pastor, and writer Eddie Lawrence gave the following prophetic word on March 12, 2004:

> The Lord says there is about to be a shift in the courts, even the Supreme Court of the United States. There will be the shifting of the voice—the voice will swing into alignment with the voice of the courts of Heaven. The heat is being turned up! Even in the hot month—the month July, there will be a signal sounded around the earth of the shift. You will hear it—all ears will hear it. Your eyes will see new faces arising pronouncing the judgments of the Lord. Rioting and righteousness will mix and mingle but righteousness will prevail. It is time for those that wear the black robes to give way to those who first wear the robes of white. In the month that usually gives no rain, you will see the rains come from the high places flooding the valleys. The princes of the government of man will war against the coming shift, but the government of God will prevail as the Saints align their prayer with the decrees of Heaven. It will be the perpetual prayer that will unleash the power to raise the shield and swing the sword that will cut the chains and bring the change.

The shift Eddie spoke of began with the resignation of Justice O'Connor, "in the hot month . . . July." The rains and floods have begun, with hurricanes Katrina and Rita. But notice that the prophecy also declares that in spite of the war over God's shift, "the government of God will prevail as the Saints align their prayer with the decrees of Heaven. Perpetual prayer . . . will unleash the power." This is now occurring—please join us as we partner with God in the turning of America.

I listened with great interest as pro-abortion groups ranted and raved after O'Connor's resignation. They were shouting and cursing as they stated their intention of stopping any pro-life nominee from being confirmed. They declared, "We will go to all fifty states to hold rallies and make our voices heard."

I couldn't help but think with satisfaction—not arrogance, smugness, and certainly not complacency—go *ahead if you want, but we've already been there.* And I wasn't just thinking about Chuck Pierce and me. I'm referring to God's prayer army that has met in every state, making our voices heard in the spiritual realm. Wherever the enemies of life go they will find a closed heaven, just as did the followers of Baal and Jezebel in 1 Kings 18.

We can and will win this war. Great gains have been and will continue to be made. God has given America a great destiny. And He has given the church stewardship of this nation that ultimately belongs to Him. Don't sit on the sidelines. Join the cause and become a history-making king-priest, a governmental, heavenly minded, volunteer soldier for King Jesus.

It is time!

Notes

Chapter 1: The Question

1. You can read about this incredible journey in Dutch Sheets and Chuck D. Pierce, *Releasing the Prophetic Destiny of a Nation* (Shippensburg, PA: Destiny Image, 2005).

2. *Consolidated-Webster Encyclopedic Dictionary* (Chicago: Book Production Industries, Inc., 1964), 49.

3. All scriptural emphasis (italics) mine.

4. Greek *basileuô*. Spiros Zodhiates, *Hebrew-Greek Key Word Study Bible, New American Standard Bible* (Chattanooga: AMG Publishers, 1977), 936.

5. Cited in Craig Brian Larson, *Contemporary Illustrations for Preachers, Teachers, and Writers* (Grand Rapids: Christianity Today and Baker, 1996), 183.

Chapter 2: The Author

1. Spiros Zodhiates, *Hebrew-Greek Key Word Study Bible, New American Standard Bible*, 1820.

2. Many other prayer experiences of Will Ford III can be read in the book he and I coauthored: *History Makers* (Ventura, CA: Regal, 2004).

Chapter 3: The Poet

1. Craig Brian Larson, *Contemporary Illustrations for Preachers, Teachers, and Writers*, 132.

2. Gloria Sanders, *www.Inspirationstories.com*.

3. Alice Gray, *More Stories for the Heart* (Sisters, OR: Multnomah, 1977), 247.

4. You can read about this in my book *God's Timing for Your Life* (Ventura, CA: Regal, 2001).

5. Edward K. Rowell, ed., *Fresh Illustrations for Preaching and Teaching: From Leadership Journal* (Grand Rapids: Christianity Today and Baker, 1997), 217.

Notes

Chapter 4: The Assignment

1. Dutch Sheets, *Watchman Prayer* (Ventura, CA: Regal, 2000), 167–68.
2. Ibid., 167.
3. James Strong, *Strong's Exhaustive Concordance of the Bible* (Lynchburg, VA: Old Time Gospel Hour, n.d.).
4. Spiros Zodhiates, *Hebrew-Greek Key Word Study Bible, New American Standard Bible*, 1707.
5. The Hebrew word is *nathan*, *Strong's Exhaustive Concordance of the Bible*.
6. Hebrew *shamar*, ibid.
7. William Wilson, *Old Testament Word Studies* (Grand Rapids: Kregel, 1978), 236.
8. Spiros Zodhiates, *Hebrew-Greek Key Word Study Bible, New American Standard Bible*, 1774–75.
9. Ibid., 1745.
10. Dutch Sheets and William Ford III, *History Makers*.

Chapter 5: The Contest

1. Craig Brian Larson, ed., *Illustrations for Preaching and Teaching: From Leadership Journal* (Grand Rapids: Christianity Today and Baker, 1993), 48.

Chapter 6: The Ekklesia

1. Craig Brian Larson, ed., *Illustrations for Preaching and Teaching: From Leadership Journal*, 261.
2. Ibid., 258–59.
3. Bill Johnson, *www.ibethel.org*, "Tijuana Revolution" (March 2005).
4. Spiros Zodhiates, *Hebrew-Greek Key Word Study Bible, New American Standard Bible*, 1816.
5. C. Peter Wagner, ed., *Destiny of a Nation* (Colorado Springs: Wagner, 2001) 80–83.

Chapter 7: The Dynasty

1. Robert J. Morgan, *Real Stories for the Soul* (Nashville: Thomas Nelson, 2000), 215–16.
2. Spiros Zodhiates, *Hebrew-Greek Key Word Study Bible, New American Standard Bible*, 1811.
3. Dick Eastman, *The Jericho Hour* (Altamonte Springs, FL: Creation House, 1994), 124.

Chapter 8: The Voice

1. Dutch Sheets and Chuck Pierce, *Releasing the Prophetic Destiny of a Nation*, 91.
2. These words and strategies can be found in *Releasing the Prophetic Destiny of a Nation*.
3. Ibid., 91.
4. Spiros Zodhiates, *Hebrew-Greek Key Word Study Bible, New American Standard Bible*, 1719.

5. Chuck Pierce with John Dickson, *The Worship Warrior* (Ventura, CA: Regal, 2002), 108–110.
6. *Strong's Exhaustive Concordance of the Bible*, 6965.
7. R. Laird Harris, Gleason L. Archer, Jr., and Bruce K. Waltke, *Theological Wordbook of the Old Testament* (Chicago: Moody, 1980), 793.

Chapter 9: The Sword

1. Jay left the reservation's spiritual leaders with specific instructions on how to maintain this breakthrough. They complied and, as he said, had no suicides for almost three years. Then they stopped doing as he instructed and the suicides resumed, with three over the past year. He is working with the leaders again to curb this before it gains new momentum. The leaders have begun to take responsibility again, as also have the people. Parents, grandparents, and the young people themselves are being raised up as watchmen to stand guard for one another. If they continue to do their part, I have no doubt that this victory will be sustained.
2. *U.S. News & World Report,* USNews.com, "High-Stakes Players," Liz Halloran (7/25/05).

Chapter 10: The Heavens

1. Dutch Sheets and Chuck Pierce, *Releasing the Prophetic Destiny of a Nation*, 75–76.
2. Bill Johnson, *The Supernatural Power of a Transformed Mind* (Shippensburg, PA: Destiny Image, 2005), 35–36.
3. Op. cit., 76–77.

Chapter 11: The Room

1. Spiros Zodhiates, *Hebrew-Greek Key Word Study Bible, New American Standard Bible*, 1804.
2. Ibid.
3. Bill Johnson, *The Supernatural Power of a Transformed Mind*, 33–34.

Chapter 13: The Levels

1. *www.holytrinitynewrochelle.org*, 2005.

Chapter 14: The Degrees

1. Dutch Sheets, *Intercessory Prayer* (Ventura, CA: Regal, 1996), 15–18.
2. Craig Brian Larson, ed., *Illustrations for Preaching and Teaching: From Leadership Journal*, 117.

Epilogue: The Gains

1. Spiros Zodhiates, *Hebrew-Greek Key Word Study Bible, New American Standard Bible*, 1888.

Dutch Sheets is an internationally recognized author, teacher, and conference speaker. He travels extensively, empowering believers for passionate prayer and societal transformation. Dutch has pastored, taught in several colleges and seminaries, and served on the board of directors of numerous organizations. Seeing America experience a sweeping revival and return to its godly heritage is one of Dutch's greatest passions. He is a messenger of hope, encouraging believers to contend for awakening in our day and reformation in our lifetime. Learn more at www.dutchsheets.org.

Powerful Teaching from Dutch Sheets

From international prayer leader Dutch Sheets, this hands-on foundational book will help you develop the most important component of effective prayer: a strong relationship with God. You'll learn how to make prayer a vital part of your life, how to persist in prayer, how to become an intercessor, and more.

The Essential Guide to Prayer

With profound insights from the Bible and personal stories, bestselling author Dutch Sheets takes you on a thirty-day journey to cultivating—and enjoying—deeper intimacy with God. Each of the thirty short chapters reveals a simple practice or biblical mindset that will help draw you away from the noise of life and into the Lord's peaceful presence.

The Pleasure of His Company

In this powerful book that Dutch Sheets calls his life message, readers are given truths about who they are in Christ and how to become the person God made them to be. Originally titled *Roll Away Your Stone*, this book provides sound biblical teaching that shows believers how to conquer the lies that keep them defeated and walk in the Spirit.

Becoming Who You Are

BETHANYHOUSE

Stay up to date on your favorite books and authors with our free e-newsletters. Sign up today at bethanyhouse.com.

 facebook.com/BHPnonfiction   @bethany_house_nonfiction

 @bethany_house

Made in the USA
Coppell, TX
28 June 2021

58223202R00292